D1645700

T

VICTIMS' RIGHTS, HUMAN RIGHTS AND

Withdrawn From Stock

Sheffield Hallam University
Learning and Information Services

In recent times, the idea of 'victims' rights' has come to feature prominently in political, criminological and legal discourse, as well as being subject to regular media comment. The concept nevertheless remains inherently elusive, and there is still considerable ambiguity as to the origin and substance of such rights. This monograph deconstructs the nature and scope of the rights of victims of crime against the backdrop of an emerging international consensus on how victims ought to be treated and the role they ought to play. The essence of such rights is ascertained not only by surveying the plethora of international standards which deal specifically with crime victims, but also by considering the potential cross-applicability of standards relating to victims of abuse of power, with whom they have much in common. In this book Jonathan Doak considers the parameters of a number of key rights which international standards suggest victims ought to be entitled to. He then proceeds to ask whether victims are able to rely upon such rights within a domestic criminal justice system characterised by structures, processes and values which are inherently exclusionary, adversarial and punitive in natur~

ONE WEEK LOAN

16 MAR 2009
15 MAR 2011

24 OCT 2012

Victims' Rights, Human Rights and Criminal Justice

Reconceiving the Role of Third Parties

JONATHAN DOAK

·HART·
PUBLISHING

OXFORD AND PORTLAND, OREGON
2008

Published in North America (US and Canada) by
Hart Publishing
c/o International Specialized Book Services
920 NE 58th Avenue, Suite 300
Portland, OR 97213-3786
USA
Tel: +1 503 287 3093 or toll-free: (1) 800 944 6190
Fax: +1 503 280 8832
E-mail: orders@isbs.com
Website: http://www.isbs.com

© Jonathan Doak 2008

Jonathan Doak has asserted his right under the Copyright, Designs and Patents Act 1988,
to be identified as the author of this work.

All rights reserved. No part of this publication may be reproduced, stored in a retrieval system,
or transmitted, in any form or by any means, without the prior permission of Hart Publishing,
or as expressly permitted by law or under the terms agreed with the appropriate reprographic
rights organisation. Enquiries concerning reproduction which may not be covered by the above
should be addressed to Hart Publishing at the address below.

Hart Publishing, 16C Worcester Place, OX1 2JW
Telephone: +44 (0)1865 517530 Fax: +44 (0)1865 510710
E-mail: mail@hartpub.co.uk
Website: http://www.hartpub.co.uk

British Library Cataloguing in Publication Data
Data Available

ISBN: 978-1-84113-603-5

Typeset by Hope Services, Abingdon
Printed and bound in Great Britain by
CPI Antony Rowe, Chippenham, Wiltshire

PREFACE

This is an intriguing time to write any form of commentary on victims. Rarely a day goes by without reference in the media to the notion of 'human rights' generally or the 'rights' of victims of crime in particular. This book aims to unite these discourses, by considering the prospects for realising victims' rights within a human rights framework.

Since the ascendancy of human rights in the aftermath of the Second World War, the discipline has been primarily concerned with the protection of victims from the abuse of power by the State. For various reasons, victims of non-state crime or 'ordinary' crime victims have tended to be viewed outside this framework. Since their rights have been violated by individual actors, rather than agents of the State, it is assumed that the domestic criminal law will adequately protect them, as opposed to any scheme of international law. That situation has recently undergone a profound transformation. The public / private divide which once characterised both human rights law and the nature of the criminal justice system has become blurred. Increasingly, it has been recognized that 'ordinary' victims of crime have much in common with victims of abuse of power. Both sets of victims have suffered as a result of their rights being violated, and both merit some form of recognition and redress.

Against this backdrop, this book argues for a unified theory of victims' rights. Acknowledging the normative correlation between victims of state and victims of non-state crime, the study draws from both international human rights and domestic criminal justice discourses. It argues that the very concept of 'victims' rights' rings hollow unless we reconceptualise these rights as being human rights, fully protected and directly applicable within both domestic and international legal orders.

The book aims to accomplish two objectives. First, it seeks to survey the current scope of international standards, drawing from norms that relate to both 'types' of victim. Whilst it is fully acknowledged that these norms amount to neither a fully definable nor fully desirable set of standards, they do give us some indication of international consensus as to what constitutes best practice.

Secondly, the book considers the extent to which such rights might be realistically mainstreamed within the English criminal justice system. While successive governments have embarked on a number of efforts to boost the position of victims in the criminal justice system, the compatibility of the structures and their underlying theoretical foundations with the human rights paradigm is very much open to question. The emphasis placed on oral evidence at court, the broad latitude of the parties to question victims, the bipartisan nature of criminal justice, the manner in which cases are constructed, and the narrow conceptions that are commonly held about remedies and reparation suggest that we may need to radically rethink our criminal justice system if victims' rights, as human rights, are to be taken seriously.

This book begins with a chapter charting the ascendancy of the victim from history into contemporary criminal justice policy. It examines the way we think about victims, their rights, and how criminal justice generally has changed over the centuries. It also unpacks some of the awkward ideological questions that are typically posed by those who are sceptical of the place of victims' rights within contemporary law and policy. The importance of human rights and the need for a broader, international perspective when engaging in such debates is also explained.

The four subsequent chapters are centred around four broad 'rights' which have come to feature as salient themes in both human rights and traditional victimology. These are the right to protection; the right to participation; the right to justice; and the right to reparation. Each chapter discusses the origin, scope and individual components of a particular 'right', drawing on norms in human rights law and, in places, international humanitarian law and international criminal justice. I attempt to identify pronounced controversies and points of both consensus and divergence, with a view to determining what constitutes 'best practice.' Each chapter also considers the extent to which such rights are currently present, or might be realisable, within the English criminal justice system. The argument advanced is not that these four 'rights' are necessarily 'rights' within any legal sense. Rather, they are four substantive areas which have been subject to considerable debate and either have emerged, or seem to be emerging, as new human rights for victims of state or non-state crime. I should also add that the discussion is not intended to constitute a comprehensive statement of the rights of victims in current international discourse. Such a task would, quite simply, be impossible since no absolute international consensus is present, and no doubt the four areas I have selected will be questioned by some readers. I have chosen them for two main reasons. First, because they touch on those aspects of criminal justice that seem to matter most for victims; and secondly, because they pose some of the most difficult questions regarding how they might be effectively realised within the parameters of an adversarial system of justice.

In conclusion, my final chapter summarises the nature of the four emergent rights discussed in the book. It is argued that the adversarial paradigm represents a poor vehicle for their delivery, both actual and potential. The primary reason for this is that it locates the interests of the victim in a position that is subservient to that of the State. As such, the bipartisan adversarial system is structurally flawed, and is inherently incapable of safeguarding the rights of third parties. In order for such rights to be fully effective, we need to radically rethink the way in which we conceive the structures and values at the heart of the criminal justice system.

With this is mind, the chapter advocates a shift towards two alternative approaches, restorative justice and the inquisitorial method, as fairer and a more holistic means of delivering justice. While neither of these approaches may represent a wholesale panacea for the problems facing victims, it is argued that they are structurally and conceptually better placed to accommodate and provide better protection for victims in the criminal justice system.

Admittedly, this work may raise more questions than it answers. Many of the 'rights' discussed herein are still in emerging form, and as such even some of the questions raised may themselves require redefinition or clarification in years to come. It is hoped, however, that the book will make a positive contribution to contemporary debates by casting a human rights perspective upon the role of the victim within criminal justice.

The first three chapters of the book are drawn in part from my doctoral thesis, and I wish to thank Professor Sean Doran and Professor John Jackson for their conscientious supervision and direction during my time as a research student at Queen's University Belfast. Advice and / or comments have also been gratefully received from Professor Christine Bell of the University of Ulster, Dr Claire McGourlay of the University of Sheffield and Dr Lorna Fox of the University of Durham. Thanks also to my father, Connor, for helping with proof-reading and to Erica Grinberg and Liz Moffat for their valuable research assistance. I also extend my sincere gratitude to Richard Hart and his team who have offered outstanding support, advice and flexibility throughout the project.

As ever, I am very much indebted to Lauran, Ben, and the rest of my family for their love, encouragement and support.

CONTENTS

1

The Evolution of Victims' Rights

IN RECENT YEARS, the phenomenon of 'victims' rights' has been catapulted to the forefront of policymaking on both domestic and international platforms. While the criminal justice system has traditionally been conceptualised as a mechanism for the state to resolve its grievances against suspects, defendants and offenders, it is now broadly accepted that justice cannot be administered effectively without due recognition of the rights and interests of other parties affected by the criminal action. This shift has affected the extent to which their interests are represented in the formulation of criminal justice policy, in that an increasing number of initiatives are undertaken in the name of victims, seeking to bolster their position within the system. These developments raise a number of key questions and fundamental issues concerning the structural and ideological basis of our criminal justice system, not least as to whether the very concept of 'victims' rights' is inherently compatible with a system that is ideologically constructed as a bipartisan contest between the State and the accused.

The phrase 'victims' rights' has now entered into widespread usage among politicians, academics and the media. Unfortunately, the terminology tends to be deployed in an imprecise manner, and is often resorted to as a form of emotive polemic. Consequently, discussions around the idea of 'victims' rights' frequently produce more heat than light, and rarely succeed in eliciting the precise scope or legal nature of such 'rights' or the extent to which construction of such rights can be realised within the normative and structural framework of the existing criminal justice system. This book aims to shed some light upon the meaning of victims' rights and their place within the criminal justice system, taking into account international and human rights perspectives. While the subsequent chapters take the form of thematic discussions that attempt to trace the scope and content of a number of selected rights, this introductory chapter aims to clarify how the concept of victims' rights might be interpreted, and what it should mean in practice, for victims to be able to exercise rights within the legal order. As a starting point, it may be useful to provide a brief overview of the interaction of historical, sociological and political factors that have positioned the victim at the forefront of contemporary criminal justice debates. The following is not intended to constitute an exhaustive analysis of the historical position of the victim, nor a detailed account of the victim's ascendancy in criminal justice policy. That task has been admirably accomplished elsewhere.[1] Nevertheless, before outlining the theoretical framework that underpins the study, it may be worth setting the scene in order to contextualise the deeper formalistic questions about the role of the victim.

I. The Victim through History

The origins of the modern day criminal law as a form of public law designed to regulate and punish offending behaviour has its origins in the early law of tort. In the absence of a central state authority, the victim / offender conflict was historically conceptualised as a private matter outside the State's immediate interests. For its part, the early State tended to concentrate on the eradication of blood feud, and the provision of a legal framework for victims to pursue compensation for injuries through the courts.[2] This legal framework was essentially a system of private law designed to facilitate the resolution of a private dispute, and bore little resemblance to the modern day criminal law, where the State itself undertakes the responsibility for punishing offenders for their wrongdoing. This philosophy underpinned the legal system of Anglo-Saxon England. Under localised dispute resolution systems, most offences were emendable: offenders could redeem themselves through the payment of compensation, known as a *bot* or *wergild*.[3] These were early forms of damages, payable by the accused to the injured party or his family group, and were calculated on the nature and extent of the wrong.[4] Where crimes were intentional, a *wite*, or public fine, was also payable to the king or feudal lord.

This system underwent a seismic shift during the Middle Ages. Under the reign of Henry II (1154–1189), a process of centralisation was instigated which culminated in the Assize of Clarendon of 1166. This ordinance clearly delineated a number of serious offences as crimes (as opposed to torts) which would fall under the king's jurisdiction. Although the move did not abolish any private rights of action, it nonetheless marked the beginning of an era when the State gradually usurped the role of the victim. Various reasons have been suggested for this shift from local to centralised law and for the emergence of a distinction between criminal and civil liability. As Ashworth suggests, the transition probably owed:

---

[1] Regarding the historical position of the victim, see Schafer (1968); Young (2001), Seipp (1996); Klermann (2000); Kirchengast (2006). In relation to the ascendancy of the victim in the modern criminal justice policy, see Walklate (2001); Dignan (2005), 42–93; Goodey (2005), 121–51; Spalek (2006).

[2] Young (2001), 6; Baker (2002), 500.

[3] This essentially constituted a private prosecution—see Pollock and Maitland (1898) II, 451. Some serious offences, such as arson and treason, were *botless*, which meant that they were irredeemable, and only punishable by death or mutilation.

[4] Whereas the *wergild* was payable to the family group in cases of serious injury or death; the *bot* was a generic compensation payment usually reserved for less serious injuries.

less to doctrinal legal distinctions than to the usefulness of criminal jurisdiction as a source of funds for the Crown . . . and to the social significance of the administration of criminal justice as a mark of royal authority.[5]

As society became larger and more complex, the development of the criminal law became a useful tool for the State to regulate the behaviour of its citizens in order to promote peace and the security of the nation.[6] However, it has also been suggested that the shift was not a conscious process, but came about over time as a result of the interaction of a number of factors, including the dilution of the ties of kinship, jurisdictional squabbles between the church and the king, and social inequities.[7]

The 'Pleas of the Crown', created by Henry II, changed the nature of the early criminal law, moving it from the sphere of private law into a form of public law enforceable by the state. Certain offences were now conceptualised in law as wrongs committed against the king, rather than private parties. Royal justices were commissioned to visit the counties and inquire into alleged criminal offences, and prosecutions were then brought as 'indictments of felony.'[8] Victims were, however, still able to take a private action against their offenders, through the 'appeal of felony', which was essentially a form of private prosecution. Although instigated by the victim, the penalties were usually death or a fine payable to the king.[9] As such, victims who brought a successful appeal had to be content with the incorporeal satisfaction that some form of justice had been done. Although appeals of felony continued to be brought until the early nineteenth century, their heyday was the late twelfth and early thirteenth centuries. Schafer describes the Middle Ages era as 'the golden age of the victim',[10] in so far as the system was based on the principle of restitution to the party who had suffered a loss. Yet, his analysis appears somewhat optimistic given that the burden and expense of prosecution and proof lay squarely on the victim's shoulders, and by the end of the thirteenth century, relatively few criminals were prosecuted by appeal. The decline of the appeals system can be attributed to a number of factors, including: changes in the judicial attitude towards private settlements; the archaic nature of the law; the emergence of 'presentment', which meant that crimes could be prosecuted even where the victim did not appeal; and the introduction of writs of trespass, which allowed victims to pursue civil damages in tort from the middle of the thirteenth century.[11] In many instances, victims could therefore choose whether to pursue a criminal or a tortious action, depending on whether they were motivated primarily by vengeance or compensation.[12] Royal officers could also prosecute

---

[5] Ashworth (1986), 90.
[6] Van Ness (1996), 66.
[7] Young (2001), 6.
[8] Ashworth (1986), 90.
[9] Klerman (2000), 9.
[10] Schafer (1968), 7.
[11] Baker (2002), 60.
[12] Seipp (1996), 84.

criminal offences using the 'indictment of felony' or 'indictment of trespass' where the victim chose not to do so, but normally only chose to do so if the offence was considered important enough to affect the interests of the king.[13]

During the fourteenth and fifteenth centuries, the appeals system was gradually supplanted by indictment.[14] As society became increasingly complex, the State's interest in regulating behaviour and punishing offenders rapidly increased, and the power to prosecute was shifted from the victim to the State.[15] From the late seventeenth century, the State began to take a more proactive role in encouraging victims to bring actions against offenders through a system of 'rewards and immunities' for those who prosecuted felons.[16] The main avenue for pursuing such an action was through 'laying an information.' This procedure could be used by a victim or by any other common informer.[17] Nonetheless, commencing criminal proceedings in this way was an expensive and slow process, and in the vast majority of cases, the offence was unlikely to be pursued.[18] This situation was eased in the eighteenth century by the formation of local associations for the prosecution of felons, which:

> aspired to promote the enforcement of the criminal law by spreading the costs of investigation and prosecution among the membership.[19]

Essentially, citizens would pay a subscription which would go towards the expenses of a criminal investigation and prosecution should one of the members fall victim to an offence.[20] In summary then, by the beginning of the eighteenth century the State had come to assume the role that the victim once had in the prosecution of crime, and the interests of the victim were relegated to a subservient position to those of the State.

Shifting Ideologies: The Political State

Ideologies concerning the role of the state within criminal justice matters underwent a further period of change during the eighteenth century. Political thought during the Enlightenment inflated the role of the state to that of the benevolent

---

[13] *Ibid*, 60.

[14] Baker (2002), 504–5. The appeals system was finally abolished in 1819.

[15] Some legal historians have concluded that that one of the main reasons for the proliferation of the criminal law during this period was economic, with judicial fines making up one-eighth of the entire revenue received by the king (Young, (2001)). Schafer (1968) asserts that this amounted to little more than power play in which the State enriched itself at the expense of victims, citing the 'violent greed of feudal barons and medieval ecclesiastical powers' as major factors in the usurpation of the rights of the injured party (at 12).

[16] Bentley (1998), 7.

[17] Baker (2002), 506.

[18] Some victims were able to engage a 'thief taker.' Thief takers were private individuals who lived off rewards from courts and victims for bringing offenders to justice (Langbein, (2003), 152–3).

[19] Langbein (2003), 132.

[20] *Ibid*, 133.

protector of the public.[21] As a result, the government began to intervene much more readily to attempt to put in place an effective criminal justice system that was capable of protecting the public good. Incentives were devised to encourage actions against perpetrators, including the opportunity to recover costs.[22] Other private parties (ie, non-victims) were also able to instigate cases as informers, with the prospects of fines being split with the king.[23] Although such actions were now brought in the name of the king, the criminal justice system remained heavily dependent on the role of victims to report crime and testify against offenders.

Policy at this time was heavily influenced by the Italian jurist, Beccaria,[24] who believed that the role of the criminal justice system was to serve the interests of society as a whole, as opposed to providing redress for victims on an individualistic basis. Thus where the interests of the public good conflicted with those of the victim, this was viewed by utilitarians such as Beccaria as being largely irrelevant, since the individual victim's interests were subservient to those of the nation state.[25] The punishment of the attack on the supreme power of the nation state far outweighed the provision of redress to individual victims.

This shifting perception of the role of the state was reflected in a sea change which occurred in the prosecution of criminal offences during the nineteenth century. The Metropolitan Police Act of 1829 had created a new police force that rapidly became the main prosecutor for public order and vagrancy offences, and, over the course of the nineteenth century, increasingly usurped the role of the victim as a private prosecutor. Although England still lacked a system of public prosecutions, in the latter half of the nineteenth century the police and local magistrates began undertaking an increasingly proactive role in overseeing prosecutions.[26] Consequently, victims became more dependent on the police to track down the suspect and gather evidence. As a result, the victim's prosecutorial function was gradually subsumed, thereby transforming his role from a 'policeman, prosecutor and punishment beneficiary to that of informant and witness only.'[27]

Just as the prosecution system underwent a major change, so too did the nature of the criminal trial. Historically, the accused was not permitted access to counsel, but during the eighteenth century, this prohibition was relaxed somewhat.[28]

[21] Yaroshefsky (1989), 135–40.

[22] Cardenas (1986), 360.

[23] *Ibid.*

[24] McDonald (1976), 655. Beccaria saw society based around the social contract, and called for a radical rethink of the principles underlying the system. He particularly urged that crimes should be redefined in accordance with the degree of harm caused to society, and not according to the offensiveness of the act to God. Since society was based on the social contract, the offence should be viewed as one against society at large rather than the victim, and punishments should be made proportionate to the crime, and should be strictly prescribed by law.

[25] Rock (1990), 87, who also observes that Bentham asserted that it was the duty of the State to protect the victimised citizen.

[26] Although the Prosecution of Offenders Act 1879 created the new office of the Director of Public Prosecutions, there was neither a statutory definition of functions nor even a public prosecutions system to direct. A century later, the CPS was eventually established under the Prosecution of Offences Act 1985.

[27] McDonald (1976), 656.

[28] Bentley (1998), 71.

According to the strict letter of the law, the prohibition against defence counsel in felony trials remained in effect, but by the mid-1730s the bench had begun to allow such representation although their actual role was tightly controlled[29] and they had few rights to intervene in the trial.[30] However, the rights of defence counsel received a major boost with the enactment of the Prisoner's Counsel Act of 1836, which not only recognised the right of a defendant in a felony case to counsel in law, but allowed counsel to address the jury directly.[31] The full implications of this reform did not become evident for some time, but through introducing a new actor onto the courtroom stage, the door was left ajar for trials to become a fora for bipartisanship and adversarial argument.

As counsel came to exercise an increasingly important role in the trial, the role of the judge as an active participant declined. Until the early nineteenth century, judges themselves were responsible for conducting most of the questioning.[32] Indeed, King adds that they were 'often highly proactive examiners who pointedly questioned witnesses and directed the hectic flow of evidence', and he also points out that it was not unusual for the judge to be seen as a counsel for the prisoner.[33] By the middle of the nineteenth century however, the majority of prosecutions were conducted by barristers, although they were usually instructed by the police rather than victims directly.[34]

The involvement of counsel in the courtroom precipitated a major change in the conduct of the criminal hearing. From the middle of the eighteenth century to the mid-nineteenth century, a complex network of evidential rules had developed; counsel had greatly honed and refined their skills as seasoned advocates, and judges exercised a much more passive role in the trial.[35] The adversarial nature of the trial had been well established by the middle of the nineteenth century, although the shift was unintentional and was largely brought about in a piecemeal and uncoordinated fashion. As May contends, the adversarialisation of the trial process 'was the result not of any deliberate intent on the part either of the State or the legal profession to refashion the felony trial as a professional contest; it was instead rooted in particular historical circumstances, prominent among which were commercial expansion and rising fears about crime.'[36]

---

[29] Bentley (1998), 71.

[30] *Ibid.*

[31] Cairns (1998), 3.

[32] Bentley (1998), 71. It was not until the latter part of the nineteenth century that prosecuting counsel appeared regularly in criminal cases. It was not unknown, however, for prosecutors to appear in earlier times. Langbein (2003) cites several instances in the early eighteenth century where the king directed the Attorney General to commission lawyers to prosecute on a number of occasions at his expense (at 120–1). He also notes that, on occasions, victims who had the resources could also make use of their solicitors to draw up papers and examine witnesses (at 123–7).

[33] Cairns (1998), 46; King (2000), 223–4.

[34] King (2000), 223.

[35] *Ibid*, 225.

[36] May (2003), 2. See also Langbein (2003), who contends that lawyerisation 'was a response to the failure to develop a reliable and effective system of pretrial criminal investigation . . . the failure to understand that criminal investigation should be a public good' (at 333).

Whatever the reasons behind the changes to the nature of the criminal justice and the criminal trial that occurred over the centuries, there has been a clear historical pattern whereby the victim has been gradually excluded from both the investigation and trial stages of the criminal process. Centuries of centralisation led to the emergence of a public criminal law administered by the State, and later by lawyers. As a result, the contemporary criminal justice system is normatively and structurally built around a contest between the State and the accused, which inherently excludes the rights and interests of the victim.[37] This historical pattern explains why victims do not have any conceptual role to play in the modern criminal justice system other than to act as witnesses to the facts. The modern day structure of the legal system is reflective of its historical origins, which have traditionally separated the functions, sanctions and philosophies of the criminal and the civil law. Ashworth describes the purpose of the criminal law as 'to penalise those forms of wrongdoing which . . . touch public rather than merely private interests.'[38] In his view, the proper approach in determining the role of the victim within the criminal justice system is on the basis of this distinction between criminal and civil proceedings, and the rights and the interests of the victim should be pursued under the civil, as opposed to the criminal law.[39] The criminal law and its penal sanctions are thus widely conceptualised as being geared to protecting the public interest in denouncing and punishing unacceptable behaviour, and not furthering the private interests of individual parties.

II. The Rebirth of the Victim

Towards the end of the nineteenth century, and during the early years of the twentieth century, widespread concern for society's most vulnerable members seemed to impact upon public consciousness. In addition to an array of legislation designed to safeguard the position of women and children,[40] many statutes made specific provision for compensating criminal injury or loss.[41] However, it was not

---

[37] See, however, Kirchengast (2006), who argues that the legacy of the victim's early common law role has continued to shape the criminal justice system over the centuries. Whilst most contemporary literature recognises that, on a normative basis, prosecution and sentencing are functions of the State, Kirchengast's genealogical analysis illustrates how the historical role of the victim continued to influence the development of prosecutorial and punitive powers over the centuries.

[38] Ashworth (1992), as cited by Cavadino and Dignan (1996).

[39] See, eg Ashworth (1998).

[40] See, eg (1853) 16 & 17 Vic, c30; Poor Law Amendment Act 1889; Infant Life Protection Acts 1872–1897; Matrimonial Clauses Act 1878; the Prevention of Cruelty and Protection of Children Act 1889.

[41] Eg, Lord Campbell's Act of 1846 recognised the right of a victim's family to claim compensation in the case of wrongful death. The Malicious Injuries to Property Act 1861 allowed the owner of damaged property to obtain recompense of up to £5. The Riot Damages Act 1886 provided for compensation to victims of riots, and the Police (Property) Act 1897 gave the courts power to order return of stolen property to its true owners, and also the power to order compensation up to the value of £10 for

until the latter part of the twentieth century that the interests of the victim really began to impact upon the shape of criminal justice reform in any meaningful way. Growing awareness of victimisation emerged in the years following the Second World War. The post-war era was marked by a 'shifting understanding of accountability and citizenship',[42] which was evidenced in the creation of the welfare state and the emergence of civil society.

Although criminal justice policy was not a widely contested political issue during this time, it was within this climate of emerging social rights that a loose association of groups and individuals became involved in campaigning for victim-specific issues. Margery Fry is widely credited for her campaigning during the 1950s for victim compensation, which was instrumental in the creation of the Criminal Injuries Compensation Scheme in 1964.[43] In the decades that followed, the feminist movement played a key role in highlighting aspects of hidden victim-isation, including domestic violence and rape. Erin Pizzey established the first Women's Aid shelter in Chiswick in 1971, and local rape crisis centres were established during the latter years of the 1970s.[44] In addition, the children's rights movement also contributed to the growing awareness of other aspects of hidden victimisation. Publicity surrounding child sex abuse emerged on a number of occasions, with various studies revealing that it was a lot more prevalent than had been thought.[45] High profile cases often centred on the abuse of children in the care of social services, or where social services had failed to intervene including Cleveland (1987), Orkney (1991), South Wales (1996) and Tyneside (1996). Throughout the 1980s and 1990s, a growing number of specific interest groups emerged, including organisations campaigning for the registration of sex offenders, incest survivor groups, relatives of murdered and missing children, relatives of victims of drunk driving, and those concerned with combating racism, homophobia and discrimination generally. While such groups were generally unconnected and pursued their own specific agendas, the net effect of their efforts was to highlight the plight of weaker and more vulnerable members of society on many different levels under contemporary legal and political frameworks.[46]

---

a variety of minor property related offences. S 4 of the Protection of Animals Act 1911 enabled the court to order compensation where animal cruelty led to damage to an animal or to any person or property, and s 14(1) of the Criminal Justice Administration Act 1914 provided that compensation could be ordered for malicious damage to property.

42 Walklate (2001), 204.

43 See discussion below at p 12, and Ch 5 below, pp 227–30.

44 There has been no attempt to unify the numerous rape crisis centres which operate throughout the UK: they all remain independent organisations, with no uniform standards, thus making funding difficult to come by (Williams (1996), 48).

45 See, eg Nash and West, (1985); Glaser and Frosh (1988) Horne et al (1991). A sample survey conducted for MORI by Baker and Duncan (1984) revealed that 8% of males and 12% of females remembered being involved in a sexual incident with an adult before they themselves had turned 16.

46 Mawby and Walklate (1994) cite the sinking of the *Herald of Free Enterprise* (1987), the Clapham rail crash (1988), the King's Cross fire (1989), the Hillsborough football stadium disaster (1989) and the sinking of the *Marchioness* (1989) as examples of specific human tragedies towards the end of the 1980s that also increased public awareness of victims (at 85).

Although there was initially a general lack of cohesiveness within the victims' lobby, the development of the voluntary organisation, Victim Support, created a new channel for campaigning for all types of crime victims. Excellent accounts of the development of Victim Support Schemes are provided elsewhere,[47] but for the purposes of this book it is worth underlining the important role the organisation has played in lobbying for better protections for victims since its formation in 1979. Traditionally, the movement was primarily welfare-orientated rather than rights-orientated, offering emotional support, information, and practical help to victims. Having rapidly expanded its operations during the 1980s and 1990s and secured a two-fold increase in Home Office funding,[48] it has become increasingly vociferous in working to promote awareness of the effects of victimisation and lobbying for better provision for victims throughout the criminal process.[49] Although technically a voluntary organisation, it performs a vital public function, reflecting a gradual blurring between the state and civil society.[50] Karmen has noted that despite the 'different priorities and world views' of the victims' lobby in the United Kingdom and the USA,[51] if viewed in an international perspective the victim's movement has reinforced a five-fold basic critique of the criminal justice system:

> (1) That criminal justice personnel—the police, prosecutors, defence attorneys, judges, probation officers, parole boards . . . were systematically overlooking or neglecting the legitimate needs of crime victims until they all began their campaign; (2) that there was a prevailing tendency on the part of the public as well as agency officials to unfairly blame victims for facilitating or even provoking crimes; (3) that explicit standards of fair treatment were required to protect the interests of complainants and prosecution witnesses . . . (4) that people who suffered injuries . . . ought to receive reimbursement . . . (5) that the best way to make sure that victims could pursue their personal goals and protect their own best interests was by granting them formal rights within the criminal justice system.[52]

Owing, in part, to the effectiveness of the political lobbying of the victims' movement, and broader shifts in public policy, the role of the victim was conceptually reconstructed in the 1980s. As part of a renewed government drive towards economy and efficiency in the public services, the relationship between public services and the citizen underwent a major re-orientation, moving from a welfare model

---

[47] See, eg, Reeves (1985); Rock (1990), esp 133–98.

[48] Dignan (2005), 49.

[49] Rights-orientated publications began to emerge in the mid-1990s. See, eg Victim Support (1995) *The Rights of Victims of Crime,* which was used to consolidate existing policies and set out specific rights of victims under 5 main headings: compensation; protection; service; information and responsibility.

[50] Crawford (2000), 292.

[51] The victims' lobby in the USA has been traditionally perceived as being much more pro-active and rights-focused than its United Kingdom equivalent. The National Organisation for Victim Assistance (NOVA) was founded in 1975. It has been prominent in a campaign of 'national advocacy' through championing the victim's cause and exerting pressure on federal and state authorities. Since 1980, all 50 states have adopted over 1,000 pieces of legislation to protect victims of crime, and foremost amongst them are 'bills of rights' for victims.

[52] Karmen (1992), 159.

towards a provider / consumer dichotomy.[53] However, the accuracy of the parallel between victims and consumers is questionable since there are important distinctions to be made. Unlike consumers, victims do not have a free market to choose from, and they are 'trapped' in the criminal justice system in so far as they have no alternative service-provider on which they can rely.[54] Furthermore, claims that such a model will automatically deliver a better service to victims are undermined by the fact that, for the most part, many criminal justice agencies tend to work in isolation and are culturally geared to exercising complete control over traditional 'fiefdoms.'[55]

Nevertheless, it can be said that the consumer-based conception of criminal justice has brought certain benefits to victims and has acted as a catalyst in the formulation of new victim-centred policies within government circles and criminal justice agencies. MacCormick and Garland argue that the construction of the private citizen as a consumer of criminal justice services means that it is becoming increasingly difficult for the criminal justice system to treat individuals en masse as undifferentiated 'cases' to be processed.[56] Instead, a more flexible type of service is demanded by the consumer, whereby the individualised private interest is taken into account. As part of the drift towards this 'new managerialism,'[57] criminal justice agencies are increasingly placed in a position whereby they must justify their budgets by measuring the satisfaction of victims as consumers of their services, rather than by use of de facto statistics, such as the levels of clear-up rates.[58] Within policy circles, it is now perceived that a more flexible criminal justice service is demanded by consumers, whereby their individualised private interest is taken into account.[59] The full impact of the rise of the individual interest within public policy remains to be seen, but it is clear that this trend also produces tensions at a theoretical level, in so far as it remains unclear to what extent the interests of private parties are capable of being incorporated as part of the overall collective interest that has traditionally governed the deliverance of public services.[60]

As a result of these shifting conceptions of victims, the political appeal of the victim has become incrementally more attractive. As Geis describes:

> [t]he plight of the crime victim is dramatic and determinable. Their relief is feasible. It has strong political, social and personal appeal. Any of us, at any time, could become a crime victim.[61]

---

[53] See further Zauberman (2000), Walklate (2001).
[54] Walklate (2001).
[55] See generally Shapland (1988), (2000).
[56] MacCormick and Garland (1998).
[57] See generally Clarke et al (2000).
[58] Zauberman (2000); Walklate (2001), 208.
[59] MacCormick and Garland (1998).
[60] On recent changes to the conception of citizenship generally, see Clarke et al (2007).
[61] Geis (1990), 260.

Propelled by media coverage of moral panics concerning, inter alia, paedophilia, rising crime rates, and the perceived rise in 'anti-social behaviour',[62] the language used in recent official publications illustrates that policymakers have become increasingly keen to be seen to be protecting and promoting victims' rights. Since the Labour government came to power in 1997, sound-bites such as 'tough on crime, tough on the causes of crime', 'rebalancing the criminal justice system', and 'putting victims at the heart of criminal justice' have become familiar. It is feared, however, that governments throughout the western world are increasingly willing to use the crime victim as a front so that they are perceived as doing something about crime.[63] In this sense, official rhetoric may be used as a mask to introduce policies that are primarily aimed at securing the interests of the state as opposed to victims.

Successive governments have embarked upon piecemeal and hurried approaches to statutory reform in the name of the victim, in order to maximise the political appeal of certain policies and, arguably, to increase conviction rates. The limitations and the dangers of such policies are largely ignored, and weak legislation is rushed through Parliament in order to enhance the perception that governments are taking action to address a criminal justice system that appears to be spiralling out of control. Indeed, Koffman has warned that piecemeal measures couched in the language of victims' rights make it appear that the Government is addressing concerns over apparently rising crime whilst avoiding having to incur the major outlay of expenditure that would be required for more far-reaching reviews of the criminal justice system or major programmes of reform.[64]

From a human rights perspective, another concern is the way in which reforms undertaken in the name of 'rebalancing' the criminal justice system have placed significant curbs upon the due process rights of suspects and defendants without carrying any obvious benefits for victims. The ascendancy of zero tolerance policing, increased use of imprisonment, measures to encourage guilty pleas from defendants, increased disclosure obligations on the defence, and the removal of certain evidential protections for the accused have arguably been examples of astute political manoeuvring rather than a desire for an enhanced role or better protection for victims.[65] This focus on what Bottoms has labelled 'populist punitiveness'[66] has unfortunately meant that efforts to identify and remedy the structural problems and complex value-based questions have been significantly hampered.

---

[62] A moral panic begins with a deviant or criminal act, which threatens to spiral out of control. See generally Cohen (1972).

[63] Elias (1986a), (1990); Garland (2001).

[64] Koffman (1996), cited by Ellison (2001a), 4.

[65] Jackson (2003), 313.

[66] Bottoms (1995).

Victims in Contemporary Criminal Justice Policy: The Realisation of Rights?

The factors outlined above have acted as catalysts in the formulation of contemporary criminal justice policy and government rhetoric, much of which is heavily steeped in the language of victims' rights. Many of the earlier measures introduced, such as compensation and practical support, were less contentious, and were aimed at addressing the unmet needs of victims, thereby only touching upon their passive or indirect role. These measures generally refrained from conferring any new legal rights upon victims, and (despite the lack of any legal status), these earlier needs-based reforms have been frequently described as 'social rights' or 'service rights.'[67] However, more recent times have witnessed a shift in policy. With the commencement of the Human Rights Act 1998, it is increasingly apparent that, in addition to accessing certain services, victims ought to be entitled to certain substantive or procedural rights. These types of rights are potentially more controversial, since they would be enshrined in law and would thus be enforceable by victims within the criminal justice system, for example, in the context of a criminal trial.

The first 'service' right emerged in the form of the Criminal Injuries Compensation Scheme, which was created in 1964. The Scheme was established to provide a method of compensation for 'innocent' victims of violence as an acknowledgement of society's sympathy for, and obligation towards them.[68] Compensation was awarded to victims on a case-by-case basis through assessing individual harm suffered and expenses incurred. However, victims never had any legal right to access compensation under the scheme, as payments have always been made on an ex gratia basis and are only available to those who meet strict eligibility criteria. The Criminal Justice Act 1972 extended the possibility of seeking restitution by providing the criminal courts with powers to order an offender to pay a victim compensation for 'any personal injury, loss or damage resulting from the offence.'[69] Other forms of reparation in relation to juvenile offenders are provided for under the Crime and Disorder Act and Part I of the Youth Justice and Criminal Evidence Act 1999. Like the Criminal Injuries Compensation Scheme, these mechanisms are also imperfect and do not amount to a legal right for victims, but they do underline a long-term shift in policy that now reflects a widespread recognition that victims should be entitled to recompense.[70]

In addition to these mechanisms designed to deliver some form of compensation, the Government published a 'Statement of the Rights of Victims of Crime' in

---

[67] Ashworth (1998); Sanders et al (2001); Sanders (2004), 98.

[68] Compensation for criminal injuries has been justified on various grounds, including the idea that the Government has breached its 'social contract' with the individual or that the interests of social welfare or social obligation require the Government to aid victimised individuals. See further discussion at Ch 5, below, p 227.

[69] Criminal Justice Act 1972, s 35.

[70] The above mechanisms are discussed within the context of 'the right to reparation' in Ch 5.

the form of the 1990 Victim's Charter.[71] The document referred to four key 'rights' to which victims would be entitled within the criminal process. These were the right to receive information; the right to make a statement about the effects of the crime; the right to be treated with respect and sensitivity in court; the right to emotional and practical support. The extent to which this list constituted a 'statement of rights' is debatable. As with the 'right' to compensation, victims had no means of securing access to any of the Charter's guarantees through the legal process. In any case, the 'rights' laid down were so vague and ill-defined that, even had some mechanism of enforcement been available, it would have been relatively straightforward for a criminal justice agency to defend themselves against any allegations that they had breached the standards laid down in the document.[72] Nonetheless, the 1990 document constituted a significant measure in so far as it was the first proper attempt by a UK government to lay down in one document a set of aspirational principles, which had some bearing on the directions of future policies. In signalling a drift away from a needs-based or welfare-orientated approach, the adoption of the language of rights, however ill-defined, would come to dominate criminal justice policy in the years to come.

A second edition of the Charter was published in 1996.[73] Wisely, the Government revoked its use of rights-based language and instead used the Charter to commit to a set of standards which victims could legitimately expect in relation to criminal justice services. Much broader than its 1990 predecessor, the 1996 version contained standards relating to, inter alia, the police, Victim Support, compensation, prosecution, and conviction / release of an offender. However, its provisions remained unenforceable and their implementation was largely dependent upon the discretion of individual criminal justice agencies.

One of the most significant aspects of the 1996 edition of the Charter was its aim to provide victims with better access to information, an issue which has long been recognised as one of the greatest sources of dissatisfaction for victims and witnesses.[74] One particular difficulty in providing for such a right is that criminal justice agencies tend to have discrete responsibilities at different stages of the criminal process.[75] This means that information is not readily shared, let alone made available to victims. As part of their commitment to the Charter, the Home Office established the 'One Stop Shop' initiatives, whereby victims were given one port of call as a means of accessing information. Under the pilot scheme, which ran in five areas, the police were charged with providing victims with information about the charges, trial, outcome of proceedings and any sentence imposed, with information being passed to them by other agencies. Having been subject to a mixed evaluation,[76] the Scheme as it stood was never rolled out nationally and most of

---

[71] Home Office (1990).
[72] See generally Fenwick (1995).
[73] Home Office (1996).
[74] See Maguire (1985); Shapland et al (1985).
[75] Dignan (2005), 69.
[76] Hoyle et al (1998).

the responsibility for providing information to victims was transferred from the police to the CPS. This reflected a broader re-orientation of the relationship between victims and the CPS, which had been discernable in England and Wales for several years beforehand. In addition to providing basic information about prosecution and charge, the Service is now also under an obligation to provide an explanation for any decision to prosecute, although currently this only applies to families of homicide victims.[77]

The direction of contemporary victim policy has largely been governed by the 2002 White Paper, *Justice for All*, which promised to 'rebalance the criminal justice system in favour of the victim and the community so as to reduce crime and bring more offenders to justice.'[78] The precise means by which the system would be rebalanced were outlined in a subsequent publication the following year, *A New Deal for Victims and Witnesses*.[79] This paper contained plans for a new national strategy for victims and witnesses, a new statutory Code of Practice to replace the Victims' Charter, and the appointment of an independent Commissioner for Victims and Witnesses.[80] Since the publication of these documents, there has been a further raft of policies, protocols, and legislation designed to implement a range of victim-orientated reforms. These have included the establishment of a Victims' Advisory Panel;[81] the development of a 'Victims' Fund';[82] and the rolling out of the Witness and Victim Experience Survey (WAVES), to provide local data in all areas of England and Wales to assist the Government in targeting areas for policy improvement. In 2004, the Government introduced Witness Care Units, a latter day renaissance of the 'One Stop Shop' initiative. Established under the *No Witness, No Justice* programme,[83] the Units are staffed by CPS and Police Witness Care Officers, and create a single point of contact for victims and witnesses to facilitate the sharing of information.[84] In recent years, the experience of victims attending court has also been enhanced, with significant improvements made to services and facilities. Buildings, infrastructure and general facilities have been widely upgraded with plans in place for further improvements,[85] and Victim Support has also received a substantial boost in funding enabling it to provide a

---

[77] The changing nature of the relationship between victims and Crown prosecutors is discussed further below. See Ch 3, p 120–130.

[78] Home Office (2002a), para 0.3. As discussed later, the metaphor of balance has been subject to considerable criticism since it incorrectly implies that victims and defendants have locked horns in a 'zero sum game'—see further below, Ch 6, p 246–9.

[79] Home Office (2002a).

[80] Although a recruitment campaign began in Jan 2006, by Nov 2007 no appointment had been made.

[81] The Victims' Panel, set up in 2003, is a mechanism that allows victims to put their views directly to government ministers through a series of workshops.

[82] The Victims' Fund, which draws money from the proceeds of crime, was specifically aimed at developing local services to support victims of sexual offending.

[83] Home Office, (2004a).

[84] See further below, Ch 3, p 128.

[85] Cf Shapland and Cohen (1987); Shapland and Bell (1998); Plotnikoff and Woolfson (1998); Home Office (2002a); Angle et al (2003); Hamlyn et al (2004).

much more comprehensive service, including extending its Witness Support service to all Magistrates' Courts.[86]

The high watermark for victims, at least in terms of service-based reforms, came with the enactment of the Domestic Violence, Crime and Victims Act 2004. The legislation provides for a new Code of Practice to replace the Victims' Charter,[87] conferring statutory rights to support, protection, information and advice in relation to all the major criminal justice agencies.[88] Specific obligations include the need for the police to give victims information concerning the arrest of suspects,[89] progress updates on any investigation,[90] and notify them of the outcome of any bail decisions.[91] For their part, the CPS is under a duty to give reasons for decisions to drop or alter charges,[92] and should meet victims in particularly serious cases.[93] Witness Care Units are charged with informing victims whether they will be required to give evidence,[94] and with communicating the outcome of court hearings.[95] If victims feel the Code has not been adhered to by any criminal justice agency, they can file a complaint in the first instance, with the respective agency, and then, via their MP, with the Parliamentary Ombudsman.[96] In addition, the legislation has created the office of an independent commissioner for victims 'to promote the interests of victims and witnesses.'[97] Exercising an oversight role, he or she will also be responsible for reviewing the Code on a regular basis and encouraging good practice.[98] However, the limited extent of the powers conferred on the Commissioner underlines concerns that the Code fails to provide for any effective enforcement mechanism.[99] Section 34 of the Act provides that a failure by any agency to abide by a duty contained in the Code 'does not of itself make [any person] liable to criminal or civil proceedings.'[100] There is thus no freestanding right to enforce the Code through the courts: the rights contained within it are external to the criminal justice system, rather than falling within it.[101]

---

[86] Home Office (2002a); Home Office (2005a).

[87] Office for Criminal Justice Reform (2005).

[88] S 32. The original Bill was introduced in the 2002/03 session of Parliament, but was subsequently withdrawn as a result of a lack of parliamentary time: *The Guardian*, 10 Mar 2003. A revised version of the Bill received its First Reading in Parliament on 1 Dec 2003. The Code of Practice took effect in Apr 2006. Plans are in place to supplement the new Code of Practice with a separate Witnesses' Charter (Home Office, 2005a).

[89] Office for Criminal Justice Reform (2005), [5.14]

[90] *Ibid*, [5.9–5.12]

[91] *Ibid*, [5.16–5.17]

[92] *Ibid*, [7.4]

[93] *Ibid*, [7.7] See further below, Ch 4, p 128.

[94] *Ibid*, [6.3]

[95] *Ibid*, [6.7–6.8]

[96] S 47; Sch 7.

[97] S 48.

[98] S 49.

[99] See, eg criticism by Liberty (2003b).

[100] S 34(2), however, proceeds to stipulate that 'the code is admissible in evidence in criminal or civil proceedings and a court may take into account a failure to comply with the code in determining a question in the proceedings.'

[101] Hall (2007), 57.

It therefore remains the case that victims are unable to enforce the types of rights set out above through the courts and, as such, it is questionable whether the existing 'service' rights can be said to constitute proper 'rights' at all. In addition, these 'rights' also tend to be couched in vague language, which makes it impossible to measure whether criminal justice agencies are performing according to the necessary standard or not. Nevertheless, the theoretical basis for these rights is largely accepted on the grounds that, as 'consumers' of a public service, those who take it upon themselves to report an offence and assist in the criminal investigation have a legitimate interest in the way that they are treated by criminal justice agencies.[102] Access to information, compensation, support and better facilities available in courthouses can all be attributed, in part at least, to the construction of the victim as a consumer of criminal justice services.[103] To this end, such measures have generally received a broad welcome, since they are capable of ameliorating the plight of the victim without interfering with due process rights of the accused or the fundamental facets of the criminal justice system.

Yet, in many respects, the idea that victims should *only* be able to rely on 'service' rights has already been overtaken by events. The central purpose of the Human Rights Act 1998 was to offer victims of Convention violations recourse to protection within domestic courts. Section 3 of the Act requires that UK courts must read primary legislation in a manner which is compatible with the European Convention on Human Rights, and section 2 stipulates that they must take account of the jurisprudence of the Strasbourg court in reaching their decisions. Furthermore, the Act has legal repercussions for the way in which victims are treated from the point when they enter the criminal process. The police, courts, the Crown Prosecution Service and other criminal justice agencies count as 'public authorities' within the meaning of section 6(3) of the Act, and will be under a duty not to act in a way incompatible with the Convention. Actions may also be pursued on grounds of a failure to act in accordance with Convention duties. Thus, if victims are entitled to either substantive or procedural rights under the Convention, they should also be able to rely upon those same rights in UK courts.[104] It is demonstrated at various points of this book that Strasbourg case law has clearly established that victims have already acquired a number of substantive rights. As such, victims can expect to have these entitlements safeguarded in domestic law, and the State is under a positive obligation to see that this is done.[105]

In this sense, the Human Rights Act has encouraged commentators, policymakers and the courts to increasingly construe certain victims' rights as forms of human rights. Given that victims are now in a position to judicially review the actions of public bodies if they feel their Convention rights have been violated, we

---

[102] Zauberman (2000).

[103] Shapland and Bell (1998).

[104] Note, however, that courts are only obligated to take account of the Strasbourg jurisprudence. Courts are not bound by it. Thus the courts do not have the power to set aside primary legislation.

[105] See Ch 2, pp 39–44.

appear to be entering new pastures where the concept of victims' rights will be developed and refined in forthcoming years, and will be fully justiciable in English courts. Whilst, at the current point in time, the full effects of this new conception of victims' rights as a form of human rights remain uncertain, already law and policy have been influenced by many of the ideas that have underpinned these newly emerging rights. For example, it was widely acknowledged during the 1990s that more had to be done to offer better protection for victims testifying as witnesses in court. A range of special measures is now available for eligible witnesses under Part II of the Youth Justice and Criminal Evidence Act that may shield such witnesses from the glare of the accused and mitigate the astringencies of the adversarial process. The legislation also placed limits on the questioning that complainants in sex cases could be subjected to at court. The Criminal Justice Act 2003 introduced an 'enhanced relevance test' to ensure that non-defendant witnesses could not be asked irrelevant questions about their character, and also extended the circumstances whereby witnesses could rely on video links or pre-recorded evidence as alternatives to live testimony.[106]

The introduction of alternative methods of testifying, like the delivery of earlier 'service rights', have nonetheless not altered the public character of the criminal justice system; the trial remains loyal to its normative paradigm of a contest between the State and the accused. While it is true that these measures are positive indicators of some degree of formal acknowledgement of the victim's needs, few of them carry any legal effect and they are thus seen as being unlikely to impact upon the due process rights of the accused.[107] More problematic are those rights which human rights scholars would typically classify as 'procedural' in nature,[108] which would raise much deeper questions concerning how far the victim's interest ought to be accommodated within the traditionally dichotomous nature of the criminal trial between the State and the accused. Yet many proponents of victims' rights view such developments as long overdue, and argue that the idea of victims' rights should be developed one step further, entailing some form of procedural right of participation within criminal proceedings.

Ironically, one anomaly of the public nature of the criminal justice system has been the survival of the right to pursue a private prosecution. This procedural right has survived the State's historical appropriation of the victim / offender conflict, although for various reasons it is rarely resorted to in practice.[109] However,

---

[106] All of these developments are discussed within the context of a 'right to protection' in Ch 2.

[107] There is, however, the potential for some substantive rights to conflict with the rights of the accused. See below, Ch 2.

[108] Traditionally, commentators and courts have adopted a distinction between 'substantive' and 'procedural' rights. Whereas the former are generally concerned with freedoms to do certain things or freedoms from state interference in certain situations, the latter can be viewed as rights of access to certain procedures and safeguards that may be attached to those procedures. Eg, while the right of privacy and the right to be free from inhuman and degrading treatment are regarded as substantive rights, rights to due process and various fair trial guarantees are usually regarded as procedural rights.

[109] See Ch 3, pp 124–6.

recent steps have been taken to offer victims a more proactive role within public decision-making processes. Many criminal justice agencies, most notably the CPS, have been placed under an obligation to seek out the views of victims, and take their interests into consideration.[110] A further example is provided by section 69 of the Criminal Justice and Courts Services Act 2000, under which local probation boards are obliged to 'take all reasonable steps' to ascertain whether the victim of a violent or sexual offence wishes to make representations concerning any conditions placed on the release of such offenders from prison, and should also take pro-active steps to keep these victims updated about any conditions or requirements to which the offender is to be subject on release.

More contentious still are various new mechanisms that allow victims to have a direct input into sentencing. Following the establishment of several pilot schemes in England in the late 1990s, the Government introduced a nationwide *Victim Personal Statement Scheme* in October 2001, which allows victims to explain the impact of the crime upon them by way of a personal statement made to the police.[111] The statement is then forwarded to the judge to give a better overview of the impact of the offence that can then be factored into the sentencing process. It should be noted, however, that the scheme only allows participation at a practical level, in that the judge will have the opportunity to read how the crime has affected the victim: he or she is still unable to enforce any right of allocution at any stage of the criminal process.[112] However, in September 2005, the Government announced a pilot scheme for victims' advocates to participate on behalf of relatives of victims in cases of murder or manslaughter. In its consultation paper, *Hearing the Relatives of Murder and Manslaughter Victims,*[113] the Government envisaged that these advocates would have two roles: to assist the relative in making an oral victim impact statement in open court at the sentencing stage of proceedings, and providing advice and support to the relative throughout the trial to enable them to be more engaged in the process. However, the victim advocates will have no role within the trial process itself, and the degree of participation in both the trial and sentencing stages is still relatively minimal and compares unfavourably with models used in the United States and continental Europe.

Aside from participating in the criminal process itself, the right of access to an effective remedy has also been subject to increased discussion in recent times. The right is enshrined under Article 13 of the European Convention, although has become increasingly integrated into the substantive provisions of the Convention, most notably through Articles 2 and 3. Although Article 13 was omitted from incorporation under the Human Rights Act, the very concept of a 'right to a remedy' is now so closely linked to the substantive rights of the Convention that the

---

[110] Crown Prosecution Service (2004), paras 5.12, 10.2. However, there is no general duty in the United Kingdom for the prosecution to represent formally the victim's view at any stage of proceedings. See further Ch 3, pp 120–22.

[111] See below, Ch 3, pp 150–51.

[112] See below, Ch 3, *ibid.*

[113] Department of Constitutional Affairs (2005). See below, Ch 3, pp 146–7.

Strasbourg jurisprudence on the issue has exerted a strong influence on the formulation of domestic law concerning remedies for victims whose rights have been subject to interference. Thus both the Government and the courts have recognised the procedural obligations under the Convention to ensure that effective procedures are now in place to prosecute and investigate crime where victimisation has occurred. It is now settled law that any criminal investigation should be independent, effective, and reasonably prompt, particularly where a loss of life is concerned. This will have a direct bearing upon police investigations, coroners' inquests and public inquiries that may be set up in the aftermath of a killing. It has also been established, as part of the 'right to a remedy' that victims may seek a judicial review of any decision of the CPS not to bring charges, although it is rare for such a challenge to succeed.[114]

Yet, in domestic law, the longer-term impact of these developments upon victim-related policymaking remains unclear. To date, successive UK governments have introduced a range of schemes designed to bolster the so-called 'social' or 'service' rights of the victim, such as improved access to information, upgraded court facilities, and entitlements to compensation. A range of statutory measures provides for some degree of protection for victims in court, and there are a number of avenues open to victims through which they are able to pursue compensation. Moves have also been made to give victims a voice in decision-making processes. While it may be true to assert that the victims have certainly risen to a position of prominence on the contemporary policymaking agenda, it will be contended in the course of this book that victims' rights on the domestic platform are still considerably underdeveloped if we measure them against international benchmarks. While policymakers and politicians readily adopt the language of rights in relation to victims, this masks the fact that historical suppositions of the victim's role continue to prevent the full realisation of their rights within the criminal justice system.

III. The Normative Basis for Victims' Rights

One of the core arguments in this book is that the prospect of realising rights for victims is intimately connected with ideas about the proper role they ought to play within criminal justice. For that reason, it is worth probing in some further detail some of the semantic difficulties inherent in the very concept of 'victims' rights.' While the concept is used widely in contemporary academic discourse, political rhetoric, and everyday speech, this usage is often imprecise, decontextualised and ill-defined. Where 'victims' rights' is alluded to in non-legal discourses, it tends to muddy the waters in resolving normative questions concerning the proper role of victims' rights within the criminal process. For that reason, it may be useful to

---

[114] *R v DPP ex parte C* [1995] 1 Cr App R 141. See below, Ch 4, for a discussion of the right to a remedy.

begin by considering what is meant when certain actors are labelled as 'victims' within different contexts, and what it means in practice for them to be able to exercise certain 'rights.' Such questions have posed considerable difficulties for policymakers, lawyers and academic commentators alike; it is undoubtedly easier to fudge the answers rather than to attempt to address them in an explicit manner.

Defining 'Victims'

The task of designating an individual as a 'victim' is more complex than it might prima facie appear. Certainly, there is no authoritative definition that can be applied across the legal order. Generally, those definitions that do exist tend to imply that the victim is one who has suffered injury or loss as the result of an illegal act.[115] On occasions, use of the term will be relatively non-contentious. Even within the setting of a criminal trial, such definitions are unproblematic where both parties accept that the complainant has suffered a criminal wrong. For example, it could be the case that although the defence acknowledges that the accused caused injury or loss to a particular person, the implication that the accused committed the crime with the requisite mens rea may still be contested by counsel. In these types of cases, there is little problem attaching victim status to an individual who has clearly been harmed by the acts of another: the presumption of innocence does not necessarily assert that there has been no victim until an accused person has been convicted.[116]

However, in other cases, the term could prove much more factious in that the designation may give rise to an inherent implication that the allegations made by that person ought to be accepted as the historical truth before the tribunal of fact has arrived at its determination as to the guilt of the accused. It could be, for example, that the defence disputes the identity of the injured party, or the very commission of a criminal offence. In these circumstances, there is a risk that the factfinder may draw conclusions concerning the guilt of the offender. For example, in a rape case where the defence alleges consent on the part of the victim, it would be wholly inappropriate for the prosecution or judge to refer to the complainant as a 'victim' since that would infer that she had not consented to the intercourse. In such circumstances, it would seem sensible for courts to exercise

---

[115] In the USA, a victim is defined under s 3771(e) of the Justice for All Act 2004 'a person directly and proximately harmed as a result of the commission of a federal offense'. Arizona defines a victim as 'a person against whom the criminal offense has been committed, or if death occurred or the victim is incapacitated, the victim's spouse, parent, child or other lawful representative' (Arizona Revised Statute 13-4401) and Wisconsin defines a victim as 'a person against whom a delinquent act or crime has been committed (Wisconsin Constitution, Art 1 (938.02)). One of the few definitions to exist under English law is found under s 7(7) of the Human Rights Act, which rather unhelpfully defines a 'victim' by reference to Art 34 of the European Convention. However, for the purposes of the Act, it seemingly includes one who has whose rights under the Act have been violated as a result of an act of a public authority contrary to s 6 of the Act.

[116] Eg, in a murder case where the deceased was clearly the victim of an individual criminal action, there would be little reason to dispute the use of the term 'victim' to refer to the deceased.

caution when referring to the 'victim' within a trial setting lest the factfinder should be unduly prejudiced against the accused. As such, it is commonplace to hear lawyers refer instead to 'injured parties', 'plaintiffs' or 'complainants.'[117] Although use of these terms may avoid the potential for confusion in some ways, it has been suggested that some of these terms can also be demeaning, in that they 'have an impersonal flavour and a pejorative connotation of one who complains or whinges.'[118]

Whilst in law, the labelling of an individual who alleges that he or she has suffered a criminal injury as a 'victim' may prove dangerous without reference to any formal process of proof, the term is still widely used in a relatively loose fashion in everyday speech, particularly within journalistic and political discourses which fail to take account of the precise connotations which the term may carry in law. The sociologist, Niklas Luhmann, contends that the law and the media are essentially closed systems of communication, which are incapable of duplicating the meaning of each other's precise meanings.[119] Adopting Luhmann's theoretical framework of analysis, Nobles and Schiff have analysed the media reporting of Court of Appeal decisions and have demonstrated the different bases upon which law and the media each construct communications about the same events.[120] The authors found that legal and journalistic discourses did 'not share a common meaning and understanding of what constitutes miscarriage of justice.'[121] For example, where a conviction is quashed by the Court of Appeal, the appellant is usually deemed 'not guilty.' In law, this term carries a particular legal definition and essentially means that the prosecution has failed to discharge the burden of proof. In contrast, media communication frequently represents both acquittals at first instance and successful appeals as authoritative statements of innocence and full acceptance of the defence cases, thereby both reinforcing and responding to the general public expectation that a miscarriage of justice equates to innocence of an alleged crime. Precise legal meanings are therefore often lost in the reportage of crime, and it can be assumed that the 'victim' is often used in a similar way that bears little resemblance to the outcome of the legal process of fact-finding.

The imprecise conception of the 'victim' within the media can be contrasted with a much narrower, legalistic meaning when used in an 'official' capacity, for example, as part of legislation or non-statutory protocols that seek to grant victim services or protect victims' rights. For various public policy reasons, the State will often seek to distinguish between 'deserving' and 'undeserving' individuals to ensure that only the most worthy of them will be able to benefit from the increasing number of rights that are being made available to victims.[122] Elias contends that official definitions are frequently intertwined with protecting the State's

---

[117] Joutsen (1987b), 19–20.
[118] Miles (1995), 198.
[119] See generally Luhmann (1989).
[120] Nobles and Schiff (2000).
[121] *Ibid*, 109.
[122] See Elias (1986a), 302.

interest in effective social control in order to avoid threatening the fabric of the State. He warns that governments will, as far as possible, take steps to avoid any linkage between the concept of victimhood and existing political structures.[123] For this reason, policymakers have been traditionally reluctant to formulate official concepts of the crime victim that diverge too far from the social view of the 'ideal' victim.

According to Christie, the 'ideal' victim is characterised by five main attributes.[124] First, the victim should be in a weak or vulnerable position, such as being sick, old or very young. Secondly, the victim is most likely to be performing a respectable or worthwhile project, such as caring for a sick person or on their way to school. Thirdly, the victim may often be somewhere that he or she could not be blamed for being; for example at school during the day or at a church service. Fourthly, the offender is usually physically stronger and has a questionable social background or morals. Finally, the offender may be known or unknown to the victim, but they should not be in any personal relationship. Christie concludes that:

> [t]he ideal victim consists of a category of individuals who—when hit by crime—most readily are given the complete and legitimate status of being a victim.[125]

Brennan records the ideal characteristics as 'innocence, passivity, vulnerability, individuality, integrity and articulacy.' Such attributes, she argues:

> contrive to attain sympathy for the victim, making his voice deserving of attention, trustworthy, relevant to decision-making and a counter to any case being put forward by or on behalf of an offender.[126]

Such constructions are commonly reflected in official policy in such a way so as to reinforce the State's preferred definitions of social harms and problems and to strengthen existing power structures.[127] As a result of this State-sanctioned exclusion, many types of victims remain unacknowledged within the criminal justice system, and the 'ideal' or 'official' conception of the victim fails to reflect the experiences of the majority of individuals who have suffered injury or loss as the result of crime. Furthermore, since the State is responsible for delineating the parameters of the criminal law, it is also possible that many individuals who have suffered harm or loss as a result of another's conduct are incapable of receiving the acknowledgement and possible benefits that 'victim' status carries if there has been no breach of domestic law. Just as ideas of what constitutes victimhood are socially

---

[123] Elias (1986a), 301. Such a restrictive definition is reflected in the criteria regarding the operation of criminal injuries compensation in the UK. Under the scheme, compensation may be payable to the victims of certain violent offences providing that the victim is free from blame, thus effectively rendering some victims more equal than others. Victims may have their award reduced or refused on the basis of their conduct or character, including past unconnected criminal behaviour. See further Ch 5, pp 228–30.

[124] Christie (1986).

[125] *Ibid*, 18.

[126] Brennan (2001).

[127] Elias (1986a), 301.

constructed, it is now broadly recognised that the criminal law itself is largely for-mulated on the basis of social conventions and political motivations.[128]

In contrast to the narrow conceptions of victimhood used to control access to criminal injuries compensation, the concept of the 'victim' tends to be much broader and more inclusive within international human rights instruments. Although such definitions are generally not subject to the confusion or caveats that apply within media, political and policy discourses, they still tend to insist that the 'victim' is an individual whose status as an injured party is not in doubt. Frequently, however, such definitions will encompass both potential and indirect victims. For example, under the UN Declaration of Basic Principles of Justice for Victims of Crime and Abuse of Power,[129] victims are defined as:

> persons who, individually or collectively, have suffered harm, including physical or mental injury, emotional suffering, economic loss or substantial impairment of their fundamental rights, through acts or omissions that are in violation of criminal laws operative within Member States, including those laws proscribing criminal abuse of power.[130]

Under this definition, we can assume that both natural and legal persons, individ-uals and collective groups, and the families and dependants of injured parties would also constitute 'victims.'[131] In the same way, Principle 8 of the 2006 Basic Principles and Guidelines on the Right to a Remedy and Reparation, defines 'victims' in the following terms:[132]

> Victims are persons who individually or collectively suffered harm, including physical or mental injury, emotional suffering, economic loss or substantial impairment of their fundamental rights, through acts or omissions that constitute gross violations of inter-national human rights law, or serious violations of international humanitarian law. Where appropriate, and in accordance with domestic law, the term 'victim' also includes the immediate family or dependants of the direct victim and persons who have suffered harm in intervening to assist victims in distress or to prevent victimization.[133]

---

[128] Rock (1998), 186; Miers (2000), 79; Brennan (2001).

[129] UN Doc A/40/53.

[130] *Ibid*, Principle A.1.

[131] Principle A.2 also states that 'a person may be considered a victim, under this Declaration, regardless of whether the perpetrator is identified, apprehended, prosecuted or convicted and regard-less of the familial relationship between the perpetrator and the victim. The term also includes, where appropriate, the immediate family or dependants of the direct victim and persons who have suffered harm in intervening to assist victims in distress or to prevent victimization.'

[132] Basic Principles and Guidelines on the Right to a Remedy and Reparation for Victims of Gross Violations of International Human Rights Law and Serious Violations of International Humanitarian Law, UN Doc A/RES/60/147.

[133] See also, eg, the Convention Against Torture provides that '[a] person is a "victim" where, as a result of acts or omissions that constitute a violation of international human rights or humanitarian law norms, that person, individually or collectively, suffered harm, including physical or mental injury, emotional suffering, economic loss, or impairment of that person's fundamental legal rights . . . A per-son's status as "a victim" should not depend on any relationship that may exist or may have existed between the victim and the perpetrator, or whether the perpetrator of the violation has been identified, apprehended, prosecuted, or convicted' (UN Doc A/39/51). Art 1 of the European Framework Decision on the Standing of Victims in Criminal Proceedings designates a victim as 'a person suffering

Thus international human rights standards typically encompass a much broader range of victims than domestic law and policy. As Brennan suggests, there is a clear danger in attempting to define victimhood in such holistic terms that could mean that 'almost anyone can be a victim of anything.'[134] This could, for instance, cover all victims of breaches of civil law and their families. The lack of clear boundaries does mean that this may indeed be so; but this need not be viewed negatively. The effects of victimisation are overwhelmingly subjective, and official definitions should reflect the fact that individuals, particularly if they are so-called 'indirect' victims, may be affected in vastly different ways; and all will share a desire to see that justice is delivered. Yet even more important than this, is the need to acknowledge the harm that injured parties have suffered. Such acknowledgement is widely assumed to carry a cathartic effect for victims in helping them overcome the psychological impact of their victimisation.[135]

In this book, the term 'victim' is used to describe an individual in recognition of his or her complaint that he or she has suffered harm as the result of the criminal action of another. As in most other pieces of academic writing, it is used here as a form of criminological shorthand for 'alleged victim.'[136] In spite of the semantic difficulties surrounding the use of the term, it is argued that these should not pose an obstacle in describing those who make a complaint to the police as 'victims.' As Brienen and Hoegen argue, conceptualising the victim in this way is an important aspect of the effective protection of his or her rights throughout the criminal process:

> The presumption of being a 'non-offender' is necessary to protect the rights and interests of the accused and to enable him to effectively exercise his right of defence. However, if the presumption of being a 'non-victim' is used, it does not advance the interests of the victim. On the contrary, it prevents him from effectively exercising the defence of his rights and has a detrimental effect on his position in the pre-trial and trial stages. For this very reason, the analogy with the defendant's status as a 'non-offender' until proven otherwise should not be followed with respect to the victim of crime . . . A crime is first and foremost, to be regarded as a violation of the individual rights of the victim.[137]

It is thus vital that those who report crime are afforded some form of special recognition by the criminal justice system, the very raison d'être of which would seem to be the provision of a forum where those who report crime can participate in seeking a redress for criminal loss or injury.

---

physical or mental harm because of a violation of the criminal law of the State.' Under Art 34 of the European Convention on Human Rights, the victim is referred to as 'any person, non governmental organisation or group of individuals *claiming* to be the victim of a violation.'

[134] Brennan (2001), citing Bayley (1991), 53.

[135] Antkowiak (2002), Roht-Arraiza (1990), Aldana-Pindell (2004).

[136] Joutsen (1987b), 18.

[137] Brienen and Hoegen (2000), 30.

Defining 'Rights'

Unfortunately, just as the word 'victim' is used with little precision in non-legal discourses, so the term 'right' tends to be brandished about in popular media with very little thought as to what it actually means in law.[138] In a nutshell, the problem stems from the fact that little recognition is given to the status of a legal right (an entity that is enforceable through the courts) as something fundamentally different from what might be regarded as a moral right. As is illustrated throughout this book, it is clear that victims have already acquired a number of de facto rights, fully enforceable within the domestic legal system. Yet not all the 'rights' referred to are of this nature. Much of the discussion herein relating to 'rights' focuses on those processes or values that have already emerged, or are currently evolving, as human rights within the international order. Admittedly, from a positivist perspective, few of these could be defined as 'rights' in domestic law. Many exist on paper only; very few have any enforcement mechanism; and fewer still are legally binding within the United Kingdom.[139] Yet even if one does not accept the moral legitimacy of human rights or the uncertain legal platform on which they stand, it is important to bear in mind that many can be said to represent international consensus on the rights victims ought to have within domestic processes. In other words, while many 'human rights' of victims are not technically enforceable, it may be argued that they nonetheless represent statements of shared values that bear an increasingly strong influence upon the formulation of domestic law and policy.

Klug has identified a further benefit in conceptualising victims' rights as human rights. She argues that while analysing victims' rights as a form of human rights will not always provide clear-cut answers to difficult questions, the approach does provide a framework whereby competing rights can be assessed.[140] For example, there are occasions where the defendant's right to a fair trial may hinge upon the elicitation of relevant evidence in court which, because of the adversarial nature of the court process, could conceivably jeopardise the victim's right to privacy and /

---

[138] This situation has perhaps been confounded by the fact that there is, as yet, no fully entrenched 'bill of rights' in the UK, and the idea of effective protection of any definable set of human rights standards by the courts was largely alien until the Human Rights Act took effect. There is, of course, a large body of jurisprudential literature discusses the origin, nature and form of 'rights' which falls outside the scope of this work. See generally Hohfeld (1919); Dworkin (1978); Jarvis Thomson (1992); Kramer (ed) (2001).

[139] International legal commitments are only binding in United Kingdom law if they have been incorporated by statute. The European Convention was incorporated into United Kingdom law by the Human Rights Act 1998, giving its provisions full legal effect in domestic courts. Most treaty commitments are internationally binding, but are ineffective in UK law and unenforceable in domestic courts. Often, these commitments are referred to as 'hard law', and include eg the United Nations Convention against Transnational Organised Crime and the UN Convention on the Rights of the Child. Other various declarations, principles, codes of conduct and general comments issued by bodies such as the United Nations or Council of Europe are generally referred to as 'soft law' and are not binding under domestic or international law.

[140] Klug (2004), 123.

or freedom from inhuman or degrading treatment under the Convention. While it is fundamentally inaccurate to depict the criminal process as a zero-sum game between victim and defendant, the need to balance competing rights is a persistent feature in this context, and it is proper that the legal system should provide a principled framework in which such conflicts of rights can be resolved.[141]

Even if we adopt a human rights framework for analysing the rights of victims of crime, it is also necessary to consider deeper questions concerning how far such rights may impact upon the paradigm of common law criminal justice systems, which have traditionally revolved around a dichotomous contest between the State and the accused. If we consider that one of the primary functions of the criminal justice system ought to be the punishment of the guilty and the acquittal of the innocent, then some thought must be given as to precisely which rights the victim ought to have in the criminal justice system, given that, as noted above, his or her status as a 'victim' is somewhat uncertain prior to the determination of guilt. It is certainly true that the risks of injustice are not the same for the victim and the defendant, and, as such, the accused must always be at the centre of proceedings.[142] However, this does not mean the criminal justice system should not take account of other interests or objectives. Spencer argues that the subsidiary aim of proceedings should be to inflict 'as little pain as possible . . . to everyone concerned.'[143] Since the criminal justice system requires the co-operation of victims in their capacity as witnesses, there is a strong case for advocating that the structures and practices that prevail within it should be geared to supporting and protecting victims, as well as ensuring that the accused is given a fair trial.

However, one potential difficulty with such an approach is the perceived danger that victims' rights will endanger the objectivity of the criminal law and collective interests which it supposedly embodies. The raison d'être of the criminal justice system is to punish offending behaviour on the basis that crime is harmful to society. The penal measures imposed by the court are thereby conceived of as an official denunciation of the offender's wrongdoing by the collective public. Victims also form part of this collective interest, but it has long been considered that the subjective desires of victims do not enter into the equation lest these should impact negatively upon the core values of objectivity, consistency and due process. Many commentators have perceived a risk that these key objectives of the criminal justice system would be jeopardised if the public interest were to be compromised by the recognition of private interests,[144] as the following passage summarises:

> Even if it is the case that we are encountering frustrations in delineating the terrain between public and private interests, to allow squatters and anarchists to run wild, they assert, would destroy any process we have made in gaining control over the process of resolving our conflicts. Their view is that introducing civil liberties into the criminal

---

[141] On interest-balancing and the 'zero sum game', see Ch 6, pp 246–9.
[142] Jackson (2004), 70.
[143] Spencer (2004), 37.
[144] See, eg Garland (1990), 252; Von Hirsch (1993), 6; Simester and Sullivan (2003), 3.

process is in effect to tribalise once again the relationship between victim and offender . . . For in their perspective the long and short will be that the level of discretion of the participants in the system will be so enlarged that an *ad hoc* populism will replace the impersonal rigour of codified and judicially made law.[145]

However, in real terms, our present day conception of the basis for theoretical distinction between the two forms of law derives from the historical separation that took place in the Middle Ages between crime and tort. What constitutes a 'crime' as opposed to a 'tort' is thus purely dependent upon how crime is defined within any given society. It is a subjective judgement call, and it is not as easy as it may first appear to make a sound distinction between public and private interests. Indeed, the abstract notion of the 'public interest' is itself every bit as illusive and ill-defined as the idea of 'victims' rights.'[146] Irrespective of how we define the 'public interest', it is inextricably linked with the private interest, since without the holder of the private interests (ie the victim) reporting the offence, no 'public interest' can arise. If the same victim then fails to provide information and testify at court, the public interest would ultimately flounder. As Goldstein observes, in both fora, the State creates a legal framework and a remedy, and both civil and criminal liability are based on overlapping concepts of fault, recklessness and strict liability.[147] In this sense, both tort and crime can be viewed as variations along the same continuum of fault,[148] and the very idea of criminal behaviour is essentially artificially constructed by the State.

This normative blurring of public and private interests is reflected in contemporary legal practice in a number of ways. Over the course of the past three decades, the concept of victim / offender restitution has made significant inroads into the formulation of the criminal law. Since 1972, criminal courts have been empowered to order an offender to pay a victim compensation for any personal injury, loss or damage resulting from the offence,[149] and criminal courts are now obliged to consider whether it would be desirable to make a compensation order and must give reasons for refusing to do so.[150] So too, the explosion in restorative justice initiatives has presented victims with much greater opportunity to seek

[145] Weisstub (1986), 205.

[146] See further below, Ch 3, pp 121–2.

[147] Goldstein (1982), 530.

[148] See Weisstub (1986), 206: 'On reflection we begin to realise that many of the decisions in tort law are fully involved with public interests, even to the point where tort law is dictated to by criminal law statutes or by public policy infused with criminal law standards, or by public sentiment, which is affected, even unconsciously, by the current state of criminal law thinking. In a similar vein, we can locate myriads of cases in criminal law where, if we were given some leeway and the benefit of common sense, we would prefer to deal by negotiation or conciliation, and with a restitutional component, if it suited the purpose of resolving the conflict to the proper satisfaction of the victim.'

[149] The court may make a compensation order, instead of, or in addition to, any other penal sanction. Where the offender has insufficient means to pay both, the court shall give preference to the compensation order (s 130(12) Powers of Criminal Courts (Sentencing) Act 2000). The powers were originally set out in Criminal Justice Act 1972.

[150] S 130, Powers of Criminal Courts (Sentencing) Act 2000. S 130(4) of the Act states that compensation 'shall be of such amount as the court considers appropriate, having regard to any evidence and to any representations that are made by or on behalf of the accused or the prosecutor, the Court.'

reparation directly from the offender. In the last decade, such projects have become widespread and have been placed on some form of statutory footing in many jurisdictions.[151]

It is increasingly acknowledged that such shifts are part of a wider trend, whereby the systems of private and public law are becoming increasingly less discrete, to take account of changing perceptions of the function of criminal justice and the need to ensure that individual interests are adequately protected within legal processes. In their examination of the Race Relations (Amendment) Act 2000, Field and Roberts argue that a 'subtle but important shift' has taken place, whereby the criminal justice system is becoming increasingly geared 'toward a more interactive relationship between the individual rights of victims and their families on the one hand, and collective interests on the other.'[152] Indeed, the House of Lords itself has already recognised the reality of a 'triangulation of interests',[153] conceding that decision-making now involves taking into account the interests of the accused, the victim, and the general public. Unfortunately, there remains a lack of any principled attempt to clarify the hierarchy of potentially competing rights and interests. What has become apparent, however, is that the ascendancy of private interests within processes that have traditionally been (incorrectly) perceived as being purely public in nature thus necessitates a rethink of the roles of the State and the public interest within our conception of the criminal justice system.

The International Perspective

As a result of these changing understandings, the goals, values and structures which underpin the criminal process are being increasingly questioned, and it can be argued that these efforts to accommodate victims constitute a microcosm of a much broader and ongoing realignment of the parameters of criminal justice. In recent years, these parameters have been expanding rapidly, enveloping developments in human rights discourse and drawing extensively on practices in other jurisdictions and international fora. Increasingly, academics and policymakers are looking beyond their own jurisdictional and disciplinary confines for solutions to problematic questions and policymakers themselves seem increasingly anxious to move beyond formal international legal commitments to comply with best practice.[154] Indeed, within the field of criminal justice, there has been a proliferation of standards and norms over the past three decades, which might be said to reflect something approaching a consensus on best practice in terms of the values, structures and procedures that underpin our approach to dealing with criminal

---

[151] For an international overview, see Roche (2003), Ch 1. The merits of restorative justice as an alternative paradigm are considered in Ch 6, pp 254–65.

[152] Field and Roberts (2002), 495.

[153] *Attorney General's Reference No 3 of 1999* [2001] 2 AC 91, 118 per Lord Steyn.

[154] Jackson (2005), 737.

investigations, trials, sentencing, and victimisation.[155] With regard to crime victims, international concerns about their role and treatment within criminal justice have influenced the formulation of new international (though normally non-binding) standards, and have also driven victim-focused developments in international courts and tribunals. In turn, these international developments have percolated domestic legal orders, acting as a catalyst for reform. As Roberts notes, 'the nice, neat tripartite division between 'domestic', 'foreign' and 'international' law can no longer safely be relied on by any lawyer.'[156]

Policymakers are not only looking upwards towards international norms and international criminal justice, but also seem more willing to look sideways to what is seen to work well in other jurisdictions. The comparative exploration of laws, procedures, policies, structures and values can give us new insights into how our criminal justice system might be refined and improved to meet the needs and protect the rights of stakeholders in the justice system. While such benefits may seem fairly self-evident, there are inherent risks in cultural 'borrowing' and legal / policy transplants.[157] Furthermore, the temptation to deem all products of harmonisation as affirmative standards of best practice should be avoided. As Findlay has argued, international criminal justice developments have often appeared 'expedient rather than experimental, rationalised rather than rational.'[158] Care should thus be taken not to make automatic assumptions about international norms being inherently positive. In the context of victims' rights, this means that we should justify a newly emergent right not solely on the basis that it is a product of international consensus, but on the grounds that it would genuinely enhance the way we do justice.

We are not only looking beyond our own national borders, but we are also coming to appreciate the value of interdisciplinary approaches. Concepts, values, ideas, and approaches are increasingly being enhanced through interaction with other disciplines. From the perspective of the crime victim, the cross-fertilisation that is occurring between victimology and human rights carries huge potential to drive forward and refine the concept of victims' rights. At first glance, the relationship between human rights and the idea of victims' rights appears somewhat awkward. The victims' lobby has been traditionally perceived as a conservative or right wing force, entrenched in ideas of retributivism and vengeance with little concern for the rights of the offender. By contrast, human rights discourse has been paradoxically perceived as liberal or left wing and perhaps even apathetic towards victims of non-state crime. It is true to a large extent that, traditionally, crime victims rarely featured within human rights instruments, although suspects, defendants and offenders did receive a considerable degree of attention. One such example is Article 6 of the European Convention, which encapsulates the right to

---

[155] See Rehman (2002); Jorg et al (1996); Amann, (2000); Jackson (2005). With regard to convergence generally, see Markesinis (ed) (1994).

[156] Roberts (2002), 560–1.

[157] See Ch 6, p 289.

[158] Findlay (2002), 241.

a fair trial, but restricts this right to the accused. No corresponding provision is made within the Convention relating to the idea of a fair trial for victims or witnesses; and thus the relationship between these actors and the interests of the state, and those of the accused, has never been defined. This position is reflected in a range of other international instruments.[159]

This neglect was attributable to two main factors. First, the criminal trial has been traditionally viewed in both international and domestic law as a contest between the State and the alleged perpetrator. Victims have been seen as mere witnesses to the State's case against the accused, with little or no consideration given to their interests. Secondly, whereas victims of abuse of power are in a direct vertical relationship with the State, victims of non-state crime are in a horizontal relationship with the perpetrator. Whereas domestic criminal law concerns the relationship between two individuals, human rights has focused on the state as a perpetrator, with the victim the one who has been abused by the state. As Rock argues, protection for victims of non-state crime was perceived as being 'axiomatically built into the substance of the heat of the state as the policing and prosecuting authority.'[160]

Human rights and victimology have, until recently, tended to view both types of victims through discrete lenses. There has been relatively little exchange of ideas between the disciplines, and both have tended to adopt distinct terminologies and modes of analysis. However, shifting disciplinary parameters of both human rights and victimology have presented a new opportunity to formulate a unified concept of victims' rights. Human rights discourse has been transformed in order to take into account the ongoing international fluctuations in loci of power, the growing role of non-state actors and the corresponding increase in opportunities afforded to individuals to utilise formal complaints mechanisms. New procedural and substantive rights have thus emerged for victims of human rights abuses. Once central to the discipline, the vertical / horizontal divide has become increasingly blurred, and the scope of human rights protection has expanded considerably.

In the same way, the study of victimology has undergone a significant change, moving away from the typologies and stereo-typing of earlier days, towards a more integrated and holistic discourse taking into account the numerous relationships in the criminal justice system between victims, offenders and the State, as well as the underlying importance of human rights and due process for all stakeholders. As Robert Elias first acknowledged two decades ago, both victims of state and non-state crime will ultimately benefit, as the disciplines of victimology and human rights expand:

> to provide crime victims with more rights, and victims of oppression with greater protections. The two fields can gain individually and mutually through their interactions.[161]

---

[159] Eg Art 10, UDHR; Art 14(1), ICCPR; Art 8, IACHR. However, as noted below, the European Court has since developed its jurisprudence under Art 6 to extent the concept of a fair trial to victims as well as accused persons.

[160] Rock (2004), 233.

[161] Elias (1986b), 267.

As a result of this mutual expansion, there has been a widespread recognition that the plight of crime victims has much in common with the plight of victims of so-called 'state crime', or abuse of power. In terms of their experiences, there are several striking similarities between both types of victims. Both suffer similar emotional and psychological responses, such as self-blame and outrage; the impact of the offence on their lives may be similar; and both feel the need for some form of redress from the offender.[162] Furthermore, victims, whether they are victims of crime or victims of abuse of power perpetuated by the State, are often subject to the same feelings of alienation and exclusion during any subsequent legal proceedings. Physically, financially and psychologically, these two types of victims have much in common.

This parallel expansion in the parameters of victimology and human rights is now evident in a range of international instruments, dating back to the 1985 UN Declaration of Basic Principles for Justice for Victims of Crime and Abuse of Power,[163] its very name serving to illustrate the reconceptualisation of victimhood as a notion inclusive of those who had been victimised by the State as well as by private individuals. The Declaration defines crime prevention as a victims' rights issue, and guarantees victims access to justice and fair treatment, a right to information, assistance, and access to informal dispute resolution methods.[164] The provisions in this instrument were further developed by two UN reports, Theo Van Boven's 1993 report on the 'Right to Restitution, Compensation and Rehabilitation for Victims of Gross Violations of Human Rights and Fundamental Freedoms',[165] and the more recent concluding report of Cherif Bassiouni to the Commission of Human Rights on the same subject.[166] These reports underlined the link between the right to reparation and the prevention of human rights violations, and emphasised the importance of seeking redress from the perpetrator and the need for measures by the State to prevent future violations. In highlighting the link between reparation, conflict resolution and deterrence, Bassiouni noted:

> [T]he obligation to respect, and to see that human rights are respected imposes the obligation on States to take appropriate legislative and administrative measures in order to prevent violations . . . to investigate violations and take action against the perpetrator . . . to provide victims with equal and effective access to justice . . . to afford appropriate remedies to them; and provide or facilitate reparations.[167]

The Reports culminated in the formulation of the Basic Principles and Guidelines on the Right to a Remedy and Reparation for Victims of Gross Violations of International Human Rights Law and Serious Violations of

---

[162] *Ibid*, 194.

[163] GA Res 40/34, 29 Nov 1985.

[164] Eg, the Declaration provides that the use of such mechanisms should ensure that the 'outcome is at least as beneficial for the victims as would have been the case if the formal system had been used' (para A.7).

[165] Van Boven (1993).

[166] Bassiouni (2000).

[167] *Ibid*, 4.

International Humanitarian Law, adopted by the UN General Assembly in December 2005.[168] Aside from these victim-specific instruments, many other international documents require the interests of victims to be taken into account in a variety of different ways. These include the Basic Principles for the Treatment of Prisoners,[169] the UN Convention against Transnational Organised Crime and the Standard Minimum Rules for Non-Custodial Measures,[170] and the Vienna Declaration on Crime and Justice.[171]

More attention has also been paid to the interests of victims in the rapidly growing body of international criminal law. The United Nations was responsible for formulating victim-sensitive rules in the Rules of Evidence and Procedure for the tribunals for the former Yugoslavia and Rwanda,[172] the Statutes of which acknowledge a relationship between the accused's right to a fair hearing and the need to protect victims and witnesses.[173] The Rome Statute of the International Criminal Court would seem to confirm that the interests of victims and witnesses are now in the process of being fully integrated into international criminal process. Not only does the Statute contain an extensive range of protective measures that victims can rely on in their capacities as witnesses, but it also confers upon victims the right to present their views and concerns at certain stages of the proceedings.

At European level, both the Council of Europe and the European Union have also been involved in standard-setting. In 1983, the former organisation was responsible for formulating the European Convention on the Compensation of Victims of Violent Crimes which lays down minimum standards for the provision of state compensation to victims of crime. Signatory states to the Convention are required to ensure that victims suffering serious bodily injury or impairment of health receive compensation for at least the loss of earnings, medical and funeral expenses and the loss of maintenance to any dependants.[174] The Convention was followed in 1985 by the adoption of Recommendation 85(11) on the Position of the Victim in the Framework of Criminal Law and Procedure,[175] and since then

---

[168]   GA Res 60/147, 16 Dec 2005.

[169]   Principle 10 states: 'With the participation and the help of the community and social institutions, and with due regard to the interests of victims, favourable conditions shall be created for the reintegration of the prisoner into society.'

[170]   R 8(1) states: 'The judicial authority, having at its disposal a range of non-custodial measures, should take into consideration in making its decision the rehabilitative needs of the offender, the protection of society and the interests of the victim, who should be consulted whenever appropriate.'

[171]   Vienna Declaration and programme of Action UN Doc A/CONF.157.24 (1993), see esp paras 27–8.

[172]   The Rules of Procedure and Evidence of the Tribunal for the former Yugoslavia apply, mutatis mutandis, to the Rwanda Tribunal (Art. 14 of the Statute of the International Tribunal for Rwanda).

[173]   See Art 21(2) which stipulates that the right to a fair and public hearing is subject to the range of protective measures for victims and witnesses contained in Art 22.

[174]   Compensation is available to all victims whose injuries are 'directly attributable to an intentional crime of violence.' See Arts 2 and 4.

[175]   Brienen and Hoegen (2000), 11. The authors note that the Recommendation (85) 11 is split into 2 distinct parts. The first contains explicit guidelines for reviewing legislation and the recommended course of action in the member states of the Council of Europe. The second part consists of a call to the governments to examine the possible advantages of mediation and conciliation, and to promote research on the efficacy of provisions affecting victims.

many more recommendations have followed, setting down a range of standards in relation to the provision of support, protection and assistance for victims and witnesses. In addition, the Strasbourg Court has been responsible for developing a line of jurisprudence, using the European Convention of Human Rights to create a range of new rights for victims and witnesses. During the latter part of the 1990s and in the earlier part of this century, issues affecting victims and witnesses appeared before the court on a frequent basis, which have culminated in a number of new legal rights expressly recognised by the Court, even if they are not categorically spelled out in the Convention.

Turning to developments within the European Union, in 1999 the Commission issued a communication to the European Parliament entitled *Crime Victims in the European Union: Reflections on Standards and Action.*[176] This document contained seventeen proposals grouped under five main headings: prevention of victimisation; assistance to victims; standing of victims in the criminal procedure; compensation issues; and general issues (information, language, training), and called on all member states to implement fair and effective legislation in these areas. Following its adoption by the Parliament, the Justice and Home Affairs Council adopted the Framework Decision on the Standing of Victims in Criminal Proceedings in March 2001.[177] While some of its provisions have been drafted in a vague or imprecise manner to ensure a basic level of compatibility with different legal cultures, its significance should not be underestimated. Unlike many international standards, all of the rights contained within the Framework Decision are binding and are directly applicable within the domestic legal order.

The exponential expansion in victim-related norms underlines the prominent position that the victim has now assumed in international human rights and criminal justice discourse. However, it remains the case that many of these norms tend to be non-binding, and adopt ambiguous language which makes their scope uncertain. For that reason, it is often difficult to gauge whether specific jurisdictions are complying with such standards or not. Furthermore, it is apparent that some of these newly emergent 'rights' are subject to a greater degree of consensus that others. For example, it is noted in the course of this book that, while it is broadly acknowledged that victims ought to be entitled to protection during the criminal process and some form of reparation as a result of their victimisation, the idea of participatory rights in trials or sentencing procedures is still contentious, with any such 'right' still very much in the developmental stage. Thus, while there can be said to be a widespread consensus that victims ought to be entitled to certain broadly defined rights, the specific meaning and content of such rights remains uncertain.

---

[176] European Commission (1999).
[177] Council Framework Decision 2001/220/JHA.

IV. Victims' Rights and the Adversarial Process

The Anglo-American criminal justice system is said to be 'adversarial' in nature.[178] The focal point of the adversarial tradition is the trial itself, described by Landsman as a 'sharp clash of proofs presented by litigants in a highly structured forensic setting'.[179] Parties in the adversarial system enjoy a high degree of freedom of proof, which largely extends to the manner in which witnesses are cross-examined. At the heart of the trial lies the principle of orality, which provides that evidence should generally be received through the live, oral testimony of witnesses in court. The entire criminal process is designed to culminate in a confrontational showdown between the prosecution and the accused, and such postures can serve only to deepen the existing conflict.[180]

One of the major aims of this book is to question the extent to which the emergent rights of victims and witnesses may be realised within the adversarial criminal justice system of England and Wales. Globalisation and harmonisation are already a reality, impacting upon the formulation of law and policy, but it is impossible to divorce these pragmatic questions on the victims' role without simultaneously examining underlying structures and conceptions of criminal justice. Writing in the early 1980s, McBarnet recognised that the proposed solutions have been overly centred on addressing visible problems within the criminal justice system as opposed to 'the deeper structures that help create them.'[181] McBarnet regarded these structures as symbols of law and order that must be upheld despite the victim's wishes.[182] Thus the victim who will not co-operate within the given adversarial paradigm is threatened with criminalisation.[183] McBarnet's ideas have been instrumental in encouraging other commentators to examine the 'deeper structures' to which she referred. For example, in *The Adversarial Process and the Vulnerable Witness*,[184] Louise Ellison argued that as long as orality and cross-examination are regarded as sacrosanct features of the English criminal trial, victim-witnesses in court are unlikely to be relieved of secondary victimisation. She maintains that effective solutions to the problems facing vulnerable witnesses can only be found by looking beyond the adversarial system, since there is an inherent:

> basic conflict between the needs and interests of vulnerable witnesses and the resultant evidentiary safeguards of the adversarial trial process.[185]

---

[178] An important caveat should be noted. The English system is not a prototype legal model: like other common law jurisdictions, the term 'adversarial' refers to the general structure of the proceedings. It is not used to set up the English mode of trial as some form of definitive norm, and it would be a misconception to state that the English trial model is purely adversarial, since it does possess some 'inquisitorial' features. See McEwan (1998), 1.

[179] Landsman, (1984), 2.

[180] Frehsee, (1999), 236.

[181] McBarnet (1983), 303.

[182] *Ibid*, 300–2.

[183] *Ibid*, 301. Eg, a victim who refuses to testify can be punished for contempt of court.

[184] Ellison (2001a).

[185] *Ibid*, 7.

In the same way, many advocates of restorative justice have contended that the exclusionary structures of the sentencing system make it fundamentally impossible to implement practices which are capable of providing comprehensive reparation to victims.[186]

The arguments set out in this book largely concur with these analyses, and identify a number of structural and normative barriers that lie at the heart of the adversarial paradigm which may impede its ability to give effect to the new rights for victims which are currently being constructed on the international platform. Owing to the conceptualisation of crime as an offence against the state, the criminal justice system is traditionally viewed as a system to facilitate a conflict between the state and the accused. The victim is thereby inherently excluded. Furthermore, trials are typically characterised by a highly competitive and confrontational atmosphere, which renders them fundamentally ill-equipped to address emotional trauma and private conflicts that have arisen as a result of the offence. The contest culture of the courtroom is not at all conducive to *listening* to the accounts of individual witnesses, let alone healing conflicts. Instead, the culture of the courtroom concerns the criminal liability of the accused.

If the accused is convicted, the bipartisan contest will continue into, and beyond the sentencing process. The prosecution will seek to impose a sentence that, theoretically at least, reflects the public interest. For their part, defence counsel will generally enter a plea in mitigation. Only recently have policymakers sought to integrate the interests of victims into sentencing, largely through the introduction of Compensation Orders and Victim Personal Statements.[187] Victims continue to be largely excluded from the process and usually stand to receive very limited or no reparation directly from the offender. Furthermore, without root and branch reform, existing structures cannot easily be adapted to accommodate the meaningful participation or effective protection of any third party.

Conceptually, victims have no role to play in the modern criminal justice system other than to act as 'evidentiary cannon fodder.'[188] In contrast to many continental systems, they have no 'right to be heard' or give a narrative account,[189] and they are denied any form of proactive participation in the trial, since their interests are deemed to fall outside the remit of the criminal trial as a forum for the resolution of the dispute between the State and the accused. Victims have been 'conscripted' into an operational role within the criminal justice system, and are generally treated as its servants or agents.[190] In the view of criminal law purists, the 'rights' and the 'interests' of the victim should thus be pursued under the civil, as opposed to the criminal law, using the law of tort. Therefore, although many victims may feel as though they are 'owed' a right to exercise a voice in decision-making processes, such as prosecution, reparation and sentencing, the criminal

---

[186] See, eg Zehr (2005); Walgrave (2002); Braithwaite (2003).
[187] See Ch 5, pp 232–6; and Ch 3 pp 150–51 respectively.
[188] Braithwaite and Daly (1998), 154.
[189] See discussion below, Ch 6, pp 269–94. See generally Spencer, (1997).
[190] Faulkner (2001), 226.

justice system places such rights or interests in a firmly subservient position to the collective interests of society in prosecuting the crime and imposing a denuncia-tory punishment.[191] In spite of the many reforms introduced in the name of bolstering the role of the victim, victims' rights remain on the periphery of the traditions, norms, structures and processes of the adversarial paradigm.

---

[191] Cavadino and Dignan (1997), 237.

2

The Right to Protection

THIS CHAPTER EXAMINES the emergence of a 'right to protection' for victims of crime. The concept of 'protection' has assumed a prominent role in contemporary criminal justice debates. According to some commentators, we are living in a 'risk society',[1] where fear about social wellbeing and general security has come to dominate politics and the media.[2] To some extent, this is attributable to a contemporary climate of fear of crime, which is a major preoccupation for western cultures.[3] Such a fear may or may not be proportionate to the actual threat, and may have come about as a result of direct or indirect experience, but, for those who have already experienced victimisation, a sense of powerlessness to prevent a repeat attack or subsequent intimidation remains very real.[4]

There is, undoubtedly, an expectation on the part of the general public that the state ought to take proactive measures to protect them from crime. Such a view has its origins in social contract theory, which emerged from the seventeenth century philosophies of Hobbes and Locke. The philosophy basically states that individuals surrender certain freedoms to the State in exchange for the latter's role in protecting society from others who breach the contract.[5] Thus the government acquires the role of benevolent protector of its citizenry, and is charged with the duty of preventing victimisation and punishing perpetrators of crime. This expectation of a sense of security is regarded as fundamental to a democratic society, and within a contemporary context, it is also intimately connected with human rights and the concept of fair treatment. Indeed, as a consequence of the increasingly consumerist view of citizenship outlined in the previous chapter,[6] there is a growing expectation on the part of the public that the state ought to do more in fulfilling its role in the social contract by taking greater steps to protect citizens from criminal behaviour.

This chapter examines the idea of a 'right to protection' in two main contexts. First, we consider the need for protection from *becoming* victims of crime in the first place. Drawing from both international standards and domestic practice, we

---

[1] Beck (1992).

[2] See further Bauman (2006).

[3] See eg Hale (1996); Hope and Sparks (2000); Garland (2001).

[4] Ferraro (1995); Farrall and Gadd (2004).

[5] Hobbes argued in *Leviathan* that individuals had ceded individual rights in return for protection from outlaws. The philosophy was particularly influential in eighteenth century Europe, where it was expounded by Jean-Jacques Rousseau. See generally Skryms (1996).

[6] See Ch 1, pp 9–10.

examine the nature of the obligation of the state to put appropriate mechanisms in place to safeguard us against both primary victimisation and repeated or continuous victimisation. Of course, in a strict sense, this is not a right that is limited to victims of crime; rather, it is a right to which all citizens are entitled, since all are potentially victims of crime.

Secondly, the chapter reflects on the concept of 'secondary victimisation,' which is a label commonly applied to describe the additional suffering of victims that has been incurred as a result of the institutional response to an offence. For the most part, the chapter focuses on protection for victims in their capacities as witnesses in court. While not all crime victims will be asked to give evidence in court, there are a significant number who will face this prospect. In the light of a considerable body of research documenting the plight experienced by victims in their capacities as witnesses,[7] the past two decades have witnessed a discernable trend where jurisdictions have introduced an array of measures designed to alleviate the stress and anxiety that have been associated with testifying. These statutory protections have, in part, been inspired by a growing body of international standards in the area. However, this chapter argues that the capacity of the adversarial system to fully comply with such standards in the longer term is highly questionable given the structures and values inherent in the adversarial paradigm.

I. Protection from Victimisation

The idea of 'protection' or 'security' is so wide that it is difficult to define its parameters. While it may refer generally to the idea of safeguarding one's physical integrity, it may take different forms.[8] A 'right to protection' may be seen to include, for example, the collective security of the nation (eg from terrorism or invasion), and in this context, the right may need to be balanced alongside specific individual rights contained within any one instrument. It may also be framed in a different sense, as the right to liberty and / or security of the person, a right that was devised primarily to protect individuals from excessive or unlawful use of force by the state.[9] This emphasis is reflected, for example, in the case law surrounding Article 5 of the European Convention, which has been mostly concerned with the actions of police officers, soldiers, or security forces. However, in the context of protecting society from the criminal actions of other individuals, the collapse of the vertical / horizontal divide and expanding duties upon the state have opened the door for victims of non-state crime to have their right to protection safeguarded within the framework of human rights law.

---

[7] See below, pp 51–64.

[8] See Powell (2006), who contends that the concept of security is primarily about safeguarding other substantive values, but that a right to security itself has little independent content.

[9] Examples include Art 3 UDHR, Art 9 ICCPR, Art 5 ECHR and Art 6 of the African Charter of Human Rights and People's Rights.

Positive Obligations: The Duty to Protect Life

The idea that the state should be ultimately responsible for preventing and punishing crime is now commonly accepted within human rights discourse, and it is clear that there are now many circumstances where the State is under a duty to put in place legislative frameworks, together with practical measures, to protect individuals from serious forms of crime that threaten their life or physical integrity. Such preventative obligations are particularly commonplace in circumstances where vulnerable parties are perceived to be at heightened risk. Children,[10] those at risk from domestic violence,[11] and those at risk from intimidation or repeat victimisation,[12] have all been subject to some form of special recognition within international instruments.

At Council of Europe level, the obligation to protect victims and potential victims of crime makes very specific demands upon signatory states. Recommendation 06(08) provides:

> States should ensure, at all stages of the procedure, the protection of the victim's physical and psychological integrity . . .

> Specific protection measures should be taken for victims at risk of intimidation, reprisals or repeat victimisation.[13]

The primary obligations are, of course, to be found in the Convention itself, and these have largely unfolded through the doctrine of positive obligations. The doctrine, which stems from the decision in *X and Y v Netherlands*,[14] stipulates that signatory states are under a positive duty to put in place preventative measures to ensure that non-state parties do not breach the human rights of others.[15] In this

---

[10] Eg, under Art 19 of the Convention on the Rights of the Child, states are obligated to put effective and appropriate measures in place to protect children from all forms of physical or mental violence.

[11] See eg Council of Europe Rec (2000)1450, which calls for the State to introduce legislation outlawing all forms of domestic violence, criminalising marital rape, and ensuring greater protection for women through the use of restraining orders. Art 6 of the Convention on the Elimination of All Forms of Discrimination against Women (CEDAW) requires states to 'take all appropriate measures, including legislation, to suppress all forms of traffic in women and exploitation of prostitution of women.' Building on Arts 2 and 3 of the Convention which aims to eliminate discrimination in all its forms, 2 General Recommendations of the CEDAW Committee further oblige signatory states 'to protect women against violence of any kind occurring within the family, at the workplace or in any other area of social life' (UN Docs A/44/38 and A/47/38). As part of this obligation, states are asked to provide information on legislation and other measures that may be capable of counteracting the threat of domestic violation.

[12] Recommendation (97)13, [14] requires States to put in place witness protection programmes. See further discussion below at pp 71–72.

[13] At [10.1–10.2].

[14] [1985] 8 EHRR 235. It was stated that: 'there may be positive obligations inherent in an effective respect for private or family life. These obligations may involve the adoption of measures designed to secure respect for private life even in the sphere of the relations of individuals between themselves' (at [23]).

[15] For an account of the history and development of the doctrine, see Mowbray (2004). Regarding its specific application to domestic criminal law in the post-HRA era, see Rogers (2003).

case, the Court found that the State had failed to safeguard the victim's right to privacy through the failure to protect a woman with learning disabilities from sexual abuse. Although the case concerned Article 8 of the Convention, it is now widely accepted that the doctrine applies to all provisions, including the right to life.

Described by the UN Human Rights Committee as 'the supreme right of the human being,'[16] the right to life is undoubtedly the most fundamental of all human rights. As the European Court of Human Rights noted in *McCann and others v United Kingdom*,[17] the right is one of the most fundamental rights contained in the Convention and enshrines a basic value common to all democratic societies.[18] Although it is the regional human rights fora that are most commonly credited with driving forward the scope of the right to life, in 1955, when the phrase 'positive obligations' was unknown in human rights law, the UN referred to the right comprising the 'duty of the State to protect human life against unwarranted actions by public authorities as well as by private persons.'[19] This duty has since been reiterated and further developed in international and regional human rights law through both hard and soft law instruments and case law.

Under Article 2 of the European Convention, states must not only refrain from taking life,[20] but must also take steps to protect life against threats from third parties. This will involve putting in place effective criminal law measures aimed at deterring and preventing crime that may pose a threat to life. The seminal case is that of *Osman v United Kingdom*,[21] which concerned the murder of Ali Osman who was shot dead by his son's former teacher. Osman's widow and son complained that the police had failed to take reasonable measures to prevent the accused killing him. Although the Court found no breach of Article 2 on the facts, it adopted a number of important principles relating to victims of crime. These included the extension of the State's obligation under Article 2 in circumstances where authorities failed to do all that could reasonably be expected of them to avoid a 'real and immediate' risk to life that they knew about or ought to have known about in certain defined circumstances.[22] The State was therefore under an obligation 'to take preventive operational measures to protect an individual whose life is at risk from the criminal acts of another' and secure the Article 2 rights of particular persons who are known to be at risk.[23] Furthermore, the Court found

---

[16] United Nations Human Rights Committee (1982).

[17] (1995) 21 EHRR 97.

[18] At [147].

[19] United Nations (1955).

[20] Except in circumstances outlined in Art 2(2). The proviso does not, however, define instances where the State is permitted to intentionally kill an individual, but rather describes the situations in which it is permitted to use force, which incidentally may involve the taking of life. See, eg *Ergi v Turkey*, Decision of the Court, 28 Jul 1998 (App No 23818/94).

[21] (1998) 29 EHRR 245.

[22] See [90–2].

[23] See, eg, *Kilic v Turkey*, Decision of the Court, 28 Mar 2000 (App No 22492/93). Here, a journalist who had received death threats sought protection from the local Governor before his murder. The Court upheld a complaint that the Turkish authorities had failed to take reasonable measures available to them to prevent a real and immediate risk to life (at [77]).

that the blanket immunity in English law which restricted an individual from bringing a claim in negligence against the police was unjustifiable,[24] and this was held to constitute a breach of the right of access to a court for victims under Article 6 of the Convention.

In contrast to its reasoning in *Osman,* the Strasbourg Court rejected the applicant's case in *Z v United Kingdom,*[25] which concerned a neglect of duty by child protection authorities. It was held that the inability to sue public authorities in negligence stemmed from 'the applicable principles governing the substantive right of action in domestic law' rather than any immunity, and in this instance it was held that domestic courts had legitimately decided to restrict the access to a remedy through the application of the *Caparo* test .[26] As such, no 'civil right' could be said to exist in domestic law under Article 6 of the Convention.[27]

There must therefore be a pre-existing right in place in domestic law before Article 6 can come into play.[28] However, the decision in *Z* does not negative in any way the duty of the state to take effective steps to prevent the loss of life; this obligation was reiterated by the Court in *Mahmut Kaya v Turkey.*[29] The applicant's brother, a doctor suspected of assisting the PKK, had been assassinated by contra-guerrillas, who allegedly were acting with the knowledge and support of the security forces. While the Court found that it had not been established that the state was involved in the killing, it held that the authorities had failed to comply with a positive obligation to protect the deceased from a known risk to his life. As someone who was suspected of aiding and abetting the PKK, the deceased was at particular risk of falling victim to an unlawful attack. Since the authorities were aware, or ought to have been aware, of this risk, and a range of preventive measures would have been available to the authorities, the state had failed to take reasonable measures to prevent a real and immediate risk to the life of the victim. Highlighting the need for effective criminal law provisions to be in place 'to deter the commission of offences . . . backed up by law-enforcement machinery for the prevention, suppression and punishment of breaches',[30] the Court found that there had, accordingly, been a violation of Article 2 of the Convention.

---

[24] A principle established in *Hill v Chief Constable of West Yorkshire* [1989] AC 53: see discussion below.

[25] (2002) 34 EHRR 3.

[26] *Caparo Industries v Dickman* [1990] 2 AC 605. The House of Lords stipulated that the existence of a duty of care was dependent upon (1) the foreseeability of damage; (2) a relationship characterised by the law as one of proximity or neighbourhood; and (3) that the situation should be one in which the court considers it would be fair just and reasonable that the law should impose a duty of given scope on one party for the benefit of the other.

[27] At [100]. However, in *Bubbins v United Kingdom* (App No 50196/99, 17 Mar 2005) police shot dead the applicant's brother, whom they believed to be an armed burglar. While the police operation was criticised on a number of grounds, the Court concluded that the officer who shot the deceased honestly believed that it was necessary to shoot, and that his actions were therefore proportionate. Despite finding no breach of Art 2, the Court held that there had been a violation of Art 13 of the Convention since the applicants would not be able to recover compensation for the loss of life, and would thus not have been granted legal aid to pursue a civil action.

[28] See further Gearty (2002).

[29] App No 22535/93, 28 Mar 2000. See also Ch 4, pp 166–7.

[30] At [85].

The approach of the European Court was echoed shortly afterwards by the decision of the Inter-American Court of Human Rights in *Velasquez Rodriguez v Honduras:*[31]

> The State has a legal duty to take reasonable steps to prevent human rights violations and to use the means at its disposal to carry out a serious investigation of violations committed within its jurisdiction; to identify those responsible; to impose the appropriate punishment and to ensure the victim adequate compensation.
>
> The duty to prevent includes all those means of a legal, political, administrative and cultural nature that promote the protection of human rights and ensure that any violations are considered and treated as illegal acts, which, as such, may lead to punishment of those responsible and the obligation to indemnify the victims for damages.[32]

The requirements upon states to take preventative measures are not limited to restraining organs of the state. In recognising the link between the vertical and horizontal obligations, the Court noted that preventative measures should also be a means of guarding against acts of non-state actors too:

> where the acts of private parties . . . are not seriously investigated, those parties are aided in a sense by the government, thereby making the State responsible on the international plane.[33]

Likewise, it is clear under the European Convention that the positive obligations contained under Articles 2 and 3, read in conjunction with the State's general duty under Article 1 of the Convention to 'secure to everyone within their jurisdiction the rights and freedoms defined in [the] Convention' are a welcome indication that the rights to protection of victims and *potential* victims of non-state crime are being taken seriously within regional human rights frameworks.[34]

Furthermore, it can be noted that the duty to put preventative measures in place has not been limited to the right to life. The European Court has also held that the State has a duty to take positive steps to protect the rights of victims under Article 3 by ensuring that they are afforded adequate protection under the criminal law. Article 3 of the Convention prohibits states from exposing any individual to torture or to inhuman or degrading treatment. In *A v United Kingdom,*[35] a 9 year-old boy was beaten on the buttocks with a cane by his stepfather, which caused significant bruising. The stepfather's acquittal on the grounds of reasonable chastisement was held to breach the boy's Article 3 right to freedom from inhuman or degrading treatment or punishment. The Court went on to state that it was not enough for a member state to make provision of a relevant criminal charge for criminal acts, but that the Convention also requires that the criminal law itself is

---

[31] (1989) 28 ILM 291. See further discussion in Ch 4, pp 164–5.

[32] *Ibid,* [174–5].

[33] *Ibid,* [176–7].

[34] In addition, the Court has laid down a strict set of requirements relating to investigatory obligations, see Ch 4, pp 165–71.

[35] (1999) 27 EHRR 611.

effective in preventing such acts. In this particular case, the defence of reasonable chastisement in English law was too wide and ill-defined to provide a satisfactory level of protection for potential child victims.

A similar contravention arose in the case *MC v Bulgaria*.[36] Here, a 14 year-old rape victim alleged that the domestic criminal law had interfered with her rights under Articles 3 and 8 of the Convention, in deeming that physical force and active restraint were essential elements of the offence of rape. On this basis, the charges against the accused were dropped. Upholding the applicant's complaint, the Court stipulated that Articles 3 and 8 required the criminalisation of any non-consensual sexual act, whether or not there was evidence of physical resistance. Failure to do so would amount to a violation of physical integrity. The Bulgarian state had pursued a restrictive rather than progressive application of its legislative framework, and any legal systems that failed to provide an adequate degree of protection for victims of rape were in breach of their Convention obligations.[37]

Positive obligations will thus often arise in situations involving particularly vulnerable people, and are also reflected in the duties that apply where vulnerable people are detained in custody. In particular, a burden will fall on the authorities to provide a full explanation for deaths or serious injuries that have occurred during detention, with a strong presumption in place against the state.[38] It is nonetheless clear that whether or not the obligation has been violated will hinge quite substantially on the specific facts of each case. In *Keenan v UK*,[39] where the applicant's son committed suicide in a prison cell, the Court found no breach as the prison officers had done what could reasonably be expected in placing the son in hospital and under close watch when it became evident he had suicidal tendencies. Similarly, in *Younger v UK*,[40] the Court rejected the idea that all prisoners should be regarded to be 'at risk' of suicide or self-harm: this was a generic assumption that could not be universally applied. These cases can be contrasted with *McGlinchey v UK*,[41] where negligent medical treatment provided to a heroin addict in custody resulted in the death of a patient. The Court here found a breach of Article 3.

From the point of view of crime victims of non-state actors, the case of *Edwards v United Kingdom*[42] is particularly salient, since the killing was committed by another individual, rather than an agent of the state. Here, the applicants alleged that the prison authorities had acted negligently in failing to protect the life of their son, who had been killed by his cellmate while being held in prison on remand. Christopher Edwards had been placed in a cell with one Richard Linford, who had

[36] (2005) 40 EHRR 20.
[37] (2003) 36 EHRR 31. See also the earlier case of *E v United Kingdom* (2003) 36 EHRR 31, where it was held that the state had breached Art 3 of the convention on the grounds that social services had failed to intervene to prevent ongoing sexual abuse by a stepfather upon his children.
[38] *Salman v Turkey* (2000) 34 EHRR 425,[100].
[39] (2001) 33 EHRR 38.
[40] App No 57420/00, 7 Jan 2003.
[41] (2003) 37 EHRR 41.
[42] (2002) 35 EHRR 487.

a history of schizophrenia and violent outbursts. Acknowledging that the deceased had been wholly under the protection of and dependent upon the state authorities at the time of his death, the Court held that the failure to pass this information on to the prison authorities led to an inadequate risk assessment. In turn, it was found that Article 2 had been violated.

This survey of Convention case law evidences a discernable trend in recent years towards imposing much broader protective obligations upon the state.[43] However, as a general caveat, it should be borne in mind that, since the vast majority of cases before the Court concerned violence inflicted by state agents, there is relatively little guidance as to how far these obligations extend when the state is not involved in the violence itself. Evidently the State cannot be held responsible for every infringement of the criminal law. In *Osman* itself it was indicated that the duty should not impose a 'disproportionate burden' on the authorities.[44] The Court indicated in *HLR v France*[45] that the obligation exists only where it is shown that:

> 'the risk [of breach] is real and that the authorities . . . are not able to obviate the risk by providing appropriate protection.[46]

Furthermore, it would seem likely that a broad margin of appreciation may exist to allow member states some lee-way in determining how to protect the rights of individuals against the infringements of private persons.[47] It is clear, for example, that the Convention standard does not require that states take extraordinary measures to protect the right to life of individuals;[48] and it would seem that any obligation must be both reasonable and proportionate.

The scope and precise nature of the protective obligations imposed on States remain somewhat uncertain. Nevertheless, in terms of ascertaining a minimum threshold, we can be certain that the protective obligation exists where there is a known risk to an individual or a group. For example, *Osman* makes it clear that reasonable preventative steps must be taken where there is a 'real and immediate' risk to the life of an identified third party.[49] This would presumably cover most situations where credible and specific information came to hand that an individual was in some way threatened or endangered, and no protective or preventative action was subsequently taken by the authorities. It would thus appear that negligence by the police or any criminal justice agency in the course of the investigation would constitute a breach, as would bias, prejudice or a lack of independence.[50]

---

[43] The protective obligations documented in this section go hand-in-hand with the procedural obligations concerning criminal investigations. These are discussed in depth in Ch 4, pp 165–71.

[44] At [116].

[45] (1997) 26 EHRR 29.

[46] *Ibid*, [40].

[47] See *Z v United Kingdom* [2001] FLR 612.

[48] *X v Ireland* (1970) 13 *Yearbook of the European Convention on Human Rights* 792.

[49] At [116].

[50] De Than (2003), 172.

Ramifications for Domestic Practice

The police are under a common law duty to preserve the peace and, by implication, to enforce the criminal law through the investigation of crime.[51]
Unfortunately, it remains the position in civil law that the police do not owe any
generic duty of care to victims or witnesses. In *Hill v Chief Constable of West
Yorkshire*,[52] which concerned an action for negligence brought by the mother of
one of the 'Yorkshire Ripper's' victims, it was held that, for policy reasons, the
police do not hold a duty of care towards potential victims. This position was subject to challenge in *Brooks v Metropolitan Police Commissioner*.[53] Duwayne Brooks
had survived a notorious racist attack in 1993, in which his friend, Stephen
Lawrence, was murdered. He sought damages for the post-traumatic stress he had
suffered as a result of the way in which he was treated by the police during
the investigation and by their failure to apprehend the alleged killers. Although the
Court of Appeal conceded that the Human Rights Act had impacted upon the
emphasis that could be placed on the policy arguments which had underpinned
the earlier decision in *Hill*, it considered that it was still not appropriate to impose
a generic duty of care upon the police in relation to the investigation of crime.[54]
When the case came before the House of Lords, their Lordships disagreed and
opted for a wholesale application of the principles set out in *Hill*, stating that
domestic legal policy had to assume priority over the potentially valid grievances
of citizens who felt they had been mistreated by the police.

However, in line with Convention standards, the domestic courts have broadly
accepted that persons in vulnerable positions must be protected against the possibility of violence or abuse at the hands of both state and non-state actors. In
Kirkham v Chief Constable of Greater Manchester Police,[55] the police were found to
be liable for the suicide of a prisoner since they had failed to communicate his suicidal tendencies to the prison authorities.[56] The existence of this duty of care was
affirmed in *Orange v Chief Constable of West Yorkshire Police*,[57] where it was held
that the police owed a duty of care to those in its custody, which could in certain
circumstances include a duty to take reasonable steps to prevent a prisoner from
taking his own life. *Commissioners of Police for the Metropolis v Reeves*[58] concerned
the suicide of a suspect in a police cell. Martin Lynch had attempted suicide on two
previous occasions, and this was known to the police and preserved on his record.
A police doctor left instructions that he ought to be frequently observed. The

---

[51] See *R v Commissioner of Police of the Metropolis, ex p Blackburn* [1968] 2 QB 118.
[52] [1989] AC 53.
[53] [2005] 1 WLR 1495.
[54] The Court of Appeal decision is reported *in The Daily Telegraph*, 11 Apr 2002.
[55] [1990] 2 QB 283.
[56] Cf *Edwards v United Kingdom* (above). Both cases concerned a failure to pass on vital information which meant that a proper risk assessment could not be carried out.
[57] [2002] QB 347.
[58] [2000] AC 360.

Court of Appeal noted that the police owed a duty of care to anyone within their custody, and in this particular case, that extended to preventing self-harm since they knew the prisoner was a suicide risk. However, it should be underlined that the breach of the duty of care in *Reeves* only happened because the police were already aware that he was a suicide risk. In that sense, it does not have a generic application.[59] This reflects the position of the Strasbourg court that there is no basis for assuming that all prisoners should automatically be considered at risk from suicide or self-harm.[60]

The decisions in both *Kirkham* and *Reeves* were adjudicated before the Human Rights Act came into force. However, the Act has undoubtedly strengthened the common law position,[61] following the House of Lords decision in *R v Secretary of State for the Home Department, ex parte Amin*.[62] As Lord Bingham observed:

> A profound respect for the sanctity of human life underpins the common law as it underpins the jurisprudence under Articles 1 and 2 of the Convention. This means that a state must not unlawfully take life and must take appropriate legislative and administrative steps to protect it. But the duty does not stop there. The state owes a particular duty to those involuntarily in its custody . . . Such persons must be protected against violence or abuse at the hands of state agents. They must be protected against self-harm . . . Reasonable care must be taken to safeguard their lives and persons against the risk of avoidable harm.[63]

While the above cases all concerned victims of state abuse of power, they nonetheless carry significant implications for victims of 'ordinary' offences too. It is clear that where the police are aware, or should have been aware, that a specific individual is at risk, then appropriate preventative action should be taken. The last sentence in the excerpt from Lord Bingham's speech implies that the remit of the domestic criminal law must be broad enough to offer comprehensive protection from all types of harm: not just where the right to life is endangered.

A further aspect of the 'right to protection' that has come under scrutiny in light of the Strasbourg authorities on positive obligations concerns the defence of reasonable chastisement. It will be recalled that in *A v United Kingdom*, the European

---

[59] However, see *Butchart v Home Office* [2006] 1 WLR 1155. Here, a psychologically vulnerable remand prisoner was placed in a cell within another prisoner who was a known suicide risk. The second prisoner committed suicide, and the damages were claimed on the grounds that he had suffered psychiatric injury as a result of the negligence of the prison authorities. Rejecting an application by the Home Office to strike out the action on the grounds that no duty of care existed, the Court of Appeal held that a duty of care existed and included the obligation to take reasonable steps to minimise the risk of psychiatric injury. See also *Hartman v South Essex Mental Health and Community Care NHS Trust* (2005) IRLR 293.

[60] See discussion on *Younger v United Kingdom*, above.

[61] The Parliamentary Joint Committee on Human Rights published a report on deaths in custody (HL paper 15–1, HC 137) which contained a detailed overview of the Convention standards and made a series of recommendations. These included the establishment of a cross-departmental task force to monitor the law, to review good practice standards and to publish information and make recommendations to Government.

[62] [2004] 1 AC 653. This case concerned the death of a young offender who had been beaten to death by his cellmate in custody. See further Ch 4, p 172.

[63] At [30].

Court of Human Rights held that the defence was too wide and failed to provide a satisfactory level of protection to potential child victims. In light of this decision, the Government issued a consultation paper,[64] but it was initially the courts, rather than Parliament, who took the lead in changing the law. In the landmark decision in *R v H*,[65] the Court of Appeal effectively overturned the common law, and laid down new guidance as to what would constitute 'reasonable chastisement' in order that it would conform to the principles set out by in *A v UK*. It was added that the executive should not lightly interfere with the discretion of the courts in striking an appropriate balance between the interests of the child and the interests of the accused. Acknowledging the fact that the decision had led to more confusion than clarity, the Government stepped in to amend the law through the Children Act 2004. Section 58 abolishes the defence of reasonable chastisement in circumstances where actual bodily harm is caused to the child. Controversially, however, the Act retains the defence for 'moderate' or 'mild' smacks, and will not apply unless the harm exceeds the threshold for actual or grievous bodily harm under the Offences Against the Person Act 1861 or child cruelty under the Children and Young Persons Act 1933. This ambiguous legislation remains divisive and opens the door to potentially complex questions regarding statutory interpretation.[66]

The provisions of the Children Act 2004, and the preceding discussion concerning vulnerable persons in custody, are but two examples that highlight the growing emphasis in law and policy that is placed upon the need to offer protection to vulnerable persons in various capacities. Indeed, since the early 1990s, the language of 'security' and 'protection' has played an increasingly prominent role in political rhetoric and Home Office communications. In its 2006 document, *Rebalancing the Criminal Justice System in Favour of the Law-abiding Majority*,[67] the term 'protection' is repeated on some thirteen occasions.[68] The same year saw the publication of a consultation document, *Convicting Rapists and Protecting Victims*,[69] which contained a range of questions over the adequacy of current legal, procedural and evidential protection of rape complainants.[70]

It would be a huge task, far beyond the remit of this work, to examine in depth the exponential expansion of crime prevention and victim protection initiatives

[64] Department of Health (2000).

[65] [2001] 2 FLR 431.

[66] For an analysis of the new law, and the general legal response to the decision in *A*, see Keating (2006).

[67] Home Office (2006a).

[68] Examples include 'We must build a criminal justice system which puts protection of the law-abiding majority at its heart' (forward); 'The Human Rights Act and the European Convention on Human Rights—which are essential protections for all of us—have been misunderstood and misquoted, sometimes preventing the proper protection of the public.' [1.22]; 'we are conducting a thorough review of how police, probation, parole and prison services balance public protection and individual and collective rights. If necessary, we will legislate to ensure that public protection is given priority.' [2.14]; '[i]t is important that we keep good safeguards and protections for the public in the way the police work' [4.3].

[69] Home Office (2006c).

[70] See below, pp 97–107.

that have come to fruition in the past decade. Suffice to say, however, the prominence afforded to the ideas of protection and security have been instrumental in the rapid expansion of crime prevention programmes that have been rolled out across the United Kingdom since Labour came to power in 1997. Section 17 of the Crime and Disorder Act 1998 introduced a range of measures aimed at preventing crime and disorder, the most significant of which was the statutory duty imposed on local councils and police to work together at a district level to formulate a Crime Reduction Strategy and establish a partnership to implement that strategy. This was one of the factors that contributed to the current preference for a multi-agency approach to tackling crime, which has meant that professionals working within the criminal justice system have seen their role undergo radical transformation.[71] This process culminated in the creation of Multi-Agency Public Protection Arrangements (MAPPA's) under the Criminal Justice and Courts Services Act 2000. Comprising police, probation and other agencies, MAPPA authorities are charged with regularly risk-assessing and sharing information on serious offenders and publishing annual reports on the activities of particular (though anonymous) individuals.

One notable shift in policy during this era has been the willingness of the Government to use civil law in conjunction with the criminal law to clamp down on forms of intimidating behaviour.[72] One of the more prominent examples can be found under the Protection from Harassment Act 1997, which contains both criminal and civil measures designed to curb stalking and harassment. It is an offence under the Act to cause harassment, alarm or distress by a course of conduct,[73] or to cause fear of violence.[74] Furthermore, any person who is, or may become, the victim of harassing behaviour may seek a civil injunction against the offender. Such an order may provide for various means of protection to be put in place, and compensation may be ordered where there is insufficient evidence to prosecute under the criminal law.

While the 1997 Act may curb aspects of domestic abuse associated with stalking, more comprehensive measures to protect victims from domestic violence were introduced under Part IV of the Family Law Act 1996. The legislation allows courts to make an order to prohibit the molestation of an 'associated person' or a 'relevant child' and can run for any period specified by the court up to 12

---

[71] See generally Nash (2006), who documents how 'public protection has now spread its tentacles across the public sector and is a much more open process,' thereby changing the nature of police and probation work. In particular, he outlines how the police have lately assumed a much more expanded new role in risk assessment and the management of ex-offenders in the community, while the probation service has moved away from its conception as a benevolent organisation designed to assist offenders to one dominated by a language of 'surveillance, monitoring and risk management' (at p9).

[72] On the blurring of civil / criminal law in relation to sex offending, see generally Thomas (2004).

[73] It can include speech—which the alleged offender knows, or ought to know, amounts to harassment of the other.

[74] For this offence to be committed, fear of violence must be caused on at least two occasions, the fear must be caused by a course of conduct, and the alleged offender must know or ought to know that the course of conduct will cause the other to fear violence.

months.[75] The provisions of the Act were buttressed by the Domestic Violence, Crime and Victims Act 2004, which criminalises the breach of an order made under the 1996 Act. Section 5 of the Act creates a new offence of causing or allowing the death of a child or vulnerable adult, and section 12, amending the Protection from Harassment Act 1997, will grant courts the power to impose restraining orders, even where defendants are acquitted under the 1997 Act.[76]

Many of these provisions were intended to clamp down on domestic violence, and should go some way, at least, to quell fears of repeated victimisation which often renders prosecution and conviction so difficult.[77] However, in spite of these initiatives, there has been considerable criticism directed at the police and the CPS for their failure to investigate and prosecute what may be casually labelled as 'domestics.'[78] Such practice seems incompatible with the doctrine of positive obligations,[79] and, in times ahead, the increasing prominence of this duty should go some way towards ensuring that effective intervention is more commonplace in practice than has traditionally been the case.

Further protections for vulnerable victims have been introduced by the Government in response to the 'moral panic' that arose in the 1990s over paedophilia and sexual offences. The widely-publicised Sex Offenders Register, created under the Sex Offenders Act 1997, contains the details of anyone convicted, cautioned or released from prison for sexual offences against children or adults since September 1997. Latest figures suggest that around 30,000 names are currently on the Register, and subsequent years will see the Register grow significantly, both in terms of numbers and the information that is contained within it. However, despite ongoing media campaigns,[80] the Government has so far resisted calls for the public to be granted access to it.[81] Aside from the register itself,

---

[75] A range of other preventative measures are available, including occupation orders and exclusion orders. The Home Office Circular 19/2000 Domestic Violence: Revised Circular to the Police and the Crown Prosecution Service Policy on Prosecuting Cases of Domestic Violence details what issues the police and CPS respectively will take into account in deciding how best to follow up such crimes.

[76] S 5 of the Act has been in force since Mar 2005. S 12 is not in force at the time of writing, despite the Government having previously announced that it would be commenced in Jul 2007 (see comments of Lord Falconer, *Hansard*, HL Deb, 18 Dec 2006, col WS210).

[77] See generally Hoyle (1998), Burton (2000), Hester (2006), Cammiss (2006).

[78] *Ibid.*, The concept of an 'effective investigation' is examined in detail in Ch 4, pp 165–71.

[79] See further Choudhry and Herring (2006).

[80] Paedophilia has been a major source of attention for much of the tabloid press. Following the murder of eight-year-old Sarah Payne by a former sex offender in 2000, the Home Office faced a major national campaign, instigated by the *News of the World*, for a 'Sarah's Law' which would grant the public access to the Sex Offenders Register to parents. Initially dismissed by the Home Office as unenforceable following a number of vigilante-style attacks, the idea has since been rejuvenated. In Apr 2007, a story was leaked to *The Sun* which suggested that the Home Office was on the verge of launching a pilot scheme, whereby parents would have the right to find out if there were any paedophiles living in their neighbourhood although their names and addresses would not be revealed. However, this was subsequently denied by the Home Office, which stated that the pilots would only allow single mothers to check if a new partner has a criminal record for child abuse (*The Guardian*, 11 Apr 2007).

[81] The Register was significantly expanded under Criminal Justice and Court Services Act 2000 which required notification if registrants went abroad for more than 8 days. Following the Child Sex Offender Review, the Home Secretary recently announced plans to place the police and other criminal justice agencies under a duty to consider whether a member of the public needs to know about an

the substantive criminal law concerning sexual offences against children was also buttressed. With specific reference to potential child victims of sex attacks, new protections were contained in the Sexual Offences Act 2003, which created an offence of meeting a child following sexual grooming,[82] and in 2006 the Home Office established the Child Exploitation and Online Protection Centre in London, designed, inter alia, to assess and disseminate international and domestic intelligence and devise crime prevention strategies.

The above discussion constitutes a very broad sweep of just some of the measures that have been introduced in the 'risk society' with either the specific aim of protecting the public from offenders, or trounced in the broader ideal of protecting the public indirectly through reducing crime. The degree of success which the above measures have had is open to debate, and concerns have been voiced as to whether these trends actually deliver genuine improvements for victims and potential victims, or whether they are designed primarily as a political tool, designed to portray the impression that 'something is being done' about crime. These developments have been met with scepticism in some quarters; many writers have linked the rise of this 'protective' legislation agenda with the authoritarian response of 'popular punitivism' discussed in Chapter 1.[83] Certainly, many agree that much of the legislation that is prima facie conceived to combat risk has been rushed, ill-thought-out, or not grounded upon substantive evaluation or research.[84] However, what the sheer volume of measures does illustrate is that the themes of public protection and victimisation continue to feature prominently in the policymaking agenda.

It is perhaps naïve to argue that the prominence attached to protection in contemporary criminal justice policy is a trend that has been inspired solely by philanthropic ideals on the part of policymakers. Nevertheless, it must equally be accepted that criminal justice policy must be fluid, dynamic and adaptable to changing norms and consensus. Bearing this in mind, there is a need to accept that the ascendancy of the victim on the international platform and the increasing tendency to reconstruct victim's rights as forms of human rights will necessarily have a direct impact in terms of how legislation is formulated and criminal justice agencies perform their functions. If the right to protection is to be taken seriously, as a legally enforceable norm, then there is a need to accept that we should consider again the relationship between the rights of those who we consider potentially dangerous, and this new, emergent right for the public to be protected from victimisation.

---

offender's history in order to protect a child or children. Although there is no immediate prospect of members of the public having unfettered access, there will be a presumption that the authorities will disclose that information if they consider that the offender presents a risk of serious harm to a member of the public's children (see Home Office, 2007).

   [82] Sexual Offences Act 2003, s 15.
   [83] Tonry (2004), Nash (2006). See Ch 1, p 11.
   [84] Eg Bernstein (1998), Hope and Sparks (2000), Thomas (2004), O'Malley (2004), Mythen and Walklate (eds) (2006)

Policymakers, courts and criminal justice agencies must now take compelling and concrete steps to protect those at risk. It may be the case that the rights of some will need to be limited in order to uphold the right of protection for all potential victims of crime. It is a balancing exercise that is necessarily difficult to perform since 'identifying and predicting future dangerousness is a notoriously difficult task,'[85] and it may be easily open to political exploitation.[86] However, to simply deny the idea that a societal right to protection exists would sit very uneasily alongside recent international benchmarks. The priority we place upon these rights is rightfully a matter of public debate, but genuine debate there must be. If we are serious about preventing victimisation, then the starting point for criminal justice policy ought to be the social contract ideal, that has been reinforced and reinvigorated through human rights discourse and jurisprudence: the state has a positive obligation to protect us all.

III. Secondary Victimisation

Research has illustrated that the psychological impact of victimisation can be considerably exacerbated by insensitive treatment and a lack of understanding of victims' needs by agencies and organisations within the criminal justice system. From the point of entry, many different classes of victims have reported feeling increased levels of stress and anxiety as a result of the manner in which they are treated. Heightened levels of apprehension and general disquiet are especially evident in research conducted in relation to rape and domestic violence, particularly regarding treatment by the police and prosecution.[87] However, the problem of 'secondary victimisation' is arguably most acute within the court system of England and Wales. Few, if any, victims are likely to relish the prospect of appearing as witnesses in court. For the vast majority, the courtroom will be an unfamiliar and forbidding environment, dominated by lawyers and court officials. As such, many witnesses may find the process of giving evidence alienating and stressful, particularly if they are not used to speaking before an audience. The formality of procedure, the austere atmosphere, and the presence of wigs and gowns are likely to contribute to this general sense of unease. Witnesses are very much outsiders to a professionalised process.[88] A survey of vulnerable and intimidated witnesses by Angle et al conducted in 2002 found that a significant minority of victim

---

[85] Nash (2006), 3.

[86] Eg, the Prevention of Terrorism Act 2005 enabled the Home Secretary to impose an unlimited range of restrictions on any person he suspects of involvement in terrorism. There has been considerable political opposition to control orders, which have been likened to a form of house arrest. See Liberty (2005).

[87] In relation to rape, see Victim Support (1996); Jordan (2001), Ellison (2007), HMIC / HMCPSI (2007). Regarding domestic violence see Brown (1984), Buzawa and Buzawa (1990), Hoyle (1998), Hester (2006).

[88] See generally Rock (1993).

witnesses (21 per cent) felt intimidated either by the process of giving evidence or by the courtroom environment.[89] A further study by Hamlyn et al published in 2004 found that little had improved.[90] Almost three quarters (71 per cent) of those questioned found cross-examination to be 'upsetting,'[91] and just under half said they would be happy to be a witness again. It is widely accepted that feelings of stress or anxiety are likely to be exacerbated among particularly vulnerable groups of victim witnesses, with a considerable body of research charting the plight of child witnesses, witnesses suffering from physical or learning disabilities, complainants in sexual cases, and witnesses at risk of intimidation or repeat victimisation. The problems facing these categories of vulnerable witnesses are now considered in turn.

The Nature and Extent of the Problem

Child Witnesses

Of all vulnerable groups, the plight of the child witness has been most extensively documented. Flin et al also showed that, for many child witnesses, stress at the prospect of testifying sets in long before the trial actually begins.[92] In their study of cases involving 218 children in 1992, Goodman et al compared the behavioural disturbances between those who testified and those who did not.[93] Of those who testified, the researchers reported that confronting the defendant in court brought back traumatic memories, caused sleep disturbance and exacerbated feelings of pain, hurt and helplessness. More specifically, the more frightened a child was of confronting the accused, the fewer questions the child would answer.[94]

In particular, stress levels are exacerbated by the unfamiliar language used in court by barristers. Davies and Noon's study of child witnesses in England found that 25 per cent of all questions were inappropriate to the witness' age.[95] Brennan and Brennan's survey of child witnesses in Australia identified 13 different linguistic devices which were used regularly to confuse child witnesses. The use of complex sentence structures and advanced vocabulary serve to exacerbate the unfamiliar surroundings which children already experience. Questions are frequently highly stylised, and may include specific linguistic techniques such as nominalisation, juxtapositioning and multi-faceted questioning, which will obviously confuse and cause stress to many young witnesses. In the words of the researchers:

---

[89] Angle et al (2003).
[90] Hamlyn et al (2004).
[91] *Ibid*, 53. Almost half (48%) were upset 'a lot.'
[92] Flin et al (1989).
[93] Goodman et al (1992).
[94] *Ibid*, 121.
[95] Davies and Noon (1991). Only 36% of barristers made extensive efforts to adapt their language so as to make it suitable for the child.

Cross-examination is that part of court proceedings where the interests and rights of the child are most likely to be ignored and sacrificed . . . The techniques used are all created with words, since they are the only currency of the court . . . Under conditions of cross-examination the child is placed in an adversarial and stressful situation which tests the resilience of even the most confident of adults . . . The right of the lawyer to directly oppose the evidence given by the child witness, the implicit hostility which surrounds cross-examination, alien language forms, and the sheer volume of questions asked, all conspire to confuse the child. It is a quick and easy step to destroy the credibility of the child witness.[96]

A recent survey of 50 child witnesses carried out on behalf of the NSPCC by Plotnikoff and Woolfson found that over half the children interviewed said that they did not understand some words or found some questions confusing.[97] Just five of the child witnesses interviewed described defence lawyers as 'polite' but nineteen said the lawyers were not polite. Defence counsel were described as 'aggressive', 'sarcastic', 'cross', 'shouting', 'rude', 'harassing', 'disrespectful', 'arrogant', 'overpowering', 'badgering', 'scary' and 'pushy.' Cordon et al cite a number of other studies which arrived at similar findings.[98] They note that advocates will frequently try to lure child witnesses into a false sense of security, by asking non-substantive questions about the child's background and interests, before subtly moving on to elicit substantive information which contradicts the child's original testimony. They also present evidence which suggests that cross-examiners typically capitalise on children's tendencies to be suggestible and to fantasise.[99] The goal in many cross-examinations, they argue, is to 'keep the child off balance to increase the chance of inconsistencies.'[100]

Witnesses Suffering from Learning Disabilities

Such problems of comprehension are not unique to child witnesses, although their limited cognitive capacity will mean that they will be particularly susceptible to feeling the pressure during such questioning. It is perhaps not surprising that, as in cases involving child witnesses, language has also been found to constitute a considerable barrier to effective communication among witnesses with learning disabilities. Although relatively few empirical studies have attempted to gauge their experiences of the criminal justice system, it is documented that the ability of this group of witnesses to give clear and coherent oral testimony in court may be significantly diminished through the nature of the questions posed during cross-examination.[101] On comparing trial transcripts involving witnesses with learning disabilities and those without, Kebbell et al found that the questions were broadly

---

[96] *Ibid*, 91.
[97] Plotnikoff and Woolfson (2004).
[98] Cordon *et al* (2003).
[99] See also Ceci et al (2002).
[100] *Ibid*, 175–7.
[101] Dent (1986), Ericson et al (1994), Sanders *et al* (1996).

similar and that lawyers had done little to adjust their questioning style.[102] Another study indicates no significant differences in the readiness of the judiciary to intervene to clarify questioning among witnesses with learning difficulties and those without.[103] Repeated questioning, in particular, can present specific diffi- culties for witnesses with learning disabilities as Sanders et al observed:

> Repeated questioning, which is commonly used . . . to secure precision as well as to challenge what is being said, often affects the learning disabled badly. People with Down's Syndrome often perceive repeated questioning as threatening and try to appease the questioner, thus undermining their credibility. Many learning disabled people have low self-esteem and confidence, and repeated questioning sometimes emphasises their relative powerlessness and unimportance compared to those around them.[104]

As Sanders et al argue, it would appear that much of the legal profession and the judiciary have a relatively limited understanding of the specific nature of learning disabilities. This carries clear implications for the impact of such testimony; since the questioning may be unintelligible to the witness, but not the court, it could appear to the fact finder that the answers given may seem unreliable or contrived on the spot. Thus the treatment of witnesses with learning disabilities in court not only causes them a considerable degree of stress and frustration in their restricted ability to answer the questions posed, but it also risks leading to erroneous assumptions being made as part of the fact-finding process.[105]

Victims of Rape and Sex Offences

By their very nature, sexual offences are notoriously invasive, and many victims will struggle with emotional and psychological consequences of victimisation for years to come.[106] Sex crimes carry a notoriously high attrition rate,[107] so it is not only in the victim's interest, but also in the public interest, that victims feel able to enter into the criminal justice system and give evidence in court without intrusive and aggressive cross-examination. Traditionally, the daunting task of coming to terms with, and moving forward from the horror of a sex attack is made much more difficult by the prospect of being asked to testify at a trial, which may take place a year or more after the attack took place. These trials differ from other criminal hearings in a number of respects. Often, the fact that intercourse actually took place is not a contested issue. Most rape cases turn upon the issue of consent which gives rise to a number of evidential difficulties, particularly where the

---

[102] Kebbell et al (2004).

[103] O'Kelly et al (2003).

[104] Sanders et al (1996), 7–8.

[105] Kebbell and Johnson (2000).

[106] See Holstrom and Burgess (1974); Santiago et al (1985); Bohn and Holz (1996), See further Classen et al (2005).

[107] See further Lees and Gregory (1993), (1999); Kelly et al (2005); HMIC / HMCPSI (2007).

complainant and the accused have previously engaged in a consensual sexual relationship. Since the complainant and the accused will usually be the only percipient witnesses to the incident in question, the battle of credibility between the accused and the victim lies at the heart of many trials. Writing in 1978, Holmstrom and Burgess were among the first to investigate the problems plaguing rape complainants in court, and concluded that 'overwhelmingly, both adult and young [rape] victims found court an extremely stressful experience.'[108]

The prospect of a direct face-to-face encounter between the complainant and the accused in court will cause considerable anxiety for many victims. In some cases, the court hearing may be the first occasion where the accused and the complainant have encountered each other in person since the offence occurred. Yet the most stressful aspect of the court is the nature of cross-examination, which is often humiliating, distressing, and largely uncontrolled. It is not unusual for complainants to be asked to relay to the court intricate details of an invasive and traumatising attack. As one rape complainant told *The Guardian*:

> The prospect of having to stand up in court and explain what this man had done to me sexually was terrifying. These were details I had not discussed with my closest friends.[109]

In order to exploit the weaknesses in the complainant's evidence, cross-examiners frequently embark upon character assassination. As Grohovsky describes, the victim's body becomes something of a crime scene in itself 'from which evidence must be collected and analysed.'[110] She adds that:

> [l]ikewise, every aspect of the victim's life is analysed, criticised and often considered fair game for the defence to use against her at trial.[111]

One of the main methods used to attack her character is to suggest that she is sexually disreputable, alluding to loose moral values and a decadent lifestyle. In assessing this, the jury are invited to take into account a wide range of deeply personal and embarrassing details. In a survey of 116 rape complainants, Lees records a number of examples of hostile cross-examination designed to humiliate and embarrass the victim. Complainants were asked in detail about their underwear, make-up, social lifestyle, menstrual cycle and drug addiction:[112]

> Questions addressed to the women in the trials I monitored included whether she had had previous sex with men other than the defendant, whether she was a single mother, whether the man she was living with was the father of her children; the colour of her present and past boyfriends . . . who looked after her children while she was at work; whether she was in the habit of going to nightclubs on her own late at night; whether she smoked cannabis and drank alcohol . . . what underwear she had on; whether she wore false eyelashes and red lipstick; whether the defendant had 'used her previously' . . .

[108] Holstrom and Burgess (1974), 986.
[109] *The Guardian*, 29 November 2003.
[110] Grohovsky (2000), 417.
[111] *Ibid.*
[112] Lees (1996), 139–49.

details of her menstrual flow; and on one occasion whether she had a vibrator in her drawer wrapped in a purple sock.[113]

The vast majority of complainants interviewed by Lees (83 per cent) said that they felt as though they were on trial, rather than the defendant. Similarly, a 1996 survey of rape complainants by Victim Support found that 12 per cent of women said their experience in court was actually worse than the rape itself.[114] Furthermore, 41 per cent of women felt anger or that they had been revictimised in court.[115]

In a study of attitudes of the Bar towards rape complainants, one leading QC told Temkin that '[i]f the complainant could be portrayed as a 'slut', this was highly likely to secure an acquittal.'[116] The advocate will usually not go so far as to overtly suggest that the woman is decadent, indecent or immoral, but will instead deploy such questions to paint a picture of female behaviour which is inappropriate and deviates from the norm. In this sense, the jury are called to make a moral judgment on the victim's character. The jury should only use the responses to such questions in determining whether the victim should be believed or not on oath: not to determine whether or not she is likely to have consented to the intercourse in question (where consent is the issue). However, there is no black and white distinction in the human mind on such issues, and the prejudicial effect of such evidence may well have an overbearing influence on whether or not the victim was the type of woman who would have consented to intercourse on the occasion in question. The risks of such prejudice are widely acknowledged in relation to the character of the defendant: the law will, subject to certain exceptions, exclude evidence of his previous convictions and previous bad character precisely in order to prevent this 'forbidden chain of reasoning.'[117] As noted below, while steps have been taken in recent years to limit the potential for attacks on the complainant, there are concerns that these are inadequate and are unlikely to address the fundamental difficulties faced by rape complainants.[118]

The rules of evidence in many common law jurisdictions have traditionally permitted such questions as they are seen as relevant to the credibility of the complainant's testimony, that is, as to whether or not she ought to be believed on oath.[119] Defence counsel have long played on the idea that, if the witness can be shown in a bad light, the jury may well give less credence to that witness's evidence. Therefore, cross-examination often exploits the concept of an 'ideal rape' which lies at the heart of many rape trials. This is basically a notion that corresponds with the conception of a victim of rape as sexually inexperienced, respectable, and who suffered at the hands of a sexual predator. Normally, she will have been physically

---

[113] Lees (1996), 134.

[114] Victim Support (1996a).

[115] *Ibid.*

[116] Temkin (2000), 234.

[117] See generally Spencer (2006). For a good overview of some of the reasons why character evidence has been traditionally excluded, see Munday (1993).

[118] See below, pp 91–113.

[119] S 41(4) Youth Justice and Criminal Evidence Act.

hurt, will have fought back, and will have promptly reported the offence.[120] Of course, that construction does not reflect the actual experience of most rape victims, yet it is the stereotypical association with rape that seems to be widely held in society. As a general rule, the prosecution will seek to portray the 'truth' of the rape as closely as possible to match the idealised version that lingers in the back of the jurors' minds, whereas the defence will seek to highlight discrepancies between the ideal and the actual version of events.[121]

Until recently, in a small minority of rape cases, the victim's experience of testifying was hugely exacerbated where a defendant opted to conduct his own defence.[122] While self-representation in cases involving violence against children or child sex abuse was prohibited by section 34A of the Criminal Justice Act 1988, a series of high profile cases in the 1990s highlighted a number of gruelling cross-examinations that rape complainants had undergone at the hands of the accused. The rape trials of Ralston Edwards and Milton Brown, who cross-examined their victims on intimate sexual matters for days on end, received widespread media attention. Edwards wore the same clothes in court that he wore at the time of the rape.[123] In the case of *Milton Brown*,[124] who was convicted of raping two women at knifepoint, the judge expressed considerable concern that the law permitted such cross-examination to occur in the first place:

> It is a highly regrettable and extremely sad aspect of this case that despite my repeated efforts during the first two days of your trial you insisted on dispensing with the services of highly competent leading and junior counsel and solicitors, the third set you had been allocated at public expense, thereafter subjecting your victims to merciless cross-examination clearly designed to intimidate and humiliate them. In the course of your questioning you made outrageous and repulsive suggestions to both witnesses . . . Although I took what steps I could to minimise that ordeal by repeated efforts to prevent repetitious and irrelevant questioning, nevertheless the whole experience must for those women have been horrifying and it is highly regrettable in my view, and a matter of understandable public concern, that the law as it stands permits a situation where an unrepresented defendant in a sexual assault case has a virtually unfettered right to personally question his victim in such needlessly extended and agonising detail for the obvious purpose of intimidation and humiliation.[125]

In refusing leave to appeal, the Court of Appeal approved the decision of the trial judge and offered further guidance to judges in cases involving unrepresented defendants:

> The trial judge is, however, obliged to have regard not only to the need to ensure a fair trial for the defendant but also to the reasonable interests of the other parties to the court

---

[120] Adler, (1987), 119.

[121] See further McColgan (1996), 300.

[122] As a general rule, any person charged in criminal proceedings is entitled to conduct his own defence under s 2 Criminal Procedure Act 1865.

[123] *The Times*, 23 Aug 1996.

[124] [1998] 2 Cr App R 364.

[125] *Ibid*, 368–9.

process, in particular witnesses, and among witnesses particularly those who are obliged to relive by describing in the witness box an ordeal to which they say they have been subject. It is the clear duty of the trial judge to do everything he can, consistently with giving the defendant a fair trial, to minimise the trauma suffered by other participants. Furthermore, a trial is not fair if a defendant, by choosing to represent himself, gains the advantage he would not have had if represented of abusing the rules in relation to relevance and repetition which apply when witnesses are questioned.[126]

One of the last defendants in a rape case to carry out his own cross-examination before a statutory prohibition came into force was Camille Hourani. He had subjected his fiancée, a 27 year-old nurse, to a 15 hour sex attack. The following account of the trial is taken from *The Times*:

> Camille Hourani . . . forced his victim to come to court six times to prepare herself to be questioned by him. After being sent away five times because of his changes of mind, the nurse was eventually subjected to nearly a day in the witness box, in which he tormented and bullied her, frequently reducing her to tears . . . The ranting, accusations and delaying tactics of her former fiancé frequently made her tearful and sick each morning before she was forced back to court . . . For an entire day, the woman was subjected to an extraordinary array of bullying, detailed questions about her sexual activity and accusations about her affairs with other men.[127]

It was, of course, extremely rare for such a scenario to arise. However, as Lord Meston pointed out in the House of Lords, infrequency of its occurrence should not preclude action to address the situation because 'a few cases attract a large amount of publicity, and cause a great deal of distress to the victims of rape involved in those cases, and also have a tendency to deter other complainants of rape from reporting the matter to the police.'[128] Indeed, the recent report by the CPS Inspectorate underlined that the prospect of attending court will often serve to heighten victims' sense of fear of the legal process and will not assist efforts to address the notoriously high attrition rate.[129]

In summary then, the law does not have a good track record of protecting victims of rape and sexual assault against secondary victimisation in the courtroom. These victims, who are some of the most vulnerable of all, have traditionally not been perceived as having any specific rights to protect them from intrusive questioning that is designed to humiliate them and intrude on their privacy at court.

Intimidated Witnesses

One consequence of victimisation that troubles many victims is the fear that they will be targeted again.[130] For some victims, this fear stems from the fact that, if they

---

[126] [1998] 2 Cr App R, 371, *per* Bingham CJ.
[127] *The Times*, 5 Apr 2000.
[128] See comments of Lord Meston, *Hansard*, HL Deb, 22 Jun 1998, cols 91–2.
[129] HMCPSI (2007), [2.5].
[130] Hale (1996), Borooah and Carcach (1997).

report the crime or give evidence at trial, they or their families could be subject to intimidation. The extent of the problem of witness intimidation within the criminal justice system is only now becoming clear. Following decades marked by a clear dearth of research, it has now become clear that intimidation is more commonplace than has been previously imagined. During the 1990s, witness protection programmes became considerably more commonplace, and two new offences, intimidating a witness and harming or threatening to harm a witness, were created under the Criminal Justice and Public Order Act 1994.[131]

Following the publication of *Speaking Up for Justice,*[132] protocols were put in place to offer improved protection for victims at risk of intimidation, through imposing restrictions on bail conditions, providing panic alarms or CCTV systems, and even offering housing relocation with new homes, new jobs and new identities where the risk to their safety was serious or life-threatening. These powers were placed on a statutory footing in the Serious Organised Crime and Policing Act 2005.[133] Section 82 makes provision for 'protection providers' to make appropriate arrangements for the protection of witnesses and other persons involved in criminal investigations or court proceedings.[134] To be eligible for protection, the individual's safety must be at risk. This is assessed according to four factors laid down in section 82(1): the nature and extent of the risk to the person's safety; the cost of the arrangements; the likelihood that the person and family will be able to adjust to any change in circumstances as a result of the arrangements; and, if the person is or might be a witness in legal proceedings, the nature of the proceedings and the importance of his testimony.

In more recent times, there appears to be a growing consensus that the problem (or at least awareness / detection of it) is on the increase. A Home Office publication, *Working with Intimidated Witnesses,*[135] envisages that the number of cases for perverting the course of justice (which includes witness intimidation) rose by over 30 per cent between 2000 and 2005. Working from the 1998 British Crime Survey, Tarling et al concluded that intimidation occurs in just under 10 per cent of reported crime and 20 per cent of unreported crime.[136] Angle et al's survey found that a quarter of all witnesses felt intimidated by an individual,[137] which was actually higher than the 21 per cent who reported feeling intimidated by the process of giving evidence.

---

[131] See also ss 39–45 of the Criminal Justice and Police Act 2001, which created new offences intended to increase the protection of witnesses in civil proceedings.

[132] Home Office (1998). See discussion below at pp 77–8.

[133] In addition, the National Witness Mobility Service, launched in 2003, now assists in those cases where a witness is in need of protection.

[134] Sch 5 of the Act contains an exhaustive list of those categories of people who may be protected under these provisions. It includes witnesses, jurors and other people involved in the legal system, law enforcement and other officers, informants, and persons who have or have had a significant connection with a person falling within any of those categories, such as family members.

[135] Home Office (2006b).

[136] Tarling et al (2000).

[137] Angle et al (2003). Of these witnesses, 56% stated that they were intimidated by defendants and 35% by 'official sources' including lawyers, police, court staff, judges and magistrates.

Intimidation of victims may take various forms, from verbal taunts or threats, to physical jousting or to serious physical violence. It may range from a relatively low-key, one-off incident, to a chain of events amounting to ongoing harassment and persistent threatening behaviour.[138] Tarling et al found that approximately two thirds of incidents featured verbal abuse, 16 per cent physical assaults and 9 per cent damage to property. However, the reasons underlying intimidation are unclear. In only a small minority of cases (8 per cent) did the victim believe that the reason behind the intimidation was to prevent them giving evidence. In nearly 50 per cent of cases victims thought it was simply that the offender wanted to 'annoy' or 'upset' them. For a further quarter, the intimidation was viewed as part of an ongoing series of offences against them, for example in cases of domestic violence.

Recent studies suggest that certain groups of people, or witnesses who testify in particular types of cases, are at risk from intimidation. Levels of intimidation appear to be highest amongst poorer socio-economic groups,[139] victims (particularly victims of violence),[140] racial and sexual minorities,[141] and women—particularly in cases involving domestic violence—are susceptible to repeat attacks,[142] as are those involving sexual offences.[143] Where organised crime or terrorist activity is involved, the criminal justice system typically relies heavily on informants for both crime prevention and the apprehension of suspects, and for that reason terrorist groups and other organised criminal gangs will often look to take decisive action against those who endanger their activities.[144]

Even if intimidation itself is only a reality in a small proportion of cases, it can be assumed that the *fear* of intimidation may act to prevent many victims reporting crime or giving evidence in court. Although intimidation is more often seen as a pre-trial problem, Hamlyn et al noted that those who were intimidated were more likely to suffer secondary victimisation at court,[145] and victims were more likely to suffer than other witnesses.[146] Despite national initiatives to ensure separate waiting facilities for victims and defendants, meetings in the court precinct still seem to be commonplace.[147]

Anxiety is increased by the longstanding construction of the adversarial trial as a public spectacle, with witnesses generally having to give their names and addresses in court. In response to the increasing recognition of this problem, many

[138] Maynard (1994); Tarling et al (2000); Fyfe and McKay (2000).
[139] Tarling et al (2000), Hamlyn et al (2004).
[140] Elliott (1998); Angle et al (2003).
[141] Elliott (1998).
[142] Elliott (1998); Tarling et al (2000); Hoyle (2002); McKee (2005).
[143] Lees (1996), 108.
[144] For a popular overview of the role of informers in criminal justice, see Morton (1996). During the Northern Ireland conflict, the state was heavily reliant upon information supplied to them by informants (see further Boyd, 1984; Greer, 1995). These 'touts' or 'snitches' were regularly subject to summary execution by paramilitaries.
[145] Hamlyn et al (2004), xi.
[146] *Ibid*, 19.
[147] *Ibid*.

jurisdictions have adopted both legal and non-legal measures designed to max-imise protection of witnesses who are deemed to be 'at risk.' Indeed, if witnesses fear for their safety or life, it would seem that the international norms noted in the previous section now require that the State should take whatever proactive steps are necessary in order to protect them. Although recent years have seen concerted efforts to combat intimidation of victims and witnesses outside the courtroom, it can recur within the court precinct, where public justice is regarded as a para-mount principle. One troubling finding from recent observational research con-ducted by Fielding was that many of the court-based professionals seemed unsure how to react and viewed it as someone else's problem.[148]

Other Victim-Witnesses

The problems experienced by these various classes of 'vulnerable' victim witnesses are particularly well documented, although they are by no means the only wit-nesses who experience secondary victimisation. Since many of the difficulties for witnesses highlighted above seem to stem directly from the adversarial nature of the trial, all witnesses who testify are likely to experience the cross-examiner attempt to undermine their testimony:

> Discrediting techniques are not something especially reserved for rape victims in particular or even victims in general. Everyone who enters the witness box is a 'victim' of the court in this sense and there is a danger of isolating the legally defined victim from the rest of the participants involved and explaining degradation by his or her personal role as victim of some particular offence, rather than by his or her legal role as witness . . . Crimes against the person merely exacerbate this vulnerability to discrediting cross-examination. Since both victim and offender are directly and personally involved, there is a wide scope for not just generally discrediting but for specifically blaming the victim. This is not confined to the offences of rape.[149]

McBarnet's argument is buttressed by research carried out by Brereton, who undertook a comparative analysis of the transcripts of 40 rape trials and 44 assault trials in Victoria, Australia in 1989–1991. Substantial similarities were found in the cross-examination strategies employed by defence counsel in both types of trial, and in both types of case 'counsel appeared to rely primarily on a limited number of generic, 'tried and true' cross-examination strategies.'[150] Whereas com-plainants in assault trials were likely to be portrayed as troublemakers and bullies, rape complainants were depicted as 'sexually provocative risk takers, and / or as persons of suspect morality who did not live a normal lifestyle.'[151] Similar pro-portions of rape and assault complainants were asked about their general drinking and drug taking habits, and their mental and emotional stability. More of the

---

[148] Fielding (2006), 215.
[149] McBarnet (1983), 294.
[150] Brereton (1997), 242.
[151] *Ibid*, 254.

assault complainants were questioned about prior criminal history, regardless of whether they were for offences of violence. Brereton concludes that the information elicited during cross-examination appeared to be of little relevance to the case at hand, and was often used to show that the victim was untrustworthy or even 'deserved what had happened to him.'[152]

In his study of proceedings at Wood Green Crown Court, Rock found that 'as a matter of course, and in most ordinary trials, gravely wounding allegations would be put to witnesses.'[153] Witnesses, he reported, were frequently bullied, harassed and felt as though they were on trial in 'the most charged of all secular rituals.'[154] Often, witnesses were not permitted to give their evidence at a greater rate than the desired pace of the transcriber, and on occasions were told to slow down their evidence.[155] Rock also observed that 'nothing was allowed to remain tacit, elided, discreet or *sotto voce*,'[156] with witnesses being asked to 'speak up' if they failed to make themselves audible to the entire court.[157] Evidently, if witnesses are relaying to the court intimate details of their private lives, including past indiscretions, or even something as mundane as their addresses and occupations, they may be reluctant or embarrassed to make certain facts public knowledge.[158] Rock noted that this can cause particular awkwardness in witnesses where they are required to flout the taboos of language, with the Court hearing details of 'all the violent doings and language of the bedroom, street and public house, witnesses having to cite the heedless and profane speech of angry relationships.'[159] For most judges and legal professions, distress was a perfectly natural aspect of criminal trials.[160]

In more recent times, Fielding has carried out a similar ethnographic study to Rock, specifically examining trials involving violent offences,[161] which identified many consonant themes and patterns. Feelings of stress and alienation seemed to be commonplace for many who testified, and was not limited to specific types of vulnerable witnesses. Many victims generally reported feeling anxious, as though they were on trial,[162] and distress and anxiety were, once again, seen by lawyers and judges as unfortunate, but essential, aspects of the court hearing.[163] On occasions, judges would attempt to mitigate the experience by 'pacing' proceedings, offering tissues or water, or sympathetic words,[164] but Fielding describes how the 'fear factor' seemed to enhance credibility, with advocates engaging in a range of

---

[152] Brereton (1997), 253.
[153] Rock (1993), 88.
[154] Rock (1991), 267.
[155] Rock (1993), 49.
[156] *Ibid.*
[157] *Ibid.*
[158] Compare Fielding (2006), who found that having one's address made public caused many victims anxiety (at 214).
[159] Rock (1993), 50.
[160] *Ibid*, 151–3.
[161] Fielding (2006).
[162] *Ibid*, 35.
[163] *Ibid*, 38; 45–6.
[164] *Ibid*, 45–50.

well-established techniques, including 'rapid fire questioning', with witnesses being visibly upset by public interrogation about very intimate or private matters:

> Trials are not, of course, subject to regular etiquette. Virtually any characteristic of the principal parties is fair game, body language is exploited, and innuendo is freely indulged despite judges' interventions.[165]

With the notable exception of witness intimidation, secondary victimisation within the courtroom is mostly inadvertent. As Fielding noted, it was not specifically callous on the part of lawyers since 'there is an inevitable conflict between trial imperatives and acknowledging the feelings involved.'[166] We should thus be slow to point the finger at lawyers, judges or other criminal professionals for the plight of victims and witnesses, since they are working within a culture where the systemic structures and values of the adversarial system demand that they treat witnesses in a particular way. Ellison's description of the working culture of the Bar describes why the adversarial criminal trial is such a difficult environment for outsiders to give evidence:

> [A]dvocates are attitudinally and ethically committed to winning the contest rather than to some other goal such as the discovery of truth or fairness to the opposing side. This standpoint has spawned a decidedly gladiatorial view of court-room advocacy, as evidenced in the metaphors lawyers select to describe litigation. Cross-examination is compared to a physical fight between advocate and witness with frequent references to 'verbal pugilism,' 'forensic duels,' and 'verbal combat.' Advocacy manuals speak candidly of 'butchering,' 'breaking' and 'destroying' opposing witnesses.[167]

As Ellison argues, it is therefore the adversarial paradigm itself that renders the experience of testifying so distressful for so many witnesses. Victim-witnesses should normally give live evidence in an alien environment dominated by lawyerised rituals and partisan conflict. They are compelled to play their part in the drama, and to relive, before an audience, experiences which may be harrowing and painful to recall. As a successor to medieval trial by ordeal, cross-examination is frequently likened to a physical fight.[168] Witnesses are also placed under close control of counsel, and their testimony is carefully kept in check to ensure they do not divulge information that might detract from the questioner's story. In an empirical study of six American criminal trials carried out in 1976, Danet and Bogoch attempted to measure the degree of combativeness in the questioning conducted by attorneys. The researchers formulated a measure of categorising questions into two groups: 'coercive' and 'non-coercive' questions, based upon the degree to which the advocate attempted to constrain or control the witness. In their findings, the authors concluded that 87 per cent of questions asked during cross-examination were 'coercive.'[169]

---

[165] *Ibid,* 127. See also 40–1.

[166] *Ibid.*

[167] Ellison (2001a), 104.

[168] See eg Ellison (2001a), 105; Jeans (1975), cited by Danet and Bogoch, (1980), 42; Du Cann (1993), 61.

[169] Danet and Bogoch, (1980), 48.

Perhaps then, the findings of the empirical studies into the experience of victims and witnesses in court should not surprise us. Clearly, much more thought needs to be given as to how we conduct trials in a manner that offers witnesses a more comprehensive form of protection when they are asked to testify. Nevertheless, in the longer term, perhaps we can afford to be more optimistic about the prospects for change. As the discussion below highlights, attitudes have undergone something of a sea-change, both on the international platform and (though perhaps to a lesser extent) within domestic policy circles too.

International Standards

International instruments now require the interests of victim-witnesses to be taken into account in a variety of different ways, although traditionally they have tended to adopt obscure or imprecise language, and to lay down generic, but unspecific, duties to treat victims and witnesses with respect and sensitivity in court.[170] In more recent years however, there are some indications that instruments are becoming increasingly specific in terms of their demands. This is attributable to the fact that human rights fora are increasingly recognising victims' rights as a form of human rights, as underlined by the Council of Europe's Recommendation 06(08):

> States should ensure the effective recognition of, and respect for, the rights of victims with regard to their human rights; they should, in particular, respect the security, dignity, private and family life of victims and recognise the negative effects of crime on victims.[171]

The Recommendation then proceeds to lay down fairly particular demands under a range of headings.[172] In terms of protections relevant to victims testifying at court, it will be recalled that states are called upon to 'ensure, at all stages of the procedure, the protection of the victim's physical and psychological integrity.'[173] The instrument also recognises that 'particular protection may be necessary for victims who could be required to provide testimony.'[174]

The provisions of the EU Framework Decision, while not very detailed, are more specific than has previously been the case in outlining how procedures should be adapted to protect the rights of victims. Unlike the Council of Europe's recommendations, its provisions bind Member States. The instrument commits them to ensure that 'victims are treated with due respect for the dignity of the individual during proceedings' and that 'victims who are particularly vulnerable can

---

[170] Eg, Principle 4 of the UN Declaration on Victims provides that 'victims should be treated with compassion and respect for their dignity.' whilst Guideline C.8 of the Council of Europe's Recommendation No R(85) provides that a victim of crime has the right to be 'questioned in a manner which gives due consideration to his personal situation, his rights and dignity.'

[171] At [2.1].

[172] The Recommendation deals, inter alia, with victim assistance, information, access to remedies, state compensation, protection, and privacy.

[173] At [10.1].

[174] *Ibid.*

benefit from specific treatment best suited to their circumstances.'[175] Under Article 3, victims have the right to be heard during proceedings and to supply evidence, and should only be questioned insofar as necessary for the purpose of criminal proceedings. Article 8 is specifically concerned with the 'right to protection' and contains a number of provisions designed to ensure the victim's privacy, to protect victims from the effects of giving evidence in open court, and ensure that contact between victims and offenders within court premises may be avoided.

Following the decision of the European Court of Justice in the case of *Pupino*,[176] it is apparent that the rights contained within the Framework Decision should be justiciable by victims within domestic courts. The case concerned criminal proceedings in Italy against a nursery school teacher for offences relating to cruelty to children in her care. Like the English legal system, Italian law stipulates that evidence should be heard in an oral form at trial. There was a procedure—*incidente probatorio*—through which the court did have the power to order pre-trial witness examination in exceptional circumstances. The prosecution sought to have a number of the child witnesses examined in this way, but the court refused on the grounds that under the Criminal Code, none of the exceptional circumstances applied in the instant case. The case thus concerned the compatibility of the relevant provisions of the Italian Criminal Code with the Framework Decision.

The European Court of Justice held that the Framework Decision:

> must be interpreted as meaning that the national court must be able to authorise young children, who, as in this case, claim to have been victims of maltreatment, to give their testimony in accordance with arrangements allowing those children to be guaranteed an appropriate level of protection, for example outside the trial and before it takes place.[177]

The Italian court was therefore under an obligation to interpret the terms of the Criminal Code 'in the light of the wording and purpose of the Framework Decision'.[178] On account of the former reluctance of the European Court of Justice to be too prescriptive in relation to domestic criminal procedure, the decision in *Pupino* is particularly welcome, and underlines the fact that the right of victims to be protected from secondary victimisation is now a standard that is directly applicable in the domestic legal order.

Child Victims

The decision in *Pupino* reflects the fact that international standards are becoming gradually more specific in relation to the protection that ought to be offered to specific clauses of victims or vulnerable witnesses. Increasingly, the need to afford special treatment to child victims and witnesses in particular is

---

[175] EU Framework Decision, Art 2.
[176] 16 Jun 2005, in Case C-105/03.
[177] *Ibid*, [61].
[178] *Ibid*.

recognised in international standards. Article 40 of the United Nations
Convention on the Rights of the Child and the United Nations Standard
Minimum Rules for the Administration of Juvenile Justice[179] are clear that young
witnesses should receive fair treatment through the judicial process, and European
human rights case law makes it clear that they should not be fairly expected to testify under the same conditions as their adult counterparts.[180]

In July 2005, the United Nations adopted the Guidelines on Justice in Matters
Involving Child Victims and Witnesses of Crime.[181] Based largely upon guidelines
devised by the International Bureau for Children's Rights, the instrument lays
down an array of standards aimed at ensuring that children who have been victims
or witnesses of crimes are treated in a fair, dignified and secure manner within the
criminal justice system. In addition to these generic requirements, the instrument
also contains a 'right to be protected from hardship during the justice process.'[182]
This right is particularly wide-ranging, and encompasses inter alia: the use of
'child-sensitive' procedures;[183] modified court environments that take child witnesses into consideration; recesses during a child's testimony; hearings scheduled
at times of day appropriate to the age and maturity of the child; an appropriate
notification system to ensure the child goes to court only when necessary and
'other appropriate measures to facilitate the child's testimony.'[184] In relation to
the questioning process, the instrument requires that child victims and witnesses
are questioned in a 'child-sensitive manner' that is subject to close judicial supervision. Steps should be taken to facilitate testimony and reduce potential intimidation, including the use of testimonial aids or the appointment of psychological
experts. Separate courthouse waiting rooms and private interview areas should
also be provided. It is also specified that child victim-witnesses should never be
subject to cross-examination by alleged perpetrators, and should be examined out
of their sight.

Victims of Rape and Sexual Assault

In contrast to the relatively specific range of provisions that relate to child
witnesses, there are not many international human rights instruments that lay
down specific standards in relation to victims of rape or sexual assault. This is perhaps surprising, given the widespread recognition of the problems that commonly
arise for rape victims regarding the manner of questioning in court and the use of

---

[179] See R 13.4.
[180] See also case of *T and v United Kingdom* (1999) 30 EHRR 121, where the European Commission
of Human Rights found a breach of a fair hearing in a case where 2 ten year old boys were subjected to
the full rigors of a murder trial in an adult court. See further discussion in Ch 3, p 149.
[181] GA/RES/2005/20.
[182] *Ibid*, s XI.
[183] These are defined in Guideline 9(d) as denoting 'an approach that balances the child's right to
protection and that takes into account the child's individual needs and views.'
[184] *Ibid*, Guideline 30(d).

previous sexual history evidence. However, in looking at developments within international criminal justice, we may be able to ascertain some potential indicators of consensus as to best practice.

At the International Criminal Tribunal for the Former Yugoslavia (ICTY), the Rules of Procedure and Evidence provide for the establishment of a Victim and Witnesses Unit,[185] which has two primary functions: to recommend protective measures for victims and witnesses in accordance with Article 22 of the Statute; and provide counselling and support for them, particularly in cases of rape and sexual assault.[186] In the same way, under the Rome Statute of the International Criminal Court (ICC), special protections for victims are contained in Article 68, which provides for an exception to the public hearing, in stipulating that the Chamber may conduct any part of the proceedings in camera or allow the presentation of evidence by electronic or other special means to assist victims, witnesses or the accused. A range of factors, including age, gender and the nature of the offences should be taken into account, and any measures ordered should not prejudice the rights of the defence. It is further provided that:

> such measures *shall* be implemented in the case of a victim of sexual violence or a child who is a victim or a witness, unless otherwise ordered by the Court, having regard to all the circumstances, particularly the views of the victim or witness.[187]

Thus, the Chamber is under an obligation to make provision for such measures where particularly vulnerable witnesses are giving evidence. Article 69(2) empowers the Court to receive oral or recorded testimony of a witness by means of video or audio technology, or through documentary evidence. It is added, however, that such measures 'shall not be prejudicial to or inconsistent with the rights of the accused.'

Subsequent to Article 69(2), the Rules of Procedure and Evidence make specific provision for the receipt of evidence through video technology. First, under Rule 67, the Chamber may allow a witness to give testimony by means of audio or video technology, although this must not preclude the questioning of the witness by the Prosecutor, defence or Chamber. Rule 67(3) adds that the Chamber will ensure:

> that the venue chosen for the conduct of the audio or video-link testimony is conducive to the giving of truthful and open testimony and to the safety, physical and psychological well-being, dignity and privacy of the witness.

Under Article 43(6), the Victims and Witnesses Unit will consult with the Office of the Prosecutor concerning the availability of protective measures, security arrangements and counselling for victims, witnesses and 'others who are at risk on account of testimony given by such witnesses.'

Testimony at the ICC may also be given in pre-recorded form. Rule 68 allows pre-recorded evidence to be adduced, providing that both the Prosecutor and the defence

---

[185] RPE, R 34.
[186] Specific evidential protections for rape complainants are discussed below .
[187] Art 68(2).

have had the opportunity to examine the witness either during the recording; or at a subsequent appearance in the proceedings. Specific provision for vulnerable victims is made by Rule 112(4), which provides that the Prosecutor can use audio or video recording when questioning victims of sexual or gender violence, or a child, where such measures could reduce any subsequent detrimental effects to the victim.

A further point to note concerning the treatment of rape victims in international criminal trials is that the use of previous sexual history evidence is generally prohibited. At the ICTY, a victim's previous sexual conduct is regarded as irrelevant and inadmissible.[188] Similarly, Rule 70 of the Rules of Procedure and Evidence at the ICC states that:

> [c]redibility, character or predisposition to sexual availability of a victim or witness cannot be inferred by reason of the sexual nature of the prior or subsequent conduct of a victim or witness.

Under Rule 71, the Court shall not admit the previous or subsequent sexual conduct of a victim or witness as evidence, subject to the general discretion to rule on the relevance or admissibility of all evidence under Article 69(4) of the Statute.[189] The quest to ensure that victims are questioned appropriately at the ICC received a significant boost in 2005, when judges subscribed to a Code of Judicial Ethics that requires them to:

> exercise vigilance in controlling the manner of questioning of witnesses or victims in accordance with the Rules and give special attention to the right of participants to the proceedings to equal protection and benefit of the law.[190]

In addition, judges are placed under an obligation to:

> avoid conduct or comments which are racist, sexist or otherwise degrading and, to the extent possible, ensure that any person participating in the proceedings refrains from such comments or conduct.[191]

In terms of standards that have a direct bearing on domestic law, the jurisprudence of the Strasbourg Court is of greater significance. The special need to protect victims in sexual cases has been acknowledged on a number of occasions by the Strasbourg Court. In *Stubbings v United Kingdom*,[192] it noted that:

---

[188] R 96(iv). Other rules have been formulated specifically to protect victims of rape and sexual assault. No corroboration of the victim's testimony is required in matters of sexual assault (R 91(1)), Furthermore, if a defence of consent is raised, the Tribunal may take note of factors that vitiate consent, including physical violence and moral or psychological constraints (R 96(ii)). R 34 also attempts to minimise the inevitable stress and fear felt by many sexual complainants by providing that due consideration be given, in the appointment of staff, to the employment of qualified women. This move was particularly important as rapes were extremely common in the Yugoslav conflict—see further Niarchos (1995).

[189] Art 69(4) allows the Court to rule on the relevance or admissibility of any evidence, 'taking into account, inter alia, the probative value of the evidence and any prejudice that such evidence may cause to a fair trial or to a fair evaluation of the testimony of a witness, in accordance with the Rules of Procedure and Evidence.'

[190] International Criminal Court (2005), Art 8(2).

[191] *Ibid*, Art 8(3).

[192] (1996) 23 EHRR 213.

Sexual abuse is unquestionably an abhorrent type of wrongdoing with debilitating effects on its victim. Children and other vulnerable individuals are entitled to State protection, in the form of effective deterrents from such grave types of interference with essential aspects of their private lives.[193]

It has been recognised by the Court, and in many other international instruments, that the privacy of all types of victims ought to be protected. As regards soft law standards, the Council of Europe's Recommendation 85(11)stipulates that:

Information and public relations policies in connection with the investigation and trial of offences should give due consideration to the need to protect the victim from any publicity which will unduly affect his private life or dignity. If the type of offence or the particular status or personal situation and safety of the victim make such special protection necessary, either the trial before the judgment should be held in camera or disclosure or publication of personal information should be restricted to whatever extent is appropriate.[194]

The importance of safeguarding privacy is also outlined in the more recent Recommendation 06(08):

States should take appropriate steps to avoid as far as possible impinging on the private and family life of victims as well as to protect the personal data of victims, in particular during the investigation and prosecution of the crime.

States should encourage the media to adopt and respect self regulation measures in order to protect victims' privacy and personal data.[195]

As regards the Convention itself, the leading case is *X and Y v Netherlands*. It will be recalled that a young woman was raped by a member of staff whilst in residential care.[196] The Court here recognised that private life, as defined in Article 8, 'covers the physical and moral integrity of the person, including his or her sexual life.' More significantly, it was acknowledged it was subject to a positive obligation:[197]

The Court recalls that although the object of Article 8 is essentially that of protecting the individual against arbitrary interference by the public authorities, it does not merely compel the State to abstain from such interference: in addition to this primarily negative undertaking, there may be positive obligations inherent in an effective respect for private or family life.[198]

The act of rape itself was viewed as a breach of Article 8,[199] and demanded an adequate criminal sanction. It follows that any subsequent trial should put in place mechanisms to protect the privacy rights of victims and witnesses. This position is also reflected in the EU Framework Decision and a multitude of international soft

---

[193] *Ibid,* [64]. See also *Doorson v Netherlands* (1996) 22 EHRR 330, [70].
[194] At [F.15].
[195] At [10.8–10.9].
[196] See discussion above in Ch 2, pp 39–40.
[197] *X and Y v Netherlands* (1985) 8 EHRR 235.
[198] *Ibid,* [23].
[199] Rape also constitutes a violation of Art 3 of the Convention—see *Aydin v Turkey* (1998) 25 EHRR 251.

law standards.[200] In the early case *X v Austria*,[201] it was held that a closed trial in a case involving sexual offences against children did not infringe Article 6 of the Convention. Since then, it has become increasingly clear that processes must balance the rights of the accused against the rights of witnesses or victims. Indeed, the Court has accepted that, like fearful or intimidated witnesses, rape complainants may be entitled to anonymity at court in certain circumstances.[202] It is also suggested below that Article 8 rights may be relied upon in domestic proceedings to protect victims of rape and sexual assault from questioning about intimate details of their private lives or sexual history.

Intimidated Witnesses

Like child victims and rape complainants, the particular problems faced by intimidated witnesses have been internationally recognised as a major problem in recent years. Paragraph 6(d) of the 1985 UN Victims' Declaration states that judicial processes should take measures:

> to minimize inconvenience to victims, protect their privacy, when necessary, and ensure their safety, as well as that of their families and witnesses on their behalf, from intimidation and retaliation.

The United Nations Convention against Transnational Organized Crime[203] contains a number of protections in Article 24 and 25 concerning protection of victims. States are called upon to take appropriate measures within their means to provide effective protection from potential retaliation or intimidation for witnesses in criminal proceedings.[204] These include non-disclosure of the identity or whereabouts of witnesses and the use of video links or other evidential protections.[205] Article 25 contains a general duty to:

> provide assistance and protection to victims of offences covered by this Convention, in particular in cases of threat of retaliation or intimidation.[206]

---

[200] EU Framework Decision, Art 8; UN Victims' Declaration, Principle 6(d); Council of Europe Recs 85(11), Guideline F.15; 03(13), Principle 8; 06(08), Principle 10.8.

[201] *X v Austria*, (1913/63), 2 Digest of Strasbourg Case Law 438, 30 Apr 1965.

[202] See below, 72–76. The potential of protective mechanisms to interfere with the rights of the accused is also considered in greater depth here.

[203] UN Doc A/145/49, which was adopted by the General Assembly on 15 Nov 2000.

[204] Art 24(1).

[205] Art 24(2).

[206] Similar provisions are to be found in the Convention Against Torture, Art 13 of which states: 'Each State Party shall ensure that any individual who alleges he has been subjected to torture in any territory under its jurisdiction has the right to complain to, and to have his case promptly and impartially examined by, its competent authorities. Steps shall be taken to ensure that the complainant and witnesses are protected against all ill-treatment or intimidation as a consequence of his complaint or any evidence given.' See also the Updated Set of Principles for the Protection and Promotion of Human Rights through Action to Combat Impunity. E/CN.4/2005/102/Add.1. Principle 10 provides that 'effective measures shall be taken to ensure the security, physical and psychological well-being, and, where requested, the privacy of victims and witnesses'.

Both the European Union and the Council of Europe have also formulated standards to combat witness intimidation. Under Article 8 of the EU Framework Decision, Member States are called upon to ensure:

a suitable level of protection for victims and, where appropriate, their families or persons in a similar position, particularly as regards their safety and protection of their privacy, where the competent authorities consider that there is a serious risk of reprisals or firm evidence of serious intent to intrude upon their privacy.[207]

The Council of Europe has dealt with the question of formulating responses to intimidated witnesses in a number of its Recommendations. The first, R (85)11 on the position of victims in criminal proceedings states that:

Information and public relations policies in connection with the investigation and trial of offences should give due consideration to the need to protect the victim from any publicity which will unduly affect his private life or dignity. If the type of offence or the particular status or personal situation and safety of the victim make such special protection necessary, either the trial before the judgment should be held in camera or disclosure or publication of personal information should be restricted to whatever extent is appropriate.[208]

Guideline G.16 further provides that victims and their families should be protected against intimidation and retaliation by the offender, particularly where organised crime is concerned.[209]

A second instrument, Recommendation (97)13, specifically concerns the 'intimidation of witnesses and the rights of the defence.' The provision is wide-ranging, yet its stipulations are also much more categorical than those contained in the 1985 Recommendation. They include a number of general principles, including the need to put in place 'appropriate legislative and practical measures . . . to ensure that witnesses may testify freely and without intimidation.'[210] 'Intimidation' is defined as:

any direct, indirect or potential threat to a witness, which may lead to interference with his / her duty to give testimony free from influence of any kind whatsoever.[211]

This definition would seemingly encompass both intimidation resulting from threats made by an individual as well as that which resulted from a particular process per se. Sections III and IV of the Recommendation deal with 'organised crime' and 'vulnerable witnesses and crime within the family' respectively. In respect of witnesses falling into the former category, a number of alternative means of giving evidence are outlined in Principle 9, including recording pre-trial statements to take the place of live testimony; late or selective release of details as

---

[207] Art 8(1).

[208] Guideline F.15.

[209] Guideline G.16. Recommendation 2000(19) on the role of public prosecution in the criminal justice system imposes this particular duty on prosecutors, who 'should take proper account of the interests of the witnesses, especially take or promote measures to protect their life, safety and privacy, or see to it that such measures have been taken' (at [32]).

[210] Principle 1.

[211] Pt 1.

to the identity of witnesses; or the exclusion of the media and/or the public from all or part of the trial. Principle 10 provides for certain witnesses to give evidence anonymously as an 'exceptional measure,' and underlines the need to preserve a fair balance between the needs of criminal proceedings and the rights of the defence.[212] Witness protection programmes should also be put in place where appropriate.[213] In relation to 'vulnerable witnesses and crime within the family', it was noted above that the instrument lays down specific stipulations concerning the availability of special measures and the need to control cross-examination. In addition, it provides that:

> [a]dequate legislative and practical measures should be taken to ensure protection against intimidation, and to relieve pressure on witnesses giving evidence against family members in criminal cases.[214]

The European Court has also upheld the use of anonymity orders to protect the Article 8 rights of witnesses who are particularly fearful about the prospects of testifying. As noted previously, witnesses may be intimidated either by a process or by an individual. It follows that some victims who would be classed as particularly 'vulnerable' by virtue of age or the nature of the crime committed against them may also be regarded as 'intimidated.' The discussion below is thus relevant not only to those witnesses who are fearful of being attacked or harassed by a particular person, but who are fearful about the nature of the process of giving evidence. As such, the principles will apply not only to intimidated witnesses, but also to child witnesses, complainants in sex cases, and other victims who are fearful of testifying. Such standards should thus be seen as further buttressing those documented above.

Under the Convention, anonymity orders will not normally contravene Article 6, providing there are counter-balancing measures in place that allow the evidence to be challenged by the accused or his lawyers.[215] In *Kostovski v The Netherlands*,[216] the anonymous evidence was presented at the criminal trial in hearsay form, with the defence only permitted to submit written questions to the magistrate's hearing, and only the magistrate was available at the trial for questioning. Here, the counter measures in place were found to be wholly inadequate. However, the Court found no breach of Article 6 in *Baegen v Netherlands*,[217] *Finkensieper v The Netherlands*,[218] or *Doorson v Netherlands*.[219] In these cases anonymous witnesses were used, but adequate counter-measures were found to be in place for the defence.

---

[212] See discussion below, pp 85–90.

[213] Principle 14.

[214] Principle 17. See also Principle 10.2 of Rec 06(8), which provides that 'specific protection measures should be taken for victims at risk of intimidation, reprisals or repeat victimisation.'

[215] See, eg, *Unterpringer v Austria* (1986) 13 EHRR 175, [31]; *Kostovski v Netherlands* (1989) 12 EHRR 434, [41].

[216] (1989) 12 EHRR 434.

[217] App No 16696/90, 27 Oct 1995.

[218] App No 19525/92, 17 May 1995.

[219] (1996) 22 EHRR 330.

In *Baegen*, a rape complainant was granted anonymity and permitted not to testify in the trial against the accused after she was threatened with a reprisal attack. Although she did give evidence before an examining magistrate, the accused alleged that his right to a fair trial had been denied by an inability to question her at the trial. Finding there was no violation of Article 6, the Commission noted that:

> The Court has had regard to the special features of criminal proceedings concerning sexual offences. Such proceedings are often conceived of as an ordeal by the victim, in particular when the latter is unwillingly confronted with the defendant. These features are even more prominent in a case involving a minor. In the assessment of the question whether or not in such proceedings an accused received a fair trial, account must be taken of the right to respect for the private life of the perceived victim. Therefore, the Court accepts that in criminal proceedings concerning sexual abuse certain measures may be taken for the purpose of protecting the victim, provided that such measures can be reconciled with an adequate and effective exercise of the rights of the defence.[220]

A similar situation arose in *Finkensieper*, a rape case involving four different complainants. As in *Baegen*, the complainants did not appear to give evidence in court, but three of the four had been questioned by the examining magistrate. Taking into account the traumatic nature of the offences and the distress caused to the victims, the Court held that Article 8 imposed a positive obligation which did not interfere with the fair trial rights of the accused under Article 6.[221]

In *Doorson v Netherlands*,[222] the Court pointed out that defence counsel was permitted to attend the magistrates' hearing and put questions to the anonymous witnesses through the magistrates. Consequently, the Court held that such procedures did not contravene Article 6 although, significantly, the Court also highlighted the fact that the conviction in this case was not based solely or to a decisive extent on the anonymous evidence.[223] In determining whether such an

---

[220] At [77]. The specific issues raised by anonymity are discussed below, pp 108–109.

[221] Although arising through a very different context, *Z v Finland* (1997) 25 EHRR 371 provides an illustration of a case where the rights and interests of the innocent party had to be weighed not against the right to a fair trial, but against the public interest in a criminal prosecution. The applicant had been married to a man who was being tried on several counts of manslaughter through engaging in sexual acts with others whilst knowing that he was HIV positive. When her former husband refused to give evidence, the authorities seized the applicant's medical records and ordered her medical advisor to give evidence at the trial to establish the date when the applicant knew he was HIV positive. The accused was convicted, but the court ordered that the judgment remain confidential for a 10 year period to protect the identity of the applicant. The Finnish Court of Appeal upheld the 10 year confidentiality order, but unintentionally disclosed the applicant's name and medical condition through a fax to the press. Before the Strasbourg Court, the Finnish authorities accepted that Art 8 had been breached, but contended that the measures were 'necessary in a democratic society' to prevent crime and to protect the rights of others. The Court agreed that the public interest in the investigation and prosecution of crime and the public interest in the publicity of court proceedings can outweigh medical confidentiality, but only in limited circumstances and where safeguards exist to protect the rights of patients. The Court found no violation of Art 8 in relation to the seizure of the applicant's medical files and the order compelling her advisors to give evidence, but did find a violation in relation to the 10 year confidentiality order, which the Court felt was too short, and through the (albeit unintentional) disclosure of the applicant's name in the Court of Appeal judgment.

[222] See further discussion below at p 112.

[223] At [76].

intervention would interfere with the accused's fair trial rights, the Court must undertake an interest-balancing exercise:

> It is true that Article 6 does not explicitly require the interests of witnesses in general, and those of victims called upon to testify in particular, to be taken into consideration. However, their life, liberty or security of person may be at stake, as may interests coming generally within the ambit of Article 8 of the Convention . . . Contracting States should organise their criminal proceedings in such a way that those interests are not unjustifiably imperilled. Against this background, principles of fair trial also require that in appropriate cases the interests of the defence are balanced against those of witnesses or victims called upon to testify.[224]

Yet the dilution of the rights of the accused should not be undertaken lightly since the accused stands to lose a lot more than the victim if the trial process is flawed. In *Van Mechelen v Netherlands*,[225] it was held that any measures restricting the rights of the defence should be strictly necessary, and if a less restrictive measure can suffice, then it is that measure which should be applied.[226] In *Visser v Netherlands*,[227] the applicant complained that he had not been afforded a fair trial since he had been denied the right to test the evidence against him under Article 6(3)(d). Neither he nor his counsel had been given the opportunity to see the anonymous witness, and had thus been unable to observe his demeanour under cross-examination. However, more than five years had passed since the witness first gave a statement to the police, while the applicant's co-accused, whom the witness was purported to fear, had been released from prison in 1988. The Court found that there was no cause for anyone to believe that they might be targeted by him, and went on to hold that, since the conviction was based primarily on the evidence of the anonymous witness, the principles set out in *Doorson* had been contravened in this specific case. By contrast, in *Bubbins v UK*,[228] the grant of anonymity to police officers at a coroner's inquest did not undermine the fairness of the proceedings, since they were cross-examined in sight of the Coroner, the family's lawyers, and the jury.

As the Strasbourg Court has observed on a number of occasions, breaches of the right to a fair trial are unlikely to be found on the basis of evidential or procedural rules, but the Court should look instead at the trial process as a whole in order to ascertain whether the fundamental requirements of fairness have been observed.[229] On the basis of recent trends, anonymity orders for witnesses ought only to be made in the most exceptional of cases, but the right of an accused to know the identity of his or her accuser should not normally be regarded as an absolutely essential component of a criminal hearing.

---

[224] At [70].
[225] (1998) 25 EHRR 657.
[226] *Ibid*, [59].
[227] App No 26668/95, 14 Feb 2002.
[228] (2005) 41 EHRR 24.
[229] *Barbera, Messegue and Jabardo v Spain* (1988) 11 EHRR 360.

The view of the Strasbourg court that anonymity will not necessarily breach fair trial rights is also reflected in the rules and jurisprudence of most international criminal tribunals. Given the heinous nature of some of the offences dealt with by these courts, it is recognised that it may be prudent to hold proceedings in camera and hold back the identity of the victim, or to admit written evidence as an alternative to requiring the witness to attend court. To this end, the Rules of the ICTY contain a number of very specific protections in relation to arrangements that may be made to protect the identity of witnesses. Rule 75 provides that a Judge or a Chamber may, of its own motion or at the request of either party or of the witness him / herself, order appropriate measures for the privacy and protection of certain witnesses, providing such measures do not impugn the rights of the accused.[230] Furthermore, Rule 69 provides that the identities of witnesses who may be at risk should not be disclosed to the accused until such time as the witness can be brought under the protection of the Tribunal (subject to Rule 75). Rule 79 provides that in 'exceptional circumstances' the prosecution and the defence are permitted to submit evidence by way of deposition for witnesses who are unable or unwilling to testify subsequently in open court.[231]

The Rome Statute makes no express provision concerning witness anonymity, but does stipulate that, during the investigation, the Prosecutor is required to respect the interests and personal circumstances of victims and witnesses, including age, gender and health, and take into account the nature of the crime, in particular where it involves sexual violence, gender violence or violence against children.[232] This power of protection also includes the authority to conceal the identity of the witnesses or informers whenever it is deemed appropriate.[233] In relation to the trial itself, not all witnesses who are deemed to be 'at risk' must attend. Article 68(5) states that where the disclosure of evidence or information may lead to 'the grave endangerment of the security of a witness or his or her family', the Prosecutor may 'withhold such evidence or information and instead

---

[230] A Chamber may thus hold a voir dire hearing in order to determine which measures may be necessary in this regard. Examples may include expunging names and identifying information from the Chamber's public records; non-disclosure of certain information to the public; use of image / voice altering devices or CCTV, and the assignment of a pseudonym. See further Shaw (1998). In the case of *Tadic*, Case No IT-94-1-T, 17 Jul 1995, the Prosecutor's office had filed a motion seeking protective measures for a number of witnesses, including confidentiality and anonymity. The defence rejected the requests for anonymity on grounds that this would infringe the right of the accused to know the identity of his or her accuser. The Chamber also held that witness anonymity did not violate the right of the accused to examine, or have examined, witnesses against him, although at the same time acknowledged that the Chamber had restricted the rights of the defence.

[231] Depositions may be taken by means of video-conference if appropriate (R 71). In order to protect the equality of arms and the rights of the accused, this procedure also applies to cross-examination .

[232] Art 54(1)(b).

[233] Art 54, s 3 provides that the Prosecutor may '(e) agree not to disclose, at any stage of the proceedings, documents or information that the Prosecutor obtains on the condition of confidentiality and solely for the purpose of generating new evidence, unless the provider of the information consents; and (f) take necessary measures, or request that necessary measures be taken, to ensure the confidentiality of information, the protection of any person or the preservation of evidence.'

submit a summary thereof.'[234] If the witness does testify, Article 68(2) creates an exception to the principle of public hearings and stipulates that the Court may conduct any part of the proceedings in camera. Other measures include withholding the name of the victim or witness from the court,[235] or expunging the identity of the victim, witness or other person at risk from the records.[236] Article 69(2) provides that such measures 'shall not be prejudicial to or inconsistent with the rights of the accused.'

On the basis of current trends in European human rights law and international criminal justice, provision should be made to enable fearful witnesses to testify anonymously under certain circumstances. There appears to be no absolute requirement that the accused must know the identity of his accuser. Undoubtedly knowing the identity of all witnesses should be broadly accepted as the 'norm' in the vast majority of criminal hearings, but there are, and must, be exceptions to this principle. As Spencer argues, a fair trial does not mean a trial which is free from all possible detriment or disadvantage to the accused. The law 'is bound to recognise at least some exceptional cases where the courts can hear the evidence of absent witnesses, because if it did not, criminal justice would be paralysed in the face of some of the most dangerous criminals.'[237] While the accused's right to a fair hearing is in no way subservient to the rights of victims, the preferred international approach would indicate that both rights should be considered in a principled and consistent manner on a case-by-case basis.

Domestic Practice

On the domestic platform, the main drive to protect vulnerable witnesses began with a flurry of initiatives in the late 1980s and early 1990s. As noted earlier,[238] it was at this point in time that the victim began to re-emerge in the public consciousness, and became a focal point in criminal justice discourse. In response to this public concern, new Criminal Justice Acts were enacted in 1988 and 1991, which contained various provisions enabling child witnesses to give their evidence via a televised link or have their examination-in-chief substituted by pre-recorded video testimony.

The nature of these reforms was generally untidy and piecemeal, with many of the provisions criticised on grounds that they were overly complex, poorly drafted, and contained numerous legal lacunae. For example, whereas the live link and the use of video-recorded evidence were limited to trial on indictment and in youth

---

[234] Under Art 68(6), a state may make an application for 'necessary' measures to be taken to protect its servants and to protect confidential information.
[235] R 87(3)(c) and (d).
[236] R 87(3)(a).
[237] Spencer (1994).
[238] See Ch 1, pp 8–11.

courts, no provision was made for children who had to testify in magistrates' courts.[239] Another major omission was the lack of any comprehensive guidance or criteria, other than the rather ambiguous 'interests of justice' test.[240] Likewise, no mechanisms were in place for ascertaining the child witness's expectations or desires; there was no guidance as to whether the views of the child should be taken into account, or indeed how such views were to be ascertained. Such omissions and complexities resulted in an uncertain regime where judicial discretion had a key role to play. In the absence of comprehensive guidelines, the prevailing climate of uncertainty and inconsistent practice was bound to be exacerbated.

The failure of the Government to introduce a more comprehensive system of protecting complainants can perhaps be attributed to their fear of opposition from the legal profession, and possibly within some quarters of the Government itself. The legislation was nonetheless significant in so far as it did mark the beginning of a broader trend in criminal justice, whereby the value placed on live oral evidence has increasingly been called into question. The introduction of video technology constituted a significant crack in the prototype adversarial paradigm, and marked the beginning of a much more far-reaching process whereby the fundamental tenets of adversarialism, including the principle of orality,[241] have been increasingly subjected to gradual statutory erosion.

Special Measures

On 13 June 1997 the then Home Secretary Jack Straw announced the setting up of a Home Office Interdepartmental Working Group, to examine and make recommendations on the treatment of vulnerable and intimidated witnesses within the criminal justice system. Its terms of reference included the identification of measures at all stages of the criminal justice process which would improve the treatment of vulnerable witnesses, and further measures that might encourage witnesses to give evidence in court. Members of the Group were drawn from a range of Government departments, and included representatives of Victim Support and the Association of Chief Police Officers. Special conferences were held to facilitate discussion with the judiciary and legal profession, and in drawing up their recommendations the Group drew heavily on the findings of a number of academic studies. It published its report, *Speaking Up for Justice*, in June 1998.[242]

The Report made a total of 78 recommendations, 26 of which required legislation. It highlighted the need for training for all those involved in the criminal justice system to assist them in responding to the needs of vulnerable witnesses, including children. A plethora of recommendations included measures to combat witness intimidation and a wide range of measures to protect vulnerable and

[239] Criminal Justice Act 1988, s 32A(1)(a), as inserted by s 54 of the Criminal Justice Act 1991.
[240] Criminal Justice Act 1988, s 32A(3)(c), as inserted by s 54 of the Criminal Justice Act 1991.
[241] See Ch 1, p 34.
[242] Home Office (1998).

intimidated witnesses within the trial itself. The Committee identified two categories of witness who should be entitled to receive assistance. First, the Report concluded that those witnesses whose vulnerability related to the effects of age, disability or illness ('Category A' witnesses) would automatically be entitled to some form of special protection. However, in the case of witnesses who may be vulnerable or intimidated for reasons relating to their particular situation or the circumstances of the case ('Category B' witnesses), it was recommended that the trial judge retain discretion in determining whether or not the granting of such measures would be appropriate.[243]

In contrast to the half-hearted attempt to implement the Pigot Report in 1991,[244] most of the *Speaking Up for Justice* recommendations were implemented in Part II of the Youth Justice and Criminal Evidence Act 1999. The 1999 Act extends both the range of witnesses who can make use of procedural protections, and the range of measures available to such witnesses. In keeping with the recommendations of the Working Group, the eligibility of a witness for a special measures direction will depend upon the characteristics of an individual witness, rather than hinging on whether or not the witness falls within a list of closed categories.[245]

Like the 1988 / 1991 regime, the provisions concerning eligibility for special assistance are complex. In determining whether or not to issue a special measures direction, the court has to concern itself with three issues: the eligibility of the witness; the availability of the range of special measures; and the desirability of making a special measures direction in the circumstances of the case.[246] Under section 16(1)(a), a child witness is eligible for special measures if he or she is less than seventeen years old at the time of the hearing. However, once it has been established that a child is eligible, the court must then consider which special measure(s) should be made available. The apparent simplicity of section 16 then gives way to an extremely complex framework of presumptions and rules, contained in sections 21 and 22. The effect of these provisions is that in cases where a person under seventeen must give evidence against a defendant accused of a sexual offence, the court will be under an obligation to make a special measures direction under section 28 unless the witness wishes to give live evidence in court.

Section 21 sets out a three-tiered hierarchy for child witnesses. At the top of this hierarchy are children testifying in sexual offences.[247] Next, provisions are made concerning the eligibility of children testifying in offences involving physical assault, neglect, kidnapping, false imprisonment or abduction under the Child Abduction Act 1984,[248] and they are followed at the bottom of the hierarchy by

---

[243] Home Office (1998), [3.25].

[244] Pigot (1989).

[245] S 18(5) gives the Home Secretary wide powers to amend these provisions, including the right to abolish any of the existing special measures and invent new ones.

[246] Either party may apply to the court to use such mechanisms, although the court can also grant special measures of its own motion.

[247] Youth Justice and Criminal Evidence Act, s 21(1)(b)(i).

[248] Youth Justice and Criminal Evidence Act, s 21(1)(b)(ii).

child witnesses who fall outside these categories and who are therefore assumed not to be 'in need of special protection.'[249] No distinction is made between children who are alleged victims and those who are eyewitnesses to offences against others.

Thus, as Birch has warned, the courts must 'navigate a statutory minefield of presumptions . . . as to which measures are deemed to be desirable.'[250] Children in all three cases have access to the full range of special measures directions. However, the difference between child witnesses in sexual and non-sexual cases is crucial in determining the scope of judicial discretion as to which measure(s) ought to be applied. The primary rule in section 21 determines that child victims of sexual abuse must be entitled to a video-taped interview and be cross-examined on video tape before trial unless they themselves decline that measure. There is no need for the court to consider whether the measure should improve the quality of their evidence under section 19(2)(a).[251]

Children in cases of abduction, cruelty or neglect have the benefit of a presumption in favour of videotaped interview and live link, though not videotaped cross-examination. As with children in cases of sexual offences, it is not necessary to show that the quality of their evidence would be improved. For all other children who are deemed not to be in need of special protection, there is a presumption that they give all their evidence by way of live link, which the defence may rebut.

The distinction in section 21 between sexual and non-sexual offences is arbitrary, and contravenes the Working Group's recommendation that the availability of special measures should relate to the age of the child and not the nature of the offence.[252] As Hoyano contends, this was a rather odd anomaly in the legislation, given that both the Scottish and New Zealand Law Commissions have recommended erasing all statutory distinctions between sexual and non-sexual offences.[253] However, recently the Government announced its intention in a consultation paper to amend the rule so that all applications for special measures would be based on the 'assessed need' of the witness.[254]

Following the application of section 21 as it currently stands, the court must then take the decision as to which special measures ought to be applied. That choice is governed by the criteria in section 19(2). The main consideration for the

---

[249] Youth Justice and Criminal Evidence Act, s 21(1)(b).

[250] Birch (2000), 240.

[251] S 21(5). S 16(5) defines 'quality of a witness's evidence' to mean its 'completeness, coherence and accuracy.' and also defines coherence as referring to 'a witness's ability in giving evidence to give answers which address the questions put to the witness and can be understood both individually and collectively.'

[252] Home Office (1998), [10.8].

[253] See Hoyano (2000), 251: 'It is difficult to justify the distinctions between child witnesses depending on categorisation of the offences according to sexual contact, physical violence and other offences. It is not self-evident that a child aged 15 will suffer trauma in testifying against or being cross-examined by her father in relation to sexual, but not physical abuse.' See Scottish Law Commission (1990), [1.7], [4.55]; New Zealand Law Commission (1999), [447], as cited by Hoyano, at 261.

[254] Office for Criminal Justice Reform (2007), [4.11].

court is whether the measure in question would improve the quality of the witness's evidence, and if so, determine which of those measures would be likely to 'maximise so far as practicable the quality of such evidence.' In arriving at this determination, section 19(3) states that the court must consider any views expressed by the witnesses, and whether the proposed measure(s) would make it more difficult for the opposing party to test the evidence of the witness effectively.

The provisions within the Act for child witnesses are a considerable step forward from the more restrictive provisions under the 1988 / 1991 regime, where the broad judicial discretion led to 'excessive and ill-defined excuses to decline to use the special provisions.'[255] Most child witnesses will undoubtedly benefit from the presumption in section 21 which should ensure that, subject to the interests of justice, videotaped interviews will be deemed admissible, and that children will be cross-examined via the live link, unless the courts opt for pre-trial cross-examinations instead.[256] In turn, this should help child witnesses feel less fearful about the prospect of testifying given that they should know in advance that they will not have to give live evidence against the accused in the same room.

In relation to adult witnesses, if the court considers that the quality of the evidence given by a witness is likely to be diminished by reason of any circumstances falling within section 16(2) or 17(2), they too may also be eligible for a special measures direction under sections 16 or 17. The section under which a witness applies for special measures will determine which measures may be granted to them. Section 18 states that the full range of eight special measures is made potentially available to all witnesses who are eligible under section 16, but only the first six of them where the witness is eligible under section 17.[257]

Section 16(2) implements the recommendations of the Working Group that, like children, those suffering from mental or physical disability should automatically be entitled to special measures.[258] Such witnesses are basically those affected by mental disorder or impairment of intelligence and social functioning,[259] and those affected by a physical disability or disorder.[260] The court should consult witnesses prior to trial in relation to their wishes,[261] although it remains to be seen what weight, if any, might be attached to the evidence of expert witnesses, or carers. The appropriateness of any special measure will effectively depend on the nature of the disability.

Section 17 provides that a witness is eligible for special measures if the quality of his or her evidence 'is likely to be diminished by reason of fear or distress . . . in

---

[255] Hoyano (2000), 261.

[256] Subject to its future enforcement (see below). In all other cases where the child is not deemed 'in need of special protection' the court should order whichever measures that will 'maximise the quality of the child's evidence so far as practicable': Youth Justice and Criminal Evidence Act, s 19(2).

[257] Thus witnesses eligible under s 17 cannot make use of an intermediary under s 29, nor aids to communication under s 30.

[258] Home Office (1998), [3.29].

[259] Youth Justice and Criminal Evidence Act, s 16(2)(a).

[260] Youth Justice and Criminal Evidence Act, s 16(2)(b).

[261] Youth Justice and Criminal Evidence Act, s 16(4).

connection with testifying in the proceedings.' The fact that a witness produces evidence that he / she suffers from fear or distress about the prospect of testifying does not give rise to automatic eligibility. The Court must determine whether this is the case by referring to a range of factors contained in section 17(2).[262] If the witness is the victim of a sexual offence, section 17(4) creates a presumption that the witness is eligible for special measures. This provision is particularly welcome, in that police can now guarantee sexual complainants that if they have to go to court, they should normally be eligible at least for one or more of the special measures.

Once the court determines that the adult witness is eligible for a special measures direction, the decision must be made as to which measure(s) would be likely to optimise the quality of that witness's evidence under section 19. In doing so, it should have regard to all the circumstances of the case, including in particular any views expressed by the witness and whether the measure or measures might tend to inhibit such evidence being effectively tested by a party to the proceedings.[263] In summing up, the trial judge should give the jury such warning as he considers necessary to ensure that the fact that the direction was given does not prejudice the accused.[264]

A variety of measures are provided for in sections 23–29 of the Act. These are:

Screening the witness from the accused;
Giving Evidence by live link;
Giving Evidence in private;
Removing wigs and gowns;
Video recording the evidence-in-chief;
Video recording the cross-examination or re-examination;
Examining the witness through an intermediary;
Providing aids to communication.

Some of these measures are new, whereas others have existed at common law or under previous legislation. Certain measures will clearly be of greater benefit to vulnerable witnesses than others. It is self-evident, for example, that the use of screens and orders to remove wigs and gowns would clearly have less impact upon the experience of the complainant in court than more radical measures such as having all testimony pre-recorded or delivered through an intermediary.[265]

---

[262] These are: (a) the nature and alleged circumstances of the offence to which the proceedings relate; (b) the age of the witness; (c) such of the following matters as appear to the court to be relevant, namely—(i) the social and cultural background and ethnic origins of the witness, (ii) the domestic and employment circumstances of the witness, and (iii) any religious beliefs or political opinions of the witness; (d) any behaviour towards the witness on the part of—(i) the accused, (ii) members of the family or associates of the accused, or (iii) any other person who is likely to be an accused or a witness in the proceedings. In addition, s 17(3) provides that the court must also consider any views expressed by the witness.

[263] Youth Justice and Criminal Evidence Act, ss 19 (2) and 19(3).

[264] Youth Justice and Criminal Evidence Act, s 32. Where an application for a special measures direction is made, the reasons for granting it or refusing it must be stated in open court and the magistrate's court must state its reasons in the register of proceedings—s 20(5).

[265] For a critical overview of each of the measures, see Ellison (2001a), 40–64.

The majority of special measures were implemented as part of a phased introduction which began in July 2002. At the time of writing, only pre-recorded cross-
examination (s 28) and the use of intermediaries (s 29) have not yet been rolled
out nationally. Early research findings have been broadly positive. Hamlyn et al[266]
have found that high proportions of witnesses found live links and video-recorded
evidence helpful, and witnesses who used special measures were significantly more
confident that the criminal justice system was effective in bringing those who commit crimes to justice and effective in meeting the needs of victims. One third of all
witnesses using special measures said they would not have been willing and able to
give evidence without this help, and this figure was expanded to 44 per cent where
the witnesses were victims of sexual offences. Similar positive findings have been
reported by Burton et al.[267] These researchers found that, overall, special measures
were having a positive impact in improving the experiences of witnesses at court,
but argued that processes for identifying vulnerable witnesses needed to be
improved, and better steps had to be taken to ensure that the views of witnesses
were individually ascertained.

In spite of this positive reception, the Act will only come to the aid of witnesses
who fall within the legal definition of an 'eligible witness' laid down in the statute,
and it also makes an apparently arbitrary distinction between sexual offences and
violent offences committed against children. Even for those witnesses who do fall
under the ambit of the legislation, the excesses of the adversarial trial are only partially reduced, rather than removed. Even if witnesses give evidence via a television
link, for example, they will still be then subjected to the same techniques and
devices commonly used to disorientate or intimidate witnesses during cross-
examination. Other witnesses, outside the remit of the legislation, will still have
to give live evidence before courtrooms of lawyers, jurors and court officers. The
Government's attempt to mitigate the asperity of the adversarial system for some
witnesses but not for others means that the vast majority will continue to give evidence under the usual adversarial conditions.

Whilst the use of screens, television links and pre-recorded evidence-in-chief
have now been in place for some years with relatively few opponents, the
pre-recording of cross-examination under section 28 of the Act and use of intermediaries in court under section 29 are particularly contentious. Both mechanisms are alien to the confrontational tradition of the adversarial process, which
perhaps explains why they have not been implemented to date. As regards the use
of intermediaries, a major perceived risk is that the traditional role of counsel
would be significantly undermined, since questions would be put to the child by
the intermediary, who would be free to use very different voice tones and interrogative techniques than those which defence counsel may believe to be in the
interests of his or her client. Following a relatively positive evaluation of pilot

---

[266] Hamlyn et al (2004).
[267] Burton et al (2006).

schemes,[268] the Government finally announced in June 2007 that intermediaries would be rolled out from September of that year.[269]

As for section 28 of the Act, this has not yet been brought into effect, and it appears that it never will be. The provision sought to give effect to the Pigot principle that children should never be forced to testify in open court.[270] However, the legislation provides for a very different model from that envisaged by Pigot. As outlined above, Pigot had envisaged that all of the child's evidence should be taken at a pre-trial hearing. The entire hearing would be pre-recorded and then played back to the court during the trial. Instead, Cooper describes how Parliament chose to confer 'evidentiary status on police interviews with child witnesses and complainants', [271] which has also formed the basis of the 1999 legislation. This, she argues, carried two unforeseen consequences. First, that the police, rather than the courts, came to act as 'gatekeepers' to the scheme since they make the original decision as to whether the evidence should be recorded, and secondly, that prosecuting counsel was deprived of the opportunity of structuring the witness's narrative.[272] However, the main problem with section 28 would appear to be the lapse of time that would occur between the Memorandum interview and the pre-recorded cross-examination. This time lapse may well have an adverse impact on the perceived reliability of the initial interview, if children's memories are negatively affected by the potentially long intervening period of time.[273]

As a result of these envisaged difficulties, the Government announced in 2004 that it had decided not to implement the measure as it stood. In December of that year, the Home Office minister Baroness Scotland announced that the mechanism was to be re-assessed as part of a wider review into children's evidence. As a starting point, Di Birch and Rhonda Powell were asked to prepare a briefing paper considering key issues.[274] The researchers concluded that there was little reason to believe that piloting section 28 would provide tangible benefits for vulnerable witnesses, and recommended that section 28 would ultimately fail to achieve the intended policy goals. In their view, the Pigot principles of accelerating the exit of child witnesses from the criminal justice system and the facilitation of their evidence in non-intimidatory surroundings had been largely achieved by legal and procedural changes introduced in the intervening years.[275] Indeed, it was feared that procedural delays resulting from pre-recorded cross-examination might interfere with efforts to expedite the criminal process for young witnesses.[276]

---

[268] Plotnikoff and Woolfson (2007).

[269] *Hansard*, HL Deb, 12 Jun 2007, Col WS105.

[270] Pigot (1989), [2.12].

[271] Cooper (2005), 460.

[272] *Ibid*.

[273] Spencer (2000). Spencer argues that significant modification is needed to the pre-trial process as well as the actual trial process itself, in order to fully implement the Pigot proposals.

[274] Birch and Powell (2004).

[275] *Ibid*, [15–16]. In particular, other measures in the 1999 legislation, changes to disclosure rules, and efforts to fast-track particularly difficult cases had largely operated to minimise the degree of secondary victimisation suffered by child witnesses.

[276] *Ibid*, [133].

In its subsequent, if somewhat belated, consultation paper,[277] the Government pro-posed to retain section 28, but only for 'a small group of the most vulnerable wit-nesses' which would include 'very young children, those with a terminal or degenerative illness and those suffering from some form of mental incapacity'.[278]

As Hoyano argues, the reports of both Birch and the Review Group seemed to overlook two crucial facts: that most vulnerable witnesses actually *desire* pre-recorded examination, and that such schemes have operated with relative success in other jurisdictions.[279] The question as to how precisely the modified version of section 28 might operate in practice has been left open to consultation, but it is not clear how restricting the categories of witness eligible to make use of it would over-come the envisaged procedural complications. The new proposal, if it does indeed form the basis for an amendment to the 1999 Act, may mean that the Government has done enough to avoid infringement of European law following the decision in *Pupino*. However, it will ultimately fail to enable prosecutors to provide a guaran-tee to all child witnesses, as Pigot recommended, that they should not be required to testify against their will in open court.

Alternatives to Oral Testimony: Witnesses in Fear

Aside from potentially being able to access special measures, witnesses who are deemed to be 'in fear' may, in certain circumstances, avoid testifying before a court at all. Instead, section 116 of the Criminal Justice Act 2003 permits the admission of previous statements of a witness who would, ordinarily, have been called upon to testify, but is unable to attend court.[280] Subsection (2)(e) may apply where a person is reluctant to give oral evidence through fear. For the purposes of this pro-vision, 'fear' is to be widely construed and (for example) includes fear of the death or injury of another person or of financial loss, although the court may only give leave if it considers that the statement ought to be admitted in the interests of jus-tice having regard to a range of factors set out in section 116(4).[281] The case law

---

[277] Office for Criminal Justice Reform (2007), [3.4–3.7].

[278] At [3.5].

[279] Hoyano (2007), 855–6.

[280] A statement made out of court may be admissible under s 116 (subject to the additional condi-tions to be considered) if the person who made the statement (the relevant person) is dead (sub-s (2)(a)); physically or mentally ill (sub-s (2)(b)); outside the United Kingdom (sub-s (2)(c)); cannot be found despite taking reasonably practicable steps (sub-s (2)(d)); or if he / she does not give oral evid-ence through fear (sub-s (2)(e)). Subsection (1) requires that two conditions be satisfied in addition to any of the above five conditions being satisfied. First, that oral evidence given in the proceedings by the person who made the statement would be admissible as evidence of that matter (sub-s 1(a)) and that the person who made the statement (the relevant person) is identified to the court's satisfaction (sub-s 1(b)).

[281] The court must have regard: (a) to the statement's contents, (b) to any risk that its admission or exclusion will result in unfairness to any party to the proceedings (and in particular to how difficult it will be to challenge the statement if the relevant person does not give oral evidence), (c) in appropriate cases, the fact that a special measures direction under s 19 of the Youth Justice and Criminal Evidence Act could be made in relation to the relevant person, and (d) to any other relevant circumstances.

relating to its predecessor, section 23 of the Criminal Justice Act 1988,[282] is likely to continue to govern the circumstances where a fearful witness wishes to avoid attending court altogether. Thus, we can assume that 'fear' is largely regarded as an intuitive condition, and is not subject to a requirement of reasonableness.[283] Instead, it is:

> sufficient that the court, on the evidence, was sure that the witness was in fear, as a consequence of the material offence or of something said or done subsequently in relation to it and the possibility of the witness testifying as to it.[284]

On this basis, it would seem that, like section 23, section 116(2)(e) requires a connection between the fear and the offence or the giving of evidence in relation to that offence.[285] However, the fact that the average witness would not be in fear or that the fear of the witness in question is wholly unreasonable is irrelevant. The fact that the witness is timid or vulnerable because of age or other factors is relevant, but the test can still not be said to be subjective in nature. It is simply that it is easier to prove that such witnesses are in fear as a result of the crime or the possibility of testifying as to it. Certainly, the provision is not limited to protecting those witnesses traditionally viewed as being at heightened risk of reprisals, such as those testifying in cases involving terrorism or organised crime. While it should be stressed that the provision was never intended to cover witnesses who are merely nervous about the prospect of being questioned in open court, it is conceivable that it could be relied upon to protect the young, the elderly or infirm, or those who have been psychologically traumatised by the crime and fearful of giving evidence in open court in front of their assailants.

Relationship with Fair Trial Rights

The advent of special measures, and the provision in section 116 that permits the substitution of live evidence with hearsay evidence for witnesses in fear, have received a generally positive reception. Broadly speaking, they can be said to reflect international good practice. However, a number of commentators have advanced the argument that such protections risk interfering with the accused's fair trial rights. For many lawyers, the value of a face-to-face encounter between the

---

[282] S 23(3) of the Act permitted a written statement to substitute the evidence of the person who made it if that person did not 'give oral evidence through fear or because he is kept out of the way.' Prior to its repeal by the Criminal Procedure and Investigations Act 1996, s 13(3) of the Criminal Justice Act 1925, in conjunction with s 102(7) of the Magistrates' Courts Act 1980, permitted the written statements of witnesses to be read out in cases where the witness was proved that the witness had been 'kept out of the way by means of the procurement of the accused or on his behalf'. These provisions were not all that helpful to the prosecution whose witness had disappeared. Even if it could be proved that the witness had been abducted by friends of the accused, the section did not come in to play unless it could also be proved that they had done so 'at the instigation of or with the accused's knowledge and approval' (*R v O'Loughlin* [1988] 3 All ER 431).

[283] *R v Acton Justices and others* (1991) 92 Cr App R 98.

[284] *Ibid*, at 105.

[285] *Neill v North Antrim Magistrates' Court* (1993) 97 Cr App R 121.

accused and the accuser is seen as injecting a vital element of individual dignity into the criminal trial,[286] and there is also a fear that shielding devices make it easier for witnesses to lie or more difficult for the jury to detect lies. For example, Lord Thomas commented in the House of Lords that such measures can 'cotton wool' or 'insulate' witnesses from cross-examination.[287] Underpinning many of these objections is the assumption that the observation of the demeanour of the witness can act as a reliable indicator of his or her truthfulness. In common law cases, demeanour continues to be regarded highly by lawyers and the judiciary,[288] and juries are often instructed to observe the demeanour of the witness.[289] In the Canadian case of *Laurentide Motels v Beauport (City),*[290] L'Heureux-Dubé J instructed the jury that they were at liberty to consider 'the movements, glances, hesitations, trembling, blushing, surprise or bravado' of witnesses as indicators of veracity.[291] Wigmore contended that 'a witness's demeanour, without any definite rules as to its significance, is always assumed to be in evidence.'[292]

Given that so much importance is attached to demeanour, it is unsurprising that many advocates will aim to exploit the demeanour of complainants, either to make them appear more vulnerable or more nervous. In more recent times, it has been increasingly subject to question whether demeanour can properly be regarded as a reliable factor in determining the veracity of witness testimony. It may be the case that a witness who appears to be well spoken, relaxed, and answers questions in full is perceived by the tribunal of fact as being more believable when he is, in fact, lying. Conversely, a witness who appears flustered and hesitant may be perceived as lying when he or she is telling the truth. It may also be natural for witnesses who have had previous experience of giving evidence to appear more relaxed and composed than someone who is appearing in court for the first time. It does not necessarily follow, of course, that the experienced witness should be treated by the trier of fact as being more reliable just because he or she appears more composed. Complainants who are subjected to ruthless and zealous advocacy techniques for the first time are more likely to be placed in a stressful situation. As such, physical reactions which the tribunal of fact may consider to be evidence of lying might be nothing more than a reaction to the stress of testifying.[293] Moreover, the link between the witness's demeanour and the veracity of his or her account is not supported by empirical evidence. Wellborn's extensive review of research on the point led her to conclude that 'demeanour diminishes rather than enhances the accuracy of credibility judgments.'[294] Other

---

[286] See, eg Massaro (1988); Freedman (1975).

[287] *Hansard,* HL Deb, 8 Feb 1999, Col 17.

[288] Fielding (2006), 109–11.

[289] Rock (1993).

[290] [1989] 1 SCR 705.

[291] *Ibid,* [245].

[292] Wigmore (1940), [946].

[293] This was recognised by the Privy Council in *Attorney General of Hong Kong v Wong Muk Ping* [1987] AC 501. See also the Canadian cases of *R v Levogiannis* [1993] 4 SCR 475, and *R v Toten* (1993) 16 CRR (2d) 49, 58.

[294] Wellborn (1991), 1075. See also Spencer and Flin (1993), 280; Ekman (2001).

attempts to survey the psychological evidence have largely arrived at the same conclusion.[295]

Other concerns over the use of televised evidence stem from the fear that the overall quality of the testimony may be reduced by making the evidence seem remote and less compelling to the trier of fact. Concerns have thus been expressed that use of televised evidence may result in loss of impact on the trier of fact; loss of immediacy;[296] loss of rapport between questioner and the witness;[297] loss of eye contact;[298] or some degree of artificiality in the testimony.[299] In cases involving child witnesses, it has also been suggested that the use of televised links may not permit the judge or jury to see the size of the child and so it may leave the jury unaware of the vulnerability of the child as against the accused.[300] Indeed, there is evidence to suggest that some prosecutors believe that the appearance of a visibly distressed child witness makes a jury more likely to convict.[301] This has given rise to fears that this loss of emotional impact may act as a disincentive for the prosecution to apply to use the link mechanism.[302]

Closely linked to the principle of orality and the value traditionally placed on demeanour is the idea that the accused has a right of confrontation, that is, that he or she has a right to be physically present to view the opposing witnesses when they are giving evidence against the defendant. While this is a constitutional right in the US,[303] such a right does not have any grounding under the common law or under the European Convention on Human Rights. Instead, both parties to the trial are said to have the right to put forward and challenge effectively the evidence adduced by the opposition. Face-to-face confrontation should not therefore be regarded as an indispensable element of common law trials.

There are few English cases that deal directly with the issue of confrontation. In *R v Smellie*,[304] Lord Coleridge denied the existence of any such right at common law.[305] While the common law has traditionally recognised the right of the accused to be present during his trial,[306] there is no authority to suggest that this right should entail physical confrontation. Wigmore was adamant that it did not:

---

[295] See eg Spencer and Flin (1993), 110; Renaud (2001); Ellison (2001a), 76–7; Bingham (2006), 335–7.

[296] Davies and Noon (1991), 78.

[297] See Short *et al* (1976).

[298] Davies and Noon (1991), 78.

[299] *Ibid.*

[300] Australian Law Reform Commission (1992), [14.105].

[301] *Ibid.*

[302] Davies & Noon (1991), 134.

[303] In the US, the Sixth Amendment states that 'the accused shall enjoy the right . . . to be confronted with the witness against him.' This right has been described by the Supreme Court as 'one of the fundamental guarantees of life and liberty . . . long deemed so essential for the due protection of life and liberty that it is guarded against legislative and judicial action by provisions in the constitution of the United States.' *Kirby v United States* (1899) 174 US 47, 55. The scope of this right is broad, and it embodies a number of different demands: that testimony should be given under oath, subjected to cross-examination, given in the presence of the accused and in the presence of the trier of fact.

[304] (1919) 14 Cr App Rep 128.

[305] *Ibid*, 130.

[306] See comments of Lord Atkin in *Lawrence v R* [1933] AC 699, 708; see generally *R v Lee Kun* [1916] 1 KB 337.

There was never at common law any recognised right to an indispensable thing called confrontation as distinguished from cross-examination. There was a right to cross-examination as indispensable and that right was involved in and secured by confrontation; it was the same under a different name.[307]

Similarly, the right of confrontation does not form part of the fair trial requirements of the European Convention. While Article 6(3)(d) gives the accused the right:

to examine or have examined witnesses against him and to obtain the attendance and examination of witnesses on his behalf under the same conditions as witnesses against him,

the wording of the Convention itself gives little guidance as to whether physical confrontation is an element of Article 6(3)(d). While some of the earlier case law would appear to place an emphasis on the need for witnesses to at least attend the trial and be available to have their evidence challenged,[308] it does not bear out the argument that confrontation is an essential ingredient to meaningful cross-examination.[309] In *Van Mechelen v Netherlands*,[310] noted above, it was held that special measures to shield vulnerable witnesses from the accused will not contravene the Convention providing that they are strictly necessary. If a less restrictive measure can suffice, then it is that measure which should be applied.[311]

This position has been confirmed by three recent cases, all involving sexual offences against children. In *SN v Sweden*,[312] the Court held that, whilst the testimony of the victim was virtually the sole evidence on which the defendant had been convicted, the fact that his counsel had been allowed to test the evidence by putting questions indirectly to the victim through a police officer acting as a conduit meant that the applicant had not been denied a fair trial. However, in *PS v Germany*,[313] where the applicant had also been convicted solely on the basis of testimony of an 8-year old girl, the fact that she had never been questioned by either the trial judge or the defence did amount to a breach of the fair trial. Similarly, in *Bocos-Cuesta v The Netherlands*,[314] the applicant's conviction was partly based upon the statements of four children to the police, which was admitted as written evidence. The domestic court rejected a defence request that the children appear in person to be cross-examined, but this was rejected on the grounds that it risked putting them through a traumatic ordeal at the courtroom. The applicant was convicted, but alleged his right to a fair hearing had been subject to interference since his lawyers had no opportunity to question the four

---

[307] Wigmore (1940), [1397].

[308] *Delta v France* (1990) 16 EHRR 574; *Kostovski v Netherlands* (1989) 12 EHRR 434.

[309] Indeed, cross-examination has no conceptual equivalent in many European jurisdictions. See Ch 6, pp 278–81.

[310] (1998) 25 EHRR 657.

[311] *Ibid*, [59].

[312] App No 34209/96, 2 Jul 2002.

[313] App No 33900/96, 20 Dec 2001.

[314] App No 54789/00, 10 Nov 2005.

children. In finding that his right to a fair trial had been breached, the Court underlined that he had not been afforded an opportunity to follow the manner in which the children were heard by the police. For instance, it was pointed out that the defendant could have watched from another room through a one-way mirror or televised link. More significantly, the fact that his lawyers were unable to question the witnesses was a fundamental breach of Article 6.

The compatibility of special measures with Convention standards was recently considered by the House of Lords in the case of *R (on the application of D) v Camberwell Green Youth Court*.[315] Here, the applicants argued that the requirement of the court under section 21(5) of the Youth Justice and Criminal Evidence Act to give a special measures direction in favour of video-recording the evidence-in-chief where child witnesses were 'in need of special assistance' was essentially incompatible with Article 6.[316] Their Lordships held that it was well established that the common law provided for exceptions to the general principle of orality and the use of special measures did not contravene Article 6 of the Convention. Whilst acknowledging that it was 'usual' for witness testimony to be received live in open court, the 'critical element' of the Convention case law was that the defence should have ample opportunity to challenge and question all prosecution witnesses at some stage in the procedure.[317] It was not necessary that the accused be physically present.[318] Counsel for the appellants suggested that the case law should be read in the light of the adversarial tradition, whereby the core principle was that all evidence was received orally in front of the accused, but this argument was dismissed by the court which stated that Parliament had determined that there were sound policy grounds to depart from the 'norm' of oral testimony in the accused's presence.[319]

This is unlikely to be the last challenge to the compatibility of special measures. Once the government has devised an appropriate alternative to section 28 of the Act, that too, is likely to be challenged in the appellate courts; although it seems improbable that the outcome should be any different.[320] Once section 29 of the Act, which provides for the use of intermediaries, is completely rolled out, it can be expected that it will also be tested. Where the use of an intermediary is directed, a third party, rather than defence counsel, will relay the questions from the advocate to the witness. There is clearly a real risk that this 'filtration' process could result in the meanings and emphases of particular words and phrases being

---

[315] [2005] 1 WLR 393.

[316] See also the cases of *R (DPP) v Redbridge Youth Court, R(L) v Bicester Youth Court* [2001] 4 All ER 411, where the Divisional Court held that the defendant's right to a fair trial was preserved by allowing the defence the opportunity to challenge by cross-examination all pre-recorded evidence.

[317] *Kostovski v Netherlands* (1989) 12 EHRR 434.

[318] *Hols v Netherlands*, App No 25206/94, 19 Oct 1996; *SN v Sweden*, App No 34209/96, 2 Jul 2002.

[319] [2005] 1 WLR 393 at [52]-[53].

[320] For a comparative overview of how such challenges have been dealt with in other common law jurisdictions, see the New Zealand case of *R v Accused* [1989] 1 NZLR 660; the Canadian case of *R v L (DO)* [1993] 4 RSC 419; and the South African case of *Klink v Regional Court Magistrate NO and others* [1996] 3 BCLR 402 (SE).

compromised, which may spawn questions as to how effective a defence the accused is able to mount in these circumstances.

As for mechanisms which permit the admissibility of hearsay statements of fearful witnesses, the courts have also refused to entertain any argument that they interfere with the rights of the accused. In *Sellick*,[321] the trial judge found that certain identified witnesses, well known to the accused, had been deterred from attending court at his murder trial. His earlier statements were admitted under section 23 of the Criminal Justice Act 1988, and the defendant was convicted. He appealed, contending that the judge should not have admitted the statements because the defence had not been given an adequate opportunity to challenge the statements at any stage of the proceedings. There had thus been a violation of his right to cross-examine witnesses under Article 6(3)(d) of the Convention. Rejecting this argument, the Court of Appeal noted that, through his intimidatory actions, it was the defendant who had denied himself the opportunity to examine the witness and so could not complain of a violation of his Convention rights. In any case, there was no absolute rule that, even where the hearsay evidence was the sole or decisive evidence, its admission should automatically lead to a violation of Article 6(3)(d). In a decision that reflects both the common law and Convention standards on confrontation, the Court of Appeal pronounced that the right to examine witnesses was not free-standing, but merely a constituent element of a fair trial. Similar decisions have since followed in the cases of *Campbell (Neville)*[322] and *Xhabri*.[323]

From the perspective of vulnerable and intimidated witnesses and victims, it is particularly welcome that, in all of the cases to date before the domestic courts and the Strasbourg court, the key requirement under Convention jurisprudence seems to be that the defence must be given sufficient opportunity to challenge the evidence of such witnesses. It is not necessary for a face-to-face encounter to take place as part of a public trial; the benchmark in all cases is whether the fairness of the trial requires cross-examination. It follows that courts should strive to achieve a balance between the contents of the statement and the risk of unfairness to any party from the inability to cross-examine if the statement is admitted or excluded.[324] Providing this approach is followed in future years, courts will still have an opportunity to hear the evidence of some of the most vulnerable witnesses in trials concerning some of society's most serious offences.

---

[321] [2005] 1 WLR 3641.

[322] [2005] EWCA Crim 2078.

[323] [2006] 1 Cr App R 26.

[324] In conducting this exercise, the quality of the evidence in the statement will be the crucial factor. The higher the quality of the evidence in the statement, the less risk there will be of unfairness through the lack of the ability of any party to cross-examine the maker of the statement. The degree of quality will also impact on the question whether it is in the interests of justice to admit the statement: the higher the quality the more important the statement will be to the issues in the case, and the more likely it will be that the evidence should be admitted in the interests of justice.

The Regulation of Questioning

It was noted previously that witnesses have often reported that they feel as though they are on trial themselves, and have been upset and hurt by the aggressive nature of cross-examination. Special measures have little, if any, impact on the manner and tone of cross-examination, and can do very little to prevent the intimidation of witnesses through gestures, facial expressions, voice intonation or other forms of non-verbal communication. The Code of Conduct for the Bar of England and Wales,[325] reinforced by the Written Standards for the Conduct of Professional Work,[326] lay down certain ethical standards to which barristers are expected to adhere in conducting cross-examinations. Neither of these instruments is legally binding, and nor do they constitute an exhaustive set of parameters by which barristers are bound to conduct their case. However, the rules are generally followed in practice and do have some bearing upon the manner in which witnesses are questioned.

Although cross-examination is not discussed extensively, there are a number of specific rules concerning the conduct of barristers and their duty to the court which are directly relevant to the manner of cross-examination. Unsurprisingly, perhaps, there is no obligation to put witnesses at ease or to help them give clear and coherent testimony. However, rule 7.08(g) provides that a barrister 'must not make statements or ask questions which are merely scandalous or intended or calculated only to vilify, insult or annoy either a witness or some other person.'

Rule 7.08(j) further states that counsel:

> must not suggest that a victim, witness or other person is guilty of crime, fraud or misconduct or make any defamatory aspersion on the conduct of any other person or attribute to another person the crime or conduct of which his lay client is accused unless such allegations go to a matter in issue (including the credibility of the witness) which is material to the lay client's case and appear to him to be supported by reasonable grounds.

However, unlike certain other Codes of Practice, the English Code imposes no requirement for allegations to have an evidential basis.[327] On the contrary, there would seem to be considerable latitude on what may constitute 'reasonable grounds':

> If his instructing solicitor tells him that in his opinion the imputation is well-founded or that he believes it to be true then he has the necessary 'reasonable grounds.' If someone other than his instructing solicitor gives him the information then he should not make the imputations unless that person can give 'satisfactory reasons' for his statement to him.[328]

---

[325] General Council of the Bar (2004a).
[326] General Council of the Bar (2004b).
[327] See, eg, R 10.02 of the New Zealand Code of Practice.
[328] Du Cann (1993), 123.

In spite of the Code's attempts to prevent counsel from making unfounded allegations against witnesses, it is nonetheless clear from the research discussed above that such allegations continue to be put to witnesses on a frequent basis. The witness's credibility may be attacked from any angle. As Ellison argues, the Code of Conduct is an ineffective limitation on cross-examination because the underlying structures of the adversarial system dictate that the provisions will be subject to the zealous advocacy that is required in a party-based contest:

> [M]any barristers perceive a conflict between their duty to a client and a responsibility towards opposing witnesses. In the terms of the Code of Conduct, provisions counselling restraint in cross-examination of opposing witnesses are perceived to conflict with the duty to provide a fearless defence. As a result the former are . . . 'neutralised' and 'circumvented.'[329]

During the latter part of the 1990s, the ineffectiveness of the Code in preventing character attacks on victims and witnesses became increasingly evident, and the case for some form of legislation intervention was bolstered. Under a scheme proposed by the Law Commission,[330] and enacted by Pt 11 of the Criminal Justice Act 2003, witnesses are now legally protected against allegations of misconduct extraneous to the events that are the subject of the trial, and which have only marginal relevance to the facts of the case.

Section 100 sets out the circumstances in which evidence can be admitted of the bad character of a person, other than a defendant.[331] Evidence of their previous misconduct is not to be given without the permission of the court,[332] and can only be admitted under subsection (1) if it is important explanatory evidence; if it is of substantial probative value and is of substantial importance in the case; or if the prosecution and defence agree that the evidence should be admitted.

The first criterion invokes the concept of 'explanatory evidence'. This term describes evidence that does not directly concern the question of the defendant's guilt, but is nonetheless necessary for the trier of fact to hear in order to place other evidence in the case within its appropriate context.[333] For such evidence to be

---

[329] Ellison (2001a), 111, citing Blake and Ashworth (1998), 32.

[330] Law Commission of England and Wales (2001).

[331] 'Bad Character' is defined by s 98 of the 2003 Act as 'evidence of, or a disposition towards, misconduct on his part, other than evidence which has to do with the alleged facts of the offence with which the defendant is charged, or is evidence of misconduct in connection with the investigation or prosecution of the offence.' Under s 112, it is clear that 'misconduct' is intended to be broadly defined and to cover evidence that shows that a person has committed an offence, or has acted in a reprehensible way (or is disposed to do so) as well as evidence from which this might be inferred. This may include previous convictions, as well as evidence on charges being tried concurrently and evidence relating to offences for which a person has been charged, where the charge is not prosecuted, or for which the person was subsequently acquitted. See *R v Z* [2000] 2 AC 483. For the purpose of deciding whether the evidence has sufficient relevance for leave to be granted, the same criteria apply to defendants and non-defendants. Under s 101 however, defendants have additional protection from the prejudicial impact of such evidence, to reflect the fact that it is their liability to criminal sanction which is at stake.

[332] S 100(4).

[333] See eg *R v M (T)* [2000] 1 WLR 42; *R v Sawoniuk* [2000] 2 Cr App R 220.

admissible it must be such that, without it, the magistrates or jury would find it impossible or difficult to understand other evidence in the case.[334] If, therefore, the facts or account to which the bad character relates are largely understandable without this additional explanation, then the evidence will not be admitted. The explanation must also give the court some substantial assistance in understanding the case as a whole, and should not be admitted merely to appreciate the context of some trivial piece of evidence. This measure should, in theory at least, provide a basic level of protection for victim-witnesses to prevent needless and irrelevant inquiries into their background.

Under the second criterion of 'substantive probative value', evidence of bad character is most likely to be relevant where a question is raised about the credibility of the victim or witness as this is likely to affect the court's assessment of the issue on which the witness is giving evidence. It might also cover attempts by the defence to engage in so-called 'victim-blaming' tactics, which are particularly well documented in cases involving rape and domestic violence.[335] In order for such evidence to be admitted, it must satisfy the 'enhanced relevance' test set out in s 100(1)(b). This basically means that the evidence must be of substantial probative value and the matter to which it relates must be of substantial importance in the context of the case. Thus evidence of no real significance to an issue, or of only marginal relevance, would not be admissible, nor would evidence that goes only to a trivial or minor issue in the case.

Section 100(3) directs the court to take into account a number of factors when assessing the probative value of evidence of a non-defendant's bad character. These include the nature and number of the events to which it relates and when those events occurred. When considering evidence that is probative because of its similarity with evidence in the case (which might be the case if the defendant were suggesting that someone else was more likely to have committed the offence), the court should take into account the nature and extent of the similarities and dissimilarities.[336] Similarly, where the evidence is being tendered to suggest a particular person was responsible, the court must consider the extent to which the evidence shows or tends to show that the same person was responsible each time.[337]

Under the previous law, evidence of the victim's or witness's past would be routinely adduced in order to challenge their credibility as a witness, particularly in cases where the defendant did not himself have any previous convictions. Under the 'enhanced relevance' test, the defence is now required to articulate how the evidence meets the required threshold. Thus, the outcome might be that a witness will be saved a public humiliation for a cause which could not sensibly have been thought to advance the defendant's case; at very least the defence will be forced to sharpen the focus of its attack.

---

[334] S 100(2).
[335] See in particular Abrahms et al (2003) on rape; Cascardi and O'Leary (1992) on domestic violence.
[336] S 100(3)(c).
[337] S 100(3)(d).

It should be underlined, however, that this distinction between evidence of substantial relevance and that of marginal relevance has not always been clear cut. It is noted below that, in the cross-examination of victims of rape, one reason for the prostration of a statutory attempt to limit cross-examination on previous sexual history was the failure to distinguish between evidence of substantial relevance to the issue, usually consent, and evidence of only marginal relevance.[338] In *R v A*,[339] discussed below, the House of Lords held that the exclusion of evidence of marginal relevance to the defence does not necessarily involve a breach of Article 6(2) of the European Convention. Such a decision must turn on the facts of each individual case. Similarly, the exclusion of evidence of marginal relevance to the credibility of a witness will not affect the fairness of the trial. However, where the 'bad character' in question is regarded as a central issue in the case, section 100 is unlikely to prevent its admissibility. Whilst, overall, the introduction of s100 seems to offer some degree of additional protection to victims, its long-term impact is still difficult to ascertain. There is already some evidence that the appellate courts veer towards admissibility where the line between material issues and credibility is blurred,[340] and this may continue to be the predominant approach in cases of sexual and domestic violence where it is commonly alleged that the defendant's behaviour is often precipitated by the victim's conduct.[341]

The Protective Function of the Trial Judge

A further potential source of protection against aggressive questioning is the trial judge. Judges are under a common law duty to intervene to prevent unduly oppressive, offensive, vexatious or irrelevant questioning during cross-examination.[342] In *Mechanical and General Inventions Ltd* and *Lehwess v Austin* and *Austin Motor Co Ltd*,[343] Lord Sankey stated:

> Cross examination is a powerful weapon entrusted to counsel and should be conducted with restraint and a measure of courtesy and consideration which a witness is entitled to expect in a court of law.[344]

Lord Bingham commented in *Milton Brown* that 'judges do not lack power to protect witnesses and control questioning' and went on to state that judges should also take the necessary steps to 'minimise the trauma suffered by other participants.'[345] The Royal Commission on Criminal Justice also recommended that

---

[338] See below, pp 97–103.

[339] [2002] 1 AC 45.

[340] See eg *R v S (Andrew)* [2006] 2 Cr App R 31.

[341] See eg Fielding (2006), 104–5, who observed a number of such instances.

[342] *R v Kalia* [1975] *Crim LR* 181; *Mechanical and General Inventions Ltd and Lehwess v Austin and Austin Motor Co. Ltd* [1935] AC 346; *Wong Kam-ming v R* [1980] AC 247 at 60; *R v Milton Brown* [1998] 2 Cr App R 364.

[343] [1935] AC 346.

[344] *Ibid*, 359.

[345] [1998] 2 Cr App R 364, 371.

'judges should act firmly to control bullying and intimidatory tactics on the part of counsel.'[346]

Concerns have nonetheless been expressed that there is a considerable gap between law and practice in relation to judicial intervention. Excessive judicial interference with counsel's questioning sits very uncomfortably alongside the orthodox view of the judge as an 'umpire'; excessive judicial intervention risks usurping the functionality of the adversarial process.[347] The appellate courts themselves have readily warned about the dangers of judicial intervention. In *Jones v National Coal Board*,[348] Lord Denning stated that 'interventions should be as infrequent as possible' and that judges should exercise restraint in intervening as it risked giving witnesses 'time to think out the answer to awkward questions.'[349] It was added that the 'very gist of cross-examination lies in the unbroken sequence of question and answer.'[350]

In *R v Sharp*,[351] the judge frequently interrupted the defence counsel's cross-examination of prosecution witnesses, and left the jury in little doubt as to what he thought of the lack of merit in the defence case. In quashing the conviction, the Court of Appeal specifically alluded to the dangers of intervention in the cross-examination of witnesses:

> [T]he judge may be in danger of seeming to enter the arena in the sense that he may appear partial to one side or the other. This may arise from the hostile tone of questioning or implied criticism of counsel who is conducting the examination or cross-examination, or if the judge is impressed by the witness, perhaps suggesting excuses or explanation for a witness's conduct which is open to attack by counsel for the opposing party.[352]

There is a perceived risk among the elements of the judiciary that too much intervention in cross-examination could compromise the role of the judge as a neutral arbiter, which may, in turn, provide a fruitful ground for appeal. Rock observed that many judges believed that 'cross-examination cannot be a soft activity, they cannot prevent questions being put, and above all they cannot appear to shield any one witness or groups of witnesses.'[353] Fielding also noted a general reluctance to prevent hostile questioning,[354] and other studies focusing on the classic categories of vulnerable witnesses have arrived at similar conclusions.[355] In their study of Diplock trials in Northern Ireland, Jackson and Doran found that judges were

---

[346] Royal Commission on Criminal Justice (1993), [182].
[347] See generally Damaska (1973); Landsman (1984).
[348] [1957] 2 QB 55.
[349] *Ibid*, 65.
[350] *Ibid*, 65.
[351] [1993] 3 All ER 225.
[352] *Ibid*, 235.
[353] Rock (1991), 269.
[354] Fielding (2006), 40.
[355] Regarding complainants in rape cases, see Brown *et al* (1992), 58. See Davies *et al* (1999), 60–1 in relation to child witnesses, and Sanders *et al* (1996), 78 regarding witnesses with learning disabilities.

'acutely conscious of the danger of appearing partisan.'[356] The authors found that such a view was widely held among both judges and practitioners:

> It is the parties and not the judge who are perceived as being responsible for the development of the issues, and a judge's interference comes from an incomplete understanding of the overall picture which counsel wish to construct.[357]

The researchers also state that where interventions did occur, 'the objection intruded very little on the questioning.'[358] For example, if counsel was required to clarify a line of questioning, he or she would simply rephrase the same question using different terms.[359] Rock also observed that judicial interventions were infrequent, and those that did occur were generally non-consequential, having little bearing on how witnesses were treated:

> In practice, judges do intervene from time to time, correcting counsel for the use of disagreeable language and displays of gratuitous rudeness. They may offer a witness tissues, water or a seat. But their interventions are designed as much to preserve the general decorum of the courtroom as to protect witnesses.[360]

An inherent conflict therefore exists between the trial judge's paradigmatic role in adversarial proceedings and his power to intervene to protect vulnerable witnesses from abusive cross-examination. As Jackson and Doran contend, whilst judges do not lack the power to intervene, they do lack the authority to do so.[361]

The recent case of *R v B*,[362] however, perhaps marks something of a turning point, with the appellate courts being seemingly prepared to accept a more interventionist approach in order to protect victims. Defence counsel in this rape case had carried out a lengthy, repetitious and detailed cross-examination of the complainant. Eventually, the judge intervened, and ordered counsel to bring the questioning to an end within ten minutes. The accused was convicted and appealed, contending that the intervention of the judge had unfairly restricted the ability of his counsel to put forward fearlessly his defence. Rejecting the appeal, it was held that the judge had been right to exercise his discretion, and there was no obligation on counsel to put every point of a defendant's case to every witness who testified. In such circumstances, the Court of Appeal would not interfere unless there was evidence of unfairness to the defendant.

The decision in *B* should undoubtedly be welcomed, but there are very few cases where the higher courts have had to adjudicate on this issue. Unfortunately, effective intervention to protect complainants is still unlikely ever to become commonplace within trials, since the adversarial trial is founded on the principle of free proof. Having come from the ranks of the Bar themselves, judges understand

---

[356] Jackson and Doran (1995), 113.
[357] *Ibid.*
[358] *Ibid,* 112.
[359] *Ibid.*
[360] Rock (1991), 269.
[361] Jackson and Doran (1995), 128.
[362] [2006] Crim LR 54.

the partisan nature of the contest and, even if sanctioned to protect victims through legislation or appellate decisions, they may be reluctant to do so in practice. Still, it can be hoped that in light of the degree of publicity surrounding secondary victimisation in court, judges will begin to intervene more readily than has traditionally been the case. A certain measure of guidance from on high may go some way in encouraging them to do so. However, despite the call in *Speaking Up for Justice* for the Lord Chief Justice to issue a Practice Direction 'giving guidance to barristers and judges on the need to disallow aggressive and / or inappropriate questioning',[363] seemingly there has been no attempt to address this specific issue to date.

Previous Sexual History Evidence

Research discussed previously in this chapter has consistently highlighted questioning about sexual history as being one of the most distressing aspects of testifying for rape victims. Often, victims have been subjected to lengthy and detailed cross-examination on sexual activity and the nature of previous relationships. The Government first introduced legislation to regulate such questioning in the 1970s. Section 2 of the Sexual Offences (Amendment) Act 1976 provided that sexual history evidence could only be admitted where:

> it would be unfair to that defendant to refuse to allow the evidence to be adduced or the question to be asked.

The vague nature of that test gave judges a large degree of judicial discretion in determining when such questioning might be 'unfair', and in the years that followed the provision was largely emasculated by the courts with the consequence that applications by the defence to admit such evidence were regularly accepted.[364]

In 1998, *Speaking Up for Justice* paved the way for a major overhaul of the law regulating sexual history evidence.[365] Section 2 of the 1976 Act was repealed and replaced with section 41 of the Youth Justice and Criminal Evidence Act 1999. The provision prescribes a basic rule designed to prevent such questioning in section 41(1), but then goes on to list four somewhat narrow exceptions in subsections 3 and 5. Application must be made to the court to allow the questioning and the court must then be satisfied that the evidence or questioning falls within one of the four exceptions. These will come into play if the evidence is relevant to (a) an issue in the case other than consent;[366] (b) sexual behaviour at or about the time of the

---

[363] Home Office (1998), [8.53].

[364] See in particular *R v Lawrence* [1977] *Crim LR 492* and *R v Viola* [1982] 3 All ER 73. On those decisions and the inadequacy of s 2 generally, see Adler (1987); McColgan (1996); Temkin (2002), 196–201.

[365] Home Office (1998), [9.72].

[366] S 41(3)(a). This may, however, include circumstances surrounding the *Morgan* defence, as s 41(1)(b) specifies that *belief* in consent is not an issue of consent. Temkin (2002) also points out that this exception may also cover evidence relating to identity, motivation to lie and cases where consent is not the issue (at 211–12).

incident in question;[367] (c) previous behaviour which is 'so similar . . . so that similarity cannot be explained by coincidence;'[368] and (d) the need to rebut prosecution evidence.[369] Section 41(4) also provides that evidence will not be regarded as relating to a relevant issue in the case:

> if it appears to the court to be reasonable to assume that the purpose . . . for which it would be adduced or asked is to establish or elicit material for impugning the credibility of the complainant as a witness.

In addition, the judge must also be satisfied under section 41(2):

> that a refusal of leave might have the result of rendering unsafe a conclusion of the jury . . . on any relevant issue in the case.

The new provisions were always going to be surrounded by a considerable degree of controversy. At first, the legislation was broadly welcomed as a significant improvement for rape complainants on the previous regime. The prejudice that had been evident in the exercise of judicial discretion under the previous legislative regime had apparently little prospect of re-emerging under a literal interpretation of the new provision. However, there was considerable criticism of the Bill in the House of Lords, signalling that the road ahead would be less than straightforward. Lord Thomas of Gresford warned that a total absence of judicial discretion was dangerous since 'no legislature has the prescience to foresee every eventuality.'[370] Other commentators pointed to a potentially problematic lacuna in the legislation in that there was no requirement upon judges to consider whether the probative value of the evidence may be outweighed by its prejudicial effect.[371] In addition, the legislation did not make any distinction between prior sexual behaviour with the accused and prior sexual behaviour with other men.[372] Concerns were also raised as to whether the provisions have been drawn too widely to make a significant difference to rape complainants,[373] and, in particular, whether the gateway under section 41(1)(a) which allows evidence concerning *belief* in consent could act as a pretext for introducing sexual history that otherwise might be ruled irrelevant.[374]

---

[367] S 41(3)(b). This is obviously a very vague phrase which has been subject to criticism. It is not clear whether this time span of 'at or about' means within the hour, the day, the month or year. The House of Lords also failed to address the point to any real extent in *R v A (No 2)* [2002] 1 AC 1 (see discussion below), although Lord Hope indicated that it should not be interpreted any more widely than 24 hours before or after the incident in question (see also discussion below).

[368] S 41(3)(c). This exception was not included in the original Bill, but was added in response to comments made in the House of Lords by Baroness Mallalieu. She gave the somewhat curious example of a complainant who alleges she was raped after the accused climbed into her bedroom from the balcony before having sex with her. If the defence should allege that the woman was in the habit of inviting men back to her home to re-enact the scene from *Romeo and Juliet*, he should be permitted to produce this fact in evidence: *Hansard*, HL Deb, 8 Feb 1999, Col 45.

[369] S 41(5).

[370] *Hansard*, HL Deb, 8 Mar 1999, Col 20.

[371] Easton, (2000), 186.

[372] McEwan (2000).

[373] Temkin (2002), 204.

[374] *The Times*, 13 Jul 1999.

Shortly after the introduction of the provisions, their compatibility under the Human Rights Act was challenged before the House of Lords in the case of *R v A (No 2)*.[375] Here, the defendant applied to have the complainant cross-examined about a previous sexual relationship that he allegedly had with her. His counsel admitted that there was no way that the relationship could fall under any of the exceptions to section 41, and as such this undermined his right to a fair hearing under Article 6 of the European Convention since it meant that relevant evidence was excluded under the statute. The trial judge gave leave to appeal 'with enthusiasm.' Whilst the Court of Appeal held that such questions were inadmissible on the issue of consent, it framed the following question for the House of Lords: 'is or may previous sexual behaviour with the accused be relevant to the issue of consent?'

Four of the five law lords took the view that the answer to this question was 'yes.' As Lord Steyn surmised:

> As a matter of common sense, a prior sexual relationship between the complainant and the accused may, depending on the circumstances, be relevant to the issue of consent. It is a species of prospect and evidence which may throw light on the complainant's state of mind. It cannot, of course, prove that she consented on the occasion in question. Relevance and sufficiency of proof are different things ... It is true that each decision to engage in sexual activity is always made afresh. On the other hand, the mind does not usually blot out all memories. What one has been engaged on in the past may influence what choice one makes on a future occasion. Accordingly, a prior relationship between a complainant and an accused may sometimes be relevant to what decision was to be made on a particular occasion.[376]

The inherent weaknesses of the statute were also alluded to by His Lordship:

> The statute did not achieve its object of preventing the illegitimate use of prior sexual experience in rape trials. In retrospect one can now see that the structure of this legislation was flawed. In respect of sexual experience between a complainant and other men, which can only in the rarest cases have any relevance, it created too broad an inclusionary discretion. Moreover, it left wholly unregulated questioning or evidence about previous sexual experience between the complainant and the defendant, even if remote in time and context. There was a serious mischief to be corrected.[377]

The logic as set out by Lord Steyn seems straightforward. It is more likely that a woman will consent to intercourse with a person whom she knows well and has had a previous sexual relationship with, than to intercourse with a total stranger. Therefore, this type of previous sexual history between the complainant and the defendant will, on some occasions, be relevant to the issue of consent.

In a nutshell, the difficulty for the court was that a literal interpretation of the Act would lead to the exclusion of this relevant evidence. The Court believed that such a construction could amount to a breach of the accused's fair trial rights

---

[375] *R v A* [2002] 1 AC 1.
[376] *Ibid*, 10.
[377] *Ibid*, 12.

under the European Convention, so the House of Lords construed section 41(3)(c) of the Act somewhat creatively, through exercising its interpretive obligation under section 3 of the Human Rights Act 1998. This provision requires courts to interpret legislation in a way that is compatible with Convention rights, insofar as possible. In future, therefore, section 41(3)(c) is to be read subject to the proviso that the previous sexual history evidence should nonetheless be admitted where 'it is nevertheless so relevant to the issue of consent that to exclude it would endanger the fairness of the trial under Article 6 of the Convention.'[378] Interestingly, however, the House of Lords declined to take into consideration the fact that the complainant had an arguable Convention right not to be questioned about her previous sexual activity. Both Article 3 (the right to be free from inhuman or degrading treatment) and Article 8 (the right to privacy) could have come into play on this occasion, although all of their Lordships' analysis chose to steer a wide berth around what might have proved an intricate and thorny rights-based conflict to resolve.

It could further be argued that the decision of the House of Lords seemed more concerned with the apparent loss of the judiciary's role in determining the relevance of a particular piece of evidence rather than the accused's Article 6 rights to a fair trial. The literal wording of section 41 does not sit easily alongside the traditional value placed on the determination of relevance by the judge in an adversarial system. In effect, the judicial role in determining relevance had been usurped by the legislation. In *R v A* however, the literal construction of the legislation was usurped by the House of Lords. They chose not to make a declaration of incompatibility, and thereby avoided sending out a dangerous signal about judicial attitudes to questioning of this type. In deploying their interpretative obligation under section 3 of the Human Rights Act, their Lordships stated that the legislation must be read as being subject to the common law concept of relevance. On the facts of that case, perhaps there was indeed little choice, but their Lordships gave no guidance as to when such questions would be relevant, and when they would be irrelevant. The problem in relation to the concept of relevance is that the courts and the legislature alike have been reluctant to draw a clear dividing line between what is deemed to be relevant solely to the credit of the complainant, and what is relevant to the issue of consent. Where the complainant's testimony forms the main body of evidence against the defendant, the line becomes blurred, and his or her credibility thereby becomes a relevant issue.[379] While to the lay observer, the evidence may appear prima facie to go solely to credit, the judicial application of the concept of relevance in rape cases has meant that complainants continued to be questioned extensively about their sexual history. As such, the door is left slightly ajar for future interpretations of the legislation which may stretch well beyond what Parliament had originally intended.

[378] *R v A* [2002] 1 AC 1, 15, *per* Lord Steyn.

[379] See comments by Lord Lane in *Viola* [1982] 3 All ER 73: 'Inevitably in this situation, there is always a grey area which exists between the two types of relevance namely relevance to credit and relevance to an issue in the case' (at 82).

It remains to be seen whether judicial attitudes have changed sufficiently to sustain this approach in the longer term. Although some of the early cases suggested that the higher courts would not emasculate the legislation as they did the 1976 Act,[380] some of the more recent appeals have been successful. Many of these have tended to centre on the distinction between questions 'about' any sexual behaviour and questions which relate to a previous statement concerning sexual behaviour, but which do not then probe the truth of those statements.

It now appears to be firmly established that section 41 does not cover those cases where the defence has an evidential basis for alleging that the complainant has made an untruthful statement in relation to an alleged act. In *R v Martin (Durwayne)*,[381] the Court of Appeal emphasised the distinction between the *main* purpose of adducing the evidence and *one* of the purposes. Here, the defendant alleged that the complainant had pestered him for sex and that it was his rejection of her advances which led to her making a false allegation against him. The trial judge refused to permit cross-examination of the complainant as to the alleged sexual acts on the basis that the main purpose of the cross-examination was to impugn the credibility of the complainant. The Court of Appeal held that, although one purpose of the proposed questions was to impugn the credibility of C, another purpose was simply to strengthen the defence case. Accordingly, the judge had erred in his decision to disallow the questioning.[382]

Similarly, in *R v Mukadi*,[383] the complainant approached a supermarket security officer wearing a short skirt and a vest top. They went to a park where they drank a bottle of wine, before a sexual encounter took place at the defendant's flat. While the complainant admitted the oral sex and kissing was consensual, she claimed the intercourse was not. In order to support the defence of consent, counsel attempted to adduce evidence that, before the complainant had entered the store that day, she was approached by an older male driving a luxury car whilst standing on the pavement. The complainant got in, and they drove to a filling station.

At first instance, the trial judge refused to admit this evidence because it had no bearing on the issue of consent. However, on appeal it was held he was wrong to have reached this conclusion. In the view of the Court of Appeal, it would have been possible for the jury to draw the proper inference that when the complainant got into the car with the defendant she had anticipated some sexual activity with the occupant. This could potentially rebut her claim that she went to the defendant's flat merely to get to know him with a view to becoming friends. Ultimately, the conviction was considered to be unsafe, since, had the jury heard about

---

[380] See eg *R v Mokrecovas* [2002] 1 Cr App R 20; *R v Minhas and Haq* [2003] EWCA Crim 135; *R v Singh* [2003] EWCA Crim 485; *R v W (Daniel James)* [2005] EWCA Crim 2134.

[381] [2004] 2 Cr App R 22.

[382] However, the Court of Appeal declined to overturn the conviction on the grounds that the defendant did not give evidence and the judge would have directed the jury that the question, if allowed, did not result in any evidence on which the jury could act.

[383] [2004] Crim LR 373.

the previous incident, that might have led them to a different conclusion when assessing that part of her evidence.[384]

Subsequent decisions have confirmed that false allegations are not 'evidence about sexual behaviour' but refer instead to a general propensity to be untruthful.[385] Providing the defence merely use such evidence to show that a particular statement was likely to be false, section 41 will not prohibit its use in this way. This position reflects earlier criticisms that the wording of the Act was simply too abstract to properly regulate the use of sexual history evidence in court. As Grohovsky noted shortly after section 41 was enacted, it is 'both vague enough and broad enough to permit almost limitless irrelevant and prejudicial evidence.'[386] Although in the immediate aftermath of *A* it seemed very unlikely that previous sexual history evidence with third parties could ever be used in court under the law as it currently stands, the increasingly blurred distinction between matters going to issues and matters relating to credibility means that the future success of section 41 in restricting the widespread use of sexual history evidence seems very questionable indeed.

It is a matter of further concern that empirical research suggests sexual history evidence is still frequently admitted in the lower courts. A recent study by Kelly et al into the operation of section 41 suggests that the legislation is not operating as Parliament intended.[387] Applications to admit sexual history evidence were made in a third of all rape trials, and two-thirds of these were successful. Moreover, interviews with 17 judges revealed that many had very little knowledge of the legislation prohibiting or allowing the use of sexual history evidence. This explains another alarming finding, namely that barristers frequently asked questions about sexual history without seeking permission from the judge at all. Three quarters of the cases contained some use of sexual history evidence without the judge intervening, even in some cases involving child victims.

Furthermore, it seems that some elements of the judiciary are reluctant to enforce the new legislation as Parliament intended. Kibble has observed how judges he interviewed 'were highly sceptical of the argument that sexual history evidence was overwhelmingly prejudicial and should therefore generally be excluded.'[388] The legislation was described by judges as 'an impenetrable maze,' 'a

---

[384] If this act constituted sexual behaviour, it would be admissible under s 41(3)(b) and a refusal of leave under s 41(2)(b) would have had the effect of rendering unsafe a conclusion of the jury on the issue of consent. If it was not sexual behaviour it would not have fallen within s 41 and was relevant and admissible. The Court of Appeal took the view that, in the circumstances, C's behaviour shortly before 'picking up' M probably was 'sexual behaviour' coming close to acting as a prostitute picking up clients for sex and was clearly relevant to the issue of whether C consented to intercourse with M.

[385] See also *R v T; R v H* [2002] Crim LR 73; *R v Garaxo* [2005] Crim LR 883; *R v W* [2005] Crim LR 965.

[386] Grohovsky (2000), 421. See also comments by Redmayne (2003), who contends that the provision is so 'deeply obscure' that 'even without the Human Rights Act this section would have caused immense difficulty' (at 101).

[387] Kelly et al (2006).

[388] Kibble (2004).

dog's breakfast,' and a 'nightmare.'[389] As a result, irrelevant evidence relating to previous sexual behaviour was still commonly being used in rape trials. Thus, even if Parliament had succeeded in formulating legislation under which the various evidential restraints *were* well balanced on paper, their success would ultimately depend upon the willingness of the judiciary to apply them. Regrettably, it seems that judicial attitudes continue to undermine efforts to protect rape complainants in court.

Protection from Cross-Examination in Person

It will be recalled that a number of high-profile cases came to light in the 1990s of defendants who conducted their own cross-examination of complainants in court.[390] The Youth Justice and Criminal Evidence Act 1999 restricted the right of the accused to self-representation. Unrepresented defendants are now not permitted to cross-examine child witnesses at all, nor can they cross-examine adult witness in certain types of cases. Furthermore, a broad discretion has been created to prohibit cross-examination by unrepresented defendants in other circumstances as the judge sees fit.

Under section 34 of the Act, no person charged with a sexual offence may cross-examine a witness who is the complainant in that offence.[391] This section also replaces and extends the scope of section 34A of the Criminal Justice Act 1988, which had originally prohibited self-representation in cases concerning child violence or child sex abuse. Section 35 replaces and extends this provision to cover a much broader range of offences against children.[392]

The discretion contained in section 35 of the Act permits courts to issue directions prohibiting unrepresented defendants from cross-examining complainants in circumstances other than those covered in section 34. Such a direction may be given following the application by the prosecution or of the court's own motion, if the court is satisfied that the criteria set out in section 36(2) are met. This provides that the court may prohibit the accused from cross-examining any witness where it appears that the quality of evidence given by the witness on cross-examination is (a) likely to be diminished if the cross-examination is conducted by the accused in person, and would be likely to be improved if a direction were given under this section, and (b) that it would not be contrary to the interests of justice to give such a direction. Section 36(3) sets out a list of criteria which the court should take into account in assessing this.[393] A direction under this section

---

[389] *Ibid.*

[390] See above, pp 57–8.

[391] Or in relation to any other offence with which that person is charged in the proceedings.

[392] These are extended to include kidnapping, false imprisonment and abduction.

[393] In arriving at its determination, the court should have regard, inter alia, to a range of factors set out in s 36(3) (a)–(d), those being: (a) whether the witness has expressed any opinion as to whether or not he or she is content to be cross-examined by the accused in person; (b) the nature of the questions likely to be asked; (c) any behaviour on the part of the accused at any stage of the proceedings, both generally and in relation to the witness; and (d) any relationship between the witness and the accused.

may be appropriate where the complainant was in a particularly vulnerable frame of mind, was in fear of the accused, or was the complainant in a stalking-type case. Sections 37 to 40 of the Act deal with practical matters relating to these directions, and include the power of the court to appoint a representative for an accused in these circumstances where he declines to do so himself.[394]

The tests laid down in the Act contain a number of safeguards for the accused, including the duty imposed on the trial judge under section 39 to give such a warning as he considers necessary to prevent prejudicial inferences being drawn against the accused by the jury in such circumstances. There have nonetheless been suggestions that this provision may contravene Article 6 of the European Convention.[395] However, the case law, most notably the decision of the European Court of Human Rights in *Croissant v Germany* does not seem to support such a view.[396] Here, the Court held that restricting the choice of counsel for the accused did not affect his ability to challenge the evidence against him.

While this reform is to be welcomed, over-focusing on this relatively rare occurrence has meant that 'the intimidatory and intrusive antics employed daily by defence lawyers in a range of contexts have escaped examination.'[397] As with the intermediary proposal, opponents have attacked this protection on the grounds that it unduly interferes with the right of the accused to conduct a full and effective cross-examination.[398] Like many objections to the shielding measures discussed earlier in this chapter, such arguments tend to be based on misconceptions about the value of adversarial practices and fail to take into account the lack of any right to confront a witness either at common law or under the European Convention. International trends and psychological discourse should, if anything, cast doubt upon the high value that is still afforded to adversarial cross-examination.

The Protection of Identity

For rape complainants and many other vulnerable witnesses, special measures and the other mechanisms outlined above will not prevent them from having to give their name and address in court. In the vast majority of cases, they will appear in person in the witness box, their identity will be revealed, and they will be visible by all parties to the proceedings as well as to the public gallery. Moreover, there is a presumption that any information they give, including their name and address, may be reported by the press.[399] This is likely to prove stressful for many victims, irrespec-

---

[394] Youth Justice and Criminal Evidence Act 1999, s 38.

[395] *The Daily Telegraph*, 21 May 1998, as cited by Ellison (1998), 611. She also notes that the proposal was condemned by the Criminal Bar Association and Bar Council.

[396] (1993) 16 EHRR 135. There would seem to be no absolute right for an accused to access a lawyer of his own choosing. See also *Philis v Greece* (1991) 13 EHRR 741.

[397] Ellison (2001a), 125. A similar argument is made by Jackson (2004), who suggests that the entire focus of victim policy around victims who are perceived to be vulnerable tends to mask deeper problems that are common to all victims.

[398] See, eg Friedman (1998).

[399] *Attorney-General v Leveller Magazine Ltd* (1979) 68 Cr App R 342.

tive of whether they are intimidated by the process of giving evidence in itself or fearful of the consequences of doing so. However, two groups of vulnerable victims may be prone to even greater anxiety. First, victims in sex cases are unlikely to want the fact that they were attacked made freely available to the press and the public, let alone the intimate details of their personal and sexual lives that are so frequently elicited in court. For other victims, particularly those testifying in cases involving organised crime and terrorism, the risks of their identities being revealed are even greater; many may fear for their lives or the well-being of their families.

The idea of 'open justice' has always been considered a cardinal principle of the adversarial tradition. It is a vital mechanism for ensuring accountability, transparency and legitimacy within the criminal process. As Lord Steyn noted in *Re S*:[400]

> A criminal trial is a public event. The principle of open justice puts, as has often been said, the judge and all who participate in the trial under intense scrutiny. The glare of contemporaneous publicity ensures that trials are properly conducted. It is a valuable check on the criminal process. Moreover, the public interest may be as much involved in the circumstances of a remarkable acquittal as in a surprising conviction. Informed public debate is necessary about all such matters. Full contemporaneous reporting of criminal trials in progress promotes public confidence in the administration of justice. It promotes the values of the rule of law.[401]

There are, however, certain exceptions to this principle. It is a criminal offence under the Sexual Offences (Amendment) Act 1992 for any organisation to publish the victim's name, photograph or other details which may be used to identify an individual throughout their lifetime.[402] Child witnesses, including victims and defendants, are subject to similar protections. Section 44 of the Youth Justice and Criminal Evidence Act 1999 Act automatically prohibits the reporting of any matter which might lead the public to identify a person under the age of 18 as a potential defendant, victim or witness as soon as a criminal investigation has begun.[403] In a welcome departure from the tendency to only legislate for the well-established categories of vulnerable witnesses, section 46 of the Youth Justice and Criminal Evidence Act 1999 gives the court power to restrict reporting about certain adult witnesses (other than the accused) in criminal proceedings on the

---

[400] [2005] 1 AC 593.

[401] *Ibid*, [30].

[402] Although originally limited to offences of rape, the prohibition was extended to other sexual offences by the Criminal Justice and Public Order Act 1994, sch 9, para 52. The Act now applies to the vast majority of offences under the Sexual Offences Acts of 1956 and 2003 and includes participatory and inchoate offences.

[403] This provision replaces s 39 of the Children and Young Persons Act 1933, which granted a court the power to prohibit the reporting of the name, address, school or other particulars identifying children and young persons under the age of 17 who are involved in proceedings. There were, however, no reporting restrictions that applied during the investigatory stage of proceedings, save the media's own self-regulatory codes. With regard to practice at the Youth Court, the blanket prohibition contained in s 49 of the Children and Young Persons Act 1933 continues to apply, subject to amendment by s 48 and sch 2 of the Youth Justice and Criminal Evidence Act. The automatic prohibition on identification of a young person concerned in the proceedings will now only apply until the 18th birthday of the young person concerned, and the particulars listed which might identify the child or young person are not prohibited from publication per se.

application of any party to those proceedings. Such a witness will be eligible for protection if the quality of his evidence or his co-operation with the preparation of the case is likely to be diminished by reason of fear or distress in connection with identification by the public as a witness.[404]

It will, however, be apparent that there will be occasions where the victim's desire to keep details out of the public domain will conflict with the desire of the press to report them. Both the right to privacy and the right to freedom of expression are protected under the Human Rights Act, and Parliament envisaged the potential for conflict between them. Under section 12(4) of the Act, courts should pay particular regard to the importance of freedom of expression when deciding whether to impose restrictions upon media reporting. In addition, courts should also have regard to the extent to which material has or is about to become available to the public, the extent of the public interest in such material being published and the terms of any relevant privacy code in place.[405]

In *Re S*, the House of Lords considered the question as to whether the publication of the identity of a woman charged with the murder of one of her children was likely to cause psychological harm to her remaining son. According to Lord Steyn, four key principles should govern the rights-balancing exercise:

> First, neither Article has as such precedence over the other. Secondly, where the values under the two Articles are in conflict, an intense focus on the comparative importance of the specific rights being claimed in the individual case is necessary. Thirdly, the justifications for interfering with or restricting each right must be taken into account. Finally, the proportionality test must be applied to each. For convenience, I will call this the ultimate balancing test. This is how I will approach the present case.[406]

Having applied the test to the facts, the House of Lords dismissed the appeal and concluded that the press should be given the freedom to report the proceedings. However, it was made clear that such decisions should be made on a case-by-case basis. In this particular instance, it was held that a restriction on reporting would make little sense as the facts were already in the public domain, and there had already been considerable publicity which included the naming of the child and the child's school.

---

[404] Quality of evidence relates to its quality in terms of completeness, coherence and accuracy (sub-s 12(b)). The court may make a reporting restriction direction in respect of such a person if the making of such an order is likely to improve the quality of the evidence of the witness or his co-operation in the preparation (s 3). Under s 4, the court must have regard to: the nature and circumstances of the offence; the age of the witness; the social and cultural background of the witness and his ethnic origin, if relevant; the domestic and employment circumstances of the witness, if relevant; any religious beliefs or political opinions of the witness, if relevant; any behaviour towards the witness by the defendant, his family or associates or anyone likely to be a witness or defendant in the proceedings; and any views expressed by the witness. The court must also consider whether the making of a reporting direction would be in the interests of justice and consider the public interest in avoiding the imposition imposition of a substantial and unreasonable restriction on the reporting of proceedings (s 8).

[405] Eg that of the Press Complaints Commission.

[406] At [17].

A more recent scenario arose before the Court of Appeal in *R (Gazette Media Company Ltd) v Teesside Crown Court.*[407] In the court proceedings concerned, the defendants had been charged with conspiracy to rape and making and distributing of indecent photographs of a child. The applicant had appealed against a court order made under section 39 of the Children and Young Person's Act 1933, which had been made to protect the victim, and required the media to refrain from reporting on facts of the case or identifying any of the participants. From a victims' rights perspective, the court's decision, and particularly its process of reasoning, is somewhat regrettable.

Allowing the appeal, the Court concluded that the wording of the order went beyond the scope of the statutory provision, and it was therefore unlawful. The Court rejected the Attorney-General's submission that it was nonetheless obliged to protect the Article 8 rights of the victim. Whilst acknowledging Article 8 rights did come into play, the court found that Article 10 prevailed and had to override the victim's right to privacy:

> [T]he interference with the child's Article 8 rights, albeit distressing, was indirect and not of the same order when compared with cases of juveniles directly involved in criminal trials; . . . By contrast, the Article 10 rights at issue concern the freedom of the press, subject to statutory restrictions, to report proceedings at criminal trials, which was a valuable check on the criminal process and promoted public confidence in the administration of justice.[408]

In the analysis of Gillespie and Bettinson, the court seemed to overlook two crucial facts in their reasoning.[409] First, it failed to recognise that Article 8 carries positive obligations for victims; and secondly, that in addition to protecting the right to privacy, Article 8 also protects the physical and mental integrity of the victim. Given that the Strasbourg court has recently acknowledged the special position of victims of sex offences under Article 8, the presumption that it should inherently carry less weight than its Article 10 counterpart seems flawed. The preferred approach would be to assess each case on its individual merits. As the law currently stands, unless the reporting of a trial is subject to an outright prohibition under the 1992 Act, victims have few guarantees that details will not be reported in the media. Furthermore, it should be emphasised that the statutory restrictions only cover reporting of the witness's personal details. They do not exempt him or her from having to give their name and address in open court. For that reason, reporting restrictions are unlikely to ease the concerns of those witnesses who fear intimidation from defendants, or their family and friends. In particular, if individuals have roots in a particular locality and are well known in an area, the value of such protection is questionable. For some witnesses, they will only be willing to give evidence at trial if their identity is entirely concealed.

---

[407] [2006] Crim LR 157.
[408] *Ibid*, [11].
[409] Gillespie and Bettinson (2007).

Anonymity

In order for witnesses to testify anonymously, an application must be made to the court. The exception to the general rule that administration of justice should take place in open court was laid down by the House of Lords in *Scott v Scott*.[410] It was held that a decision to grant anonymity should be based 'upon the operation of some other overriding principle which . . . does not leave its limits to the individual discretion of the judge.' In the more recent case of *R v DJX, SCY, GCZ*,[411] Lord Lane CJ laid down a number of principles which courts ought to consider in deciding whether to grant anonymity:

> The learned judge has the duty on this and on all other occasions of endeavouring to see that justice is done. Those are high sounding words. What it really means is he has got to see that the system operates fairly: fairly not only to the defendants but also to the prosecution and also to the witnesses. Sometimes he has to make decisions as to where the balance of fairness lies. He came to the conclusion that in this case the necessity of trying to ensure that these children would be able to give evidence outweighed any possible prejudice to the defendants by the erection of the screen.[412]

In *R v Taylor*,[413] the Court of Appeal upheld at first instance a decision to grant anonymity where the witness's evidence was regarded as decisive since it was the only independent corroboration of the removal of the victim's body from a pub where a murder was alleged to have occurred. Applying *DJX*, the Court held that courts should take a number of factors into account before granting anonymity. These should include: the question of the potential consequences of revealing the identity of the witness; the importance of the evidence he or she is providing; and that no undue prejudice is caused to the defendant (although it was recognised that *some* degree of prejudice will be inevitable). In taking all of these factors into account, the court should balance the need for anonymity—including the consideration of other ways of providing witness protection (eg, screening the witness or holding an in camera hearing or screen) against the unfairness or appearance of unfairness in the particular case.

The most recent authority on the use of anonymity orders is the English Court of Appeal decision in *R v Davis; R v Ellis*.[414] A number of witnesses at both trials had their anonymity protected by voice modulation and screens. The appellants contended that, since their conviction was based solely or substantially on the evidence of anonymous witnesses, the practice was incompatible with Article 6 of the Convention. Dismissing their appeal, the Court held that the use of anonymity in trials was an acceptable practice where witnesses were in a state of 'justifiable and genuine fear' and whose testimony could be tested in the adversarial

---

[410] [1913] AC 417.
[411] (1990) 91 Cr App R 36.
[412] *Ibid*, 40.
[413] [1995] Crim LR 253.
[414] [2006] 1 WLR 3130.

process.[415] Providing appropriate safeguards were in place, the trial would not be considered to be unfair. While the Court acknowledged that witness protection programmes could provide a useful alternative to anonymity in some cases, it stressed that they were best suited for professional criminals giving evidence against former associates. If these notoriously difficult cases are to come to court, then it will often be the case that anonymous testimony may be the only realistic option.

The case law remains, however, somewhat vague as to which specific circumstances could justify anonymity or which counterbalances should be in place in order to admit such testimony. As such, many human rights commentators and non-governmental organisations have expressed fears that anonymity orders endanger the fair administration of justice, the due process rights of the accused, as well as the age-old legal maxim that justice must not only be done, but must also be seen to be done.[416] While an absolute right to know the identity of one's accuser cannot be located either in international instruments or at common law, in the interests of certainty for victims, witnesses and defendants, it is hoped that the courts will clarify the precise circumstances where anonymity may be justifiable in the not too distant future. As the law currently stands, it is most probably Convention-compliant insofar as it only permits anonymity in exceptional circumstances. Undoubtedly, the use of anonymity orders should remain exceedingly rare, but their value to a small minority of victim-witnesses should not be underestimated. Likewise, anonymity is an invaluable mechanism for the criminal justice system in that it enables prosecutions in cases where they might not have otherwise proceeded owing to a fearful victim who would be unwilling to testify openly.

Discussion

Recent domestic developments to combat secondary victimisation in court provide welcome evidence that policymakers and courts are taking the idea of protecting victims more seriously. It is clear that efforts have been made which, on paper at least, offer some victims the possibility of testifying in more congenial surroundings, thereby reducing secondary victimisation. Empirical evidence suggests that special measures have improved the lot of many vulnerable witnesses, despite continuing problems in terms of their practical roll-out. It is particularly welcome, for example, that certain vulnerable witnesses, including children and complainants in sex cases, can now be guaranteed that they should be able to rely on some form of special measure at court. This reflects the minimum standard found in most international human rights instruments and, from a child's perspective, in the UN Convention on the Rights of the Child and the UN Guidelines on Justice in Matters Involving Child Victims and Witnesses of Crime. Regrettably, however, video-recorded cross-examination has never been introduced. The decision in

---

[415] *Ibid*, 3148.
[416] See, eg, Costigan and Thomas (2000); Amnesty International (1996).

Pupino suggests that the Government should act urgently to find an alternative mechanism that enables children to testify without attending court at all, lest they should find themselves in violation of the EU Framework Directive. The two year delay in issuing a consultation paper on the matter hardly bodes well in relation to the pace of reform. Eight years after Part II of the Youth Justice and Criminal Evidence Act received royal assent, it is pitiful that some of its central innovations for protecting vulnerable witnesses are not readily accessible.

Of greater concern still is the manner in which victims of rape and sexual offences are routinely treated at court. Section 41 of the Youth Justice and Criminal Evidence Act was an attempt by Parliament to impose an outright ban on the questioning of rape complainants in relation to their previous sexual history, albeit subject to four narrowly defined exceptions. It was certainly clear that something had to be done if the notorious attrition rate which has plagued sexual assault and rapes was ever to be addressed. While drafted imperfectly, the measure reflected the position in international criminal justice whereby such evidence is inadmissible, and offered a much better means of protecting the privacy rights of victims and sparing them from the types of ordeal that had become so widely reported in the 1990s. In the wake of recent judicial decisions and empirical findings, the long-term success of the measure in improving the experience of rape victims at court has to be doubted. Overall, the domestic protections in place for rape victims would appear to fall short of the standard required by certain international provisions. The experience of cross-examination, even if no sexual history evidence is adduced, is still notoriously difficult given the conflict paradigm of the adversarial system. Few victims, one assumes, would agree that their cross-examination amounted to being 'treated with compassion and respect for their dignity,'[417] or that they had been 'questioned in a manner which gives due consideration to his personal situation, his rights and dignity.'[418]

More significantly than these soft law provisions however, is the substantive right to protection that can now be located in domestic law both under the EU Framework Decision and, by virtue of the Human Rights Act, the European Convention. While the majority of international standards focus on specific vulnerable classes of victims, crucially these legally binding instruments provide instruction in the way all victims ought to be treated. Furthermore, it is apparent that current criminal practice in England and Wales could breach either of these instruments in a number of ways. Under Article 3 of the Framework Decision, it is stipulated that any questioning of victims should be 'necessary for the purpose of criminal proceedings.' The way in which witnesses are routinely denigrated and humiliated about events which have at best a very tenuous degree of relevance to the issues before the court can hardly be said to comply with this standard. Cross-examination has been traditionally used to allow a wide range of questions to be put to complainants concerning their previous behaviour and intimate details of

---

[417] UN Basic Principles (1985), Principle 4.
[418] Recommendation No R(85), Guideline C.8.

their private lives which go far beyond a 'need to know' basis. It is not inconceivable that domestic cross-examination practice could be subject to a future challenge on this point, particularly in a case involving a child or victim of rape.[419] Such a challenge may seem improbable given the extent to which robust questioning is a sine qua non of the adversarial paradigm and the traditional reluctance of the European Union to make specific stipulations in relation to the format of criminal procedure. However, once again, the decision in *Pupino* serves to remind us that the era when the European Court of Justice took a back seat in relation to domestic criminal justice processes may well have passed.

It could be further argued that the duty to protect victim-witnesses is also inherent under both Articles 3 and 8 of the European Convention on Human Rights. Case law under Article 3, which states that 'no one shall be subjected to inhuman or degrading treatment or punishment' has largely been centred on allegations of some form of physical abuse or maltreatment. Nevertheless, there is also an argument for stating that it may be applied to cover psychological abuse which may affect witnesses as a result of the manner of questioning in court. In *Ireland v United Kingdom*,[420] the Court found that techniques used in Northern Ireland detention centres in the 1970s, such as deprivation of food, water and sleep, were designed to impose severe mental and physical stress on the body in order to obtain information. The Court acknowledged that psychological injury brought about by physical acts may amount to torture, even if those physical acts by themselves did not pass the required Article 3 threshold. However, the manner of ill-treatment 'must attain a minimum level of severity' and whether this is so:

> depends on all the circumstances of the case, such as the nature and context of the treatment, its duration, its physical or mental effects and, in some instances, the sex, age and state of health of the victim.[421]

In this particular instance, it was found that the techniques were degrading for the purposes of Article 3, since they were 'such as to arouse in their victims feelings of fear, anguish and inferiority capable of humiliating and debasing them and possibly breaking their physical or moral resistance.'[422] Certainly, it is not inconceivable that this description could be applied to many vulnerable victims who are required to testify in adversarial proceedings. Such an argument was put forward in *T and V v United Kingdom*,[423] where two defendants, aged ten and eleven years were tried and convicted in an adult court of the murder of toddler Jamie Bulger. In that case however, the Court rejected their argument that the nature of

---

[419] Aggressive cross-examination of a rape complainant by the accused was the basis of the applicant's action in *M v United Kingdom* (1999, Unreported). However, following the government's decision to introduce s 34 of the Youth Justice and Criminal Evidence Act, the case was withdrawn.

[420] (1978) 2 EHRR 25.

[421] *Ibid*, [162].

[422] See also *Labzov v Russia* App. No 62208/00), 16 Jun 2005. Other Art 3 cases have alluded to the psychological impact of deporting individuals where they may be subjected to torture or the death penalty. See eg *Soering v United Kingdom* (1989) 11 EHRR 439 and *Cruz Varas v Sweden* (1991) 14 EHRR 1.

[423] [2000] Crim LR 187.

adversarial spectacle amounted to a violation of their Article 3 rights. However, it did find that the trial had interfered with their ability to participate effectively within the proceedings.[424]

In relation to Article 8, no exhaustive definition of privacy has been given by the court, which means that the right is potentially very broad under European human rights law. The court has made clear that it seeks to protect an individual's physical and psychological integrity,[425] and, as noted above, it considers the right to privacy to be of utmost importance in cases involving sexual violence. While the specific circumstances whereby a positive obligation will arise 'do not lend themselves to precise definition,'[426] the degree of long-term trauma and emotional distress commonly associated with certain types of serious victimisation such as rape and child abuse would seem to suggest that there is clear potential for the Article to apply if these same victims are subsequently subjected to an aggressive and highly degrading cross-examination at court.

Whether the thresholds for either Article 3 or 8 would be crossed by the way in which vulnerable victims are routinely treated in the adversarial trial is a matter for debate; a specific case of a failure to adapt national laws or procedures to protect victims when testifying has not to date come before the Strasbourg Court. However, the manner in which cross-examination has been used in the past to manipulate, humiliate and embarrass victims suggests it may not be far from the mark. For example, a rape complainant who was subjected to a lengthy and aggressive cross-examination which included questions about the intimate details of her sexual habits, may well have a strong case based on either Article 3 or Article 8. In the same way, a failure to offer anonymity or some lesser form of special measure to an intimidated witness who had been threatened with physical violence could also breach Article 3; and potentially Article 2 could also come into play. To date, the Strasbourg Court has been reluctant to make any specific pronouncements about the preferred format of a criminal trial or lay down any boundaries in relation to such matters. However, as the European Court of Justice found in *Pupino*, sidestepping the astringencies of the adversarial process may not be sustainable in the longer term.

Of course, if we accept the reality of a substantive right to protection for victims under the Convention, we must also realise that there are occasions when the defendant's right to a fair trial may compete for priority. This was precisely the scenario that arose in *R v A*, and it is unfortunate that the House of Lords opted for a straightforward application of Article 6 of the Convention without considering possible corresponding rights of the complainant under Articles 3 or 8. It is well established before the Strasbourg Court, and, indeed, in most other human rights fora, that the right to a fair trial does not automatically assume priority over other competing interests. The decision in *Doorson* makes it absolutely clear that principles of a fair trial require that the rights of the accused should be balanced against those of victims and witnesses. In effect, this means that longstanding rules of pro-

---

[424] See further Ch 3, p 149.
[425] *Pretty v United Kingdom* (2002) 35 EHRR 1.
[426] *Stjerna v Finland* (1994) 24 EHRR 185, [38].

cedure and evidence should be adjusted or replaced to take account of these newly emergent rights. Unfortunately, the decision in *A* illustrates the fact that, while the courts have always perceived their role as protecting the defendant's fundamental rights in order to ensure a fair trial, the idea of embracing any corresponding rights for victims under Articles 3 or 8 of the Convention may be a bridge too far for the appellate courts.

Given the well-documented difficulties of the judiciary in exercising a protective function, it may very well be the case that the new measures contained in the 1999 and 2003 Acts will not be sufficient if we are to comply with both our formal European legal commitments, as well as other standards of best practice emerging in international criminal justice. Toying with evidential rules, tightening trial procedures, or altering the professional codes of conduct and protocols are unlikely to alter the way in which victims are treated in the criminal trial. It is difficult, for example, to envisage how legislation could possibly regulate the language used by questioners, the hostile tone of their voices, or non-verbal communication such as frowns, gestures, sneers or a raising of the eyebrows. As a tool that is frequently used to confuse, embarrass and denigrate witnesses, cross-examination is probably the single greatest excess of the adversarial process for complainants and it is difficult to see how it can ever be controlled effectively within the adversarial paradigm. In the longer-term, it is evident that a more systematic method of reform is needed which will re-evaluate adversarial values and processes, as well as the normative perceptions that underpin them.

III. Conclusions

The idea of protecting victims, and potential victims, of crime is now deeply rooted within international standards and jurisprudence. It has received a mixed reception in English domestic law. As regards the right to protect individuals from physical attacks, there is certainly some evidence that policymakers have undertaken a number of initiatives to increase public confidence that society is safer. The idea that the criminal law should constitute an adequate basis for protecting victims should ensure that policymakers respond to changing social conditions and new data concerning the nature and extent of victimisation. The courts, too, have been largely receptive to new Convention standards relating to the positive obligations of criminal justice agencies. Overall, it is true to say that the substantive law has been improved in recent years in terms of the protections it now offers victims and potential victims of crime. It will be shown in Chapter 4 that the doctrine of positive obligations not only requires an effective criminal law framework to be put in place, but also imposes additional procedural requirements relating to how criminal investigations are carried out, how they are prosecuted and how they are punished.[427]

---

[427] See Ch 4, esp pp165–180.

In terms of addressing the problem of secondary victimisation, efforts of policymakers and the courts have been less successful. Victims are still subjected to intrusive and insensitive questioning at court, and victims involved in sex cases are still routinely asked questions related to previous sexual history. In particular, it seems that too little regard has been paid to the rights of victims under Articles 3 and 8 of the Convention. Although the advent of special measures and legislation designed to regulate questioning may ease the pressure of testifying, they are unlikely to impact hugely upon the culture of the courtroom. The insensitive treatment of complainants in the adversarial trial is primarily a structural problem, exacerbated by working cultures and normative perceptions about the place of the victim in the criminal process. It is absolutely vital, not only for victims, but for the sake of the legitimacy of the criminal justice system, that secondary victimisation is minimised as far as possible.[428] It is suggested in the final chapter of this book that in order to address problems caused by secondary victimisation in a more comprehensive manner, we should seek to mainstream alternative responses that are arguably better placed to safeguard the rights of victims without compromising those of the offender.

---

[428] On this point, see McEwan (1998): '[T]he goodwill of witnesses is necessary for the protection of society. Fear of humiliation in cross-examination could affect their willingness to come forward or to report crimes. If a genuine victim suffers a stinging attack from the defence during a trial, it looks as if he or she is being punished for objecting to the crime, and that is surely not the object of the exercise' (at 14).

3

The Right to Participation

MORE CONTROVERSIAL THAN the reforms discussed in the previous chapter is the idea that victims ought to be able to exercise a right of participation within the criminal justice system. The concept of 'participation' is something of an abstract term and lacks any concrete definition. Edwards has suggested that it may be perceived as stemming from the broader concept of citizenship, and may include 'being in control, having a say, being listened to, or being treated with dignity and respect'.[1] Interpreted in this way, 'participation' in criminal justice may appear both feasible and desirable, but the debates around the *extent* of participation to which victims ought to be entitled touch upon the much deeper issue of how far the victim's interests should be accommodated in the bipartisan contest between the State and the defendant. At first glance, our intuitive sense of logic would seem to dictate that victims ought to be able to exercise a voice in relation to the offence that was committed against them. After all, the injured party will be the person who has suffered most directly and primarily. However, such a participatory role cannot easily be accommodated in an adversarial system. Whilst the paradigm may conceptualise their interests as part of the general collective interest embodied by 'the State', adversarial processes are normatively and structurally geared to facilitate the two-way contest between the State and the accused, and will thus tend to inherently exclude victims. In addition, it has been mooted that core values, such as certainty and objectivity, would be jeopardised, and the role of core criminal justice agencies would have to undergo significant reform were the system to expand its parameters to accommodate third parties.

However, as noted in the introductory chapter, the 'public' nature of key decision-making processes has been increasingly influenced by private interests, with victims in some jurisdictions having acquired the right to make a 'victim impact statement'.[2] This is discussed in greater depth below, but the notion of victim 'participation' implies much more than contributing to the sentencing process. Indeed, relatively little attention has been given to pre-trial participatory rights, such as the right to pursue a private prosecution or to intervene in plea negotiation; or to the position of victims within the trial itself. The concept of victim involvement at these stages of the criminal process is fraught with particular difficulties on account of the myriad of competing aims of criminal justice, which

---

[1] Edwards (2004), 973.
[2] See Ch 1, 27–8.

include the objective adjudication of guilt, the desirability of truth-finding, the preservation of public interests, and the need to preserve due process rights for the accused. It is additionally complicated by the fact that the complainant's status as a 'victim' is somewhat uncertain prior to the determination of the accused's guilt.[3]

Since the issue of victim participation in criminal justice is potentially so contentious, international standards have tended to shy away from laying down explicit requirements in terms of stipulating that victim participation ought to be enshrined as a generic standard or value. The concept of participation does not feature at all in any of the Council of Europe's recommendations. Those instruments that touch on the issue tend to do so in a relatively vague or non-prescriptive manner. For example, Principle 6(b) of the UN Declaration on Victims states that the judicial process should allow:

> the views and concerns of victims to be presented and considered at appropriate stages of the proceedings where their personal interests are affected, without prejudice to the accused.

Likewise, the EU Framework Decision grants victims a 'right to be heard and supply evidence'.[4] Neither instrument, however, offers specific details as to how such rights are to be realised in practice or as to what stage(s) of the process they are to be applied. In terms of United Nations hard law standards, they too tend to be framed in an equally uncertain manner. For example, Article 25 (3) of the Convention Against Transnational Organised Crime echoes the UN Victims' Declaration in requiring only that:

> each State Party shall, subject to its domestic law, enable views and concerns of victims to be presented and considered at appropriate stages of criminal proceedings.[5]

and Article 6 of the Convention's Protocol to Prevent, Suppress and Punish Trafficking in Persons, Especially Women and Children provides that, in appropriate cases, victims of trafficking shall be 'assisted to express their views and concerns at appropriate stages of criminal proceedings in a manner not prejudicial to the rights of the defence'.[6]

Before making any argument in favour of more specific participatory rights for victims, it should be asked whether victims actually *want* such a right. While studies tend to confirm that victims do not actually seek decision-making power,[7]

---

[3] See Ch 1, pp20–24, noting that the very designation of an individual as a 'victim' may give rise to an inherent implication that the allegations made by that person ought to be accepted as the historical truth before the tribunal of fact has arrived at its determination as to the guilt of the accused.

[4] Art 3.

[5] UN Doc A/45/49.

[6] See also, eg, the UN Principles on the Effective Investigation and Documentation of Torture and Other Cruel, Inhuman or Degrading Treatment or Punishment (GA/RES/55/89). Principle 4 provides that victims and their legal representatives have rights both to be informed and to have access to any hearing or relevant information about the investigation, and are entitled to present additional evidence.

[7] Shapland et al (1985); JUSTICE (1998); Wemmers and Cyr, (2004).

they do seem to desire recognition, acknowledgement and some form of participation.[8] A range of empirical studies confirm that victim participation in the criminal justice process enhances satisfaction with justice through giving victims a sense of empowerment and official, albeit symbolic, acknowledgement.[9] It should be underlined, however, that proponents of victims' rights are not calling for the victim to carry some form of veto through the criminal process. Indeed, some of the victims' movements argue for participation primarily for empowerment to express oneself and communicate messages to other criminal justice stakeholders, rather than any actual decision-making power. Roberts and Erez, for example, propose a 'communicative' model rather than an 'impact' model,[10] which emphasises the therapeutic benefits of participation for both victims and offenders. If this was to be followed, it would be vital that victims were made aware of the limited purpose and extent of their participation. A number of studies have identified a real risk that victims may end up frustrated and even more isolated if they feel their expectations have not been met.[11]

The positive effects of victim participation may not only empower victims, but may also enhance the legitimacy of the criminal justice system generally. Arguing that the notion of the 'participation' of a wide range of stakeholders within criminal justice is inherently positive, Walker and Telford contend:

> Participation is clearly an important concept in criminal justice as an instrument for assisting in the achievement of other ultimate objectives. For example, without the involvement of the public in reporting crime the criminal justice system would be fatally handicapped in its pursuit of the security objective. Similarly, participation in the criminal process also serves to legitimise the system by engaging interested, and often aggrieved parties in resolving a dispute, or as a form of external audit to help ensure equitable procedures . . . [T]he concept of participation, in the sense of involvement in the public life of the community and polity with the sense of dignity and personal respect which this brings, is also a good in itself. Furthermore, insofar as there is a non-state or informal sector in criminal justice, participation is a key good in this context also, again both as a means of securing other key objectives and in its own dignitarian terms.[12]

---

[8] Kilpatrick et al (1998). It may be noted, however, that data from a number of participatory initiatives, such as restorative justice schemes and victim statement schemes do contain relatively low take-up rates by victims (see eg Morgan and Sanders, 1999, Newburn et al, 2001; Hoyle et al 2002). However, this may be because of the way in which such schemes were implemented in practice. See further discussion below at 150–56.

[9] See Kury and Kaiser (1991); Erez and Bienkowska (1993); Shapland et al (1985); Erez and Rogers (1999) Wemmers and Cyr (2004). Bacik *et al* (1998) noted a number of key advantages for victim representation for rape complainants. They found that participants with some form of legal representation experienced fewer difficulties in obtaining information about case developments; had a clearer understanding in relation to their role at trial; reported higher levels of confidence and articulateness when testifying; experienced less hostility from the accused's lawyer; and were much more satisfied with their overall treatment within the legal process (at 39–40). A study of victims by Webbers (1995) in the Dutch criminal justice system has also suggested that many victims feel that procedures which even allow *passive* participation in the criminal trial carry a certain symbolic importance for many victims which, in turn, can reduce feelings of exclusion and unfairness (at 338).

[10] See eg Roberts and Erez (2004).

[11] Erez and Tontodonato (1992); Sanders et al (2001).

[12] Walker and Telford (2000), 10.

This chapter explores a range of issues relevant to the concept of 'participation' including the scope for private prosecutions; the recent unravelling of the prosecutor / witness relationship; and prospects for participation in both the trial and sentencing processes. Whilst there are a variety of structural and normative reasons why victims have traditionally been unable to participate in common law criminal justice systems, recent years have witnessed a major shift in attitude about the merits of victim participation at both domestic and international level.

I. Prosecution and Pre-Trial Processes

Influencing Prosecutorial Decisions

The relationship between public prosecutors and victims is fraught with a number of tensions. These tensions arise primarily from the normative function of the prosecutor as a 'minister of justice',[13] who represents the public interest as opposed to the private interests of any one party. In theory at least, prosecutors should ensure that innocent defendants are not convicted. There are, of course, some very sound reasons for this role to be exercised in such a way. Objectivity, certainty and the need to safeguard against punitivism are all laudable principles for any contemporary criminal justice system, and it is right that an agent of the state should ensure that they are upheld.

At first sight, it may appear that the rights and interests of the victim as a private individual sit very uneasily alongside the notion of a fair and objective system of public prosecutions. If the victim were to act as prosecutor, or if indeed his or her concerns were to be the basis on which decisions to prosecute, or drop or alter charges were made, serious questions would need to be addressed as to whether it would be fair to the accused to recognise the legitimacy of such an input, when the practice could so easily interfere with the objective pursuit of justice. As such, many commentators are sceptical about the prospect of victims exercising any procedural right that would interfere with the public nature of the prosecutions system:

> The victim's personal view should be no more relevant . . . than the personal view of any other individual . . . A particular victim may be vindictive or forgiving, demanding or afraid of the offender, and it would be an abdication of the State's responsibility to allow such individual feelings to influence the sentence. The same reasoning applies to the key stages of the criminal process, such as the decision to investigate, the decision to prosecute, and the acceptance of a plea to a different charge: the rule of law requires these decisions to be taken impartially and independently, and not influenced by the wishes of a particular individual.[14]

---

[13] *Randall v The Queen* [2002] 1 WLR 2237, 2241; *R v Banks* [1916] 2 KB 621.
[14] Ashworth and Redmayne (2005), 50.

[A] victim who forgives his attacker may discontinue his civil suit for damages, but cannot stop the prosecution of that attacker. Criminal offences are not merely a private matter. The public as a whole has an interest in their prevention and prosecution.[15]

The argument is particularly strong when applied to those types of cases, including domestic assaults and sexual offences, where there has been a longstanding high attrition rate. Often, these cases involve suspects who are in a position where they can easily gain access to the victim and subject him or her to pressure not to testify. In addition, as noted in the previous chapter, these vulnerable victims are more susceptible to having their character attacked at court, and being subjected to 'victim-blaming' tactics during cross-examination. For that reason, many victims may be reluctant for the CPS to pursue a prosecution against the offender,[16] and it is increasingly recognised that one means of addressing this problem may be through the more widespread use of so-called 'victimless' prosecutions.[17]

It is certainly true to state that any legitimate criminal justice system should ensure that its decisions are rooted in consistency and objectivity, and offering the victim some form of 'veto' on pre-trial decision-making would endanger both the public interest in punishing crime and the accused's interest in being treated in a fair and consistent manner. However, since the State is partly reliant upon the victim for the production of evidence, and since the public interest in prosecuting certain cases might be outweighed by the private interest of allowing parties to resolve issues without State interference, it is vital that the victim is not left out of the equation altogether. Indeed, it seems there is a growing recognition that victims can and should be able to participate within criminal justice decision-making without jeopardising core principles of fairness, consistency and objectivity. Increasingly, both domestic and international standards indicate that the role of the prosecutor has undergone a considerable expansion—not only in terms of having to take into account the interests of the victim, but also in terms of administration and public bureaucracy.[18]

As noted above, although many international standards have traditionally fudged the issue of participation, some standards do require prosecutors to consider the views of victims as part of pre-trial decision-making processes. For example, the Council of Europe's Recommendation (85) 11 requires that public prosecutors should give due consideration to the prospect of the victim obtaining compensation.[19] Thus, if in practice a case were to cross a prosecutor's desk where his / her instinct may be not to proceed because of a lack of evidence or for failure to reach the de minimus threshold, the ramifications of such a decision upon the ability of the victim to obtain compensation should be taken into account. The views and interests of the victim are also required to be taken into account by

---

[15] Simester and Sullivan (2003), 2.
[16] See Cretney and Davis (1997); Hoyle (1998); Temkin (2002).
[17] See further Ellison (2003).
[18] Goldstein (1982).
[19] Guideline D.5.

Recommendation 00(19),[20] the UN Guidelines on the Role of Prosecutors,[21] and the International Association of Prosecutors' Standards of Professional Responsibility and Statement of the Essential Duties and Rights of Prosecutors.[22] In addition, all of these instruments place prosecutors under an obligation to ensure that victims are kept informed of all relevant decisions relating to their case.[23]

Charging Decisions

While, as a matter of course, the police will generally seek the victim's views about prosecution,[24] the ultimate decision on initiating proceedings lies with the CPS. Crown prosecutors must apply a two-fold test in determining whether to prosecute a case. The first limb of the test asks whether there is enough evidence to provide a 'realistic prospect of conviction', and the second limb of the test asks whether it would be in the public interest to proceed.[25] If there is no realistic prospect of conviction, a prosecution will not proceed, even in the most serious offences. In applying the notoriously vague and ill-defined 'public interest' limb of the test,[26] the Crown Prosecution Service should always take into account the consequences for the victim of the decision whether or not to prosecute, and any views expressed by the victim or the victim's family:

> The Crown Prosecution Service does not act for victims or the families of victims in the same way as solicitors act for their clients. Crown Prosecutors act on behalf of the public and not just in the interests of any particular individual. However, when considering the public interest, Crown Prosecutors should always take into account the consequences for the victim of whether or not to prosecute, and any views expressed by the victim or the victim's family.[27]

The Farquharson Guidelines on The Role of and Responsibilities of the Prosecution Advocate reiterate this position:

> When a decision whether or not to prosecute is based on the public interest, the CPS will always consider the consequences of that decision for the victim and will take into account any views expressed by the victim or the victim's family.[28]

---

[20] Principle 33 states that 'public prosecutors should take proper account of the views and concerns of victims when their personal interests are affected and take or promote actions to ensure that victims are informed of both their rights and developments in the procedure'.

[21] Guideline 13(d).

[22] At [4.3].

[23] Regarding the pre-trial rights of victims at the ICC, see Stahn et al (2006).

[24] Sanders (2002), 212.

[25] Crown Prosecution Service (2004), [5.1–5.2].

[26] For an in-depth discussion of some of the problems with the 'public interest' test, see Ashworth (1987).

[27] Crown Prosecution Service (2004), [5.12].

[28] Crown Prosecution Service (2002a), Guideline 1.14.

The nexus between the victim's views and the public interest is ambiguous. Clearly, the CPS as an institution believes that the concept is sufficiently broad to include the interests of victims. Yet these interests may be conceivably extremely diverse. Not only may individual victims have particular views on what charges (if any) ought to be brought, there may be other substantive rights at stake. For example, as the previous chapter noted, all victims have rights to privacy under Article 8 of the Convention that ought to be taken into account in any decision-making process.[29] Thus if the alleged offence is sexual in nature, or involves domestic assault, the need for these rights to be fully protected will be particularly important for many victims.

Such rights and interests are, however, only one of a number of elements that constitute the elusive 'public interest'. Paragraph 5.9 of the *Code for Crown Prosecutors* outlines 16 'non-exhaustive' factors which the CPS may consider in making charging decisions, and paragraph 5.10 contains nine public interests factors which may make a prosecution less likely. Yet the weight attributed to each of these factors in establishing whether or not there is a sufficient public interest to prosecute is a matter of subjective assessment, and is wholly dependent upon the judgement of individual prosecutors:

> Crown Prosecutors must balance factors for and against prosecution carefully and fairly. Public interest factors that can affect the decision to prosecute usually depend on the seriousness of the offence or the circumstances of the suspect. Some factors may increase the need to prosecute but others may suggest that another course of action would be better.[30]

Deciding on the public interest is not simply a matter of adding up the number of factors on each side. Crown Prosecutors must decide how important each factor is in the circumstances of each case and go on to make an overall assessment.[31] However, the decision-making process will also be subject to the procedural requirements laid down by Articles 2 and 3 of the European Convention, which are considered in detail in the next chapter. For the purposes of this discussion, it should be underlined that the Convention requires that criminal investigations should normally be undertaken with a view to prosecution,[32] and it is conceivable that a failure to prosecute where there is sufficient evidence to do so may constitute a breach of convention rights, particularly if the criminal conduct in question amounts to a violation of Articles 2 or 3 of the Convention.

Of course, there may be perfectly legitimate reasons for the state deciding not to prosecute, but the task of balancing these factors alongside any related Convention will fall to the individual prosecutor. While it may be the norm for serious cases involving a killing or endangerment to life to be subject to prosecution, there may well be extenuating circumstances which will render prosecution unlikely. For

---

[29] See Ch 2, pp109–13.
[30] Crown Prosecution Service (2004), [5.8].
[31] *Ibid*, [5.11].
[32] See eg *Aydin v Turkey* (1998) 25 EHRR 251, discussed below in Ch 4, pp165–71.

example, where a prosecution of someone suspected in the involvement of organised crime has been built around evidence of informers, the risk of the retaliatory action against witnesses would need to be weighed against the public policy interest in prosecuting such cases.[33]

In practice however, the victim's views are only likely to be considered as a major factor when the prosecutor thinks ahead to how those views are likely to impact upon how the case can be argued at court. Thus a victim who is reluctant to testify may well have an impact upon the prospects of a case going to court; but a victim who is eager that a prosecution should proceed despite other evidential or public interest considerations is unlikely to have a significant bearing upon the decision. If the victim is unhappy with a decision of the Service, he or she has no right to appeal such a decision. The decision may be challenged on grounds of judicial review,[34] although this only sets aside the previous decision and obliges the prosecutor to reconsider. Courts in the past have displayed a marked reluctance to grant applications[35] and, even where they do so, the final decision may not be any different. However, it is not the failure to give appropriate weight to victims' desires that may amount to a potential breach of Articles 2 or 3 in such circumstances, but the failure to prosecute cases where the taking of life or degrading/inhuman treatment has arisen. In sum then, the victim has no rights to become involved in any charging decision that is taken by the State, although the latter is obliged to consider the victim's interests in deciding whether or not to prosecute.

Plea Negotiation

The interests of the prosecution and the victim may also clash where so-called plea negotiation occurs. 'Negotiated justice' may take a variety of forms. The defendant may agree to plead guilty in return for a lesser sentence; or in exchange for a less serious charge or less counts on an indictment. Ashworth and Redmayne also point to the use of 'fact bargains', whereby the prosecution agree to present the case a particular way and not to mention particularly aggravating factors to the sentencer in exchange for a guilty plea.[36] Under the Prosecution of Offences Act 1985, prosecutors are permitted to vary or discontinue charges.[37] Although Crown

---

[33] The relatives of the 29 people killed in the Omagh bomb attack in August 1998 have expressed considerable frustration over the lack of progress in the police investigation. It would appear that one of the main reasons for the fact that no successful prosecutions have been brought in Northern Ireland to date is that the police are anxious to protect the anonymity of informers (*Irish Times*, 31 Jan 2002). This highlights the delegate balance which the Court has to strike between upholding the right to an effective investigation and charging suspects on the one hand, whilst bearing in mind that this may risk endangering the Art 2 rights of others if a criminal prosecution were to proceed, along with jeopardizing the receipt of further information. See further the case of *Rowe and Davis v United Kingdom* (2000) 30 EHRR.

[34] *R v DPP ex p C* [1995] 1 Cr App R 136, discussed below in Ch 4, p177.

[35] *Ibid.*

[36] Ashworth and Redmayne (2005), 274.

[37] Prosecution of Offences Act 1985, s 23.

prosecutors are under an obligation to accept guilty pleas only if 'they think the court is able to pass a sentence that matches the seriousness of the offending',[38] there are a number of incentives that encourage guilty pleas at an early stage in proceedings.

For example, section 144 of the Criminal Justice Act 2003 stipulates that, in determining the sentence, magistrates' courts must take into account the stage in proceedings where the offender indicated an intention to plead guilty. More significantly, previous common law rules, that prevented the judge from giving an indication of any likely sentence discount, have now been reversed.[39] Under Schedule 3 of the Criminal Justice Act 2003, defence lawyers acting in summary cases can request an indication from the court as to whether a custodial sentence would be any less likely if the defendant were to plead guilty. An extended version of this principle is now applicable in indictable offences, following the Court of Appeal decision in *Goodyear*.[40] Before a plea is entered, the defence may seek an indication from the judge as to what sentence may be imposed on a particular set of facts. In light of these changes, it can be expected that the proportion of guilty pleas is set to rise significantly in years to come.[41]

Thus the formalistic position of the prosecutor as a 'minister of justice' sits awkwardly alongside a process whereby efficiency and costs act to discourage lawyers from bringing cases to trial. While the CPS is put under increasing pressure by the government to see that more offenders are 'brought to justice', prosecutors are also charged with ensuring that they act as objective arbiters, proceeding against individuals where the public interest demands it, yet taking no action in cases where it does not or where the evidence appears weak. This 'role conflict' is essentially a structural problem,[42] and produces a tension in the everyday working culture of prosecutors. As Edwards submits:

> both sides become socialised in a culture which shies away from too much conflict because it undermines individuals' standing in the place where they carry out a large amount of their professional work.[43]

Empirical evidence tends to buttress the suggestion that trial avoidance plays a prominent role in contemporary criminal practice.[44] Since, strictly speaking, the practice is not regulated by law, it cannot be subject to any appeal process or judicial review.

While the use of plea negotiation may spare some victims the prospect of giving evidence in court, the practice also underlines the marginal position of victims in

---

[38] Crown Prosecution Service (2004), [9.1].

[39] The rule under *Turner* [1970] 2 QB 321 stipulated that, in any pre-trial indication of likely sentence to the defence, judges should not differentiate on the basis of the plea.

[40] [2005] 1 WLR 2532.

[41] For a discussion of some of the factors underpinning guilty pleas, and the potential for official statistics to mislead, see Ashworth and Redmayne (2005), 266–9.

[42] Sanders and Young (2007), 334.

[43] Edwards (1999), 127.

[44] See eg Brownlee et al (1994).

the criminal justice system. Any decision to alter or vary charges lies entirely with the Crown prosecutors. Currently, there is no statutory duty upon prosecutors to inform or consult with the victim where plea negotiation takes place. While the Attorney General's 2005 *Guidelines on the Acceptance of Pleas and the Prosecutor's Role in The Sentencing Exercise* imposes a duty on the prosecution to 'speak to the victim or the victim's family, so that the position can be explained' and to inform them of any position to reject or accept the plea, victims do not have any formal input into the decision.[45] Conceptually, as with any charging decision, the victims' interests may be taken into account as part of the general public interest, and the Attorney General's Guidelines reiterate that:

> the views of the victim or the family may assist in informing the prosecutor's decision as to whether it is in the public interest . . . to accept or reject the plea.[46]

However, the concept of the public interest is so vague and ill-defined that it is impossible to measure the extent to which the views of victims are actually factored into any decision to drop or alter charges. The emphasis in the Guidelines is very much on the provision of information rather than including the victim in the decision-making process.

Victims have a legitimate expectation that society will punish offenders for the crime that they committed, and not for a lesser offence on the basis that the prosecutor's job would be made easier, or the courts made more efficient. While some form of prosecution and punishment may still follow, it may be of a different scale or nature than victims, or society as a whole, would regard as just. To fail to prosecute perpetrators for a particular offence where there is sufficient evidence to do so will speak volumes to many victims about the piteous way the system views their injury or loss. The fact that the CPS is now under an obligation to keep victims informed about any decision to alter charges and seek out any views as to whether a guilty plea should be accepted does not detract from the fact that victims' views are not directly taken into account in any principled way when plea negotiation takes place. This may not only cause victims feelings of alienation and frustration, but may also interfere with their right to have the truth of past events officially acknowledged.[47]

Private Prosecutions

If victims feel disenfranchised by a decision not to prosecute, it may be possible for them to institute a private prosecution. Interestingly, there are no international instruments which contain a free-standing right to pursue a private prosecution. Such a right does not feature in any of the Council of Europe's Recommendations, the UN's 1985 Victims Declaration, nor the EU Framework Decision. The Council

---

[45] Attorney General (2005), S B.
[46] *Ibid.*
[47] See discussion below at p192 et seq.

of Europe's Recommendation 85(11) envisages that the mechanism may be used as an alternative to judicial review as a means to challenge decisions of public prosecutors not to prosecute,[48] although the phrasing of the provision suggests that it implies a preference for review procedures as an alternative to private prosecution.[49] The absence of such a right within international instruments is perhaps explicable by the fact that the concept is largely alien to inquisitorial jurisdictions.[50]

In England and Wales, all members of the public may exercise their historical right to institute a private prosecution by virtue of their shared interest in enforcing the criminal law.[51] In practice, this right is severely curtailed to such an extent that it is rarely used in practice, and is normally resorted to infrequently where the CPS have decided not to institute proceedings. Various obstacles stand in the way for a victim who is considering going down this route. First, they will not receive legal aid for private prosecutions, and severe limitations are placed upon their powers to access investigative materials or prosecution files.[52] Secondly, surmounting the criminal standard of proof will not be easy, and the victim must invest sufficient time and effort in order for the case to come to court. Furthermore, the Attorney General, the Director of Public Prosecutions or the magistrate issuing the original summons may withhold consent or order that the proceedings be discontinued if their continuation would be contrary to the public interest.[53] Alternatively, the prosecution may be challenged on the grounds of abuse of process.[54]

These factors explain why private prosecutions remain very much on the fringes of the English legal system. In particular, they are extremely rare in cases involving alleged indictable offences,[55] although more recently there have been a number of examples of high profile (albeit unsuccessful) attempts, including an action against three people suspected of involvement of the Stephen Lawrence killing, an attempt to prosecute police officers on duty at the time of the Hillsborough tragedy, and an action brought by the families of those killed in the 1998 Omagh bomb. The effect of the residual right to pursue a private prosecution carries little practical effect in the contemporary criminal justice system, and the fact that it remains an avenue open to victims is primarily of symbolic value. However,

[48] See [B7]. See also Rec 2000(19), [34].

[49] Brienen and Hoegen (2000), 16.

[50] See Ch 6 below, p269.

[51] Prosecution of Offences Act 1985, s 6. See Smith and Hogan (2005), 12.

[52] See further Field and Roberts (2002), 499. The authors note that although the private prosecutor can compel police to produce all relevant documents in their possession under the Criminal Procedure (Attendance of Witnesses) Act 1965, there is no duty to disclose any materials before committal, and any such application could be opposed on grounds of public interest immunity. See also *R v DPP ex p Hallas* (1988) 87 Cr App R 340.

[53] Prosecution of Offences Act 1985, s 6(2).

[54] See *R v Tower Bridge Stipendiary Magistrate ex p Chaudry* [1994] QB 340.

[55] Bryett and Osborne (2000), 9. Where a trial does proceed at the Crown Court, the victim must involve legal counsel, although it was held in *R v Southwark CC, ex p Tawfick* [1995] Crim LR 658 that the Crown Court does now have a discretionary power to allow a private prosecutor to appear in person.

Sanders and Young suggest that such a right may be of greater significance than this, and can act 'to shame those responsible and highlight the suffering of the victims and their families', and can also fulfil a broader policy function through lending momentum to political campaigns that resulted from the tragedies in the first place.[56]

In spite of these purported advantages, the mechanism remains open to the ideological objection that, in effect, the legal system permits a private party to utilise criminal law to pursue a private vengeance. In turn, this jeopardises the principle of 'prosecutorial independence',[57] which is a cornerstone of any fair and just system of prosecution.[58] The fact that the practice is not widely recognised on the international platform suggests that it is something of a hangover from a bygone era, and that there may be better ways of conferring participatory rights on victims than offering them a procedure which exists on paper, but is of little use in practical terms.

Preparing for Trial

If a case is prosecuted by the CPS and committed for trial, a considerable amount of preparation will go into it. In spite of the fact that the Crown's case will almost always be dependent to some extent on the testimony of victims, victims have traditionally experienced a lack of support by prosecutors in the run-up to the trial. The historic reasons for this are clear. There has never been any lawyer / client relationship between prosecutors and victims. The latter have been viewed as any other witness: merely a tool of evidence in the prosecutor's war-chest. Ordinarily, the vast majority of victims never had an opportunity even to meet with the prosecutor prior to the date of the trial. This was primarily because of concerns over 'coaching'. Prosecutors have long been advised to avoid talking to witnesses lest the case should become contaminated. This might occur, for instance, through the unintentional divulgence of events of which the witness was not aware, by asking leading questions in relation to the witness's account or by causing the witness to question the accuracy of his or her recollection of events.[59]

From the victim's perspective, this reluctance to provide any support heightens perceptions of alienation and exacerbates anxiety about the process of coming to court and giving evidence.[60] Many victims will never have been inside a court building before, and fewer still will have had any experience of testifying. They will thus have little idea what to expect, the types of questions that may be put to them,

---

[56] Sanders and Young (2007), 379.

[57] The principle states that prosecutors should act objectively, in pursuit of the public interest. It can be found in the Code of Crown Prosecutors as well as in many international instruments: see eg, Guideline 13, UN Guidelines on the Role of Prosecutors (1990), UN Doc A/CONF.144.28 Rev.1 at 189. See generally, Livingstone and Doak (2000), 107–8.

[58] Bryett and Osborne (2000), 75.

[59] See Doak (2005).

[60] Rock (1993), Konradi (1997), Temkin (2000).

or the expected response that they should give. When the time for them to testify eventually comes around, these agitations and anxieties that have festered for some time in advance of the trial will inevitably exacerbate the stress that occurs under questioning. In turn, this is likely to interfere with their ability to answer questions clearly and coherently.

Against this backdrop, a considerable amount of criticism has been directed at prosecutors for their failure to offer support and advice to complainants in the countdown to the court appearance. Consequently, both the Crown Prosecution Service and the General Council of the Bar have found themselves drawn into the ongoing re-alignment of the criminal justice paradigm,[61] and have re-examined their practices with a view to enhancing the degree of engagement between prosecutors and victims.

Re-casting the Prosecutor / Victim Relationship

The beginnings of the realignment of the relationship between the CPS and victims can be traced back to its 1993 *Statement on the Treatment of Witnesses and Victims*, where the Service recognised that 'making provision for the proper care and treatment of victims and witnesses' should form 'an essential part of CPS initiatives.'[62] The document outlined a number of policies which altered, on paper at least, the traditional role of the prosecutor as a minister of justice. Prosecutors were obliged to take into account the interests of victims and witnesses in any decision to prosecute; inform the court where the victim has made a claim for compensation; try to help victims and witnesses at court by giving 'appropriate and useful information'; try to ensure that witnesses attend court only when they are required to give evidence, so that they are not kept waiting too long; introduce themselves to witnesses; look after the interests of the witnesses as the trial progresses; and explain the results of cases, whenever possible, to victims at court. These same principles were reiterated in the second edition of the Victim's Charter of 1996, and in the same year, the Crown Prosecution Service Trial Issues Group produced a *Statement of National Standards of Witness Care* that outlined four primary commitments of the Service towards victims.[63]

Following recommendations made by Sir Iain Glidewell in his review of the Service in 1998, and similar recommendations in 1999 in Sir William Macpherson's report into the death of Stephen Lawrence,[64] the pace of reform gathered momentum. The main responsibility for communicating decisions to

---

[61] See Ch 1, pp26–8.

[62] Crown Prosecution Service (1993).

[63] These being: all witnesses should be dealt with sensitively, with regard being given to differences in language, expression, religion and custom of those from ethnic minority groups; witnesses will only be required to attend court to give evidence if this is essential in the interests of justice; every effort will be made to arrange trial dates that are convenient to witnesses; the time witnesses are kept waiting at court will be kept to a minimum.

[64] See Glidewell (1998), Rec 32; MacPherson (1999), Recs 35–7.

victims was transferred from the police to the CPS. Since October 2002, the Service has been writing to victims outlining the reasons for any decision to drop or substantially alter the charge and offers a meeting:

> in cases involving a death, child abuse, sexual offences or racially / religiously aggravated offences or in any other case in which the reviewing lawyer considers it appropriate.[65]

Although this obligation is somewhat limited, such an explanation coming directly from the prosecutor who made the decision (as opposed to from the police) is more likely to generate confidence on the part of the victim that full and careful consideration was given to the case.

Other new initiatives that reflect the forging of a much closer relationship between the CPS and victims include the establishment of Witness Care Units, which were rolled out throughout the country as part of the Home Office's *No Witness No Justice* programme. Staffed jointly by CPS and police personnel (though not prosecutors themselves), the Units allocate an officer to every victim or witness to inform and support them about the criminal process and all aspects of the court appearance. Under the Victims' Code of Practice, Units must conduct a full needs-based assessment with all victims where a 'not guilty' plea is entered and keep them informed throughout the process.[66] In addition, the Service has recently introduced a new ten-point pledge that codifies what victims can expect.[67] For the most part, the pledge largely reflects changes that were already introduced in preceding years, such as the obligation to take into account the impact of the crime on victims or their families when making or substantially altering a charging decision. Other aspects of the pledge reflect new changes introduced by the Victims' Code of Practice, including the obligations to apply to the court, where appropriate, to protect the identity of the victim, to answer questions on courtroom procedure, and to consult with Victim Support to facilitate communications between barristers and victims at court. The Pledge was followed by a subsequent CPS document, *A Standard for Communication between Victims, Witnesses and the Prosecuting Advocate*,[68] which summarises the new responsibilities of prosecutors in the following terms:

> Broadly stated, prosecuting advocates have a responsibility to consult and liase with victims and witnesses at all stages of the court process to ensure, in conjunction with the Witness Service, the CPS and court staff, that they are provided with appropriate information and support, and their needs are taken account of when arranging the business of the court. In particular, prosecuting advocates have a responsibility to ensure that those who are unfamiliar with courts are put at ease as much as possible, especially witnesses who are nervous, or vulnerable, or intimidated or are the victims of crime.[69]

---

[65] Crown Prosecution Service (2003a), 2. This obligation is reiterated in the new Victims' Code of Practice at [7.7].

[66] Code of Practice, s 6.

[67] Crown Prosecution Service (2005a).

[68] Crown Prosecution Service (2006).

[69] *Ibid*, 2.

Pre-Trial Contact

One of the most contentious aspects of the victim / prosecutor relationship is the extent to which prosecutors may speak to victims in advance of the trial. In order to accommodate the new service standards above, changes also had to be made to the General Council of the Bar's Code of Conduct, which originally precluded pre-trial meetings between prosecutors and witnesses. Prompted by a recommendation by the Royal Commission on Criminal Justice that the rule should be relaxed,[70] the General Council amended the Code to permit barristers to introduce themselves to witnesses prior to the trial.[71] Legal guidance subsequently issued by the Crown Prosecution Service reiterates the desirability of all prosecutors introducing themselves to their witnesses as a matter of course, and also recommends that these witnesses are introduced to defence counsel.[72] Moreover, prosecutors should also 'seek indirect information about the needs of the witness from his or her court witness supporter, relatives, friends or carers prior to the hearing if it is not provided by the police,[73] and should communicate such information to the court.[74]

However, concerns remain that many barristers are still wary of exercising this duty lest they should inadvertently overstep the mark and be accused of coaching the witness. In 1997, the Director of Victim Support, Helen Reeves, expressed the view that victims were still reporting that barristers were not introducing themselves.[75] This impression was confirmed in surveys conducted in the late 1990s by the organisation itself,[76] by Jennifer Temkin,[77] and by a more recent report of the Crown Prosecution Service Inspectorate.[78] In spite of the distinct change in ethos introduced by the CPS and reflected in the amended Code of Practice and Written Standards, these studies replicated many of the findings made in the earlier surveys by Shapland *et al*, Chambers and Millar, and Rock.[79]

It may have been the case that the full effects of the change in the Code had not been given adequate time to percolate and alter the practices of prosecutors. It is worth noting that some of the empirical research discussed above was conducted in the immediate aftermath of the implementation of the reforms. Victim Support's study was carried out in late 1995 and early 1996, and Temkin's study was conducted between 1995 and 1997. Both surveys were qualitative in nature and involved only a small number of interviewees. This is not to diminish the importance of the findings of these surveys: they remain significant in that they

---

[70] Royal Commission on Criminal Justice (1993), [50].
[71] General Council of the Bar (2004a), [6.1.2].
[72] Crown Prosecution Service (2003b), [4.51].
[73] Crown Prosecution Service (2003b), [4.18].
[74] *Ibid*, [4.27].
[75] Reeves (1997).
[76] Victim Support (1996a), 55.
[77] Temkin (2000), esp 219.
[78] HM Crown Prosecution Service Inspectorate (2002), [11.34].
[79] Shapland *et al* (1985), Chambers and Millar (1986), Rock (1993).

raise the same important issues that were highlighted in the earlier surveys by Shapland *et al* and Rock. However, it may be the case that in the intervening period, practices of prosecutors have changed significantly. It is unfortunate that there has been little recent research to evaluate whether or not this is indeed the case.

Even though prosecutors are now encouraged to introduce themselves to witnesses, they are still not permitted to engage in any substantive discussion concerning the victims' evidence. That position may prove to be unsustainable in the longer term. Following a recommendation in *Speaking Up for Justice*,[80] prosecutors can now meet with vulnerable or intimidated witnesses prior to the trial in order to determine which special measure(s) may be the subject of an application to the Court. To this end, the Home Office and Crown Prosecution Service have jointly published a guide on how such a meeting should be arranged.[81] The document states that the primary purpose of such a meeting is:

> to establish a link between the CPS and the witness and provide witnesses with reassurance that their needs will be taken into account.

It is clear, however, that any substantive issues relating to the evidence must not be discussed:

> It is imperative that there is no discussion whatsoever with the witness as to the evidence in the case. It is quite possible that the witness will wish to mention or discuss a matter relating to evidence but both the Bar Code of Conduct and the Guide to the Professional Conduct of Solicitors make it clear that there must be no discussion of evidence with the witness. Any such discussion would be likely to lead to an allegation of rehearsing or coaching of the witness . . . If the witness does wish to discuss an evidential matter, the prosecutor must explain that the witness must discuss his or her evidence with the police officer, not the prosecutor, and that arrangements for this to happen can be made.[82]

Although this specific reform represents a significant step forward on previous practice for victims and other vulnerable witnesses, it is suggested that it will be limited in its effect for three main reasons. First, such meetings will only take place at the request of the prosecutor. As previously noted, research has confirmed that barristers are reluctant even to introduce themselves to witnesses prior to the trial.[83] Given that the nature of pre-trial interviews under the Youth Justice and Criminal Evidence Act is certainly more substantial than a mere word of introduction at court, it can be assumed that many prosecutors will err on the side of caution when considering whether such a meeting should take place at all. Unfortunately, this supposition seems to be substantiated by recent research.[84] It

---

[80] Home Office (1998), Rec 27. The Working Group believed that such a meeting could benefit the conduct of the case and provide reassurance to the witness.

[81] Home Office (2002b).

[82] *Ibid*, 23–4.

[83] Temkin (2000) notes 'Some barristers were keen to avoid any prior contact with the complainant. It was felt that there was not much that could be talked about so that the meetings were awkward and that there was always a danger of being drawn into a discussion of the evidence, which was strictly forbidden'. (at 223).

[84] Burton et al (2006), 43.

thus seems that longstanding occupational cultures continue to act as a significant barrier to mainstreaming these meetings.

The second reason why the current provisions are inadequate relates to their scope. Such a meeting will be of potential benefit only to witnesses who are classed as eligible for special measures under the 1999 Act.[85] As noted in the previous chapter, it is not only vulnerable or intimidated witnesses who suffer from the excesses of the adversarial system: many other witnesses, particularly victims, will find the prospect of testifying downright terrifying.[86] Such witnesses continue to rely solely on the Witness Service or Witness Care Units for reassurance or answers to procedural questions. There would seem to be no logical basis for restricting the reform to cases involving vulnerable witnesses: vulnerability is not a pre-requisite to secondary victimisation at court. *Speaking Up for Justice* had recommended that the Bar Council alter its rules to allow for meetings to take place between prosecutors and all witnesses. It was anticipated that such a step would increase witness confidence in the criminal justice system and provide reassurance for complainants that all aspects of the case had been fully examined.[87] Although it is now permissible for counsel to reassure witnesses and discuss aspects of procedure,[88] there is no mechanism in place to ensure that this happens on a routine basis.

Finally, only pre-trial contact is permitted. Counsel is still precluded from discussing any aspect of the case with complainants after they have begun to give evidence.[89] The main points of contact they have to provide them with such information will be the police, the court staff or a volunteer from Witness Service. During the trial itself, complainants often report feeling excluded, unrepresented and unsupported.[90]

The case for a relaxation in the rules regulating pre-trial contact received a considerable boost following the report by the Director of Public Prosecutions into issues arising out of the Damilola Taylor murder trial.[91] One of the issues to arise in that inquiry centred on the extent to which the Crown Prosecution Service should have probed further the evidence and character of a 12 year-old girl, known as Bromley, before she had been called to give evidence. The Report expressed regret that the prosecution were very limited in their ability to investigate the witness's story in advance of the trial. They had to rely mostly on information obtained from police files and the co-operation of officers who had interviewed

---

[85] See further Ch 7.

[86] See above, Ch 2, pp51–64.

[87] Home Office (1998), [6.27].

[88] General Council of the Bar (2004b), [6.1.4].

[89] General Council of the Bar (2004a), r 7.05(c).

[90] Shapland et al (1985); Victim Support (1995), (1996a); Plontikoff and Woolfson (2005).

[91] Calvert-Smith (2002). This high profile case concerned 4 youths who were charged with the murder of schoolboy Damilola Taylor in south London. An inquiry was established to investigate a number of issues arising out of the manner in which the investigation and prosecution was carried out. Two such inquiries were actually established. The one under discussion here was carried out by the outgoing DPP, David Calvert-Smith. An earlier inquiry focusing on issues relating to policing in the community was headed by Bishop Sentamu.

the witness. In conclusion, the inquiry argued that careful consideration should be given to the possibility of changing the rules to allow for some discussion of the testimony before trial.[92]

In response, a three-month public consultation was instigated as to whether or not prosecutors should be permitted to interview prosecution witnesses before trial. The Crown Prosecution Service issued a paper in May 2003 outlining a number of advantages that would follow from such meetings:

> First, not only is the prosecutor in a position to assess the demeanour of the witness . . . direct pre-trial contact may also provide an opportunity to question the witness, for the purposes of clarification or expansion of detail, about the contents of the witness statement provided to the police. As a result, weak cases are more likely to be weeded out at an early stage. Secondly . . . [the meeting] would provide an opportunity to put the witness at ease, explain the prosecution process and answer any questions a witness may have. As a result a potentially reluctant witness may be more likely to support the prosecution if he or she feels reassured that all aspects of the case have been fully examined and his or her interests properly taken into account.[93]

Not all consultees, however, welcomed the proposal. Concern was expressed by the Criminal Bar Association, which argued that such meetings would bring the prosecutor into the investigatory process which has always been the domain of the police.[94] LIBERTY contended that, owing to the risks of coaching and the cost implications to safeguard against it, on balance pre-trial interviews raised 'more concerns than potential benefits'.[95]

The Consultation Paper envisaged a number of ways whereby the risk of coaching could be minimised. It was proposed, for example, that a contemporaneous video or audio recording of the discussion could be made and then be disclosed to the defence, after being edited for 'sensitive material'. This practice is currently used for the meetings mentioned above, which are used to arrange applications for special measures. Many of the responses to the CPS paper indicated the need for a thorough and reliable record to be kept. For example, the Criminal Bar Association argued that such a safeguard was required 'to protect the witness from allegations of coaching, and to protect the integrity of the witness evidence, to protect the defendant, to protect the prosecutor . . . to enable others to assess both the witness and a decision not to proceed'.[96] Grohovsky has suggested that the presence of a competent and independent third party at any pre-trial meeting would also act as a potential safeguard in this respect.[97]

---

[92] Crown Prosecution Service (2002b).

[93] Crown Prosecution Service (2003a), 7.

[94] Criminal Bar Association (2003), 1.

[95] LIBERTY (2003a), 3. They outlined a preferred solution whereby the pre-trial interview would be conducted by the police before a video recording was passed to the prosecution. See also similar concerns regarding coaching raised by the Law Society of England and Wales (2003b) and the Criminal Bar Association (2003). See generally, *The Guardian*, 2 May 2003.

[96] Criminal Bar Association (2003), 3.

[97] Grohovsky (2000), 429. It can be noted that, in Northern Ireland, a police officer will normally be in attendance at such a meeting to take a written record of the discussion.

It is suggested that some of these concerns about coaching may be somewhat exaggerated. For a start, as Grohovsky argues, the criminal process already provides a number of inherent protections. Such safeguards include the presumption of innocence, the burden of proof, the oath, the ethical obligation of prosecutors to seek justice, the use of cross-examination and the ability of jurors to make credibility determinations.[98] Furthermore, it seems somewhat anomalous and inconsistent that concerns over coaching are so deeply rooted with respect to one branch of the legal profession, but not to the other: solicitors acting in criminal cases are permitted to discuss evidence with individual witnesses.[99] It is also significant that pre-trial meetings have not been seen as particularly problematic in other jurisdictions where they are commonplace. In Northern Ireland, prosecutors are permitted to hold pre-direction consultations and consultations during the trial with all witnesses to the facts. Such meetings will usually take place if the witness is particularly vulnerable, or where intimidation is a concern. They will typically be used to clarify matters of evidence, assess the need for special support mechanisms, or evaluate the credibility of the witness.[100] Similar practices are followed in Canada, Scotland and the USA.[101] Ellison has recorded how attorneys in the US meet and coach witnesses as a matter of course. Frequently, witnesses will participate in roleplays to prepare them for both examination-in-chief and cross-examination.[102] Testimony is thoroughly rehearsed, with the consequence that many victims feel better empowered and less apprehensive about the prospect of testifying in live court.

Following the consultation period, the Attorney General announced in December 2004 that Prosecutors should be able to meet with witnesses, but only for the purpose of clarifying or assessing the reliability of the evidence they could give. A Code of Practice was drawn up in late 2005,[103] and the pilot began in November of that year. Under the new arrangements, prosecutors may conduct pre-trial interviews where this may assist them in reaching 'a better informed decision about any aspect of the case'. The Code nevertheless proceeds to state that:

> pre-trial interviews must not be held for the purpose of improving a witness's evidence or performance although a prosecutor conducting a pre-trial interview may answer a witness's questions about court procedure.[104]

[98] Grohovsky (2000), 429. Grohovsky also notes that good advocacy practice means that most prosecutors will not want to coach witnesses since it could portray them to the court in a rehearsed and artificial manner.

[99] Principle 21.10 of the Law Society's Guide to Professional Conduct states that it is 'permissible for a solicitor acting for any party to interview and take statements from any witness or prospective witness at any stage in the proceedings' (Law Society, 2003a).

[100] DPP for Northern Ireland (2003).

[101] Home Office (1998), [6.26]; Crown Prosecution Service (2003a), 12. The Criminal Bar Association (2003) has pointed out that while the material from other jurisdictions is 'interesting', they give no statistical detail nor does it establish that such interviews improve attrition rates (at 1).

[102] Ellison (2007), esp 174–7.

[103] Crown Prosecution Service (2005b).

[104] *Ibid*, [2.2]. This position is reflected in the Bar's Code of Conduct which stipulates that 'a barrister must not rehearse, practise or coach a witness in relation to his/her evidence' (General Council of the Bar, 2004a, r 7.05).

In order to prevent a repeat of the fracas that marred the Damilola Taylor trial, prosecutors may use the interviews to assess the reliability of a witness's evidence. The Code is clear that, as part of this exercise, the witness may be asked about the content of their statement or 'other issues that relate to reliability'.[105] The remit afforded to prosecutors is thereby fairly broad: steps taken to ensure reliability may include:

> taking the witness through his/her statement, asking questions to clarify and expand evidence, asking questions relating to character, exploring new evidence or probing the witness's account.[106]

As the pilots took place, the Court of Appeal also pronounced its own views on the issue in *R v Momodou*.[107] The appeal concerned a well-publicised disturbance at the Yarl's Wood Immigration Detention Centre. It came to light that a number of prosecution witnesses had received witness training from a legal consultancy following instructions from their employer. By the time advice was sought from counsel as to the wisdom of this practice, 16 potential witnesses had already undergone training. The Court made clear that, under no circumstances, was any form of training or coaching permitted:

> The witness should give his or her own evidence, so far as practicable uninfluenced by what anyone else has said, whether in formal discussions or informal conversations. The rule reduces, indeed hopefully avoids, any possibility that one witness may tailor his evidence in the light of what anyone else said, and equally, avoids any unfounded perception that he may have done so. These risks are inherent in witness training.[108]

Lip-service was, however, paid to the value of pre-trial familiarisation visits, and the court proceeded to give detailed guidance as to other forms of 'sensible preparation' that might be undertaken.[109] It was stated that such preparation should normally be supervised by a member of the legal profession who had no personal knowledge of the matters in issue at the forthcoming trial. In addition, formal records should be maintained of the scope of any such training and who organised it. Any materials used should bear no similarity to the issues in the forthcoming trial nor should anything be done that might 'play on or trigger the witness's recollection of events'.[110]

On the one hand, the decision constitutes a not insignificant acknowledgement by the higher courts of the difficulties witnesses face in giving evidence within the adversarial process. The need for some degree of preparation is recognised, and this in itself can be welcomed. On the other hand, the stern warnings given about the dangers of coaching reflect the longstanding (and, arguably, irrational) fears within the legal profession. Shortly after the judgment, the Bar Council

---

[105] Crown Prosecution Service (2005b), [2.3].
[106] *Ibid.*
[107] [2005] 1 WLR 3442.
[108] *Ibid,* 3453.
[109] *Ibid,* 3454.
[110] *Ibid.*

issued further guidance to underline the very limited nature of the interaction that should take place between barristers and witnesses before trial.[111]

This position is unfortunate in light of a significant corpus of research that highlights that witness preparation programmes tend to reduce stress and anxiety, engender confidence, and assist witnesses in giving more articulate testimony.[112] From the perspective of victims, it means that many will continue to go without the type of preparation that witnesses in other jurisdictions routinely receive, and which is also commonplace for experts within the English criminal justice system. Defendants, of course, will often have been heavily involved in preparations for trial by their legal teams. While the established Witness Care Units and the Witness Service may be able to provide sufficient reassurance for some witnesses, those who are particularly vulnerable or unfamiliar with the court system should rightfully be entitled to a better level of support than they currently receive.

II. The Trial Process

The ability of victims to actively participate in the trial process has traditionally been limited, particularly in common law jurisdictions where they are seen as conceptual outsiders to the State / offender conflict. Participation at the trial process is, however, desirable for a number of reasons. First, it offers the victim a chance to ensure that the court has a maximum opportunity to hear facts and receive evidence from all of those directly affected by the crime—not just the perpetrator and the prosecution. This would also serve to counteract the way in which testimony is manipulated and historical events are reconstructed to suit the version of events which the advocate wishes to portray to the court.[113] Secondly, it boosts the legitimacy of the criminal process through empowering the victim and acknowledging their status as a party directed affected by the alleged act of the accused. Thirdly, there may also be a longer-term, though less ascertainable, benefit for victims through the cathartic effect that participation may bring. The opportunity to give an account of traumatic past events is widely recognised as instrumental to the healing process,[114] particularly when contrasted with the 'anti-therapeutic' nature of adversarial questioning.[115]

However, in advocating this sort of participatory role for the victim, it is also necessary to consider whether it would interfere with the function of the criminal justice system in determining the guilt or innocence of the accused. It is difficult to see how such a right of allocution would interfere with the fact-finding process.

---

[111] General Council of the Bar (2005).

[112] For an overview of the literature, see Ellison (2007), 180–2.

[113] See Ch 4, pp193–201.

[114] Harber and Pennebaker (1992); Orbuch et al (2004); Harber and Wenberg (2005); Koenig Kellas and Trees (2006).

[115] Carson (2003), 131.

Indeed, any contribution by the victim should actually serve to assist the fact-finder by ensuring a broader array of information is made available to the trier of fact on which it is able to base its decision. It can therefore be argued that allowing a victim a right to testify in his or her own words at a criminal trial should also serve the broader public interest, in that it could contribute positively to the truth-finding process.[116] As a party who alleges that he or she has been subjected to a criminal offence by the accused, logic surely dictates that his or her evidence should be essential to the decision-making progress, over and above most other witnesses. As Cavadino and Dignan point out, it seems 'intuitively strange' to accord the complainant with the same locus standi as any other member of society.[117] Giving the victim a voice at trial should not, therefore, affect the primary role of the criminal process in the determination of guilt, but would certainly help alleviate some of the feelings of exclusion and alienation that victims have reported feeling at court.

In terms of international perspectives on participation at trial, it will be recalled that while the majority of international instruments do suggest that victims ought to be able to participate to some degree in proceedings, they are extremely vague. They tend to centre around the idea that some mechanism should be in place to allow the concerns and views of victims to be heard,[118] but none go so far as to require that victims ought to be considered parties to proceedings.[119] The lack of consensus on the extent to which victims ought to be entitled to participate has also been reflected in the rules governing international criminal tribunals. Victims testifying before the International Criminal Tribunals for Yugoslavia and Rwanda are unable to participate within a personal capacity, and their role is confined to testifying as witnesses. In common with the adversary model, there is no mechanism for them to relay their account to the court through free narrative; victims are entitled to speak only when questioned in the context of examination or cross-examination. Moreover, there is no right to legal representation, and no right to introduce additional evidence. It has been suggested that the minimalist nature of participatory rights granted to victims in the ad hoc tribunals is attributable to fears that the presence of victims could cause undue delay in the trial process, thereby jeopardising the rights of the accused to be tried expeditiously.[120]

The position of victims within the ad hoc international tribunals contrasts with the prominent position of participatory rights afforded to victims at the ICC. The

---

[116] See Ch 4, 186–203.

[117] Cavadino and Dignan (1997), 237.

[118] See eg Art 25(3) UN Convention Against Transnational Organised Crime; Principle 5(3) UN Victims Declaration.

[119] An exception, however, is to be found under Principle 8(d) of the UN Guidelines on Justice in Matters involving Child Victims and Witnesses of Crime. It confers on children a right to 'express his or her views, opinions and beliefs freely, in his or her own words'. Read literally, this would seem to entail a right to free narrative.

[120] Mekjian and Varughese (2005), 14.

basis for participatory rights not only offers victims an opportunity to advance their own interests, but also enables them to monitor the actions of states.[121] It is also the case that the trial system seems to be considerably less adversarial than the approach of ad hoc tribunals, with the inquisitorial tradition clearly exerting an influence on the structure of proceedings. The provisions of the Rome Statute contain a general right to participation under Article 68(3), which permit victims at the International Criminal Court to choose their legal representatives, who have a right to present their views and make submissions when their interests are likely to be affected. Such views and submissions may be made at all stages of the court proceedings with only the limitation that it would not be prejudicial or inconsistent with the rights of the accused.[122]

Rule 90 of the Rules of Procedure and Evidence stipulates victims or their legal representative may apply to the Chamber to participate in the trial in three ways: to attend and participate in the proceedings;[123] to question a witness, an expert or the accused;[124] and to make opening and closing statements.[125] While the right to attend proceedings is absolute,[126] the right to participate is discretionary.[127] Under Rule 91(2), it is for the Chamber to determine the extent to which victims ought to be able to participate, and may rule that participation is confined to written observations or submissions. The Court also has the power to scrutinise any questions or lines of examination which participating victims' counsel intends to pursue with witnesses.[128] Such a ruling may include directions on the manner and order of the questions and the production of evidence in order to ensure 'a fair, impartial and expeditious trial'.[129]

While, in practical terms, many challenges lie ahead for the ICC in realising the rights contained in Rule 91,[130] the mechanism constitutes a high-water mark in terms of what victims can now expect in international criminal justice, and reflects a significant departure from the purist adversarial approach adopted by the ad hoc tribunals. It is also significant insofar as that it illustrates that it is possible to put in place a mechanism for victim participation in a forum that largely adopts

---

[121] Aldana-Pindell (2002), 1414.

[122] Art 68(1).

[123] R 91(2).

[124] R 91.

[125] R 89(1). Where there are a number of victims, the Court may request that victims choose a common legal representative (R 90(1)(2)). If a victim is unable to afford legal representation, financial assistance may be available from the Registry (R 90(5)).

[126] R 91(2). Art 43(6) of the Statute requires that the appointment of a victims' advocate is to be effected through the Victims and Witnesses Unit. Further details on the assignment of advocates are contained within R 90.

[127] R 89, 91(3)(a).

[128] R 91(3)(a).

[129] R 91(3)(b).

[130] For an overview of potential problems, especially in relation to pre-trial procedure, see Stahn et al (2006). The authors note, however, that the Victims and Witnesses Unit could provide a crucial role in providing resources and guidance to victims to ensure they are able to exercise their rights during the proceedings.

adversarial procedures without infringing the rights of the accused.[131] The lack of an entrenched adversarial system at the International Criminal Court, and the fact that the majority of the judges and lawyers will come from inquisitorial traditions may mean that realising the right to participation for victims may not be as difficult to accommodate as had been feared. In stipulating that the trial Chamber must weigh the triangular interests of the accused, the prosecution, and the victim within decision-making, a gauntlet has been laid down to other fora to devise new mechanisms that depart from outdated conceptions about the nature of criminal offences and the purposes of a criminal trial.

Participation within the Adversarial Context

While the right to participation has now found firm footing in international trials, victims have little opportunity to participate within domestic criminal trials. As a common law jurisdiction, victims are normative outsiders to the criminal trial: the showdown between the State and the accused. Victims in England and Wales have no right to be present at the trial; no right to legal representation; no right to question witnesses and no right to present evidence. Perhaps most significantly of all in the context of this study, they lack any ability to advance arguments based on substantive Convention rights that may arise during the trial.[132] They are the only stakeholders in the offence, and are only of value as tools of evidence. As such, the main function of the victim within the adversarial trial is as a witness and, as William Pizzi has remarked, the adversarial system 'turns witnesses into weapons to be used against the other side'.[133] Their testimony must be shaped to bring out its maximum adversarial effect,[134] and victims are thereby confined to answering questions within the parameters set down by the questioner. They have no opportunity to relay their account before the court using their own words, which seems something of an irony given that logic dictates that such an account should have a key role to play in arriving at the truth.[135] In practice, counsel in adversarial trials seek to take control of the witness, and use questioning to elicit only those facts which he or she feels should be included. Questions are carefully framed to avoid the witness speaking about anything that counsel feels should be omitted from the testimony.[136] The goal, essentially, is to manipulate witness testimony in such a way that victory is made more likely. This form of control exercised by advocates over witnesses means that the conflict is entirely removed

---

[131] See further Ambos (2003), who traces a shift from a wholly adversarial model towards a hybrid form of procedure. However, see also Jorda and de Hemptinne (2002), who have identified the bipartisan nature of proceedings as being one of the main factors that is likely to obstruct the effective participation by victims at the International Criminal Court (at 1388).

[132] Eg, if their protective rights under Arts 3 or 8 of the Convention have been violated by the manner of the cross-examination. See discussion in Ch 2, pp109–113.

[133] Pizzi, (1999), 197.

[134] *Ibid.*

[135] See below, Ch 4, pp193–201.

[136] See Stone (1995), 127. Further discussion of advocates' tactics is contained in Ch 4.

from the hands of its protagonists. It is unsurprising then that many victims perceive themselves to be awkward outsiders to the criminal process.

As noted above, one of the fundamental misconceptions within common law systems is that prosecutors will represent the interests of the victim. As 'ministers of justice', prosecutors are neither obligated nor empowered to act on behalf of victims, and will not generally perceive it to be within their remit to offer support to the complainant.[137] In the adversarial trial, they are not supposed to act as legal representatives of any one particular witness since this could potentially conflict with their duty to act on behalf of the public interest. This is reflected in the *Code for Crown Prosecutors* which states:[138]

> The CPS does not act directly on behalf of individual victims, or represent them in court in criminal proceedings because it has to take decisions reflecting the overall public interest rather than the interests of one person.[139]

It is therefore unsurprising that past surveys have found that many victims have reported feeling shunned and confused by the way in which they are treated by prosecutors. In 1985, Shapland et al reported that 'the prosecutor [was] the most unsatisfactory courtroom participant as far as the victims were concerned'.[140] Rock also found that witnesses 'could not understand why they were so shunned by the lawyers whom they supposed to act for them'.[141] He concluded that complainants were a major inconvenience for prosecutors, who were either unable or unwilling to provide the level of support or protection which they expected:

> The CPS did not undertake to look after victims and prosecution witnesses. Formally, the branch Crown prosecutor maintained, victims were the responsibility of the police ... [V]ictims were taken to have an influence that might on occasion almost be described as baneful. They stirred things up around them. The great, central driving conflict of the Court transformed them into diffuse sources of difficulty and danger for all staff and users. They threatened conduct of cases. They threatened the appearance of neutrality so carefully cultivated by staff. They threatened the studied competence of counsel. They were awkward companions for the police . . . they were thrust to a distance, never fully trusted, denied knowledge about much of what transpired, relegated to safe, outer margins of the court's social organisation. Victims were outsiders.[142]

Other research suggests that many victims feel that the prosecution case was not presented as strongly as that of the defence.[143] Some victims have expressed concern about the amount of effort that the prosecutor has put into winning the case. Chambers and Millar have noted that prosecutors offered few objections to

---

[137] Temkin (2000).
[138] *Crown Prosecution Service* (1993).
[139] *Ibid*, [2.1].
[140] Shapland *et al* (1985), 67.
[141] Rock (1993), 177.
[142] *Ibid*, 160–1.
[143] See, eg Shapland *et al* (1985), Victim Support (1996a), Lees (1996).

aggressive and persistent cross-examination by defence counsel.[144] As noted in the previous chapter, studies have also indicated that complainants feel that they themselves are put on trial, especially during cross-examination.[145] In many cases, their character will be publicly called into question, and linguistic devices may be deployed as the cross-examiner tries to 'trip up' the witness.[146] Brown et al found that prosecutors in Scottish sexual offence trials will avoid frequent objections as these are not regarded as tactically astute:

> [P]rosecutors maintained that when and why they objected would very much depend on the case. They provided a number of tactical reasons for delaying in making an objection or not objecting at all, even if the defence questioning was straying into prohibited areas.[147]

Glissan and Tilmouth have pointed out that too many objections risk depriving the witness's evidence of weight; jurors may become suspicious and may want to know what counsel is trying to hide.[148] Besides, a physically distressed witness suffering at the hands of an overly zealous cross-examiner for the defence could play into the hands of the prosecution by winning the jury's sympathy for the complainant and alienating the defence.[149] Thus, the prosecutor will only object to such questioning if it is strategically advantageous to do so. As argued in the previous chapter, since judges are also typically reluctant to intervene to prevent hostile or irrelevant questioning,[150] complainants will have no one to protect their interests during cross-examination.[151]

Representation for Victims?

A better means of ensuring effective participation for victims may be to allow them to appoint and rely upon their own legal representative. Such a representative may have an important role to play in protecting the victim's interests whilst he or she is under cross-examination, as well as making submissions to the Court about, inter alia, the means of giving evidence, the need for any special protective measures, rebutting any character attacks, or objecting to unfair, intrusive or overly aggressive forms of questioning. Victims should also benefit from direct practical support from their representatives, who would be in a position to explain the rules

[144] Chambers and Millar (1986), 123.

[145] See above, Ch2, pp50–64.

[146] Murphy (2001) cites a number of examples of recent high profile cases in the USA where prosecutors have failed to intervene to protect the interests of complainants, including the William Kennedy Smith rape trial.

[147] Brown *et al* (1992), 56.

[148] Glissan and Tilmouth (1998), 169.

[149] Spencer and Flin (1993) have noted that this may be particularly common in cases involving child witnesses (at 283).

[150] See above, pp94–7.

[151] Even if prosecutors were intent on protecting complainants, it is in any case doubtful how well placed they would be to do this effectively. Prosecutors are typically ill-prepared to perform such a task given the lack of contact they will have had with the complainant prior to the trial.

of evidence and procedure and help prepare them for cross-examination, subject to reform of the above-noted rules on witness preparation. Such provisions might contribute to helping the victim feel less excluded from the trial process.

However, such representation has traditionally not been a feature of the adversarial paradigm owing to its systemic and conceptual restraints. Only the parties to a criminal action, namely the prosecution and the defence, may make direct representations to the court. Nonetheless, there have recently been calls for legal representation of rape complainants because of the way that intimate details of their character are often subject to intense scrutiny. Such a scheme would allow for a legal representative to guide the complainant through the complexities of the criminal trial and to represent his or her interests before the court. It is noteworthy that two common law jurisdictions, namely the USA and Ireland, have recently experimented with such a concept of court-based victim advocacy, albeit to a somewhat limited extent.

In the USA, a number of individual states have already adopted amendments to their constitutions,[152] and have created a special office of 'victim advocate' to enforce provisions contained in their constitutional amendments. For example, a 'victims' service advocate' was added to the New Mexico Office of the Attorney General in 1999 to provide assistance to victims of violent crime and their families. Some states make provision for the victim to rely on the presence of a legal representative at court. Washington State provides that victims of violence and sex crimes have the right:

> to have a crime victim advocate from a crime victim/witness program present at any prosecutorial or defence interviews with the victim, and at any judicial proceedings related to criminal acts committed against the victim.[153]

Similarly, Illinois confers a constitutional right on victims to have the presence in court of 'an advocate or other support person of the victim's choice'.[154] In both these cases, however, the right is confined to the mere presence of a legal representative as opposed to any actual involvement.

Other US states now take a more radical approach and permit victims to hire their own attorneys to represent them at various parts of the criminal process. This occurs mostly during parole hearings, plea negotiations and sentencing.[155] Certain states go further and permit victims' counsel to intervene in rape and sexual assault trials. Wisconsin, West Virginia and New Hampshire allow complainants' representatives to make representations when questions governing the admissibility of sexual history evidence are being considered by the court.[156] The South Carolina provision is even broader in that it permits representations from a

---

[152] As at 13 Jul 2007, the National Victims' Rights Constitutional Amendment Network listed 34 states as having adopted such amendments (http://www.nvcan.org).

[153] Washington Statute RCW 7.69.030, s 1.

[154] Art 1, s 8.1 Illinois Constitution. This provision has, perhaps surprisingly, not been replicated in the proposed amendment to the federal constitution—see below.

[155] Hillenbrand (1989), 318–19.

[156] Yaroshefsky (1989), 146 (n 31).

victims' advocate in any type of case where the defendant alleges improper or illegal conduct on the part of the victim as part of his or her defence.[157]

Calls for legal representation for complainants in the USA received a recent boost by the debate in Congress towards a constitutional amendment, which, if ratified, would provide victims of violent crime with constitutionally guaranteed rights. These rights could be enforced 'by the victim or the victim's lawful representative',[158] although there is no provision for this representative to actually participate within the criminal trial itself. In view of fairly intensive academic and political debate on the constitutional amendment, it is surprising that there has not been any recent evaluation of the extent of legal representation for victims in the USA. However, some commentators have speculated that actual participation in criminal trials by victims' attorneys throughout the states may be more common than is generally thought, and may occur more widely than is formally provided for at law.[159]

Formal legal representation is also provided for in the Republic of Ireland. Like most of the US-based schemes, the Irish provision is only available to complainants in cases concerning rape and serious sexual offences. The idea had been mooted in Ireland for some time,[160] although a more intense debate was generated in the late 1990s by a discussion paper on the Law on Sexual Offences issued by the Department of Justice, Equality and Law Reform.[161] Following a period of consultation, legislation came into force in 2001 that permitted complainants to be represented by their own counsel in a voir dire where the defence had applied to introduce previous sexual history evidence. Section 4A(1) of the Criminal Law (Rape) Act 1981 now provides:

> Where an application . . . [relating to the use of sexual history evidence] is made by or on behalf of an accused person who is for the time being charged with an offence to which this section applies, the complainant shall be entitled to be heard in relation to the application and, for this purpose, to be legally represented during the hearing of the application.[162]

---

[157] South Carolina Statute 16-3-1510. S 3F(2) states 'A victim or witness has the right to retain counsel in court to represent him in cases involving the victim's reputation'.

[158] S.J. Res 1 (2003), 'Proposing an amendment to the Constitution of the United States to protect the rights of crime victims.' These rights would include the right to be notified of proceedings in the criminal case; to attend public proceedings in the case; to make a statement at release proceedings, sentencing, and proceedings regarding a plea bargain; and to have the court order the convicted offender to pay restitution for the harm caused by the crime. See further http://www.nvcan.org [accessed 13 Jul 2007].

[159] Yaroshefsky (1989), 146 (n 33); Sebba (1996), 205.

[160] The Irish Law Reform Commission (1988) had originally considered the proposal in their 1987 Consultation Paper on rape, but rejected any suggestion that rape complainants should be separately represented at all stages of the trial. They questioned the constitutionality of such a proposal stating: 'It might . . . be constitutionally suspect, since it tilts the balance of the criminal process significantly in favour of the prosecution in a defined range of offences by permitting a dual representation hostile to the interests of the accused, thereby depriving him of one of the long standing benefits of a criminal trial conducted in due course of law' [42].

[161] Department of Justice, Equality and Law Reform (Ireland) (1998).

[162] As inserted by Sex Offenders Act 2001, s 34.

It is the responsibility of the prosecution to inform the complainant of his or her right to counsel,[163] and the judge may postpone the hearing of any such application until he or she has been afforded adequate opportunity to make the appropriate arrangements.[164]

While the Irish measure does provide some degree of protection to complainants at a crucial juncture in rape trials, the scope of the provision is extremely narrow. It will only apply in cases of rape or sexual assault, and, like many of the US provisions, only in the specific circumstance where the defence is attempting to introduce sexual history evidence. The advocate cannot participate within the trial itself. As in ordinary adversarial proceedings, only the prosecutor will thereby be able to object to overly vexatious or aggressive cross-examination. It is therefore wrong to think of such measures as actually enhancing the degree of victim *participation* within a trial. In 1998, the Irish Department of Justice, Equality and Law Reform had rejected any wider role for the victim's advocate because of fears over coaching. The Irish Law Reform Commission had expressed a number of concerns the previous year, stemming from the fear that the risk of 'coaching' would increase, whereby complainants would be advised to 'down play' or highlight certain aspects of their evidence or to answer certain questions in examination or cross-examination in a particular way.[165]

However, given that the accused has a right to counsel in many international human rights instruments,[166] it could be argued that the principle of equality of arms requires that victims should be afforded similar protection to protect their interests in court. This perhaps explains why, as noted above, victims have a right to counsel at the ICC, and seemed to be the conclusion of a 1999 UN working paper that stated:

> Looking at the rights of victims as a whole, the right to counsel seems the logical complement of the defendant's right to counsel. There is no zero-sum game between those two rights. The victim's right to be treated with respect seems to have little if any negative implications for the offender.[167]

Implementing Victim Representation in England and Wales

Victim representation, as practised in parts of the USA, Ireland or at the International Criminal Court, is virtually unknown in the United Kingdom. Prior to the formation of the Witness Service in 1988, the care of witnesses at court fell to the police and existing court staff, who were constrained by their lack of specific victim-related training and their responsibilities for performing other duties in the

---

[163] S 4A(3).
[164] S 4A(5).
[165] Irish Law Reform Commission (1997), [107].
[166] See, eg Art 6(3)(c) ECHR; Art 14(3)(d) ICCPR; Basic Principles on the Role of Lawyers, (UN Doc A/CONF.144/28/Rev.1 at 118), Principle 8.
[167] United Nations (1999), [21].

courthouse. It became increasingly clear that they were unable to provide the level of support that witnesses required.[168] In 1988, Victim Support established the Witness Service, which is staffed by volunteers.[169] The Service aims to provide witnesses with information about the case and to offer moral support throughout the trial. Its major functions include the provision of information about trial procedures, the organisation of pre-trial familiarisation visits, and ensuring that the victim is able to wait in a separate room from the defendant.[170]

While the benefits conferred on victims through the pioneering work of the Witness Service should not be underestimated, the information about the operation of the court and relevant legal procedures they can offer is limited. Volunteers are not permitted to advise victims about their evidence or prepare them for cross-examination so as to avoid allegations that the Witness Service has coached witnesses or contaminated their evidence. As Riding has observed:

> The Witness Service is constrained by the criminal justice system in what it can do to assist witnesses to prepare for, and cope with, cross-examination. Just as the Witness Service takes the view that it cannot warn them on the importance of their demeanour, it believes it cannot warn them of the nature of cross-examination. If the Witness Service did tell witnesses about the techniques of the cross-examiner, for example, constructing a 'slippery slope,' making the 'unlikely likely,' and pouncing upon the answer 'but,' lawyers would strenuously object that the Witness Service had prejudiced the trial. The objections would be stronger if the Witness Service spent time building up the confidence of the witness to mentally prepare her for the attack.[171]

The idea of putting in place some formal representation for victims has been mooted in the United Kingdom on a number of occasions. In 1984, the Criminal Law Revision Committee considered a proposal to permit a complainant's counsel a right of audience in a voir dire concerning the admissibility of previous sexual history evidence.[172] The Committee rejected the proposal on the basis that it would constitute a substantial change to accepted procedures and that this was unjustified on the basis that the proposal would be unlikely to add anything to the judge's duty to prevent oppressive or unnecessary questioning:

> The implementing of this suggestion would make a substantial change in criminal procedure which would be unnecessary and would probably have far-reaching consequences . . . Our correspondents may not have appreciated that judges have a duty to protect all witnesses from unfair cross-examination by counsel, whether they be prosecuting or defending. In our experience they try to perform their duty . . . If representation of witnesses in rape cases were allowed, it would be difficult to refuse it in other cases. Cross-examination about previous sexual behaviour may become relevant in cases of all kinds. One of our members was once counsel in what seemed a straight-

---

[168] See Rock (1991), 308; Victim Support (1988). The police, however, continue to be responsible for the protection of witnesses at risk of intimidation outside the courtroom.

[169] Initially piloted in 1988, by 1996 the Witness Service operated from every Crown Court centre in England and Wales (Victim Support, 1996b).

[170] Victim Support (1996b), 1.

[171] Riding (1999), 417.

[172] Criminal Law Revision Committee (1984).

forward receiving case. Cross-examination about past sexual behaviour revealed that the allegation of receiving had been fabricated because of sexual jealousy. Further, cross-examination about such behaviour is not the only kind of cross-examination about past conduct which may cause distress to prosecution witnesses.[173]

Temkin has argued that the reasoning of the Criminal Law Revision Committee was unconvincing insofar as legislation could easily delineate the scope of such a mechanism. She points out that statutes already provide for third parties to be legally represented in certain types of cases.[174] She also attacks the Committee's reliance upon the duty of the trial judge to exercise his discretion to protect witnesses, and points to the use of previous sexual history as an example of the prejudices and unwillingness of Committee members to take positive steps to prevent irrelevant and degrading cross-examination.

The Report by Sir William MacPherson on the Stephen Lawrence Inquiry recommended the development of the procedure as an extension to the existing common law right of private individuals to initiate their own criminal proceedings.[175] However, somewhat surprisingly, *Speaking Up for Justice* made no mention of the possible role of a victim-advocate in the United Kingdom, and the idea was rejected by Lord Justice Auld, who felt that such a proposal would be unworkable:

> It is difficult to see how such a scheme would fit our adversarial system, in which there are only two parties and the hearing is a substitute for private vengeance not an expression of it. To put an alleged victim whose account the defendant challenges—as will often be the case—in the ostensibly privileged role of an auxiliary prosecutor would be unfair. Whilst the current concern for the plight of victims in the criminal justice process and the steps being taken to right it are thoroughly justified, care must be taken, in particular when there is an issue as to guilt, not to treat him in a way that appears to prejudge the resolution of that issue.[176]

In many ways, Auld's statement epitomises the dismissive manner with which calls for radical reform have been dealt with over the years by working groups, law reform bodies, and successive governments. Such reports often acknowledge that the treatment of victims within the criminal justice system is poor, yet there would appear to be an institutional reluctance to accept the need for radical change at a structural level.[177] In the same way, the Criminal Law Revision Committee was correct to point out that rape complainants were not the only type of witness to suffer under cross-examination,[178] but rejected a course of reform because of their flawed assumptions that judges were well-placed to control the excesses of adversarial combat.[179]

---

[173] *Ibid*, [2.100].

[174] Temkin (2002), 302. Examples she has cited include s 36 Criminal Justice Act 1972; s 34 Obscene Publications Act 1959.

[175] MacPherson (1999), Rec 42. See above, pp124–6.

[176] Auld (2002), [11.74].

[177] See further Ch 6, pp285–92.

[178] Criminal Law Revision Committee (1984), [2.100].

[179] Criminal Law Revision Committee (1984), [2.100].

In examining protection for rape complainants, Jennifer Temkin has argued for a mechanism whereby the role of the victim advocate would be limited to three specific functions: objecting to pre-trial applications for third-party disclosure; contesting applications for admission of sexual history evidence and objecting to improper defence questions put to the victim at trial.[180] Such a measure could go some way to addressing the notoriously high attrition rate that characterises rape cases, through offering further protection to complainants against unduly prejudicial and hostile questioning, and may help to elicit evidence which complainants are reluctant to divulge.[181] However, in her survey of practitioners' attitudes towards rape trials, Temkin found near-unanimous opposition to this idea. Her study seemed to confirm considerable institutional resistance, since it was 'thought to be contrary to the adversarial system and counterproductive for the victim who might then be seen by the jury as a contending party rather than as a victim of the crime'.[182]

To some extent, these concerns are justified. The adversarial mode of trial would have to be significantly adapted to allow for what would essentially amount to a three-way contest. As such, it would complicate the balance of power in the criminal trial. If both the victim advocate and prosecution counsel were seen to be 'joining forces' against the accused, this could be criticised for undermining the principle of equality of arms. As such, it is difficult to envisage how a system of victim advocacy within the trial could work, given the apparently high degree of institutional reluctance to compromise the values of the adversarial system.

However, in September 2005, the Government surprised many commentators and lawyers in issuing a consultation paper, *Hearing the Relatives of Murder and Manslaughter Victims*,[183] which proposed a scheme for victims' advocates to assist relatives of homicide victims. While the document appears to envisage that the primary role of such an advocate would be to assist the victim at the sentencing stage of proceedings, it is also envisaged that the representative would provide advice and support to the relative in the run-up and during the trial to keep them informed and help them feel more engaged in the process. Potentially, such an advocate may be appointed at the charge stage or during the Plea and Case Management Hearing, and may be able to make representations to the CPS on pre-trial matters. It is also clear from the document that the victim advocate may not interject within the trial itself. Having gauged that there was 'firm support' for its proposals,[184] a pilot scheme was established in April 2006 at five Crown Court centres.[185]

---

[180] Temkin (2002), 304.
[181] *Ibid*, 292.
[182] Temkin (2000), 221.
[183] Department of Constitutional Affairs (2005).
[184] Department of Constitutional Affairs (2006).
[185] Pilots were established at Birmingham, Cardiff, the Central Criminal Court, Manchester Crown Square and Winchester.

If this scheme is rolled out nationally, it will mark a significant milestone for victims' rights campaigners. It should certainly enable some form of effective participation, and may help alleviate some of the stress associated with testifying in court—especially if the victim is a vulnerable witness. A legal representative may also help victims feel more familiar with the environment and language of the courtroom, and would give them a better idea of what to expect when testifying. In addition, prosecutors could be relieved of certain responsibilities towards victims, and as such would be less likely to encounter conflicts of interests in their role as 'ministers of justice'.

However, under the Government's scheme, the limited functions of the victim advocate reflect the fact that there are serious questions to be addressed as regards how a third party could be accommodated in a bipartisan arena. It was, perhaps, always inevitable that such a proposal would stop short of conferring powers on victim-advocates to become actively involved in the trial through cross-examining witnesses or making specific representations to the court on behalf of victims.[186] At the time of writing, although publication of the pilot results are far from imminent, a positive outcome may invigorate further discussion as to whether it would be possible to extend the right to counsel to other victims. It seems especially odd that victims of sexual offences should have been omitted from the proposal, since recent debates surrounding a possible role for victims' counsel have tended to focus on these offences.

Another beneficial effect of the pilots may be to inject a fresh perspective into whether adversarial structures really are capable of protecting victims' rights. Recently, debates have moved away from narrow legalistic perspectives and instead have tended to focus on deeper questions, concerning structures, values and working cultures. The coming years should afford us with some valuable insights from the ICC as to how effective victim participation can be within a largely adversarial framework, although the institutional reluctance of lawyers to tolerate a third party may be considerably more difficult to overcome within the domestic context, where adversarialism is much more deeply entrenched. While there can be little doubt that a victim's 'right to counsel' would sit very uncomfortably within the adversarial framework, it may, conceivably, not be so incompatible that it could not function at all.

III. Sentencing

Most debate concerning participatory rights for victims has largely taken place within the context of sentencing. In recent years, many jurisdictions have made provision for victims to make known their views to the court when the offender

---

[186] Temkin (2002) cites a number of surveys of the legal profession in the common law world which suggest that judiciary and lawyers were overwhelmingly opposed to such an innovation (at 303).

faces sentence. The function of these 'victim impact statements' is usually to inform the court of the physical, emotional or financial harm suffered as the result of an offence. There are two main types of victim impact statements: those which explain the impact of the offence on the victim alone (as is commonplace in Canada, New Zealand and South Australia); and those which, in addition, lay down specific penal demands (as in many parts of the USA and Germany). Such a statement may be tendered in writing, made orally directly by the victim, or may be presented to the court indirectly, through either prosecuting counsel or a pre-sentence report compiled by probation or social services.

The International Perspective

While there has been considerable debate lately as to the pros and cons of victim participation in sentencing,[187] these discussions have tended to examine issues from an Anglo-American perspective, omitting discussion of emerging inter-national standards and developments in other jurisdictions. However, as with the idea of participation generally, international instruments and human rights fora have traditionally fudged the issue of whether the victim ought to be allowed any input into decision-making in sentencing proceedings. While participation per se is enshrined as an inherently positive value in various instruments and inter-national criminal justice, there is nothing here to indicate that victims should have a specific legal right to intervene in sentencing.

At the ICC, for example, Rule 145 stipulates that the Court shall, inter alia, give consideration 'to the extent of the damage caused, in particular the harm caused to the victims and their families'. The requirement to consider the extent of harm is bolstered by Rule 143, which clearly envisages that victims may be actively par-ticipating at the sentencing stage of proceedings.[188] Read in conjunction with the general participatory requirements laid down by Article 68 of the ICC Statute, at first sight it seems to confirm that victims have a right to participate in sentencing. However, as noted in the previous section, the rights conferred on victims by Article 68 are limited and are dependent upon the exercise of the Court's discre-tion. There is therefore no automatic right for a victim to lodge a victim impact statement or to have their views taken directly into account by the sentencer. Once sentence is passed, the victim is unable to appeal the sentence, but may appeal any subsequent decision on reparations.[189]

---

[187] See eg Morgan et al (1996); Ashworth (2002); Roberts and Erez (2004); Edwards (2004).

[188] R 143 states: 'Pursuant to Art 76, paragraphs 2 and 3, for the purpose of holding a further hear-ing on matters related to sentence and, if applicable, reparations, the Presiding Judge shall set the date of the further hearing. This hearing can be postponed, in exceptional circumstances, by the Trial Chamber, on its own motion or at the request of the Prosecutor, the defence or the legal representa-tives of the victims participating in the proceedings pursuant to rules 89 to 91 and, in respect of repa-rations hearings, those victims who have made a request under rule 94'.

[189] See Ch 5 below, pp219–22.

In European human rights law, while victims may well have the right to challenge a sentence on the basis that it constitutes an inadequate punishment,[190] there is no corresponding right to participate. There has been only one occasion to date where the issue has arisen before the Strasbourg court. In *McCourt v United Kingdom*,[191] the mother of a murder victim complained that she had been denied a right to be involved in the sentencing process contrary to Article 8. In rejecting her complaint, the Commission found that the United Kingdom sentencing framework did not reveal any lack of respect for her right to family life,[192] and also drew attention to the fact that concern for the victim's interests had already been shown when the Parole Board came to decide on whether to grant early release.

The decision was unsurprising, since the European Court of Human Rights and the Commission have traditionally shied away from intervening in cases concerned with sentencing. However, the more recent decision of *T and V v United Kingdom*[193] would seem to mark a shift in thinking. Here, the Court permitted the parents of Jamie Bulger, a child victim in a murder case, to be present at the hearing and to make representations to the Court. Although the Strasbourg Court stopped well short of stipulating that this ought to be a requirement vis-à-vis the domestic process, Rock records the toddler's mother as saying that it was a 'magnificent gesture' that she had been allowed to intervene in Strasbourg, since she had been precluded from doing so domestically.[194] While it is unlikely that the Court will acknowledge a right for the victim to be involved in the sentencing process in the near future, as Member States enact legislation to this effect there is every chance that in the medium to long term, some form of recognisable right may emerge under Article 8. As Emmerson and Ashworth contend, it would seem that if this were indeed to happen, it would take the form of a statement to the court outlining the effects of the crime on the victim and his or her family, rather than the more radical approach used in many parts of the USA which allows victims to actually make representations as to the length or type of sentence to be conferred.[195] The Court, however, may be inclined to give any further emergent rights in this area a wide berth, as it is not inconceivable that potential conflicts may be seen to arise with the defendant's right to a fair and impartial hearing under Article 6(1).[196]

---

[190] See Ch 4 below, pp167–71.

[191] App No 20433/92, 2 Dec 1992. Note, however, that the Court did highlight the fact that victims' opinions were taken note of in the United Kingdom when the Parole Board decides on whether to grant early release.

[192] The Commission also rejected her complaint that denial of bereavement damages by the State also contravened Art 8.

[193] (1999) 30 EHRR 121. For a detailed discussion of the background to this case and its ramifications within the Home Office, see Rock (2004), 250–61.

[194] Rock (2004), 254.

[195] Emmerson and Ashworth (2001), 18–78.

[196] *Ibid*, see also Leverick (2004), 193.

Domestic Practice

Despite the conceptual and practical difficulties in granting victims participatory rights within the adversarial framework, it has been the case for some time that the level of harm suffered by the victim was a legitimate factor for the courts to take into account in sentencing. While, technically, victims' views as to the length of sentence imposed are still irrelevant, in *R v Perks*[197] the Court of Appeal noted that the effect of an offence upon an individual victim can impact upon the level of sentence imposed by the court. The opinion of the victim may be relevant 'where the sentence passed on the offender is aggravating the victim's distress, the sentence may be moderated' or:

> where the forgiveness or unwillingness to press charges provide clear evidence that his or her psychological or mental suffering must be very much less than would normally be the case.[198]

In *R v Roche,*[199] where the offender pleaded guilty to causing the death of his cousin by careless driving while under the influence of drink or drugs, it was further accepted that the court might, as an act of mercy, reduce a sentence if the relatives of the victim indicated that the punishment imposed on the offender was aggravating their distress.[200]

These cases illustrate that, for some years now, the appellate courts have accepted that victim statements may be a useful tool in furnishing the sentencer with additional information concerning the gravity of the offence.[201] However, the *opinion* of the victim remains irrelevant.[202] Moreover, until recently, there was no formal mechanism in place for such views to be made known to the court. Following the commitment in the 1996 Victims' Charter to offer victims 'the chance to explain how the crime has affected [them] and [have their] interests taken into account', the Government established several pilot Victim Personal Statement (VPS) schemes in England in the late 1990s. The schemes were implemented nationally in October 2001, and allow victims to explain the impact of the crime upon them by way of a personal statement made to the police. The Statement is then appended to the case papers.

The purpose of the VPS is purely to give sentencers better understanding of the harm caused as a result of the conduct in question. Victims are not permitted to give any indication as to the nature of the sentence that should be imposed, unlike

---

[197] [2000] Crim LR 606.

[198] *Ibid,* at 609.

[199] [1999] 2 Cr App R (S) 105.

[200] See also *Consolidated Practice Direction* [2002] 1 WLR 2870, [28].

[201] See also *R v Doe* (1995) 16 CR App R (S) 718; *Attorney-General's Reference (No 2 of 1995)* [1996] 1 Cr App R (S) 274.

[202] See eg *R v Hobstaff* (1993) 14 Cr App R (S) 605, where the Court of Appeal stressed that the effect of the offence on the victim must be demonstrable by potentially admissible evidence.

other schemes in place elsewhere. This position has been buttressed by a Practice Direction issued from the Lord Chief Justice, which stated that the:

> opinions of the victim or the victim's close relatives as to what the sentence should be are therefore not relevant, unlike the consequence of the offence on them.[203]

Potentially the limited impact of their input could serve to exacerbate feelings of disillusionment on the part of victims insofar as they may have expected their opinions on such matters to count, only to have their expectations dashed.[204] Indeed, this may explain evidence of rather erratic take-up rates among victims,[205] and lower satisfaction rates among victims after having given a statement than beforehand.[206]

While a VPS may contribute towards a more factually accurate basis for sentencing, from the victim's perspective, its function is purely expressive. Providing, however, victims are made aware of the purpose of such a statement, a purely expressive input may still prove beneficial. Not only does it avoid lumbering victims with a potentially burdensome decision, but it may also carry cathartic benefits in offering them a channel by which they can offload their feelings about the impact of the offence.[207] However, such potentially therapeutic benefits may be subjugated by the fact that a VPS must be relayed to the court indirectly, ie. through the case papers; victims are not permitted to read the statements themselves in open court. In this sense, the scheme as it stands only allows participation on paper. The victim does not have a right of allocation: that is, he or she cannot appear in person and give an oral statement before the sentencer.

A much more comprehensive form of participation at sentencing will be available through the 'Victim's Advocate Scheme', noted above. Under the proposals, victims will acquire a 'right of allocution', and will be led through their statements by the advocate. However, like Victim Personal Statements, the purpose of such a mechanism is to give the sentencer a more accurate picture of the impact of the offence and to possibly offer some cathartic benefit for the victim. No specific penal demands may be relayed to the court. As Erez has suggested, the English model for facilitating participation of the victim in sentencing makes little real difference to either victims or defendants in the criminal justice system.[208]

The Debate goes on . . .

There is a vast amount of literature debating the pros and cons of victim participation at the sentencing stage of proceedings. The arguments in favour of victim impact statements largely reflect those concerning participation generally, set

---

[203] *Practice Direction (Victim Personal Statement)* [2002] 1 Cr App R (S) 482.
[204] See Sanders et al (2001); Chalmers et al (2007).
[205] Graham et al (2004).
[206] *Ibid.*
[207] Roberts and Erez (2004).
[208] Erez (2000).

out at the beginning of this chapter.[209] In addition to boosting levels of victim satisfaction and improving the overall sense of legitimacy for the criminal justice system, it might be added that such statements ensure that courts have a fuller picture of the crime and are thereby better placed to sentence the offender or order reparation to the victim.[210] Arguably, victims also have a moral interest in seeing that punishment is effected, since this can provide some measure of reassurance to the victim that they have public recognition and support.[211]

Opponents of victim participation point out that these statements jeopardise the public interest and due process rights of the accused. This argument is often grounded in the assumption that victims are somehow primarily inspired by vengeance, and will seek a harsher punishment than the court may otherwise be willing to impose.[212] On one level, it would be foolhardy to deny that many victims do experience deeply rooted feelings of anger and desire some measure of revenge, and, by the same token, it would be patronising to dismiss these emotions as somehow invalid or irrational. In many cases, such reactions are entirely human and worthy of acknowledgement. It would be naïve in the extreme to expect that these emotions can be easily overcome and replaced by acceptance, forgiveness and reconciliation.

While these fears of a 'reversion to the retributive, repressive and vengeful punishment of an earlier age'[213] have been subject to relatively little empirical testing, some research does appear to suggest victims would seem to be no more punitive than the general public in relation to their attitudes to sentencing by criminal courts.[214] In their evaluation of the VPS pilots, Hoyle et al found that:

> rather than . . . encouraging exaggeration, inflammatory statements, and vindictiveness, the opposite appears to apply: they [victim personal statements] tend to understate rather than over-state the impact of offences.[215]

In Chalmer's et al analysis of the content of victim statements in Scotland, statements made concerning sentence tended to be unspecific and some even displayed some concern for the offender and requested a lighter sentence.[216]

Research into victim input in restorative justice schemes also suggests that the desire for vengeance rarely features within the agendas of most victims.[217] Hoyle et al noted that many victims who attended restorative conferences were less afraid about the prospect of future victimisation.[218] Indeed they cite a number of

---

[209] See above, pp115–20.

[210] Hillenbrand and Smith (1989); Chalmers et al (2007) in the Scottish scheme. Possibilities for victims to receive compensation are considered below in Ch 5, pp226–36.

[211] Cretney and Davis (1996), 178.

[212] See eg Buruma (2004), Guastello (2005), Coen (2006).

[213] Erez et al (1997), 40.

[214] Erez and Tontodonato (1992); Hough and Park (2002); Mattinson and Mirrlees-Black (2000); Mayhew and Van Kesteren (2002).

[215] Hoyle et al (1998), 28.

[216] Chalmers et al (2007), 374.

[217] Restorative justice is explored in greater depth below at Ch 6, see pp254–65.

[218] Hoyle et al (2002).

instances where 'anger turned to sympathy'. Those victims who attended were more likely to express satisfaction with reparation and the outcome of the case and many felt that 'the process was punishment enough'. In a study examining the attitudes of victims participating in youth conferencing in Northern Ireland, Doak and O'Mahony found that the vast majority of participating victims had not attended conferences to vent anger towards the offender.[219] Rather, many victims were more interested in 'moving on' or putting the incident behind them and 'seeing something positive come out of it'.[220] The frustration and anger that was expressed was mostly clearly directed at the incident and the consequences of the crime, rather than at the offender as an individual. Victims were often angry at what had happened, but they also appeared to be able to see beyond the incident and wanted to see some good come out of the whole thing. Many victims (77 per cent) even expressed a degree of empathy towards the offender. These findings broadly correlate with research conducted by Strang,[221] who reported that significantly more victims felt angry with the offender before the conference (63 per cent) than after it (29 per cent); conversely more victims felt sympathetic to the offender after the conference (48 per cent) than beforehand (19 per cent).

Far from seeking vengeance, research seems to suggest that most victims prioritise restitution or compensation over retribution and many display a desire to help the offender. Of course, the major caveat in relation to most of the research discussed above is that it was carried out within restorative processes. A curious paradox is that victim input is considered appropriate for restorative justice but not within conventional sentencing frameworks.[222] There would seem to be a distinct lack of cross-applicability to the arguments that have been used to support or oppose victim participation across the conventional / restorative divide. Whilst there are clear differences between the conventional and restorative paradigms, they also have a considerable degree in common. Both involve the assignment of responsibility and some degree of shaming; both place some value upon proportionality; both aspire to be accountable and legitimate in the eyes of the community; and both processes have been justified in terms of truth-finding. Although some commentators hold the view that restorative mechanisms should only be used in very particular circumstances (ie where petty crime or young offenders are involved) and, as such, should remain on the periphery of the criminal justice system,[223] the merits of victim participation suggest they should have a wider and more general application. Whether participating within a restorative or punitive sentencing arrangement, it is suggested that the theoretical argument for excluding victims on the basis that they may be overly punitive is fundamentally flawed.

Even if (contrary to the weight of research), victims were found to be particularly vengeful, it seems that victims' statements only have a minimal impact upon

---

[219] Doak and O'Mahony (2006).
[220] *Ibid*, 169.
[221] Strang (2002). 102.
[222] Sanders et al (2001).
[223] See eg Ashworth (1993a); Hudson (1998).

sentencers. In their interviews with judges, Chalmers et al found that many found it difficult to isolate the effect of the victim impact statement from the vast array of other factors that were built into the sentencing equation, though the researchers do note a number of incidents where judges were minded to 'consider a sentence of a different nature from the one they were initially minded to impose'.[224] Similar findings were uncovered by Erez and Tontodonato in South Australia.[225]

Admittedly, objections to victim input statements are not solely based around the myth of the vengeful victim. The idea that the use of victim impact statements is fundamentally inconsistent with the traditional rationales underlying sentencing has resulted in significant levels of scepticism within some quarters.[226] In particular, concerns have been addressed as to whether it is legitimate for sentences to vary in accordance with the potentially unforeseeable results of an offender's conduct (ie how an individual victim may respond).[227] It is feared that victim participation, particularly within the sentencing process, could introduce a new and unpredictable variable into the penalty equation and would jeopardise core principles such as 'just-deserts', certainty and objectivity. Such objections are concisely summarised in the following passage by Morgan et al:

> Most victims will lack knowledge of either the options available to the court or the wider policy considerations which must be considered in sentencing, which is supposed to reflect the moral wrong suffered by the violation of societal rules and the personal responsibility and moral guilt of the offender. Any large increase in victims' rights in sentencing might destroy this relationship; interfere with the objective decision of sentencers; and blur the difference between civil wrong and crime.[228]

The supremacy afforded to the collective interests over and above those of individual victims is justified primarily on the basis that crime is harmful to society, and that the penal measures imposed by the court are thereby conceived of as an official denunciation of the offender's wrongdoing. It is also considered vital to sideline the subjective desires of individual victims in order to maintain objectivity, consistency, and hence the overall legitimacy of the criminal justice system. From Ashworth's point of view, there is no specific rationale for conferring locus standi upon victims at the sentencing stage of proceedings:

> just because a person commits an offence against me . . . that does not privilege my voice above that of the court in the matters of the offender's punishment.[229]

Thus, many purists like Ashworth perceive a real risk in compromising the key values and objectives of the criminal justice system in order to recognise the validity

---

[224] See eg Ashworth (1993a); Hudson (1998), 376.
[225] Erez and Tontodonato (1992).
[226] See eg Abramovsky (1992); Dugger (1996); Ashworth (2000).
[227] Hall (1991); Ashworth (1993b), (2000); Buruma (2004).
[228] Morgan *et al* (1996), 315.
[229] Ashworth (2002), 585.

of furthering private interests.[230] This argument has also tended to prevail in the higher courts, as is illustrated in the following dictum of Judge LJ in *R v Nunn*:[231]

> We mean no disrespect to the mother and sister of the deceased, but the opinions of the victim, or the surviving members of the family, about the appropriate level of sentence do not provide any sound basis for reassessing a sentence. If the victim feels utterly merciful towards the criminal, and some do, the crime has still been committed and must be punished as it deserves. If the victim is obsessed with vengeance, which can in reality only be assuaged by a very long sentence, as also happens, the punishment cannot be made longer by the court than would otherwise be appropriate. Otherwise cases with identical features would be dealt with in widely differing ways, leading to improper and unfair disparity, and even in this particular case . . . the views of the members of the family of the deceased are not absolutely identical.[232]

While unpredictable variations in sentence would lead to a lack of certainty and a discernable interference with the rights of the accused, this argument tends to exaggerate the extent to which the consequences are likely to be unforeseen.[233] The very basis of the vast body of the criminal law is that we all can, to some extent, envisage the broad consequences of our actions, including how they might impact upon a victim. Fenwick suggests a compromise between due process and the victim's interests could be facilitated whereby sentencing could be influenced by a victim statement:

> only where a reasonable person endowed with the defendant's knowledge of the victim would find that the actual consequences of the offence were within the range of probable consequences.[234]

This test, it is submitted, should be capable of addressing the concerns expressed about the potentially negative impact of victim statements upon the rights of the accused. In addition, however, it should be borne in mind that few proponents of victim statements argue that the desires of the victim should prevail at all costs. In those cases where victims are making demands that appear to be overly punitive or unreasonable, the sentencer should always be able to exercise some form of veto. Judges are, after all, trained to disregard evidence that is irrelevant.[235] The interests of the victims are but one factor that ought to be taken into account alongside a range of other factors, including the seriousness of the offence, the threat posed to the public, and any circumstances in mitigation. The point being made is simply that private interests should not be considered alien to public processes.

---

[230] See eg Ashworth (1986), 86; (1998), 32; Garland (1990), 252; Von Hirsh (1993), 6.

[231] *R v Nunn* [1996] 2 Cr App R (S) *136.*

[232] *Ibid*, 140.

[233] See further Fenwick (1997).

[234] *Ibid*, at 330. The only exception to this principle envisaged by Fenwick would arise where the defendant had some clear impairment such as mental handicap, rendering him or her incapable of foreseeing matters which might arise from the offence.

[235] Roberts and Erez (2004), 237.

A further problem for this purist conception of the function of the criminal justice system lies in the fact that whatever the historical explanations for the de facto distinctions between public and private realms of law, the distinction has been artificial since its inception during the Middle Ages.[236] Indeed, a closer look at the actual nature of individual crimes and torts suggests that it is not so easy to neatly separate the public from the private interests. As Smith and Hogan note, crimes, as opposed to torts, can be defined as wrongs which Parliament or the courts have deemed to be 'sufficiently injurious to the public to warrant the application of criminal procedure to deal with them',[237] but the real issue, as Frehsee contends, is whether such separations of doctrine can 'ultimately be found in the measure of whether our stated aims and purposes have been achieved in practice'.[238] Civil and criminal liability are each based on overlapping concepts of fault and recklessness and strict liability,[239] and many crimes have their equivalent in the law of tort.[240] As Weisstub has argued, public and private wrongs may be conceived as variations along the same continuum of fault,[241] a theoretical blurring already reflected in a number of ways on both the domestic and international platforms. If concepts such as 'harm', 'reparation' and 'punishment' are viewed through a different lens, it may be that the sentencing objectives of the court could also take into account the restitutionary interests of the victim, without jeopardising the objectivity or denunciatory aspects of the penal system. This issue is revisited in Chapter 5, where it is argued that we should actively consider shifting the focus of our criminal justice system so that punishment and reparation cease being viewed as discrete entities, which are incapable of being mutually delivered within the same system.[242]

IV. Conclusions

Trends in both international human rights law and international criminal justice suggest that victim participation is increasingly viewed as a desirable value for the administration of the criminal process. It may not only help the victim feel less alienated, but may also enhance the legitimacy of pre-trial, trial and sentencing processes in the eyes of both victims and the public. This position reflects an increasingly popular view that crime should not just be conceptualised as an offence against the state, but also in terms of the harm it causes to individual victims and communities.[243]

[236] See Ch 1, pp2–4.
[237] Smith and Hogan (2005), 12.
[238] Frehsee (1999), 243.
[239] Goldstein (1982), 530.
[240] Sebba (1997), 399.
[241] Weisstub (1986), 206.
[242] See below Ch 5.
[243] See Ch 6, p253.

However, the dimensions of any 'right to participation' are still extremely vague: international standards give us little indication of the *extent* to which victims ought to be able to participate, or how far their views should hold sway. Furthermore, the instruments make little distinction about what form participation may take, and whether it should be inherent throughout the pre-trial, trial and sentencing arrangements, or whether it only ought to be applied in relation to a few specified processes. Unfortunately, this lack of clarity means that, as things currently stand, we cannot truly speak of a 'right to participation' as constituting a benchmark of international good practice. While its parameters remain so loosely defined, even the fact that the participation is enshrined as a value to be cherished in both the EU Framework Decision and Strasbourg jurisprudence,[244] as well as the ICC, is largely inconsequential for victims.

The reasons for this apparent lack of certainty are twofold. First, different legal traditions conceptualise participation and the normative role of victims in vastly different ways. While, as the previous chapter suggested, there is a broader and more defined consensus as to certain levels of protection to which victims ought to be entitled, the same cannot be said about participatory rights. Adversarial theory dictates that victims are simply the witnesses for the prosecution; inquisitorial systems view the victims' reparatory interests as a legitimate concern of the criminal hearing.[245] The second reason for a lack of concrete standards stems from the lack of consensus as to what 'participation' actually entails. As Edwards suggests, we ought to take time to reflect upon the various forms of participation. Participation does not necessarily infer an input into decision-making, let alone any form of veto over the process. Rather it can take a range of forms from a very limited expressive role to a key decision-making role. It may be undertaken orally (either in person, or through a lawyer), or in written form. It is suggested that it is not particularly useful to either promote or denigrate the concept of victim participation without being very specific as to (a) the particular form of participation we are advocating / criticising and (b) the basis on which we are doing so. For the debate to start shedding more light than heat, it is suggested that a measured approach is taken that takes into account international developments and what is perceived to work well in other jurisdictions. In addition, we need to clarify in our own minds a principled and specific framework whereby we can take account of the victim's legitimate interests alongside those of the general public and the defendant.

In time, a point of consensus may well be reached, but until then a period of theoretical reflection on the respective roles of the victim, the offender and the State may help both national and international orders acquire a better understanding of some of the reasons for the traditional exclusion of victims. Logically, it seems that the norms that underpin criminal justice, along with their accompanying structures and processes, ought to reflect the fact that crime impacts first

---

[244] These standards being particularly significant in so far as they are directly applicable within domestic courts.
[245] See Ch 6, pp272–4.

and foremost upon its direct victims. This is not to deny the legitimate public interest in punishing crime and reducing offending, but it is desirable that the structures of criminal justice, as well as their theoretical bases, should reflect the interests of individual victims as well as the broader interests of the state. The challenge that confronts both international and domestic policymakers is to review existing criminal justice structures and procedures to ascertain whether these frameworks can be adjusted to facilitate victim participation, whilst at the same time preserving judicial oversight to protect core due process values.

As ceded by Sanders et al, 'victim participation of some kind is here to stay',[246] and we can expect international norms to become increasingly prescriptive in future years. This presents a challenge, which, in time, adversarial jurisdictions will have to confront. As things stand in the domestic order, the Government's expressed aspiration that they 'want victims to be heard properly and fully in court'[247] remains a very distant prospect. The introduction of the Victim Personal Statement Scheme and, more recently, victim advocates, does indicate that the opportunities for participation are, however, slowly improving—at least in the arena of sentencing. However, a right to participation throughout the criminal justice system, and, in particular, at the trial stage of proceedings, is fundamentally impossible to realise in a meaningful way within the existing parameters of the adversarial framework. The entire paradigm is in need of a radical overhaul in order to fully accommodate a participatory model of justice.

---

[246] Sanders et al (2001), 448.
[247] Department of Constitutional Affairs (2005), 3.

4

The Right to Justice

THE NEXT TWO chapters consider the idea of a 'right to a remedy' for victims. The phrase is frequently used in human rights discourse, although its
precise meaning is somewhat unclear. Seemingly, it is often used as an
umbrella term, comprising various constituent elements that are broadly concerned with rectifying wrongs. In this sense, Shelton suggests that the concept of a
'remedy' may be understood to refer to 'the range of measures that may be taken
in response to an actual or threatened violation of human rights'.[1] These measures
can be largely classified under two broad headings. First, there are those elements
that are concerned with general and procedural forms of redress, such as the
obligation on the state not only to prevent crime,[2] but also to respond to crime in
terms of putting in place systems of investigation, prosecution and punishment.
Secondly, there is a range of remedies that is more substantive in nature and
focused on providing redress to individual victims. This second category of remedies is often referred to by human rights lawyers as 'reparation', and typically
includes both 'material' and 'moral' measures such as compensation, restitution,
rehabilitation, and satisfaction, etc. The right to reparation will form the basis of
the next chapter. This chapter focuses on the general and procedural obligations
of the state in the aftermath of a criminal offence. From a victim's perspective,
such obligations may be collectively labelled a 'right to justice'.

I. International Standards

Several international and regional human rights instruments stipulate the duty to
provide a remedy for human rights violations. Such instruments tend to guarantee both a procedural right to access investigatory procedures, as well as a substantive right to a remedy. While certain instruments give formal and express
recognition to very specific components of these rights, case law has also had a key
role to play in developing them as corollaries to other substantive rights or general
obligations. It is evident that the idea of a remedy has undergone significant development in recent years, and has increasingly been viewed as dovetailing with the

---

[1] Shelton (1999), 4.
[2] See discussion in Ch 2, pp39–44.

more specific duties to carry out a full and effective investigation and uncover the truth of past events. The interconnectivity between these duties is reflected in a range of international instruments and decisions, which underscore the fact that human rights in themselves are largely declaratory and ineffective without a corresponding mechanism of enforcement.

International Human Rights Law

The right to a remedy at international level was first formulated in 1948 as part of the Universal Declaration of Human Rights. Article 8 of the Declaration noted that everyone:

> has the right to an effective remedy by the competent national tribunals for acts violating the fundamental rights granted him by the constitution or by law.

Since then, the concept of a remedy has been included in a vast array of instruments.

Article 2(3) of the International Covenant on Civil and Political Rights requires states to ensure that:

> any person whose rights or freedoms as herein recognized are violated shall have an effective remedy, notwithstanding that the violation has been committed by persons acting in an official capacity

and to provide compensation for unlawful detention or wrongful conviction. It will be recalled from Chapter 2 that human rights instruments have increasingly placed specific obligations on states concerning the scope and remit of their criminal law.[3] For example, under Article 4(1) of the Convention Against Torture, State parties are obliged to ensure that all acts of torture, attempts to commit torture, as well as complicity or participation in torture, are classed as criminal offences under domestic law. Article 4(2) notes that the State parties 'shall make these offences punishable by appropriate penalties which take into account their grave nature'. However, as noted above, the obligation to criminalise certain forms of behaviour would be largely ineffective without appropriate enforcement mechanisms. Thus, Article 12 of CAT provides that:

> each State Party shall ensure that its competent authorities proceed to a prompt and impartial investigation, wherever there is reasonable ground to believe that an act of torture has been committed in any territory under its jurisdiction.

The individual right to make a complaint is contained in Article 13, which stipulates that:

> each State Party shall ensure that any individual who alleges he has been subject to torture in any territory under its jurisdiction has the right to complain, and to have his case promptly and impartially examined by its competent authorities

[3] See Ch 2, pp42–4.

and Article 14 specifies that states must ensure that victims are able to take legal actions for 'an enforceable right to fair and adequate compensation'.

Similar provisions can be located in many other treaties both within, and beyond, human rights law. Under international humanitarian law, the Convention on the Prevention and Punishment of the Crime of Genocide imposes a duty on contracting parties to prevent, prosecute, punish and provide for effective penalties for instances of genocide.[4] Under the Geneva Conventions[5] and the first Additional Protocol of 1977,[6] states involved in international conflicts are subject to a duty to prosecute and punish perpetrators of 'grave breaches' including torture, inhuman treatment, and depriving civilians of due process rights. Returning to the field of human rights law, the recently adopted International Convention for the Protection of All Persons from Enforced Disappearance[7] stipulates that each State party should take appropriate measures to investigate instances of enforced disappearances,[8] and ensure that enforced disappearance constitutes an offence under its criminal law.[9] Obligations on states to criminalise, investigate and pursue human rights breaches may also be found, inter alia, in the Convention on the Elimination of All Forms of Discrimination against Women,[10] the Convention on the Elimination of Racial Discrimination[11] and the Convention on the Rights of the Child.[12]

The jurisprudence of the UN Human Rights Committee has also played a key role in widening the idea of a remedy. While its jurisdiction only covers alleged infractions of the ICCPR,[13] the case law has, like that of the other bodies detailed below, helped to build a more comprehensive understanding as to what the idea of a remedy may entail. In a General Comment released in 1982 on Article 7 ICCPR, which prohibits torture and cruel, inhuman and degrading treatment and punishment, the Committee asserted that the Article should be read alongside the right to a remedy contained in Article 2, and proceeded to note that:

> States must ensure an effective protection through some machinery of control. Complaints about ill-treatment must be investigated effectively by competent authorities. Those found guilty must be held responsible, and the alleged victims must themselves have effective remedies at their disposal, including the right to obtain compensation.[14]

---

[4] GA/RES/260 A (III), Arts 1, 4 and 5.

[5] Art 49 of Geneva Convention (I) 75 UNTS 31; Art 50 of Geneva Convention (II) 75 UNTS 85; Art 129 of Geneva Convention (III) 75 UNTS 135; and Art 146 of Geneva Convention (IV) 75 UNTS 28.

[6] Art 85 of Additional Protocol II.

[7] E/CN.4/2005/WG.22/WP.1/REV.4.

[8] Art 3.

[9] Art 4. Such an offence must also be subject to punishment under the law—Art 7.

[10] See Arts 2(b) and 2(c).

[11] Art 6.

[12] Art 39.

[13] The Covenant contains a procedure whereby individuals claiming a violation of the Covenant's provisions may bring a complaint against a state before the Human Rights Committee. However, this provision is only accessible to the victim if the state has accepted the jurisdiction of the Committee through adopting the Optional Protocol to the Covenant.

[14] 37 UN GAOR Supp. (No 40) at 94, UN Doc No A/37/40 (1982).

This Comment reflects what has been noted above; the right to a remedy is composed of a number of distinct and separate elements. The relatively broad scope of the idea of a remedy has been affirmed in a number of cases before the Committee, many of which stemmed from allegations of arbitrary arrests, deaths, torture, and disappearances in Uruguay during the late 1970s. In *Hugo Rodriguez v Uruguay*,[15] a case concerning alleged torture and maltreatment, the Committee rejected the Uruguayan submission that domestic remedies had not been exhausted, and stated that the fact that no criminal investigation had been undertaken amounted to an impediment to the applicant's ability to pursue domestic remedies. Article 2(3) imposed an obligation on the state to carry out a criminal investigation where an allegation of torture or ill-treatment had been made: this was a core part of the idea of an effective remedy.[16]

Similarly, in *Bleier v Uruguay*,[17] which concerned the alleged forced disappearance of Eduardo Bleier, the Committee found that the government was under an obligation:

> to take effective steps (i) to establish what has happened to the missing person since October 1975; to bring to justice any persons found to be responsible for his death, disappearance or ill-treatment; and to pay compensation to him or his family for any injury which he has suffered; and (ii) to ensure that similar violations do not occur in the future.[18]

Past decisions of the Committee also make it clear that compensation payments by themselves are an inadequate remedy in cases involving allegations of serious human rights abuses. In such circumstances, some form of criminal sanction should be in order. *Bautista v Columbia* concerned the alleged abduction, torture, and murder of a man by armed men posing as civilians.[19] Despite the fact that the national *Procuraduría Delegado* for Human Rights found that two military officials were responsible for the disappearance of Bautista, the victim's family was offered only monetary damages. Only one of the two officials was dismissed from his post, and neither was subject to criminal proceedings. Noting that these penalties were wholly inadequate, the Committee stated that 'purely disciplinary and administrative remedies cannot be deemed to constitute adequate and effective remedies' within the meaning of Article 2(3) of ICCPR.[20] The state was under a duty to:

---

[15] Comm No 322/1988 (1994).

[16] Moreover, it was stressed that States may not deprive individuals of the right to an effective remedy, including compensation and such full rehabilitation as may be possible. See also *Laureano v Perú*, Comm No 540/1993 (1996), where it was stated that 'state parties should also take specific and effective measures to prevent the disappearance of individuals and establish effective facilities and procedures to investigate thoroughly, by an appropriate and impartial body, cases of missing and disappeared persons in circumstances which may involve a violation of the right to life' [8.3].

[17] Comm No 30/1978 (1992).

[18] *Ibid*, [15]. That obligation to investigate would come into effect in the event of 'substantial witness testimony'—[13.3].

[19] Comm No 563/1993 (1995).

[20] At [8.2]. A host of other cases before the HRC illustrate the obligation of the state to investigate and establish the truth behind past events. See *Dermit Barbato v Uruguay*, Comm No 84/1981 (1983), *Muteba v Zaire*, Comm No 124/1982, (1984); *Laureano v Peru* 540/1993 (1996); *Zelaya v Nicaragua*, Comm No 328/1988, (1994).

investigate thoroughly alleged violations of human rights, and, in particular, forced disappearances of persons and violations of the right to life, and to prosecute criminally, try and punish those held responsible for such violations.[21]

The requirement to prosecute reflects the findings in *Rodriquez v Uruguay* that amnesty laws which prevent prosecutions of serious human rights violations are incompatible with the duty of States to investigate acts of torture and to ensure that they do not occur in the future.[22] In cases involving disappearances and other violations of the right to life, administrative steps and the payment of compensation do not adequately reflect the gravity of the crime.[23]

Undoubtedly the most significant attempt to specify the rights of victims in relation to remedial action is contained in the Basic Principles and Guidelines on the Right to a Remedy and Reparation of Victims of Violations of International Human Rights and Humanitarian Law.[24] The background and the scope of the Principles are discussed in the subsequent chapter,[25] but it is worth noting at this juncture that they represent the culmination of a longstanding process to codify the rights of victims. The Special Rapporteurs on the right to restitution, compensation and rehabilitation, Theo Van Boven and Cherif Bassiouni, whose work lay behind the formulation of the principles, all highlighted the importance of the victims' right to know the truth and to hold the perpetrators accountable in their respective reports. In terms of the instrument itself, Principle 3 outlines the obligation on states to:

(a) take appropriate legislative and administrative and other appropriate measures to prevent violations (b) investigate violations effectively, promptly, thoroughly and impartially and, where appropriate, take action against those allegedly responsible in accordance with domestic and international law (c) provide those who claim to be victims of a human rights or humanitarian law violation with equal and effective access to justice . . . irrespective of who may ultimately be the bearer of responsibility for the violation; and (d) provide effective remedies to victims, including reparation.

It is thus widely accepted that states have a duty to investigate alleged human rights violations and to prosecute and punish perpetrators. However, ideas of a 'right to a remedy' have, by in large, been confined to discourses concerning victims of human rights abuses. Such language is not as widely reflected in the international standards that purport to deal either wholly or substantially with victims of non-state crime. It is a matter of some regret that the recently ratified Basic Principles and Guidelines on the Right to a Remedy and Reparation of Victims of Violations

---

[21] However, the Committee added at [8.6] that 'the Covenant does not provide a right for individuals to require that the State criminally prosecute another person'. See previous decisions in *HCMA v the Netherlands*, Comm No 213/1986 (1989) at [11.6]; *SE v Argentina*, Comm No 275/1988 (1990) at [5.5].

[22] *Hugo Rodriguez v Uruguay*, above n 15, [12.3]; *Laureano v Peru*, above n 16, [10].

[23] See also *Arhuacos v Colombia*, Comm. No 612/1995, UN Doc CCPR/C/60/D/612/1995 (1997), [8.8].

[24] UN Doc A/RES/60/147.

[25] See Ch 5, pp213–16.

of International Human Rights and Humanitarian Law departed from the example set by the earlier 1985 Declaration in failing to cover victims of non-state
crime. The instrument does make reference to the 1985 Declaration, and the
principles contained therein are broadly reflected. However, despite reconciling
victims of violations of both human rights and humanitarian law, the 2000
Declaration does not expressly extend the rights contained within it to victims of
non-state crime. While it may be legitimate to speak of a soft law basis for mainstreaming key principles such as 'restitution' and 'satisfaction' in relation to
victims of human rights / humanitarian law violations, these principles do not
apply to victims of non-state crime.

Within the 1985 Declaration, we read that all types of victims 'should be treated
with compassion and respect for their dignity' and 'are entitled to access to the
mechanisms of justice and to prompt redress'.[26] The ambiguity of this particular
principle leaves considerable leeway for interpretation. There is certainly no
express provision in the Declaration that refers to anything close to a duty on the
state to investigate, prosecute and punish crime or uncover the truth about past
events.

These standards are thus not only inadequate, but they are also problematic
insofar as they are unenforceable. Unfortunately, the EU Framework Decision,
which is legally binding on all member states, does not impose any obligation on
states to investigate, prosecute or punish crime. The concept of a remedy would
seem to be limited to the requirements concerning legal aid, compensation and
penal mediation,[27] but the instrument has very little to say on questions regarding
criminal investigation or prosecution.

Progressing the Concept

The constituent components of a right to a remedy have been expatiated in much
greater depth by regional human rights courts. Neither the European nor the
American Human Rights treaties include any express obligation on the State to
investigate alleged killings or acts of torture. Nevertheless, recent years have seen
the scope of positive obligations in relation to the right to life and its correlating
duties rapidly unfold through the case law.

Under the Inter-American Convention, Article 8, which safeguards the right to
a fair trial, has been used to secure guarantees of fairness and participation for
victims in addition to the overall duties laid down in Article 1 and the right to a
remedy in Article 25. The seminal case of *Velasquez-Rodriguez v Honduras* concerned the arrest, torture and subsequent execution of a student activist by the
Honduran military.[28] Having denied any involvement in his killing, the student's

---

[26] 1985 Declaration, Principle 4.
[27] See Ch 5, p225.
[28] (1989) 28 ILM 291. See Ch 2, p42.

family alleged violations of the rights to life, to humane treatment, and to personal liberty. Finding in their favour, the Inter-American Court of Human Rights concluded that the inclusion of the phrase 'ensure all persons' in Article 1(1) of the American Convention of Human Rights constituted a duty on signatory states to investigate, prosecute and punish violations of Convention standards:

> The State has a legal duty to take reasonable steps to prevent human rights violations and to use the means at its disposal to carry out a serious investigation of violations committed within its jurisdiction; to identify those responsible; to impose the appropriate punishment and to ensure the victim adequate compensation.
>
> The duty to prevent includes all those means of a legal, political, administrative and cultural nature that promote the protection of human rights and ensure that any violations are considered and treated as illegal acts, which, as such, may lead to punishment of those responsible and the obligation to indemnify the victims for damages.[29]

In seeking to develop the scope of the duty, the Inter-American Court of Human Rights declared in the *Street Children Case* that Article 1(1) of the Convention meant:

> that the State is obliged to investigate and punish any violation of the rights embodied in the Convention in order to guarantee such rights.[30]

Thus, the State is under an obligation to investigate situations where Convention rights have allegedly been breached. If no action is taken, then the state has failed to comply with its duty. Subsequent cases have shed light on the components of an effective investigation. In many respects, the requirements reflect those under European human rights law. Criminal offences that endanger the right to life should be investigated and the perpetrators punished. Any such investigation must be prompt,[31] effective,[32] impartial,[33] open to participation by victims' families,[34] and should be used as a general means of deterring impunity and recidivism.[35]

The Nature of Procedural Obligations

It was noted in Chapter 2 that the European Court of Human Rights has been steadily developing and refining the positive obligations on signatory states following alleged killings involving state actors. In a number of cases the Court has

---

[29] At [174–5].
[30] *Villagrán Morales Case* (The 'Street Children' Case), Series C No 63 (1999), [225].
[31] *Ibid.*
[32] *Velasquez-Rodriguez*, above n 28, [174–5].
[33] *Castillo Paez*, Series C No 43 (1998), [106].
[34] *Ibid*, [105–7]; *Street Children Case*, above n 30, [227]. As Antkowiak (2002) has observed, the emphasis placed on the Inter-American Court on the need for mechanisms to involve the victim's family stems from the fact that many Latin American jurisdictions permit victims to play a significant role in the criminal process as civil parties in order to gain reparation (at 986).
[35] *Street Children Case*, above n 30, [227].

examined the combined effect of Article 13, the right to a remedy,[36] in conjunction with the general duty under Article 1 to 'secure to everyone within its jurisdiction the rights and freedoms', alongside Articles 2 (the right to life) and 3 (the right to be free from inhuman or degrading treatment). Such cases indicate that a state's violation of its Convention duties may also breach the victim's right to access an effective remedy. Thus the remedy itself must not only be effective, but so must the system that is used to obtain it.[37] As the Court noted in *Silver and Others v United Kingdom* 'where an individual has an *arguable* claim to be the victim of a violation of the rights set forth in the Convention, he should have a remedy before a national authority in order both to have his claim decided and, if appropriate, to obtain redress'.[38]

In *McCann and others v United Kingdom*,[39] which concerned the killing of three IRA members in Gibraltar in 1988, it was held that the duty on the State was not confined to protecting the right to life and guaranteeing access to remedies for victims,[40] but also required the establishment of procedures to investigate unlawful killings by the State.[41] In subsequent cases the Court has gone further, specifically outlining how investigations should proceed in order to ensure that constituent rights under Article 2 are comprehensively protected. The investigation into the death of an alleged PKK member by Turkish authorities was held to be wholly inadequate by the Court in *Mahmut Kaya v Turkey*.[42] It was argued by the applicant, the brother of the deceased, that there was evidence to suggest state collusion in the killing and that the investigation into his death was fundamentally flawed. It appeared that no attempts were made to secure statements from the soldiers at the scene of the crime; no efforts were made to secure evidence of an exchange of shots that allegedly took place; no forensic tests were carried out; and the autopsy report was deficient in a number of respects as to the precise cause of death. The Court held that such incidents 'undermined the effectiveness of the criminal

[36] Art 13 states 'Everyone whose rights and freedoms as set forth in this Convention are violated shall have an effective remedy before a national authority notwithstanding that the violation has been committed by persons acting in an official capacity'.

[37] Aldana-Pindell (2002), 1421. The Court has, however, stopped short of obliging national authorities to undertake specific remedial actions. In *Finucane v UK* (2003) 22 EHRR 29, the Court found a violation of Art 2 in respect of an investigation into a murder of a Northern Ireland solicitor where state collusion was alleged. However, the Court refused to require the UK government to mount a fresh investigation into the death, on the basis that it was not 'appropriate to do so . . . [since] the lapse of time, the effect on evidence and the availability of witnesses, may inevitably render such an investigation an unsatisfactory or inconclusive exercise, which fails to establish important facts or put to rest doubts and suspicions'. This view has been criticised by Leach (2005), arguing that it ought not to have been assumed that a future investigation would not be effective.

[38] Series A, No 44 (1983) 5 EHRR 347, [113(a)].

[39] App No 18984/91, 5 Sep 1995.

[40] See Ch 2, p40.

[41] In *McCann* itself, above n 39, the Court concluded that the inquest constituted 'a thorough, impartial and careful examination of the circumstances surrounding the killings' (at [131]). The Court was subject to some criticism in this case for failing to award damages to the victims' families, despite finding three violations of the right to life. Compensation was denied on the grounds that the victims were planning to commit a terrorist act.

[42] App No 22535/93, 28 Mar 2000. See also discussion in Ch 2, pp39–40.

law'.[43] Although 'the scope of the obligation under Article 13 varies depending on the nature of the applicant's complaints under the Convention', the right to a remedy 'must be effective in practice as well as in law, in particular in the sense that its exercise must not be unjustifiably hindered by the acts or omissions of the authorities of the respondent State'.[44]

Similarly, in *Gulec v Turkey*,[45] the applicant's son had been killed by security forces after they opened fire on a political demonstration. The Court found that the investigation was not thorough, mostly because a number of key witnesses had not been interviewed. Like the UNHRC, the Court has held that payments of compensation alone are generally insufficient remedies for victims. In *Aydin v Turkey*,[46] the Court implied the existence of the right to an effective investigation as part of the right to a remedy under Article 13:

> [W]here an individual has an arguable claim that he has been tortured by agents of the State, the notion of an 'effective remedy' entails, in addition to the payment of compensation where appropriate, a thorough and effective investigation capable of leading to the identification and punishment of those responsible and including effective access for the complainant to the investigatory procedure.[47]

There is no prescriptive list as to what steps ought to be taken to constitute a 'thorough and effective' investigation, but the *Aydin* decision implies that an investigation is not an end in itself. The investigation is clearly envisaged as a process that will lead to 'the identification and punishment of those responsible'[48] and the full extent of the investigatory duty has become more clearly defined in recent years. In *Ogur v Turkey*,[49] the Court found a violation of Article 2 on the grounds that the state had failed to inform victims' families of the decision not to prosecute. In the eyes of the Court, this failure represented an obstacle to accessing justice since it denied the next of kin the possibility of appealing or reviewing the decision. It should be the norm that relatives have full access to investigation files for this purpose.[50]

The components of an effective investigation were again examined in four joined cases taken against the United Kingdom by relatives of those killed by the security forces during the Northern Ireland conflict: *Kelly v United Kingdom*;[51] *Jordan v United Kingdom*;[52] *Shanaghan v United Kingdom*;[53] *and McKerr v United Kingdom*.[54] In a strong indictment of Northern Ireland inquest and investigation

---

[43] *Ibid*, [98].
[44] *Ibid*, [124].
[45] (1999) 28 EHRR 121.
[46] (1998) 25 EHRR 251.
[47] *Ibid*,[98].
[48] *Aydin*, [103].
[49] *Ogur v Turkey* (2001) 31 EHRR 40. See also *Gulec*, above n 45.
[50] *Ibid*, [92].
[51] App No 30054/96, 4 May 2001.
[52] App No 24746/94, 4 May 2001.
[53] App No 37715/97, 4 May 2001.
[54] App No 28883/95, 4 May 2001.

procedures, the Court upheld the vast majority of the complaints concerning severe shortcomings in a wide range of the investigatory procedures. Among the major criticisms to emerge from the judgments were the lack of independence in the police investigation;[55] a lack of public scrutiny of the investigation and very limited access for relatives;[56] security force witnesses being non-compellable to the inquests; the non-disclosure of evidence to the relatives; the lack of legal aid for relatives; the lack of prompt verdicts in the inquests;[57] the lack of prompt or effective investigation where there was evidence to suggest collusion;[58] and the lack of public reasons given by the DPP for his failure to prosecute.[59] The rationale for laying down these requirements regarding the investigation was:

> to secure the effective implementation of the domestic laws which protect the right to life and, in those cases involving State agents or bodies, to ensure their accountability for deaths occurring under their responsibility. What form of investigation will achieve those purposes may vary in different circumstances. However, whatever mode is employed, the authorities must act of their own motion, once the matter has come to their attention. They cannot leave it to the initiative of the next of kin either to lodge a formal complaint or to take responsibility for the conduct of any investigative procedures.[60]

Following its previous decision in *Kaya*, the Court concluded in *Jordan et al* that since the State had failed in its obligations of accountability, it would never be possible for the families of the victims to prove that the killings concerned were brought about by the State contrary to Article 2. The Court also dismissed the State's argument that the possibility of sufficient redress lay open to the families through the civil courts. Although the Court recognised that civil proceedings could provide a means of ascertaining the truth underlying past events and recompensing relatives, civil actions were ill-equipped to deal with the question of identification and punishment of perpetrators.[61]

It may be that the rights of victims of state crime have a much stronger legal footing through the nature of the cases that have tended to come before the European Court of Human Rights. However, the collapse of the vertical / horizontal divide in human rights law has opened the door for victims of non-state crime to have their interests protected under Articles 2 and 3 of the Convention.

---

[55] Similar criticisms were levelled at the Turkish authorities in *Gulec*, above n 45.

[56] Regarding participation of the victims' relatives, see discussion in Ch 3, pp150–51. See also *Mahmut Kaya*, above n 42, where the investigation was criticised for lacking transparency.

[57] Considerable delays were present in all 4 cases, ranging from 25 months to 4 1/2 years. See also *Finucane v UK* (2003) 22 EHRR 29, which concerned a delay of 10 years before an inquiry was opened. Delays in taking statements were also criticised in the decisions of *Mahmut Kaya*, above n 42 and *Avsar v Turkey* (2003) 37 EHRR 53.

[58] See also *Finucane, ibid,* where the inquest was criticised for failing to consider allegations of collusion.

[59] See also *Finucane*, above n 57, [82–3]. Cf *McShane v United Kingdom* (2002) 35 EHRR 23, [117–19], where the DPP gave brief reasons for his refusal to prosecute. The Court noted that these could have been challenged through means of judicial review.

[60] *Jordan*, above n 52, [105].

[61] See also *Menson v United Kingdom*, App No 47916/99, 6 May 2003.

Significantly, from the perspective of victims of non-state crime, the obligation to investigate under Article 2 extends beyond those cases where there is clear evidence that state agents were involved. In *Ergi v Turkey*,[62] it was held that Turkey had violated Article 2 by failing to launch an effective investigation, even though the Court was not satisfied beyond reasonable doubt that the victim had been killed by security forces during an anti-terrorist operation. In *Tanrikulu v Turkey*,[63] the Court noted that the:

> mere fact that the authorities were informed of the murder of the applicant's husband gave rise ipso facto to an obligation under Article 2 to carry out an effective investigation into the circumstances surrounding the death.[64]

Similarly, in *Menson v UK*,[65] it was established that there ought to be some form of official investigation where an individual had sustained life-threatening injuries in suspicious circumstances, notwithstanding the lack of any involvement by agents of the state.

It is now clear that, under the Convention, there exists an absolute duty upon the state to investigate any murder, whether or not state agents are suspected of involvement. In *McCann*, the Court had highlighted that the duty to investigate arose 'when individuals have been killed as a result of the use of force by, *inter alios*, agents of the State'.[66] The insertion of the phrase 'inter alios' implied that the duty to investigate arose irrespective of whether state agents or private parties were ultimately responsible. This view was affirmed in *Ergi v Turkey*:[67]

> This obligation is not confined to cases where it has been established that the killing was caused by an agent of the State. Nor is it decisive whether members of the deceased's family or others have lodged a formal complaint about the killing with the relevant investigatory authority. In the case under consideration, the mere knowledge of the killing on the part of the authorities gave rise *ipso facto* to an obligation under Article 2 of the Convention to carry out an effective investigation into the circumstances surrounding the death.[68]

Edwards v United Kingdom[69] is one such case, where a prisoner died as a result of an attack by the person with whom he shared a cell. Here there had been no killing or alleged killing by state agents. However, it was alleged that the prison authorities had been negligent in failing to protect his life. The Court applied the

---

[62] (2001) 32 EHRR 18.
[63] (2000) 30 EHRR 950.
[64] *Ibid,* [103].
[65] Above n 61.
[66] At [161]. Likewise, in *Cakici v Turkey*, Decision of the Court, 8 Jul 1999 (App No 23657/94), the obligations under Art 2 were held to extend to situations where it was unclear that agents of the state were responsible for the death of the victim, an alleged member of the PKK, who was killed in suspicious circumstances in 1995.
[67] (2001) 32 EHRR 18.
[68] *Ibid,* [82]. See also *Salman v Turkey* (2002) 34 EHRR 17, where the Court stated the 'the obligation . . . [to conduct an effective investigation] is not confined to cases where it is apparent that the killing was caused by an agent of the State' (at [105]).
[69] (2002) 35 EHRR 487. See Ch 2, pp43–4.

same principles as it had done in *Jordan,* in determining whether an 'effective investigation' was carried out in this case. In finding in favour of the applicants, the Court determined that the State had breached its positive obligations under Article 2, and had violated the right to a remedy in Article 13.[70] Similarly, in *Menson v United Kingdom,*[71] the Court referred to the requirements of an effective investigation as laid down in *Jordan et al.* It proceeded to note that:

> [T]he absence of any direct State responsibility for the death of Michael Menson does not exclude the applicability of Article 2 . . . Although there was no State involvement . . . the Court considers that the above-mentioned basic procedural requirements apply with equal force to the conduct of an investigation into a life-threatening attack on an individual regardless of whether or not death results.[72]

It would thus appear that the investigatory requirements of Article 2 apply to investigations of murders whether or not state actors have allegedly been involved. However, the investigatory requirements have also been found to exist in relation to Article 3 of the Convention. In *Assenov and Others v Bulgaria,*[73] a Romany teenager alleged that he had been beaten whilst detained in police custody on suspicion of illegal gambling charges. The Court stated that, where credible evidence exists that a person has been mistreated in police custody, then there is an inherent obligation on the state under Article 3 of the Convention to carry out a full and independent investigation:

> The Court considers that . . . where an individual raises an arguable claim that he has been seriously ill-treated by the police or other such agents of the State unlawfully and in breach of Article 3, that provision, read in conjunction with the State's general duty under Article 1 of the Convention to 'secure to everyone within their jurisdiction the rights and freedoms defined in . . . [the] Convention', requires by implication that there should be an effective official investigation. This investigation, as with that under Article 2, should be capable of leading to the identification and punishment of those responsible.

Despite an apparent temporary retreat from the *Assenov* requirements in the subsequent decision of *Ilhan v Turkey,*[74] the Court has since reaffirmed the existence of investigative obligations in relation to all situations that pass the Article 3 threshold.[75] However, the scope of the investigatory obligations under Article 3 is

---

[70] The Court found in favour of the applicants: the State had breached the deceased's right to life in failing to effect a proper investigation.

[71] App No 47916/99, 6 May 2003.

[72] *Ibid,* [1]. Here, the Court found that there had been no breach of the state's investigative duty. The complaint was held to be manifestly ill-founded.

[73] (1999) 28 EHRR 652.

[74] (2002) 34 EHRR 36. See related commentary in Mowbray (2004), 61–2.

[75] See eg *Veznedaroglu v Turkey,* (App No 32357/96, 11 Apr 2000); and *Afanasyev v Ukraine* (App No 38722/02, 5 April 2005), where it was noted that the 'state is responsible for the welfare of persons in detention and that the authorities have a duty to protect such persons. Bearing in mind the authorities' obligation to account for injuries caused to persons under their control, the Court considers that failure to find State agents guilty of a crime of violence against a detainee, as in the instant case, cannot absolve the State of its responsibility under the Convention' (at [64]). For a good overview of the case law relating to the expansion of positive obligations to cover Art 3 procedural breaches, see Mowbray (2004), 59–65.

not as clear as those under Article 2, and may, in fact, be narrower. The above passage refers specifically to state actors, and it is thus open to question whether positive obligations under Article 3 would be applicable to non-state actors whose actions cross the threshold. Certainly, it may be speculated that there are certain circumstances where it would also be applicable to injuries caused by non-state actors. Had the facts in *Edwards* been not quite so tragic, perhaps the UK prison authorities would have then been in breach of Article 3, as opposed to Article 2, of the Convention.

In summary then, over a period of time the European Court has gradually developed and clarified the extent of the investigatory obligation under Articles 2 and 3 of the Convention. In doing so, it has given an indication of key components of an effective right to a remedy. However, while the duty to investigate and prosecute probably extends to violations of Articles 2 and 3 by non-state actors, it may not extend beyond this. Thus these obligations may not be replicated where less drastic violations are concerned.[76] Nonetheless, where the relevant thresholds have been met, it is clear that immediate and effective action is required on the part of state authorities. The State is under a positive obligation to prevent crime that risks infringing Article 2 or 3 rights; to undertake a thorough investigation of such infractions; and, if warranted, to press charges. While a specific mode of investigation is not prescribed, the investigation must be open to public scrutiny and involve the next of kin.[77] The criminal investigation should also be independent, effective, and reasonably prompt. Reasons should be given for any failure to prosecute.

II. The Right to a Remedy in the Domestic Legal Order

Taking these international standards into account, this section considers the extent to which these remedies are provided for in the domestic criminal justice system. However, it should be noted from the outset that, de jure, the rights contained in the Convention are directly applicable to the domestic legal order through the Human Rights Act. One notable exception is the right to a remedy itself. Article 13 of the Convention was not incorporated into domestic law under the Act, although the domestic courts have already accepted that the concept of a remedy is certainly inherent in both Articles 2 and 3.[78] Furthermore, section 6(2) of the HRA makes it illegal for public bodies to act in a way which is incompatible with a Convention right, and it is therefore clear that the legislation has the

---

[76] See further below, p174.

[77] See also *Edwards*, above n 69, where the ECHR held that the private inquiry had been insufficient for the state to discharge its duty where there was no power to compel witnesses and the family were unable to attend for all the proceedings or to ask questions.

[78] See eg *R v A; R (Anderson) v Secretary of State for the Home Department* [2003] 1 AC 837; *R (Middleton) v West Somerset Coroner* [2004] 2 WLR 800 (discussed below).

potential to impact significantly upon police investigations, coroners' inquests and public inquiries that may be set up in the aftermath of a killing.

Much of the post-HRA domestic law in this field stems from cases involving deaths in custody. Where this occurs, the Coroners Act 1988 requires a coroner to hold an inquest with a jury.[79] However, such courts are generally restrictive in nature, and only issue short verdicts without detailed reasoning. Furthermore, coroners cannot make recommendations and the scope of their investigation is generally agreed to be narrow. The principal case is *R v Secretary of State for the Home Department, ex parte Amin*,[80] which concerned the death of a young offender who had been beaten to death by his cellmate in custody. In the leading speech, Lord Bingham confirmed that the European Court of Human Rights in *Jordan v UK* and *Edwards v UK* had laid down minimum standards for Article 2 investigations, 'which must be met, whatever form the investigation takes'.[81] Having reviewed these requirements, their Lordships affirmed that the duty to instigate an effective and impartial investigation arose where an individual had been killed by an agent of the state or there was suspicion that the state had failed in its positive obligation to protect his life. Holding that an internal inquiry by the Prison Service was insufficient to discharge the Article 2 duty, Lord Bingham noted the rationale which underpinned Article 2 requirements:

> The purposes of such an investigation are clear: to ensure so far as possible that the full facts are brought to light; that culpable and discreditable conduct is exposed and brought to public notice; that suspicion of deliberate wrongdoing (if unjustified) is allayed; that dangerous practices and procedures are rectified; and that those who have lost their relative may at least have the satisfaction of knowing that lessons learned from his death may save the lives of others.[82]

The need for such an investigation was:

> to promote those interlocking aims: to minimise the risk of future like deaths; to give the beginnings of justice to the bereaved; to assuage the anxieties of the public.[83]

It is noted below that ideas of 'satisfaction' and 'truth' feature prominently in international human rights discourse, though perhaps less so under the ECHR jurisprudence than other forums. Interestingly, Lord Bingham here seems to acknowledge that part of the rationale for implementing Article 2 rights is to ensure some form of moral redress is made available to the victim's relatives.

The subsequent House of Lords' decision of *R (Middleton) v West Somerset Coroner*,[84] elaborated on the extent of the duty in its particular application to coroners' inquests. Lord Bingham observed that the European Court of Human Rights had imposed a:

---

[79] Coroners Act 1988, ss 8(1)(c), 8(3)(a).
[80] [2004] 1 AC 653.
[81] *Ibid*, [32].
[82] *Ibid*, 672.
[83] *Amin*, [53–4].
[84] [2004] 2 WLR 800.

procedural obligation to initiate an effective public investigation by an independent official body into any death occurring in circumstances in which it appears that one or other of the foregoing substantive obligations has been, or may have been, violated and it appears that agents of the state are, or may be, in some way implicated.[85]

In order to ensure that the investigation was fully effective and independent, their Lordships held that a jury's remit to decide the question of 'how' a prisoner died under the Coroners' Act 1988 should be extended 'by what means and in what circumstances' to enable jurors to examine the entire circumstances of a death. Thus, section 3 of the Human Rights Act 1998 was invoked to broaden the scope of the inquest so that the question of 'how' the death occurred should be interpreted to mean not just 'by what means' but should also include 'in what circumstances'.

The Article 2 requirements were applied in the context of a 'near-miss' in *R (D) v Secretary of State for the Home Department*.[86] Following the attempted suicide of a prisoner which resulted in extensive brain damage, the Court of Appeal held that the Article 2 requirements extended to mounting an effective investigation of the circumstances in which life threatening injuries were sustained. An investigation by the Police and Prisons Ombudsman would not suffice in such circumstances for the purposes of Article 2. In determining whether a public hearing was needed, a number of factors should be taken into account. These included whether the prisoner was known to be a suicide risk, seriousness of the incident and its consequences, and whether more could have been done. Ultimately each case must turn on its own particular facts.

It has, however, been established that the investigatory requirements only apply to those cases where the death occurred after 2 October 2000, when the Human Rights Act took effect. In *Re McKerr*,[87] the House of Lords held the requirements did not carry retrospective effect. The Court distinguished between rights arising directly under the articles of the Convention and rights created by the HRA as a result of incorporation. Whilst the former only 'existed before the enactment of the HRA and they continue to exist', the latter only 'came into existence for the first time on 2 October 2000'.[88] Thus, there was no obligation to hold an Article 2-compliant investigation where the death itself did not fall within the ambit of section 6 of the Human Rights Act.[89]

A further limitation upon the potential for victims to rely on the investigatory duties stems from the fact that the parameters of the duty are not entirely clear. Neither European nor domestic case law indicates the precise threshold for when the duty will come into play. While the duty to investigate and prosecute probably extends to violations of Articles 2 and 3 by both state and non-state actors, it may

---

[85] See [2] and [3].

[86] [2006] 3 All ER 946.

[87] [2004] 1 WLR 807.

[88] *Ibid*, 815.

[89] The decision effectively overruled the earlier cases of *R (Wright) v Home Secretary* [2002] HRLR 1, the Divisional Court in *R (Hurst) v North London Coroner* [2004] UKHRR 139, and the Court of Appeal in *R (Khan) v Secretary of State for Health* [2004] 1 WLR 971.

not extend beyond to acts which do not reach this threshold. In turn this would carry significant ramifications for victims in the domestic criminal justice system, as most have been victims of less serious offences.[90] In the absence of any authority on this point, it may be prudent to assume that prosecutors and the police will be left with some degree of discretion as to when other factors, such as the 'public interest', might dictate that no prosecution should be taken despite an offence having taken place. If the crime did not endanger life or amount to cruel, inhuman or degrading treatment, it is possible that the investigatory duties need not be applied with such rigour.

It is also clear that these obligations will not apply with equal measure in all environments. Both the domestic courts and the European Court of Human Rights have drawn a distinction between the scope of the investigatory duty to be drawn between deaths that occurred in custody and those occurring in other situations. In *R (Takoushis) v HM Coroner for Inner North London*,[91] the scope of the investigatory requirements as a result of medical negligence in NHS hospitals was outlined. Here, the coroner's original inquest was regarded as being short of full and fair; its verdict was quashed and a new inquest instated. It was noted that where a person died as a result of alleged medical negligence, the State was under an obligation to put in place a system to establish facts and determine civil liability. However, unlike cases involving death in custody, the system did not have to provide for an investigation initiated by the State, nor did the duty necessarily extend to an obligation for the coroner to install a jury and it did not follow that a criminal investigation had to be launched. The question as to whether a jury ought to be summoned would be a matter for the coroner, as would the question whether to call any expert evidence that the family sought. Recognising the distinction drawn by the European Court between victims who were in state custody and those who were not, it was held in *Calvelli and Ciglio v Italy*,[92] that the principles laid down in *Amin* and *Middleton* did not apply to this form of case. Here, the possibility of instituting civil and criminal proceedings or a disciplinary process satisfied the requirements of Article 2.

For the most part, the above decisions have indicated that the domestic courts are willing to apply the core investigatory requirements laid down by the European Court of Human Rights. As the House of Lords recognised in *R (Green) v Police Complaints Authority*,[93] the investigatory duty under domestic law was 'no less thorough', and, arose in any case involving death, a 'near miss' or torture that occurs in custody or through the state's use of force: even where a substantive breach of Article 2 was not evident.[94] All such investigations should thus conform

---

[90] Leverick (2004), 188.

[91] [2006] 1 WLR 461, where it was held that 'no separate procedural obligation to investigate under Art 2 where a death in a hospital raises no more than a potential liability in negligence'.

[92] App No 32967/96, 17 Jan 2002. See also decision in *Goodson v HM Coroner for Beds and Luton NHS Trust* [2006] 1 WLR 432.

[93] [2004] 1 WLR 725.

[94] However, their Lordships dismissed the appeal, holding that the disclosure of witness statements sought by the applicant was not necessary in this particular case to discharge Art 2 obligations.

to the requirements laid down in *Jordan* and *Edwards*: they should be independent, public, effective, prompt, and involve the next of kin. However, not all victims are able to access such rights. The decision in *Takoushis* reinforces the case-specific nature of the investigative obligations: the scope of an inquest following a death in hospital need not be as extensive as an inquest established following deaths of custody. Guidance on the scope and specific nature of such an investigation remain broad, and questions remain unanswered concerning the threshold for an investigation. It is unclear whether, for example, an injured party needs to show an arguable case for negligence on the part of the state, or merely that death / injury occurred under state care.[95] It is not even clear whether a breach of law would be required. No doubt those questions will be addressed by the courts in due course.

Victims of Non-State Crime

While much of the academic commentary surrounding these decisions has focused on the obligations incumbent on hospitals, prisons, and other state institutions, less attention has been given to the ramifications for investigating 'ordinary' criminal offences committed by non-state actors. Emphasising the grey area that exists between deaths caused by state and non-state actors, Lord Slynn in *Amin* noted that:

> It does not seem to me to be possible to say that there is a clear dividing line between those cases where an agent of the state kills and those cases where an agent of the state or the system is such that a killing may take place. The result of 'an incident waiting to happen' may just as much as an actual killing require detailed and profound investigation, though in some cases the procedure to be adopted may be justifiably different.[96]

Clearly, in *Amin*, the House of Lords recognised that Article 2 obligations are triggered in relation to 'horizontal' killings that occur within custody, but it is still not apparent to what extent the same investigatory requirements apply to a killing that may occur in society at large. However, the Strasbourg jurisprudence, most notably the decisions in *McCann* and *Ergi*, support the contention that the investigatory obligations extend to non-state actors in a range of different contexts.[97] As such, the domestic courts have recognised that the investigatory obligations arising from Articles 2 and 3 will apply to instances of state and non-state crime alike throughout the criminal process.

---

[95] See Stern and Chahal (2006), 24–5.
[96] *Ibid*, 674.
[97] See discussion above, pp166–9.

Prosecution

The Crown Prosecution Service is only obliged to institute proceedings if it is considered appropriate to do so,[98] and that decision rests on the two-fold test discussed in the previous chapter.[99] The decision on whether to charge a suspect and commence a prosecution will always require some sensitivity towards the families of a victim, and, over time, implementing policies restricting prosecutions can affect public confidence in the integrity of the criminal justice system. A victim may choose to pursue a private prosecution or a civil remedy, but for reasons discussed above,[100] these options are rarely pursued in the United Kingdom. It may, however, also be argued that Article 2 case law imposes an obligation to prosecute all persons against whom there is sufficient evidence that they have committed a killing or an act amounting to torture under Article 3 of the Convention. To fail to do so would interfere with a victim's right to justice. Indeed, failure to act would seem to contravene every international standard governing the right to life. The obligation has been justified both on the grounds that it is fundamentally just to punish serious offenders,[101] as well as on grounds of deterrence.[102] It follows that, in the domestic criminal justice system, all criminal investigations in these areas ought to be undertaken with a view to prosecution.

It will be recalled from the previous chapter that victims who are unhappy with a decision not to prosecute may not appeal such a decision. Instead, they may seek a judicial review of it. Judicial review, of course, is made extremely difficult if victims or their families are not made aware of the grounds on which a decision not to prosecute is based. In addition to the international obligation to instigate prosecutions in cases involving the right to life or serious bodily injury, a further key principle to emerge stipulates that clear reasons ought to be given for any decision not to prosecute. It was stressed in *Shanaghan* that:

> where no reasons are given in a controversial incident involving a killing, this may in itself not be conducive to public confidence. It also denies the family of the victim access to information about a matter of crucial importance to them and prevents any legal challenge of the decision.[103]

It has been common practice in England and Wales for many years for the CPS to give only a very broad, generalised indication of their reasons for declining to pursue (or for abandoning) a prosecution. Certainly there is no obligation in law to do so, although following the Glidewell Review of the CPS in 1998, and similar

---

[98] Prosecution of Offences Act 1985, s 3(2)(b).

[99] See Ch 3, pp120–22.

[100] *Ibid*, p124.

[101] See *Aydin*, above n 46, [103], where the Court stressed that the investigation must be capable of leading to the punishment of the offender.

[102] See eg *A v United Kingdom* (1999) 27 EHRR 611, [22].

[103] At [107]. *Shanaghan v UK*, above n 53 was one of the 3 cases considered alongside *Jordan*, above n 52, by the European Court of Human Rights.

recommendations contained in Sir William Macpherson's report into the death of Stephen Lawrence,[104] the Service has assumed responsibility for communicating prosecution decisions directly to victims rather than via the police.[105]

It remains the case, however, that victims have no legal entitlement to be involved in any consultation before charging decisions are made, and courts have in the past rejected challenges brought by judicial review by victims who have felt aggrieved that they were not consulted. In *R v DPP ex parte C*,[106] it was held in a judicial review decision concerning the failure to prosecute in an alleged case of buggery that such challenges would only be successful because of some unlawful policy, if the Director of Public Prosecutions failed to act in accordance with 'his own settled policy', or if it was a decision at which no reasonable prosecutor could have arrived.

In 1999, the question was considered as part of the Butler Report into deaths in police custody.[107] One aspect of the Report concerned the failure of the CPS to prosecute officers allegedly responsible in two cases, despite coroners' courts having made findings of unlawful killing. Butler found that the decision-making processes adopted by the CPS in deciding whether to prosecute were 'inefficient and fundamentally unsound' and that the evidential limb of the test had not been properly applied.[108] On that basis, the Report recommended that, in cases involving a coronial verdict of unlawful death, decisions as to whether or not to prosecute should be made by the Assistant Chief Crown Prosecutor. Where the decision was not to prosecute, this should be sent to Senior Treasury Counsel for advice.

In the aftermath of the Butler report, it appears that the courts are becoming more willing to recognise that the current lack of a legal right of victims to access reasons may be untenable in the longer term. The case of *R v DPP ex parte Manning*[109] concerned a remand prisoner, who had died in custody from asphyxia. Following an inquest finding of unlawful killing, seven prison guards were suspended, on full pay, until a decision on whether to prosecute was made by the CPS. Following a decision that there was insufficient evidence on which to base a prosecution, the family of the deceased brought a successful judicial review. The case then was referred back to the CPS, but, again, it was decided not to proceed. The CPS refused to give full reasons for the decision, and this decision was subject to further judicial review proceedings. Noting that it seemed to be:

---

[104] See Glidewell (1998), Rec 32; MacPherson (1999), Recs 35–7.

[105] See Ch 3, p128. See also the Victims' Code of Practice, [5.19–5.20], which imposes an obligation on the police to communicate the decision to victims of whether a file has been forwarded to the CPS with a view to prosecution, or whether there is insufficient evidence on which to charge a suspect.

[106] [1995] 1 Cr App R 141.

[107] Butler (1999).

[108] See [8.2].

[109] [2001] QB 330 cf the Northern Ireland case of *Re Adams* [2001] NICA 2.

wrong in principle to require the citizen to make a complaint of unlawfulness against the Director in order to obtain a response which good administrative practice would in the ordinary course require,[110]

the Lord Chief Justice concluded that the DPP's decision not to prosecute any prison officer was 'unsustainable in law'. Whilst it was acknowledged that the DPP was under no duty to give reasons for a refusal to prosecute, it should be the norm to do so, particularly in circumstances where an inquest jury had already returned a verdict of unlawful killing implicating clearly identifiable persons. In such circumstances, Lord Bingham CJ explained that the 'ordinary expectation would naturally be that a prosecution would follow'. Proceeding to acknowledge that the right to life was at the 'forefront of the Convention', the Lord Chief Justice stated:

> In the absence of compelling grounds for not giving reasons, we would expect the Director to give reasons in such a case: to meet the reasonable expectation that either a prosecution would follow or a reasonable explanation for not prosecuting be given, to vindicate the Director's decision by showing that solid grounds exist for what might otherwise appear to be a surprising or even inexplicable decision and to meet the European Court's expectation that if a prosecution is not to follow a plausible explanation will be given.

On the basis of Article 2 of the Convention, it was held that full reasons for a decision not to prosecute should be given where (1) there has been a death or ill-treatment of a person in custody; (2) the results of a prior inquiry (eg, an inquest) indicate that a state official is responsible for the harm and has behaved outside the law; and (3) the prosecution of the responsible official would be expected to follow. It was further noted that 'the standard of review should not be set too high, since judicial review is the only means by which the citizen can seek redress against a decision not to prosecute and if the test were too exacting an effective remedy would be denied'.[111]

In the wake of this decision, it is clear that the courts are rethinking their long-standing reluctance to interfere in prosecutorial decision-making. Where a verdict of unlawful killing has been reached by a jury at an inquest, the CPS is then under a considerable onus to justify any decision not to prosecute. It is self-evident that the decision of an inquest jury may well assist a prosecutor in determining whether there is a realistic prospect of conviction. The evidence is, in effect, tested prior to going before a prosecutor or a criminal court. While this need not be definitive, the link between the verdict of a coroner's court and the corresponding prosecution file is indisputable. The effect of the decision in *Manning*, however, should not be overestimated. It is clear that full reasons need only be given by the CPS if the three relatively stringent criteria cited by the Lord Chief Justice are met.

---

[110] *Ibid*, [33].
[111] [2001] QB 330 cf the Northern Ireland case of *Re Adams* [2001] NICA 2 [23].

The decision in Manning was applied in the recent high-profile case of *R (Da Silva) v DPP*.[112] The claimant applied for judicial review of the DPP's decision not to prosecute any individual police officers for murder or gross negligence manslaughter following the fatal shooting of Jean Charles de Menezes at Stockwell tube station in July 2005. The deceased had been shot dead by police officers who had mistaken him for a suicide bomber. In July 2006, the DPP announced that no individual would be prosecuted in connection with the killing, but instead the office of the Metropolitan Police Commissioner would be prosecuted under the Health and Safety at Work Act 1974.[113]

The applicant contended, inter alia, that the failure to commence prosecutions against individual officers through applying the two-fold test laid down in the Code for Crown Prosecutors contravened Article 2 of the Convention. It was also argued that the court was obliged to undertake a more intensive review of the DPP's decision than the criteria that had been laid down in *Manning*. In rejecting this argument, the Court held that the DPP had acted lawfully in applying the two-fold test, and that it could not use judicial review as a sword to strike down decisions that were both lawful and reasonable. The decision-making process had been lengthy, careful and thorough, and the final decision had been made on reasonable grounds.

The rejection in *Da Silva* of any expansion of the *Manning* principle was perhaps not surprising. It was a decision very much in line with the traditional reluctance of the courts to exercise the power of review sparingly. It does, however, highlight the fact that the CPS is fundamentally lacking in its accountability not only to victims, but to the general public as well. Both the evidential test and the public interest tests call for the exercise of subjective judgement, and the latter test is so vague that it remains extremely difficult to challenge its application in the context of a judicial review. The decision-making process lacks transparency, openness and access for the victim (or his / her family / legal counsel). Much more specific guidelines are obviously required to give prosecutors, victims and the general public some idea of what constitutes the 'public interest' and the weight that will be given to specific factors that comprise that interest.

In summary then, domestic case law broadly reflects Convention standards on procedural obligations stemming from breaches of Articles 2 and 3, and provides further evidence of the ongoing collapse of the vertical / horizontal divide in human rights discourse. The idea of a 'right to a remedy' for 'ordinary' victims of crime, as well as victims of state crime, is gradually securing a foothold within domestic law. However, as the law currently stands, it is clear that some aspects of this right to a remedy are likely to prove more operative in practice than others. The decisions in *Amin* and *Middleton* recognise the broad nature of the duty under Article 2 to investigate deaths. Nevertheless, these rights are underdeveloped in the

---

[112] (2007) 157 NLJ 31, [2006] EWHC 3204 (Admin).
[113] On 31 Oct 2007, the Metropolitan Police Service were found guilty of breaching health and safety laws and fined £175000 (see further *The Times*, 1 Nov 2007).

domestic legal order and we are still unclear as to the long-term ramifications of positive obligations in these areas. In particular, it is unclear whether the investigatory requirements cover less serious criminal offences, which fall well short of the threshold required for Articles 2 and 3. To date, there is only a limited range of cases to draw upon, and the parameters of the duty will become clearer over time. The willingness of the courts to adopt rights-based language in respect of these remedies suggests that one can afford to be optimistic in this regard. Nevertheless, we have reason to be less optimistic in respect of the right of a victim to attain reasons for a decision to drop or alter charges, or not to proceed at all with the prosecution. While the decision in *Manning* constitutes a welcome move towards transparency and a comprehensive review process, there are no signs that the CPS intends to alter its practice in being more specific as to how it takes account of the 'public interest' requirement.

III. A Right to Truth?

Many discussions of the victim's right to a remedy in domestic criminal justice tend to focus on access to justice, and the possibility of challenging decisions and obtaining reasons for failure to prosecute. Unlike many human rights and transitional justice analyses, however, there have been relatively few attempts to assess the ability of victims of non-state crime to access the truth of past events within the criminal justice system. There have been a number of commentaries which have considered the place of truth-finding within the adversarial paradigm, but few of them have attempted to consider the issue from a rights-based perspective of the victim.

In many ways, the very concept of truth-finding pervades much of the previous discussion concerning effective investigations and access to justice. In the words of former UN Special Rapporteur, Theo Van Boven:

> only the complete and public revelation of the truth will make it possible to satisfy the basic requirements of the principles of justice.[114]

By its own definition, the very concept of a criminal investigation should involve an attempt to ascertain the facts. If a criminal suspect is placed on trial as a result of that investigation, then guilt will be determined on the basis of how the law is applied to the particular version of events that the trier of fact has chosen to believe. The point made by Van Boven above underlines that truth-finding is a necessary corollary of the entire criminal process. It can be said to assist the process in a number of ways. Perhaps most importantly, it serves to create an historically accurate narrative, which is vital in determining whether there is

---

[114] Van Boven (1993), 130.

adequate evidence to prosecute or impose criminal liability. In turn, this may assist the tribunal with determining an appropriate sentence or imposing some form of reparation. Whilst debates may continue to simmer as to what extent truth ought to be pursued at the expense of other goals of criminal process, such as the right to a fair hearing, there can be little doubt that an effective and just criminal justice system should place a very high value upon the correct ascertainment of the facts.

In addition to bolstering the legitimacy of criminal justice, commentators, particularly those approaching victims' rights from a transitional justice perspective, have often emphasised the particular benefits truth-finding can bring for victims. Truth-finding may carry benefits in both collective and individual senses: not only may it serve to heal collective societal divisions and help prevent future repetition,[115] but it may also be viewed as a 'psychological premise' that must be fulfilled in order to obtain justice and reconciliation for individual victims.[116] Central to the cathartic effect of truth is the idea that it may aid reconciliation through promoting forgiveness and understanding; whether that might be between an individual victim and offender or on a collective, inter-communitarian basis. In this way, confronting the truth can help alleviate the suffering, vindicate the victim's status and encourage perpetrators to confront their past deeds.[117] Such an acknowledgement of previous wrongs may help the individual to re-organise his or her thoughts into a form of narrative that allows them to make sense of past events,[118] and move on towards healing and coming to terms with what has happened. However, in order to be effective in this sense, truth must be complete and made public, and should give some indication of *why* the violation occurred.

For these reasons, a high value is typically placed upon truth-finding in many post-conflict societies, where the uncovering of the facts of past violations, along with the circumstances and conditions in which such violations occurred, has come to be regarded as a central component of reconciliation and socio-political reconstruction. Such processes frequently assume the form of a 'truth commission';[119] but may also be effected using other devices including public inquiries[120] or special courts.[121] South Africa is perhaps the best known example of a society that chose to pursue a truth commission process that offered an amnesty in return for testimony

---

[115] Cohen (1995), Sveaass & Lavik (2000).

[116] Sveaass & Lavik (2000), 44.

[117] Aldana-Pindell (2004).

[118] Smyth & Pennebaker (1999).

[119] Recent prominent examples include Chile, Argentina and South Africa.

[120] Note, eg, the use of the public inquiry model in Northern Ireland to uncover events surrounding the deaths of 13 civilians in Londonderry on Bloody Sunday in 1972. See further Walsh (2000).

[121] See, eg, the Gacaca courts of Rwanda, which are based on a form of community justice whereby respected community elders attempt to settle disputes by communal consensus: see further Ironside (2002). The Special Court for Sierra Leone also provides an interesting example in so far as it constitutes an interesting hybrid on international and national criminal law: see further Corriero (2002). It is also worth mentioning so-called 'truth-trials' in Argentina, which, while taking the format of an orthodox criminal hearing, were geared solely to establish facts and criminal conviction was prohibited (see Aldana-Pindell (2004)).

and a request for forgiveness.[122] The predominating political viewpoint in the aftermath of apartheid dictated that the widespread prosecution of former combatants may have hindered inter-communal reconciliation and political, social and economic progress. South Africa may be the most widely reported example, but it is by no means alone,[123] and the latter part of the twentieth century tended to show that 'prosecutions are rare and that inaction, amnesties, and pardons are the norm'.[124] There is considerable debate among transitional justice scholars as to whether truth processes which are accompanied by amnesties are desirable (or even legal) in transitional societies.[125] Here is not the place to examine that debate in detail.[126] However, if (as is suggested below), the right to truth also exists for victims of non-state crime, it can be taken on board that whilst truth and justice may complement each other, that relationship may also produce certain tensions.

International Developments

As suggested above, 'truth' is not a value that has been traditionally associated with victims of non-state crime. Instead, both international and domestic standards tend to embody some form of a 'right to information'. Such a right is to be found, for example, in Article 4 of the EU Framework Decision, which provides victims with a range of component rights to be kept informed about means of support and compensation, as well as the specific right to be informed of the outcome of their complaint, the course of criminal proceedings and any sentence. The most recent Council of Europe recommendation in the field similarly outlines a commitment to:

> ensure that victims have access to information of relevance to their case and necessary for the protection of their interests and the exercise of their rights.[127]

On the UN platform, the 1985 Victims' Declaration speaks of the need to inform victims of:

> their role and the scope, timing and progress of the proceedings and of the disposition of their cases, especially where serious crimes are involved and where they have requested such information.

[122] Aldana-Pindell (2004), 1043. Ni Aolain (2002) defines a truth commission as an official body 'set up to investigate and report on a pattern of human rights abuses in a state or region frequently associated with places that have experienced serious human rights abuses over an extended period of time implicating both state and non-state actors' (at 588–9).

[123] Other notable truth commission processes have been used inter alia in Argentina, Bolivia, Chile, El Salvador, Guatemala, Haiti, Nigeria, Sir Lanka and Uganda. For further explanations and examples, see Hayner (1994).

[124] *Ibid.*

[125] For a summary of the debate, see Aldana-Pindell (2004), esp 1443–57; Roht-Arriaza (1990); Antkowiak (2002), 996–1001.

[126] Foremost amongst the findings of Diane Orentlicher, the UN independent expert appointed to update the Set of Principles for the Protection and Promotion of Human Rights through Action to Combat Impunity was that amnesties were illegal under international law (UN Doc E/CN.4/2005/102, [50]). See further Roht-Arriaza and Mariezcurrena (2006).

[127] Rec (2006) 8, [6].

At first glance, these provisions may seem to mirror to some extent the idea of uncovering the truth. However, the 'right to information' is more focused on what has happened within the criminal process itself, rather than 'information' about the circumstances of past events. In this sense, they are primarily a form of 'service' rights,[128] and cannot be said in any meaningful way to equate to a 'right to truth'.

Although relatively new within human rights discourse, the right to truth (sometimes referred to as 'the right to know') is fast becoming acknowledged as a core standard for victims who have suffered as a result of state crime. Indeed, the International Committee of the Red Cross has suggested that it is already established as a rule of customary international law.[129] Certainly, in the opinion of the United Nations High Commissioner for Human Rights, it is viewed as an inalienable right, which is non-derogable and should not be subject to limitations.[130] In his report into the principles for the Protection and Promotion of Human Rights through Action to Combat Impunity,[131] UN expert Louis Joinet was the first to pinpoint the existence of a legal right to truth within international human rights frameworks:

> Every people has the inalienable right to know the truth about past events and about the circumstances and reasons which led, through the consistent pattern of gross violations of human rights, to the perpetration of aberrant crimes. Full and effective exercise of the right to the truth is essential to avoid any recurrence of such acts in the future.[132]

As part of a subsequent expert report by Diane Orentlicher,[133] the principles were recently updated,[134] and now expressly recognise the victim's 'inalienable' right to truth.[135] Victims, and their families, are entitled to know the truth about the circumstances in which violations took place and, in the event of death or disappearance, the victims' fates.[136] States are under a corresponding obligation to 'preserve memory',[137] which includes keeping records, provide information upon request, and take all measures necessary to give effect to the 'right to know'.

While the right is not yet widely evident within international treaties, the recently adopted International Convention for the Protection of All Persons from Enforced Disappearance[138] signals a shift towards a more widespread recognition of the right, in affirming the right of any victim:

---

[128] See Ch 1, p 12.
[129] International Committee of the Red Cross (2005), 421.
[130] E/CN.4/2006/91, [44] and [55].
[131] UN Doc E/CN.4/Sub.2/1997/20/Rev.1.
[132] *Ibid*, Ann 1, Principle 1.
[133] UN Doc. E/CN.4/2005/102.
[134] UN Doc E/CN.4/2005/102/Add.1.
[135] *Ibid*, Principle 2.
[136] *Ibid*, Principle 4.
[137] *Ibid*, Principle 3.
[138] UN Doc E/CN.4/2005/WG.22/WP.1/REV.4.

to know the truth about the circumstances of an enforced disappearance, and the fate of the disappeared person, and the right to freedom to seek, receive and impart information to this end.[139]

In time, the concept of a 'right to truth' is likely to become more widely entrenched within international human rights law.

Such a process is likely to be propelled by the emphasis placed on truth-finding by regional and international human rights tribunals. In *Quinteros v Uruguay*,[140] the UN Human Rights Committee stated that it understood:

> the anguish and stress caused to the mother by the disappearance of her daughter and by the continuing uncertainty concerning her fate and whereabouts. The applicant has the right to know what has happened to her daughter. In these respects, she too is a victim of the violations of the Covenant suffered by her daughter.

The various forms of reparation, set out in Part IX of the Basic Principles and Guidelines on the Right to a Remedy and Reparation of Victims of Violations of International Human Rights and Humanitarian Law,[141] include 'satisfaction', which, according to Principle 22, places a particularly high value on truth. 'Satisfaction' may include 'verification of the facts and full and public disclosure of the truth' as well as 'the search for the whereabouts of the disappeared' and 'public acknowledgment of the facts and acceptance of responsibility'.

The development of a 'right to know' under the Inter-American human rights system may be attributable to the high instances of grave human rights violations, including 'disappearances' under military juntas that ruled many parts of Central and Latin America during the latter part of the twentieth century. The Court made a fleeting reference to such a right in *Velasquez Rodriguez*, in stating that an 'effective search for the truth by the government' was an inherent part of an effective investigation, but the Court did not identify any freestanding 'right to truth'. The Inter-American Commission, in a report on the compatibility of impunity laws with the American Convention, recommended to the Argentinean government:

> that it adopt the measures necessary to clarify the facts and identify those responsible for the human rights violations that occurred during the past military dictatorship[142]

but again declined to expand on the nature of the right of any victim. The right was more specifically identified and discussed by the Court in the 1996 case of *Castillo Paez*.[143] While the Court acknowledged that such a notion corresponded to 'a concept that is being developed in doctrine and case law',[144] it declined to develop the concept further, and seemed to imply that it formed part of the duty to investigate rather than a separate obligation in its own right. The issue was fudged in a

---

[139] *Ibid*, Preamble.
[140] Comm No 107/1981 (1983).
[141] See *Ibid*.
[142] Report No 28/92, Inter-Am Ct HR, OEA/Ser.L/V/II.83. Doc 14 at 41 (1993).
[143] Series C, No 43 (1998).
[144] *Ibid*, [86].

similar manner four years later in the case of *Bamaca Velasquez*.[145] Despite noting the connection between the denial of justice and the denial of truth, the Court went on to note that the right to the truth was not a free-standing right within the Convention, although it may incidentally be protected by Articles 8 and 25 of the Convention.

Signs of the right emerging in much clearer terms were evident from the 2001 decision in *Barrios Altos*.[146] Relying in part on Article 1(2) of the United Nations Declaration on the Protection of All Persons Against Enforced Disappearance, the Court stressed that a state's duty to investigate and punish human rights violations included an obligation to shed light on past events. This obligation corresponded to a 'right of truth' for victims and their families. In the subsequent case of *Ellacuria*,[147] the Court went as far as to find the respondent state in violation of the right to truth. Relying on Articles 1, 8, 13, and 25 of the Convention, the Court analysed the right to truth as comprising two constituent elements. On the one hand, it was a collective right 'that ensures society access to information that is essential for the workings of democratic systems'.[148] On the other, it was also a private right for victims and their families, which 'affords a form of compensation'. Linking this 'private' aspect of the right to truth to the right to a remedy under Article 25, the Court proceeded to note:

> The existence of obstacles, *de facto* or *de jure* (such as the amnesty law), to the access of information relating to the facts and circumstances surrounding the violation of a fundamental right constitutes an open violation of the right established in that article and negates remedies available under domestic jurisdiction for the judicial protection of the fundamental rights established in the Convention, the Constitution and domestic laws.[149]

While full implications of the decision in *Ellacuria* may not be known for some time, it is relevant to the discussion here insofar as it illustrates the increasing emphasis that is placed internationally upon the value of truth in conflict resolution. The recent, innovative case law from the Inter-American Court reflects the widespread consensus that the ascertainment of truth forms part of the remedy which victims may legitimately expect. The proliferation in truth commissions and related processes in transitional societies provide us with further evidence that 'truth' is increasingly viewed as a core aspect of justice; and that victims who cannot access truth may find it difficult to move on.

It may be apparent from the above discussion that, whilst the desirability of uncovering the truth has come to feature prominently within the jurisprudence of the UN Human Rights Committee and the Inter-American human rights system, there has been relatively little discussion of a right to truth by the Strasbourg Court. The lack of any recent military regimes among Council Members has

---

[145] Series C, No 70 (2000).
[146] Series C, No 75 (2001), [41].
[147] Report No 136/99, Inter-Am Ct HR, OEA/Ser.L/V/II.106. Doc 3 rev. at 608 (1999).
[148] *Ibid*, [224].
[149] *Ibid*, [225].

meant that the concept of a 'right to truth' has only arisen in a very peripheral sense before the Court. The obligations outlined in *McCann* and *Jordan* reflect that a high value is placed upon the ascertainment of facts as a corollary to an effective criminal investigation, but a free-standing right to truth has not been recognised to date. Nonetheless, if and when the opportunity should present itself, we can expect the European Court is also likely to view the concept of truth-finding as an indispensable aspect of a right to a remedy. Not only is it a necessary corollary of pursuing criminal complaints and investigations, but it is also recognised that it forms a necessary component of the healing process for many victims of serious human rights violations.

Truth in the Adversarial System

If we are to draw from best practice, the criminal justice system ought to prioritise truth-finding as one of its primary goals as a means of delivering justice to victims of crime. Commentators have been divided on the extent to which the adversarial system places a value on truth. It has been argued that the adversarial trial provides the best way to determine the truth of what witnesses are saying. Live oral evidence, given to the court, under oath, and tested by the parties is widely regarded within the legal profession as the best means of reaching the truth.[150] Whilst Jerome Frank was no great admirer of the adversary model, he nonetheless defended its ability to seek out the truth. In his eyes, parties which have a clear focus on victory will produce the best information for the tribunal of fact to make a determination:

> Many lawyers maintain that the best way for the court to discover the facts in a suit is to have each side strive as hard as it can, in a keenly partisan spirit, to bring to the court's attention the evidence favourable to that side. Macauley said that we obtain the fairest decision 'when two men argue, as unfairly as possible, on opposite sides' for then 'it is certain that no important consideration will altogether escape notice.[151]
>
> The 'fight' theory . . . has invaluable qualities with which we cannot afford to dispense.[152]

An alternative justification for the adversarial process is that although adversarial structures do not always lend themselves to truth finding, it is nonetheless the dispute-resolution model that is best placed to ensure outcomes are as fair as possible to parties to the case. Landsman, for example, is quite happy to defend the adversarial system on the basis that truth is not its primary goal:

> [A] preoccupation with material truth may be not only futile but dangerous to society as well. If the objective of the judicial process were the disclosure of facts, then any technique that increases the prospect of gathering facts would be permissible.[153]

[150] Eggleston (1996), 433.
[151] Frank (1949), 49.
[152] *Ibid*, 80.
[153] Landsman (1984), 37.

Landsman proceeds to list examples, such as the use of psychoactive drugs and / or torture as a means to produce truth. Thus, by necessity, a *truth at all costs* approach to criminal trials is unworkable given that exclusionary evidential rules,[154] coupled with certain due process protections, are designed to maintain the integrity of the criminal justice process. Instead, Landsman defends the adversarial trial on the basis that truth plays second fiddle to the overriding need for justice. Procedural requirements such as party control, an impartial decision-maker, and commitment to winning the contest mean that the process should be broadly equal. Fundamental rights are safeguarded through evidential rules, which go some way to offsetting the broader range of resources at the disposal of the prosecution, as well as maintaining integrity and public confidence in the criminal justice system. In a similar vein, Thibaut and Walker argue that the 'truth-finding' aspect of the adversarial system is subservient to the overriding goal of 'justice' or 'fairness', since the outcomes of proceedings will naturally reflect the inputs of the parties.[155] Factual truth is a pre requisite of justice, as Jeremy Bentham's image of '[i]njustice, and her handmaid [f]alsehood' underlines.[156]

The notion that 'truth' must, by necessity, be balanced against other values is questionable. Goodpaster's analysis that truth and justice are 'intimately connected' and cannot be so clinically separated seems more persuasive. Fair procedures are more conducive to accurate fact-finding, unfair procedures may lead to erroneous fact-finding.[157] Both objectives, he contends, should be considered to be twin objectives of the adversarial system: fair outcomes are fundamentally dependent upon fair processes.[158]

The problem with past debates concerning the role of truth in adversarial theory is that they have tended to centre solely on the instrumentalist function of truth, that is, how processes and outcomes are linked to ascertaining details of past events. Debates among criminal justice theorists have largely ignored the victim-related dimension to truth-finding. Emerging international practice tends to indicate that, though intimately connected to both just process and just outcome, truth also constitutes a form of reparation for victims insofar as it helps them to achieve closure and move forwards. If we are to draw lessons from human rights discourse, truth ought to be regarded as an intrinsic value in itself, and as a freestanding right for victims. Even if the adversarial system could ensure that justice would always prevail in the absence of truth, this may preserve the rights of the accused to a fair trial, but it would effectively deny victims their right to know the truth about what actually happened and why.

Before considering how the structures and processes of the adversarial system impact upon its ability to ascertain the truth, it is important to underline certain

---

[154] See below, pp 197–8.
[155] Thibaut and Walker (1978).
[156] Bentham (1827), (I)-22.
[157] Goodpaster (1987), 118–27.
[158] For an overview of the normative debate on the place of truth in the criminal justice system, see generally Duff et al (2004), 20–3.

caveats relating to the discussions concerning 'truth'. First of all, as Jung reminds us, 'truth cannot be "found" . . . it can only be reconstructed'.[159] The idea that objective 'truth' is somehow absolute and readily accessible is to be doubted, yet that assumption seems to underpin much of the law of evidence.[160] However, we cannot *know*, for example, what precisely occurred as part of the events in question, nor can we ascertain the precise thoughts that went through a defendant's mind at the time. Perhaps the 'truth' that is created through the criminal process is the *only* truth to which we have access, and it is thereby unwise to try to divorce 'the truth of the matter from our manner of apprehending it'.[161] Yet, to some extent, such normative questions risk detracting from the fact that, no matter how hard it may be to recreate the past, the pursuit of objective truth is, in theory at least, something that ought to favour victims, society and innocent defendants. As such, it should lie at the core of any criminal justice system.

Investigation and Charge

At the outset, it is worth underlining that, even before any criminal investigation begins, the 'truth' is already a fait accompli of the past. One of the functions of the criminal process is to piece together, from various sources, what occurred. The information that will be eventually assessed by the trier of fact will be obtained as part of the police investigation. Yet even before any evidence is gathered, the picture of the past has already begun to fragment. The task of reconstructing events is necessarily dependent on various forms of evidence, but the primary form of evidence will be the accounts of past events that are given to the police by witnesses. Building a picture of the past is thus highly dependent first, upon our powers of perception, secondly upon our memory and skills of retrieval, and thirdly our ability to articulate or communicate our memories effectively. All of these factors are likely to affect the quality of the information the police (and eventually the prosecution, defence and courts) will gather from witnesses. Our ability to perceive events accurately is dependent upon a number of different factors, including our senses of sight, sound and smell, and the impact of physical conditions such as distances and lighting. Furthermore, it is well established that memories are susceptible to changes over time, and become conflated with other real or imaginary events.[162] Events are interpreted and reinterpreted over time, and the time gap between the events in question, giving a statement to the police, and then testifying at trial will often run into many months or even years. This is particularly true where the event in question was of a traumatic nature. Thus some witnesses who give statements may be giving a bona fide account according to their memory, but they may still be mistaken about all the facts or certain facts. Some,

---

[159] Jung (2004), 144.
[160] Twining (1994), 73.
[161] Bankowski (1981), 262.
[162] For an overview of the psychological literature, see Loftus et al (2006).

for one reason or another, may be subconsciously prejudiced or biased in the way they perceive past events,[163] and some may actively choose to be dishonest. Other witnesses will be limited in their ability to articulate clearly what they recall, perhaps due to age, disability, or illness.[164] The accounts of others may be adversely affected by a sense of 'extreme eagerness' to assist the police with their inquiries.[165]

In a seminal, though controversial, work, McConville et al argue that the police, though normatively neutral, will seek to build a strong case for the prosecution.[166] It has been suggested that they do so by forming working hypotheses, which are formulated and modified on the basis of how they perceive the events in question, the witnesses who give statements, the suspect(s), and any real evidence. In being placed in charge of the evidence gathering process and the taking of witness statements, the police are in a position to control the investigatory process. Police officers will inevitably form opinions of those from whom they have taken statements, and views on witnesses, including the suspects, can have a bearing on the type of questioning that may occur at a future date.[167] The police will also be mindful that, if there is a trial, it is likely that they will be called to testify. As such, the investigation, including all witness statements, will be undertaken with this in mind. Investigation will be conducted to serve the needs of the criminal justice system—which effectively means to secure a conviction.[168] As Sanders and Young observe, the need to secure convictions means that police will routinely look for ways to 'strengthen cases which would otherwise be weak', and will avoid pursuing lines of inquiry that might undermine existing evidence.[169] Ericson viewed the evidence-gathering process as a form of 'information control' by the police, dependent upon:

> the investigation they do or do not undertake; the questions they do and do not ask; the interpretations they do and do not give to the answers; the written accounts they give and what they leave out.[170]

This case construction may be effected on both a conscious and a subconscious level, but ultimately the adversarial system places the police within a system where their primary concern will be collecting evidence in such a way that it confirms a predetermined case theory. In an adversarial system where 'cop cultures' have been characterised by a sense of mission[171] and a 'presumption of guilt',[172] the

---

[163] See Greer (1971).

[164] Most commonly (though not exclusively) this affects child witnesses and witnesses with learning disabilities. For a general overview, see respectively Murphy and Clare (2006) and Davies and Westcott (2006).

[165] Gudjonsson (2006), 66.

[166] McConville et al (1991).

[167] Zuckerman (1992).

[168] For an opposing view, see Smith (1997), who argues that McConville et al have based their arguments on too many unfounded assumptions.

[169] Sanders and Young (2007), 336–7.

[170] Ericson (1981), 9.

[171] Reiner (2000).

[172] Skolnick (1966).

police are likely to create for themselves a sense of 'pending conviction'.[173] Thus police interviews with suspects are commonly (and correctly) characterised as being confrontational and aggressive in nature and tone. Interviews and questioning will therefore be aimed primarily at supporting a particular case theory rather than gathering facts. In the same way as lawyers carefully craft their questions at trial to elicit particular responses, so police interviews are used 'to bring the suspect's version into accordance with the officer's own view'.[174]

Occasionally, the police investigation will stray into the territory of illegality, with 'facts' being constructed, evidence being tampered with or fabricated, suspects being intimidated into confessing, or disclosure procedures not being fully complied with. During the late 1980s and early 1990s, there were a number of high profile acquittals by the Court of Appeal, including the Birmingham Six, the Guildford Four, the Bridgewater Four, the Cardiff Three, Judith Ward, and Derek Bentley. Although the Police and Criminal Evidence Act 1984 was intended to safeguard personal liberties by placing tighter controls upon the exercise of police powers, it would be naïve to believe that it has been effective in eradicating corruption within the investigative process. It is self-evident that a failure to follow formal procedure and respect due process requirements carries risks to the fact-finding process. If left unchecked, evidence obtained improperly will then be admitted as 'facts' and will comprise part of the case against the accused in court. There is no defence of entrapment or procedural impropriety in English common law,[175] and if evidence has been unfairly obtained, the trial judge may use discretion under common law or under section 78 of the Police and Criminal Evidence Act if he / she feels that the evidence would have 'such an adverse effect on the fairness of proceedings, that it ought not to be admitted'. If levels of past miscarriages of justice are representative of the amount of improperly obtained evidence, including false confessions,[176] that manages to seep into the criminal trial, the potential for accurate fact-finding is severely undermined.

The pre-trial investigation and case construction processes are strongly rooted in the adversarial tradition, with facts being inevitably distorted or reconstructed to boost the prospects of a conviction. Some of this distortion will be intentional, whereas other aspects of it may be totally inadvertent, and will simply be a product of the working culture. However, it is not just the police and CPS who are involved in an elaborate process of case construction at the pre-trial stage of the criminal process. Just as the police and CPS will construct their case with a view to how it will be presented in court, defence lawyers will also formulate their own case constructions at an early stage in the process. The difficulty here is that the potential for the defence to embark on its own evidence-gathering process is very

---

[173] McBarnet (1981), 61.

[174] *Ibid*, 63.

[175] *R v Sang* [1980] AC 402.

[176] Confessions are subject to separate regulation. Under s 76(2) Police and Criminal Evidence Act, confession evidence that is obtained through oppression or by means likely to make it unreliable must be excluded.

much hindered in terms of resources. The defence will be highly dependent on the CPS to comply with disclosure obligations in order to sift through the evidence gathered by the police. However, as noted above, there is a risk that such evidence will already have been selectively filtered by the police or CPS, even on a subconscious level. Certain aspects of evidence which sat uneasily alongside the initial case theory may have been discarded; certain lines of enquiry may not have been probed; certain witnesses may not have been interviewed and certain questions may not have been asked. The information which the defence has on which to construct its own case theory will therefore have already been subject to a selective filtration process in the way that the investigation was undertaken.

Furthermore, it is not the role of the defence solicitor to search for the truth or question the suspect's version of events; the duty is, first and foremost, owed to the client. Lord Brougham's famous pronouncement that 'the first great duty of an advocate [was] to reckon everything subordinate to the interests of his client'[177] is largely reflected in the contemporary Codes of Practice for both branches of the profession.[178] While counsel must not mislead the court,[179] where a client privately admits guilt, the defence may still put the prosecution to proof. Moreover, it may be recommended by the lawyer that the accused relate a version of events in a substantially different way from what he or she had originally intended, perhaps including or omitting relevant facts. Any record of communication between the lawyer and client will be privileged,[180] and thus cannot be accessed by the police or prosecution, nor can it be relied upon in court.[181]

While the pre-trial investigation may seek to establish whether there is sufficient evidence on which to charge a suspect, the investigation may draw to an abrupt halt if little evidence is available. It may well be that such evidence is discoverable, but that resources or policy considerations mean that the investigation may not be thorough enough to uncover it.[182] Alternatively, such evidence may be destroyed or lost.[183] The resulting failure to charge, let alone convict, any one suspect does not mean that the complainant was not a bona fide victim of crime, or that other evidence or statements that have been gathered are somehow false or misleading. Neither the CPS nor the courts have the power to compel any further investigation. The fact that the police investigation may have drawn a blank does not, of course, alter the historical truth. Yet from the victim's perspective, there is no formal legal recognition that a particular suspect is to blame, or indeed that an offence has been committed at all. Whilst, depending on circumstances, they may be able to access compensation for criminal injuries or even pursue a civil action,

---

[177] Cited by Costigan (1931), 521.
[178] General Council of the Bar (2004a), r 3.03; Law Society (2003a), Principle 1.04. It has, however, been suggested that advocates owe a paramount duty to the court. See comments of Lord Denning in *Rondel v Worsley* [1966] 3 All ER 657, 665.
[179] General Council of the Bar (2004a), r 3.03.
[180] Police and Criminal Evidence Act 1984, s10(1).
[181] See further Dennis (2007), ch 10.
[182] Edwards (1999), 68.
[183] *Ibid.*

in the absence of a decision to prosecute there is no official declaration of, or sanction for, blameworthy conduct.[184]

Even where there is sufficient evidence to charge a suspect, material truth may be undermined for legal expediency. It would be difficult to understate the role discretion plays in the English criminal justice system. Not only do the police enjoy a vast degree of latitude in determining how they respond to reports of crime, but charging decisions are also subject to an array of interacting factors. As noted above, such decisions are made by the CPS on grounds of both evidential sufficiency and public interest. Thus, if the elusive 'public interest' should dictate that no prosecution should be instigated, the official mechanism for uncovering the truth of past events is not present.

Similarly, the practice of plea negotiation denies victims the right to have some form of independent inquiry into a defendant's past actions.[185] While few victims may relish the prospect of testifying at a full trial, the trial at least provides a forum for fact-finding to take place and communicates the message that the State has, at least, taken the victim's complaint seriously. Plea negotiation risks leaving victims feeling marginalised and irrelevant,[186] but it also removes the prospect of a public and independent fact-finding exercise. If a defendant agrees to plead guilty to a lesser charge, he or she will be presumed in law to have committed the lesser offence. Such a scenario may prove especially painful for a victim in a case where the CPS agrees to accept a guilty plea for a sexual assault where a rape charge was initially levied: the outcome of such a case will amount to a legal judgment that she has not been raped.[187] The offender cannot therefore be said to be fully accountable for those actions which he allegedly has committed, in such cases the adversarial system does not probe any further into past events.[188] Rather, the individual concerned is presumed to be guilty of a less serious offence, and presumed not to be guilty of the more serious charge.

Of course, a guilty plea or a decision to drop charges does not necessarily mean that the elements of a more serious offence did not take place. In either case, while giving suspects the full benefit of the presumption of innocence is fundamental to any liberal criminal justice system, from a victim's perspective the failure to charge a suspect with the particular offence may lead many victims to feel that there has been no official acknowledgement of the harm they have suffered. Instead, a legal truth is constructed which fails to recognise the real harm suffered by the victim.[189] This sits extremely uneasily with the emergent right to truth on the

---

[184] As a caveat, it should be added that the decision to caution may be regarded as a form of official censure.

[185] See above Ch 3, pp 122–4.

[186] *Ibid.*

[187] McConville (2002), 373.

[188] Where the prosecution and the defence are unable to agree the facts of the offence, the court may convene a *Newton* hearing to resolve the dispute, but such a hearing will not take place where the differences in the two versions of facts does not affect the sentence.

[189] Arguably, however, 'the most appropriate concept of truth is one that defines "truth" as simply that version of facts which is acceptable to all concerned' (Damaska (2004), 1029).

international platform.[190] A process of fact-finding that is complete and as accurate as possible cannot be fully realised within an adversarial system where partisan conflict and selective filtration dominate criminal practice.

The Trial

If a defendant pleads not guilty and the case proceeds to trial, a trier of fact will be appointed, and charged with the eventual task of arriving at a verdict. The 'truth' that emerges as the end product of the trial may be pragmatic, legalistic and constructed by the trier, the advocates and the evidence. As Haines J noted in the Canadian case of *R v Lalonde*:

> A trial is not a faithful reconstruction of the events as if recorded on some giant television screen. It is an historical recall of that part of events to which witnesses may be found and presented in an intensely adversary system where the object is the quantum of proof. Truth may only be incidental.[191]

Yet in spite of the many conjectural questions this gives rise to concerning the definition, value and role of truth within criminal proceedings, there remains a need for finality and for the criminal justice system to communicate 'to a wider audience a message that the system has done its best to determine the truth'.[192] From a human rights perspective, such confusion does little to clarify the extent to which the victim is able to access information about past events. Unfortunately, there are certain core facets of the adversarial trial that render its potential to uncover facts rather limited.

Party Control

Parties to the adversarial trial hold a near-complete autonomy to gather, select and present evidence before the trier of fact.[193] The commencement, conduct and termination of proceedings rest largely in their hands. The parties will decide which facts are in issue and which are not. They will determine how to go about generating proofs, and which witnesses will be called to aid them in that task. They will generally have a free hand in examining and cross-examining witnesses, including the accused and the complainant.

The State, personified by the trial judge, will generally assume an impassive stance. However, the judge can, in theory, widen the scope of the fact-finding process. For example, judges may call witnesses of their own motion,[194] although

---

[190] Interestingly, although it has been argued 'truth' is fast emerging as an international value, plea negotiation is commonplace at international criminal tribunals. See further Damaska (2004); Henham and Drumbl (2005).

[191] (1971) 15 CRNA 1,4.

[192] Jackson (2004), 137.

[193] See Ch 3, pp 138–51.

[194] *R v Wallwork* (1958) 42 Cr App R 153.

in the *Review of the Criminal Courts*, Lord Justice Auld advised that this power should be used infrequently.[195] In their study of Diplock trials in Northern Ireland, Jackson and Doran found that while the power to call witnesses is seldom used in practice,[196] it may nonetheless act as an incentive to counsel to ensure that all relevant witnesses are heard.[197] In addition to calling witnesses himself, the judge can also play a role in encouraging parties to produce their own witnesses or any other items of evidence that may not otherwise have been introduced.[198] Jackson and Doran cite a number of occasions where judges requested or suggested that counsel produce further evidence on a particular matter or conduct further inquiries.[199] The nature of the interventions, however, was 'not insistent'.[200]

It remains the case, nevertheless, that the adversarial trial is a distinctly partisan affair, which carries with it considerable ramifications for truth-finding. All witnesses, including victims and defendants, are denied the opportunity to tell their story to the court using their own words, lest they should inadvertently say something which might damage the questioner's case. In seeking to take control of the witness, counsel will try to elicit only those facts which he or she feels should be included, and will do everything to avoid the witness speaking about anything that counsel feels should be omitted from the testimony. The goal, essentially, is to manipulate witness testimony in such a way that victory is made more likely. Testimony is closely regulated through carefully crafted questions and answers, in order to keep a tight rein on the witness, as Frank describes:

> [The witness] often detects what the lawyer hopes to prove at the trial. If the witness desires to have the lawyer's client win the case, he will often, unconsciously, mould [sic.] his story accordingly. Telling and re-telling it to the lawyer, he will honestly believe that his story, as he narrates it in court, is true, although it importantly deviates from what he originally believed.[201]

It has been said that the adversarial system 'turns witnesses into weapons to be used against the other side'.[202] The party calling them will seek to control carefully what witnesses say in an effort to make sure that their testimony fits in with the narrative that counsel puts forward. Their testimony must be shaped to bring out its maximum adversarial effect,[203] and witnesses are thereby confined to answering questions within the parameters set down by the questioner. Hamlyn et al

---

[195] Auld (2002), [11.36]. See also *R v Roberts* (1984) 80 Cr App R 89.

[196] In their survey of Diplock trials in Northern Ireland, Jackson and Doran (1995) found no examples of a judge calling a witness that neither party had previously called, although on one occasion a judge did exercise his power to recall a witness (at 181). Diplock trials are criminal trials where professional judges sit without a jury for scheduled offences in Northern Ireland, thus deciding upon questions relating to both law and fact.

[197] *Ibid.*

[198] There are conflicting authorities, however, as to whether a judge may *force* either party to call a witness. Contrast *R v Olivia* [1965] 1 WLR 1028 and *R v Sterk* [1972] Crim LR 391.

[199] Jackson and Doran (1995), 181–3.

[200] *Ibid*, 182.

[201] Frank (1949), 86.

[202] Pizzi (1999), 197.

[203] *Ibid.*

found that less than half of the vulnerable and intimidated witnesses they surveyed felt they had given their evidence completely accurately, in the sense that they had been able to recall adequately and convey to the court their recollections of what they had seen.[204]

Truth is thereby compromised by the marginalisation of all witnesses, but in particular, by denying the key stakeholders in the criminal offence an effective means of relaying their account to the court. In what seems to be a counter-intuitive practice, those who have greatest insight into the commission of the offence are prevented from relaying their experiences to the court in their own words, at their own pace. The irony is that the trial system will frequently demand that victims and offenders testify in open court, swearing an oath 'to tell the truth, the whole truth, and nothing but the truth', when, in fact the nature of advocacy lays down extremely narrow parameters by which all witnesses are expected to confine their answers.

Adversarial theory also rests on the assumption that all barristers are extremely skilled advocates and will know what to ask, and what not to ask. Certain types of questions must be avoided, as Stone recognised in advising barristers how to mount an effective examination-in-chief of a witness:

> It should be noted that controlled questioning does dictate the subject of enquiry and how it progresses, it does not involve leading. It does not suggest any answers, although the evidence is controlled by selection and editing. The witness is taken through his evidence by tightly framed questions, in small steps, and in an orderly and deliberate way, to ensure that all material facts are covered, and to avoid inadmissible, irrelevant, harmful or prejudicial evidence.[205]

Of course, whether a particular advocate can accomplish the skills and techniques of good advocacy will very much depend upon the individual—one's skills, experience, education, intelligence and ability to articulate oneself will vary tremendously. Not all barristers make good advocates.[206] Some may be particularly apt at controlling witnesses and drawing out the information which they desire. Others, perhaps less experienced counsel, may not think out the correct questions, or frame them in an inappropriate manner. Perhaps they will not question a witness carefully enough, and may fail to see the potential relevance of a particular fragment of information.

Story-telling

Counsel are advised to construct a 'case theory' before a case comes to trial.[207] This is the version of events which he or she believes to have taken place, which will then be relayed to the court in form of a story. As Stone explains:

---

[204] Hamlyn et al (2004), 57.
[205] Stone (1995), 94.
[206] See generally Pannick (1992).
[207] Stone (1995), 82.

[a]ll the advocate's arts, including techniques and devices of cross-examination, should converge to tell a party's story, in such a way as to persuade the court that it is true.[208]

Supported by a substantial body of literature,[209] story-telling theory holds that juries deliberate by constructing stories based around the way the evidence is presented to them. Stories are selectively prepared to enable the jury to identify the central action in the alleged crime; to make empirical connections among evidential elements based on that storyline; and to then interpret and evaluate those connections for internal consistency, completeness, and for their collective implications for the central action.[210]

The advocate thus becomes the storyteller, and will carefully select which parts of the story to tell and which to omit. The prosecution will seek to elicit the information that will assist their version of the story; whereas the defence will seek to disparage that story, and instead will attempt to portray the evidence in such a way that casts a positive light on their own version of events. Lubet points out how the formulation of a good narrative can provide a coherent 'story frame', which organises all of the events, transactions, and other surrounding facts of the case into an easily understandable context so that it will strike a familiar chord with jurors.[211]

The centrality of a good story to good advocacy fundamentally undermines the truth-finding potential of the adversarial trial. The truth that is reconstructed in the courtroom can represent a gross distortion of past events. Recollections of past events, along with associated evidence, are routinely manipulated, decontextualised and recategorised, before an attempt is made to re-organise them so that they correspond with abstract legal principles.[212] As part of this process, counsel also seek to:

> construct and represent . . . a moral identity for the participants in violent incidents that imputes particular attributes to them and accentuates aspects of their identity that speak to these attributes.[213]

The way in which the jury perceives their testimony may then be intensified or diminished as counsel attempt to highlight or downplay respective aspects. The advocate will accentuate those parts of the evidence that can be effectively challenged, thus intensifying the effect of any flaws or inconsistencies contained within it. As McBarnet writes:

---

[208] Stone (1995), 120.

[209] See, eg Bennet and Feldman (1981); Pennington and Hastie (1993); Rieke and Stutman (1994), 94–102; Taslitz (1999), 15–18. Others have suggested alternative models for jury decision-making. Wigmore (1937) asserted that decisions were based primarily on probability, calculated through a process of inductive reasoning. See further Anderson et al (2006), Ch 9.

[210] Bennet and Feldman (1981), 67. This appears to be supported by Pennington and Hastie's research.

[211] Lubet, (2001). It is not unusual for victim-blaming to feature prominently within such stories: see eg Rock (1998); Fielding (2006), 192.

[212] Cole (2001), 2.

[213] Fielding (2006), 192.

To process a case through to conviction as quickly as possible, the prosecution requires sufficient factual information to incriminate the accused but no extras which might introduce ambiguities that surround real-life incidents. He wants the issues kept clear cut—there is an offence; there is a victim who is blameless and an offender who is guilty; there are no reasonable doubts. He thus needs a victim-witness who gives clear, precise evidence on the relevant facts as *he* defines them, who is personally credible and who is the blamelessly white side of the black and white adversarial dispute. He wants no grey areas introduced in relation to the facts, credibility or culpability for the defence to pounce on in cross-examination.

Grey areas are, of course, exactly what the defence lawyer *does* want raised and especially from the central witness, the victim. Techniques in dealing with the victim are thus developed by the prosecutor and defence to respectively play down and play up the extra information that the victim might or might not provide, and *both* can involve treating the victim in a way which he or she experiences as degrading.[214]

There is therefore a clear difference between the historical truth and the constructed truth, as told through a story. The concealment, or at very least the simplification, of the historical truth may better serve the advocate's end than its discovery.

The Rules of Evidence

Aside from any selective filtration that may occur at the hands of the parties, a further tenet of the adversarial trial that may hinder truth-finding is the existence of a stringent regime of evidential rules. Damaska famously observed how one of the key features of the adversarial paradigm was its exclusionary regime of evidentiary rules which prohibited the flow of information to the factfinder.[215] As any teacher of evidence law will be aware, one of the first rules that students need to be familiar with is that all evidence adduced must be relevant to the facts in issue. As noted previously, this is a subjective judgement call for the judge to make, and depends on whether or not the judge considers something to be 'logically probative'.[216] That is not to say, however, that all relevant evidence will be produced for the trier of fact to assess: evidential rules do not require that certain types of evidence are included; only that certain types of evidence are excluded.[217] If neither of the parties wishes to introduce a particular piece of evidence, the court cannot admit such potentially relevant evidence of its own accord. Therefore evidence that may be perceived as being 'neutral', yet may still be relevant, is often overlooked. McEwan gives the example of the evidence of a key witness whom neither side wishes to call,

---

[214] McBarnet (1983), 296.
[215] Damaska (1973).
[216] *R v Kilbourne* [1973] AC 729.
[217] Evidence can be excluded either automatically by the operation of law (eg, hearsay evidence), or under the trial judge's discretion either at common law or under s 78 of the Police and Criminal Evidence Act.

since both sides fear what he or she may do to their case.[218] Evidential rules make no provision for the admissibility of such a witness's testimony, and thus the trier of fact is unable to take this witness's testimony into account.

The law of evidence has also served to exclude evidence that is probative and relevant. For example, the case of *R v Sparks*,[219] illustrates how the hearsay rule, will, on occasions, have this effect. Here, a white man was convicted of an attack on a 3 year-old girl. The girl had described her attacker as a 'coloured boy'. Since she was not competent to give evidence herself, the only way this could come to the attention of the court was if someone else read out her statement. The Privy Council held that the statement had been properly ruled out since no matter how great the perceived injustice, a criminal court had no discretion to permit the admissibility of hearsay evidence.[220] Another basis for the exclusion of potentially relevant evidence is section 78 of the Police and Criminal Evidence Act. If the Court determines that evidence has been obtained improperly, it may use its discretion under this provision to render the evidence inadmissible. It is not necessary that the Court finds the evidence to be unreliable before deciding to exercise this discretion.[221] In the same way, proceedings may be halted on the grounds of abuse of process, even if there is highly cogent evidence against the accused.[222] The question as to whether it is legitimate to use 'fruit from the poisoned tree' as the basis of a defendant's guilt results in different answers in different jurisdictions. If the evidence is struck out, or if the trial is stopped for abuse of process, the defendant may well be set free with his record unblemished, but in spite of the operation of rules of criminal procedure or ideas about the presumption of innocence, the truth of past events will remain unaltered. The rules of evidence therefore impede the flow of information being presented to the jury. They filter various elements of a witness's account that are subject to exclusion for whatever reason and thereby compromise the historical truth.

Adversarial Questioning

The manner in which advocates conduct cross-examination is crucial to the prospects of victory, but arguably also jeopardises the pursuit of truth. Language has been described as the 'primary manipulative tool' used by lawyers to advance their case.[223] If, as McBarnet has argued, it serves the interests of the defence to

---

[218] McEwan (1998), 4. Although the judge may urge parties to call a particular witness and also has the power to call witnesses himself.

[219] [1964] AC 964.

[220] This position has now changed. Under s 114(1)(d) Criminal Justice Act 2003, the court may admit hearsay evidence where it is 'satisfied that it is in the interests of justice' to do so.

[221] In *R v Mason* (1988) 86 Cr App R 349, the suspect and his solicitor were falsely told that the police had fingerprint evidence implicating the accused in an arson attack. The solicitor then advised the suspect to make a confession, which was subsequently admitted at trial. The accused was convicted and appealed. The Court of Appeal held that while the police action did not make the confession unreliable, he hoped to never again hear of deceit such as this practised on an accused, or more so on his solicitor. The evidence, he said, should definitely have been excluded.

[222] See further *R v Beckford* [1996] 1 Cr App R 94 at 100 for a summary of the grounds when proceedings may be stayed.

[223] Eades (1995), as cited by Ellison (2001b), 354.

create grey areas, it is unsurprising that witnesses are frequently confused by the questions put to them.[224] Suggestion is a specific questioning technique where advocates put scenarios to witnesses and then ask them to comment. Some witnesses are more susceptible to suggestion than others. Research has indicated that suggestion is a particularly effective technique for the advocate to establish control in cases involving children[225] or those with learning disabilities,[226] particularly where such a witness views the questioner as an authority figure.[227] A child is more likely to respond to a question that they did not understand, rather than admit incomprehension.[228] Thus the pressure engineered by hostile cross-examination makes it more likely that witnesses, especially vulnerable witnesses, will be more open to suggestion.[229] The better honed the advocate's skills are at suggestion, the more likely it will be that the witness responds in the desired way, and the more likely the factfinder will believe that particular version of events. Having surveyed the psychological literature, Spencer and Flin concluded that the more a questioner suggests a particular response, the less reliable the answer is likely to be.[230] In this way, the prominent use of suggestion within adversarial questioning impairs its potential for truth-finding.

It might be expected that if, as is so often claimed, cross-examination is a useful fact-finding tool, the courts would take steps to restrict the manipulation of witnesses by placing boundaries on the use of suggestive questioning. However, as previously noted, there are relatively few limits on adversarial cross-examination. The use of suggestion is regarded by the courts as a valid tool of persuasion and argument. It seems somewhat illogical that suggestion can be so freely used, if, as Lord Denning suggested in *Jones*, the advocate's role was to state the case as fairly and as strongly as possible.[231] As with the other techniques and devices discussed here, the truth is obscured rather than elicited by the way in which advocates carefully control oral evidence. Persuasive cross-examination tactics are untenable in terms of the underlying truth-finding justification for cross-examination as a means of accurate fact-finding.

The use of language that is unclear or ambiguous is also a useful device for advocates who wish to establish control over a witness. This, too, can impact upon the witness's ability to relate past events in a clear and accurate fashion to the court. Du Cann gives the example of how, in the American Borden murder trial,[232] the defence counsel misled the witness as to the purpose of the questioning. The

---

[224] Hamlyn et al (2004) found that 47% of witnesses reported that many of the questions they were asked were neither clear nor straightforward.

[225] Hedderman (1987), 28; Spencer and Flin (1993), 303; Ceci et al (2002).

[226] Sanders *et al* (1996), 75–6.

[227] Milne and Bull (1999).

[228] Waterman *et al* (2000), 211–25.

[229] See Gudjonnsson (1992), (2006); Spencer and Flin (1993), 306–7.

[230] Spencer and Flin (1993), 116.

[231] *Jones v National Coal Board* [1957] 2 QB 55, 64.

[232] The Borden murder trial is one of the most famous American murder trials in history. Lizzie Borden was acquitted of the murder of her parents, even though the prosecution presented an overwhelming case of circumstantial evidence.

witness had thought she was being asked about her service record for the family, whereas to the jury counsel appeared to be asking about relationships between the accused and the victim.[233] It is also important to note *how* such language is used. Ellison points out that:

> vigorous objection, warnings, reminders, repetition of questions and the insistence of proper answers are all devices used to attain and maintain editorial control.[234]

Stone advises advocates to prevent witnesses from thinking carefully about important questions:[235]

> Rapid questioning, especially in an unpredictable order, may give a liar too little time to invent answers related to earlier evidence and the hidden truth . . . Off balance he can be led into inconsistencies, improbabilities or testimony which can be contradicted by other evidence.[236]

As was noted in Chapter 2, the way in which lawyers use language in court can act as a source of considerable stress and confusion among many witnesses. This in itself means that the witness will be 'in the worst possible frame of mind to be examined—he will be agitated, confused and bewildered'.[237] Advocates are free to behave in a hostile manner and are free to make use of a range of devices in order to upset and frustrate complainants. By implication, the jury is invited to draw assumptions about the confused and distraught state of the witness, which opens the doorway to potentially inaccurate fact-finding since there is no evidence to suggest that the witness's demeanour is a reliable factor in determining the credibility of the evidence which he or she may give to the court.[238]

Cross-examiners have a vast range of tactics at their disposal to unsettle witnesses. In doing so, they aim to establish control over the witness so that they can fully exploit the testimony, using such tactics to filter the evidence and to cast it in a favourable light. Frequently, such control will result in evidence being presented to the court in a wholly different manner from the way in which witnesses intend. In Hamlyn et al's survey of vulnerable witnesses, over half of interviewees (57 per cent) felt they were not given the opportunity to say everything they had wanted to say in response to questions. Of these witnesses, 43 per cent said that this was because the lawyer interrupted or cut off the witness.[239] Fielding's qualitative study also found that many witnesses felt that the jury had received an incomplete version of events since they were unable to tell their own story in their own words.[240] Narrative testimony, he found, was strongly disliked by lawyers, who instinctively mistrusted the witnesses they called.[241] This raises clear implications

---

[233] Du Cann (1993), 138–9, as cited by Henderson (2001), 110.
[234] Ellison (2001a), 359.
[235] Stone (1995), 129.
[236] *Ibid*, 130.
[237] Harris (1892), cited by Fielding (2006), 219.
[238] See Ch 2, pp 85–7.
[239] Hamlyn et al (2004), 51.
[240] Fielding (2006), 182.
[241] *Ibid*, a number of examples are cited at 182–7.

for the contention that the limited question / answer format of the adversarial trial is an appropriate tool for uncovering the truth about past events. Far from facilitating the process of eliciting truth, it would appear that cross-examination acts as a relatively high hurdle in preventing witnesses from communicating the whole truth to the trier of fact.

The Verdict

Since the adversarial trial is limited to two versions of events, its eventual outcome will always be framed in terms of winning and losing. The adversarial paradigm dictates that the decision-maker, whether judge or jury, must rely on the parties exclusively for all the material facts.[242] Despite having no personal knowledge of the events in question or the witnesses giving evidence, the fact-finder must determine the outcome of the trial by fully awarding complete gain or loss through a 'guilty' or 'not guilty' verdict in respect of each individual charge.[243] In theory, there is usually scope for the jury to convict the accused of a lesser charge,[244] thus, in effect, allowing the fact-finder to partly transcend the terms of the dispute as framed by the parties. However, it remains the case that the trier of fact bases any such decision on the material presented by the parties themselves. Consequently, the version of the truth that is accepted by the jury will only reflect the historical record if the parties have presented a complete picture of past events.

The means of reconstructing past events is through the presentation of the evidence at trial. It is upon the evidence (in theory at least) that the trier of fact arrives at its verdict as to whether the accused is 'guilty' or 'not guilty'. Thus if evidence or the decision-making processes are imperfect, the verdict is also likely to be imperfect. In this sense, the verdict does not 'create' guilt or innocence, since it does not recreate the facts of the crime. Verdicts themselves 'only give official sanction to a

---

[242] Although in theory jurors may question witnesses themselves, the trial is not conducive to such a practice and jurors are almost entirely dependent upon the advocates as their source of information. From their discussions with judges in Northern Ireland, Jackson and Doran (1995) found that juries were rarely encouraged to ask questions (at 175) and that they were often ignorant about their power to do so (at 177). Langbein (2003) contends that while the practice of jury intervention is reasonably commonplace in the early eighteenth century, the practice faded as the trial became increasingly lawyerised: 'Defence counsel did not want participants cluttering . . . [the] inquiry with other questions, especially with questions about the truth' (at 312).

[243] It is, of course, open to the jury to acquit the accused of some charges whilst convicting on others.

[244] By virtue of s 6(3) of the Criminal Law Act 1967, where a person is tried on indictment for any offence except treason or murder and the jury find him not guilty of the offence specifically charged in the indictment, the jury may find him guilty of an alternative offence, if the allegations in the indictment expressly or by implication amount to, or include, an allegation of the alternative offence, provided that the alternative offence falls within the jurisdiction of the court of trial. Section 6(2) of the Act deals with alternative verdicts to a count of murder. Eg, if the defendant is charged with robbery it may be possible to convict him or her of theft if the element of force is not proved. On occasions, the prosecution may also charge the accused of 2 or more offences in the alternative. In these circumstances, if the defendant is convicted of the more serious offence, the jury should be discharged from giving a verdict on the lesser charge.

particular hypothesis about those facts'.[245] Therefore, within a trial context, 'truth of alleged facts in adjudication is typically a matter of probabilities, falling short of absolute certainty'.[246] It is perhaps more appropriate to regard the verdict as an acknowledgement of the strengths and weaknesses of the parties' performances and their use of evidence, rather than a definitive account of the 'truth' about past events.

The 'truth' as contained in the verdict is not only dependent on the evidence presented, but also upon the trier's interpretation of that evidence. It will be subject to individual value-judgements, as may the law that has been explained to the jury by the judge. Such a scenario may give rise to what is commonly known as 'jury equity' or 'jury nullification'. Here, the jury may act in defiance of the weight of the evidence and / or the legal instructions given by the bench in determining the question of guilt.[247] Matravers has defended jury nullification as a means of preserving truth within a criminal trial.[248] Rather than assume that a jury is 'lying' or acting illegally in arriving at its verdict, the jury should instead be seen as answering a different type of question, which is not confined to whether the defendant broke the law, but whether he did so in a manner than merits a certain type of punishment to be handed down. While Matravers' argument will not win favour with those who place an overriding value upon the need for legal certainty, it is perhaps correct to view the existence of jury equity as one means of counteracting those processes and values which seem to do so much to distort the truth in the adversarial trial.

Even if the jury performs its function faithfully, there is still the possibility that the verdict may misrepresent past events. It is possible that (a) the jury may have erred; or (b) that the prosecution failed to discharge the burden of proof. In either event, it may be the case, for example, that the jury, whilst acting in good faith, reached an incorrect verdict, and that the defendant was, in fact, guilty of the offence charged. He is thus declared 'not guilty' according to the principles of proof under the law, and a new legal truth is thereby created that supersedes the historical truth. Conversely, the same situation could arise where the jury has erroneously concluded that the defendant is guilty. In many criminal verdicts, legal guilt and factual guilt will not necessarily be synonymous.[249] From a victim's perspective, the 'truth' that is reconstructed during the trial may take a very different form than the victim's recollection of events. While the emergence of truth and the delineation of criminal responsibility may well have a cathartic effect for victims, if the trier of fact makes a different finding in favour of the accused, the victim may be left feeling deflated and confused.

---

[245] Laudan (2006), 12.

[246] Risinger (2004), 1285.

[247] For a summary of research on the likely extent of jury equity, see Darbyshire et al (2002); Sanders and Young (2007), 535–41.

[248] Matravers (2004).

[249] This reflects what was noted in Ch 1 at p 21. Law is essentially a closed system of communication. The legal meaning of 'guilty' or 'not guilty' is, potentially, very different from the way such terms are construed in the media or by the public at large.

In summary then, the criminal trial 'produces truth, rather than finds it'.[250] The testimony of complainants, and indeed all witnesses, is filtered by a number of adversarial practices including: questioning processes; exclusionary rules of evidence; the insistence upon orality and finally, the application of the law. The interaction of these factors results in the tribunal of fact being presented with a very select and simplified version of what actually occurred. Since the facts available to the court are limited, it logically follows that the truth is also limited. In many cases, the 'truth' that emerges through the verdict may simply constitute the view of the better advocate.

Summary

It is regrettable that the victim's right to truth, which is now recognised on a widespread basis in international human rights standards, has been subject to relatively little analysis within the context of domestic criminal justice. Indeed, even if one declines to accept the existence of a 'right to truth' for victims of crime, the pursuit of justice itself cannot be accomplished without an accurate fact-finding process. The pursuit of truth must therefore be a *sine qua non* of any judicial process.

Damaska has not been alone in noting that:

> the Anglo-American method of collecting and presenting evidence not only deviates from ordinary decision-making but . . . it also strikes discordant notes with arrangements recommended by a model of inquiry aimed at obtaining only accurate, trustworthy knowledge.[251]

Judge Frankel also observed:

> [w]e proclaim to each other and to the world that the clash of adversaries is a powerful means for hammering out the truth . . . but . . . [d]espite our untested statements of self-congratulation, we know that others searching after facts—in history, geography, medicine, whatever—do not emulate our adversarial system.[252]

There are, of course, valid arguments for separating the nature of legal inquiry from other disciplines. Truth, for example, should not be considered to be the *only* goal of the legal system. Clearly, the system's integrity also hangs on other considerations too, such as the need to account for due process, fair trial rights, public policy and practical time restraints. These factors do not feature so prominently in other discourses. Nonetheless, and in contrast to the inquisitorial method, the adversarial system is remarkably ill-equipped to the uncover the truth. It is grossly inefficient in terms of its ability to search and scrutinise the available evidence, and denies many victims the opportunity to have the harm against them officially acknowledged. In this way, victims are less likely to achieve any sense of closure.

---

[250] Goodpaster (1987), 130.
[251] Damaska (1997), 101.
[252] Frankel (1975), 1036.

IV. Conclusions

The idea of an effective remedy has evolved considerably in recent years, and is now, along with many of its individual components, entrenched in international human rights law. Standard-setting has rapidly evolved in both international and regional human rights systems. As a result, there is an array of positive obligations in place which are now widely accepted as going hand-in-hand with the most fundamental of human rights. Signatory states to the European Convention are under a very clear obligation to investigate and punish alleged breaches of Articles 2 and 3 committed by both state and non-state actors. Similarly, the recent emergence of a 'right to truth', while not featuring widely in binding instruments or European jurisprudence, has begun to percolate traditional understandings about the role of the criminal process in delivering justice for victims. Increasingly, it is accepted that the truth of past events is not only necessary for just outcomes to be achieved, it is also a legitimate expectation of all victims and may play a key role in helping them to understand the causes of the offending behaviour and contribute towards the long-term healing process.

Whilst there remains some degree of ambiguity as to the full scope of such newly emergent rights, we can expect that, in time, international norms will become further refined and more specific in their demands. It is important that we do not underestimate their significance for victims. International benchmarking has played a significant role in stirring academic and policy-based debates towards a new conception of victims' rights as a form of human rights. It is becoming increasingly apparent that, in order to fully realise these rights within the criminal justice system, we may need to rethink some of our most entrenched structures and practices. While domestic courts have accepted the principle that victims of non-state crime have certain inalienable rights under the Convention, it is clear that some aspects of the right to a remedy are easier to realise than others. For example, the decisions in *Amin* and *Middleton* recognise the broad nature of the duty under Article 2 to investigate deaths. However, these rights remain underdeveloped; in particular, it is unclear whether the investigatory requirements cover less serious criminal offences, which fall well short of the threshold required for Articles 2 and 3. To date, there have only been a limited range of cases to draw upon, and we can expect the parameters of the duty to become clearer over time.

We have reason to be less optimistic in respect of the right of a victim to attain reasons for a decision to drop or alter charges, or not to proceed at all with the prosecution. While the decision in *Manning* constitutes a welcome move to a comprehensive review process, there are no signs that the CPS intends to alter its practice in being more specific as to how it takes account of the victim within the 'public interest' requirement. Similarly, questions remain as to the long-term prospect for the newly emergent 'right to truth' to penetrate domestic practice. The challenge of realising this right may prove to be troublesome in the extreme, given that accurate truth-finding appears to be an anathema of the adversarial paradigm.

Overall, however, from a victim's perspective the expansion of a right to a remedy and the corresponding ascendancy of positive obligations in both international and domestic fora mark a tremendous leap forward, in that victims' rights are now being conceived as a dimension of human rights. Consequently, the concept is no longer confined to the realms of political mantra, or declaratory soft law publications; but victims' right are now legally enforceable within the courts. Of course, the law of the books does not always reflect the law in action; and in time we will need to look again at our structures, processes and their underlying normative frameworks to ensure that the human rights of victims become a reality in practice.

5

The Right to Reparation

T HE UNDERSTANDING THAT reparation should be available to victims whose rights have been violated is widely regarded as falling 'among
the most venerable and most central of legal principles'.[1] As noted in the
previous chapter, the concept of 'reparation' may be viewed as one of two distinct
aspects of the right to a remedy. Reparation, as the root of the term ('repair')
suggests, is frequently used to describe a range of measures that aim to rectify
the harm caused and to restore the victim to his or her position before the act in
question occurred, insofar as that is possible.

This chapter examines what victims ought to expect to receive from the State or
from the offender in terms of redress for the harm that they have suffered. The
obligation of a responsible party to provide full reparation to an injured party for
any loss or damage incurred forms a core principle of both international human
rights and humanitarian law. It is also found within the criminal and / or civil law
of most domestic jurisdictions.

The rationale for reparation is derived from the violation of the victim's individual rights, which will usually have resulted in a victim suffering some form of
material or emotional loss or harm. Whilst the concept of reparation is somewhat
paradoxical in that redress is fundamentally incapable of undoing the effects of a
serious or traumatic crime,[2] it should help make the loss easier to bear for victims
and their families. It should, to some extent, help rehumanise victims and restore
their dignity.[3] There is also a strong policy argument for providing reparation,
insofar as the possibility of recompense should encourage victims to report crime
and co-operate with the criminal justice system. In addition, it may be argued that
victims are morally entitled to redress in order to restore the equilibrium that has
been upset by the offender's actions.[4]

It is not uncommon for the term 'reparation' to be used interchangeably with
terms such as 'compensation', 'damages', 'restitution', or 'restoration', which
stems from a common misconception that 'reparation' equates to financial compensation. It may well *entail* some form of compensation, but the concepts should

---

[1] Roht-Arriaza (1995), 17.
[2] Roht-Arriaza (2004). She asks 'What could replace lost health and serenity; the loss of a loved one
or of a whole extended family; a whole generation of friends; the destruction of home and culture and
community and peace?' (at 159).
[3] Bassiouni (2006), 231.
[4] Cavadino and Dignan (1997), 235.

not be construed as being synonymous. Indeed, in recent years, there is a discernable international consensus which suggests that reparation should not be defined in an overly narrow or legalistic sense. As argued below, 'reparation' may take a number of different forms and may apply in a range of different contexts.

One important aspect of reparation generally is that it represents a victim-centred approach to offending, whether such offending is committed by state or non-state actors. Thus, while reparatory measures will often impose some form of burden on the offender, their primary rationale is to empower the victim. In transitional justice discourse, reparations are often made to victims in the absence of an effective collective sanctioning or enforcement authority, and in this way they may also serve to punish and deter wrongdoing.[5] In criminal justice discourse, this is often linked with restorative justice and Braithwaite's concept of 'reintegrative shaming',[6] which seeks to 'shame' offenders:

> in such a way as to promote their integration into the community of law-abiding citizens rather than alienating them from it in the ways that conventional forms of justice often seem to do.[7]

A right to reparation, it has been argued, is not only beneficial to victims, but can carry important benefits for offenders and wider society as well through promoting the alleviation of guilt and the idea that amends have been made.[8] Cavadino and Dignan have highlighted the potential of reparation to enable 'denunciation to be expressed in a currency other than that of retributive-style punishments'.[9]

I. Reparation as an International Standard

The Origins of Reparation in International Law

The concept of reparations was originally conceived as lying within the legal framework of inter-state relations; the idea of individual victims receiving redress directly from a perpetrator was relatively unknown before the advent of modern human rights norms in the aftermath of World War II. In customary international law, the State was originally conceived as the protector of its citizens, and had a right to resort to legal and diplomatic action to obtain redress on their behalf. This position was codified in the Hague Conventions of 1899 and 1907, and confirmed in the oft-cited *Chorzów Factory Case* in 1928.[10] In a landmark ruling, the Permanent Court of International Justice stated that it was a 'principle of inter-

---

[5] Shelton (2002), 833.
[6] Braithwaite (1989). See further discussion in Ch 6 at pp 254–65.
[7] Cavadino and Dignan (1997), 241.
[8] Zedner (1994), 233.
[9] Cavadino and Dignan (1997), 241.
[10] *Factory at Chorzów (Jurisdiction)*, Series A, No 17 (1927) PCIJ No 8.

national law that the breach of an engagement involves an obligation to make reparation in an adequate form',[11] and that:

> reparation must, as far as possible, wipe out all the consequences of the illegal act and re-establish the situation which would, in all probability, have existed if that act had not been committed.[12]

Where a state has caused damage to another state or its citizens through a breach of international law, an obligation arises to compensate the injured state.[13]

Since the *Chorzów* decision, the question of reparation has been raised at the end of wars,[14] either through ad hoc claims commissions or arbitral tribunals established under peace agreements.[15] Usually such reparation prioritised specific economic losses, such as the destruction of property, infrastructure, or ships,[16] but it may also cover personal injury to individual victims by virtue of them being members of a larger collective victim community.[17] It should be stressed, however, that the nature of the obligation in international law was, and largely still is, inter-state in nature. One state may take action against another for a breach of international law on behalf of its citizens. While the beneficiary state may then choose to redistribute such funds to individual victims, there is no obligation to do so. Herein lies one major weakness of the state-responsibility framework: individual victims have not been viewed as having any legitimate claim to pursue reparations independent of them being part of a larger victimised state or community.[18] It is therefore perhaps unsurprising that there have been relatively few incidences of reparations being paid out to victims in the aftermath of mass atrocities.[19]

In more recent times, however, there are some signs that the doctrine of state responsibility is expanding, in a way that is not dissimilar to the normative realignment of human rights and criminal justice norms charted in previous chapters.

---

[11] *Ibid*, 21.

[12] *Ibid*, 47.

[13] Art 3, ILC Articles on State Responsibility.

[14] See Art 3 of the Hague Convention on Land Warfare of 1907 and each of the Geneva Conventions of 1949.

[15] Forms of reparation may also be ordered by, inter alia, the International Court of Justice, World Trade Organisation, or the International Tribunal for the Law of the Sea.

[16] Shelton (1999), 99.

[17] Examples of 'collective' reparations include payments by the Federal Republic of Germany and Austria to Israel in relation to the Nazi holocaust; and a UN Resolution requiring Iraq to pay reparations for Kuwait stemming from its invasion in 1990 (see discussion below).

[18] Bottigliero (2004) provides a few rare examples where individual victims have been viewed as direct beneficiaries, such as Hague Convention No XII (which never entered into force) and the Mixed Arbitral Tribunal (established under the Treaty of Versailles). The Central American Court of Justice, which adjudicated 10 cases between 1908 and 1918, was open to states, individuals and institutions to pursue losses for the breach of international agreements. 5 of the cases involved losses sustained by individuals; 4 of these were dismissed because of the non-exhaustion of domestic remedies. In the 5th case, the Court found against the victim. These isolated examples aside, there has been very little evidence of the existence of an obligation on states to compensate individual victims under the doctrine of state responsibility (at 82–4).

[19] Roth-Arriaza (2004). She notes 2 prominent exceptions. Germany paid sizeable reparations for crimes committed during the period of Nazi rule, and the United States paid reparations to surviving Japanese-American internees.

Increasing attention is being paid to the plight of individuals, and the law relating to state responsibility has been altered to ensure that individual victims of state violations of law are better placed to obtain some form of reparation directly. Two major developments are indicative of such a shift: the establishment of the UN Compensation Commission for Claims Against Iraq; and the formulation of new ILC Articles on State Responsibility.

The UN Compensation Commission for Claims Against Iraq was established by the UN Security Council to consider claims and administer compensation payments arising from Iraq's invasion and subsequent occupation of Kuwait in 1990–91.[20] In contrast to the position of the law on state responsibility, the Commission was empowered to adjudicate claims from, and award compensation to, individual victims in cases of human rights violations and international crimes. While individual claimants or victims still must be supported by their respective governments or an alternative international organisation, the Commission has put in place a 'priority policy', whereby individual claims for human rights abuses take precedence over government or corporate claims. In this way, the Commission, which concluded its work in June 2005,[21] has delivered a very practical form of redress to many Kuwaitis who suffered from Iraq's invasion and subsequent occupation of their country. Despite criticism in some quarters over the Commission's legality, and allegations that its establishment was politically motivated,[22] the fact that significant compensation payments were actually made stands in sharp contrast to the International Tribunal for Yugoslavia or the International Tribunal for Rwanda, discussed below, which failed to provide victims with any realistic mechanisms to obtain compensation.

The second factor to indicate an increasing concern for the 'direct victim' is evidenced in the nature of the codification of the law on state responsibility. Much of this progress can be attributed to the penetration by human rights discourse into the traditional law governing state responsibility and the international breakdown of the vertical / horizontal divide. In 2001, after several previously unsuccessful attempts, the International Law Commission adopted the Articles on State Responsibility. While the focal point of the Articles is the relationship between one state and another, it is clear that the Articles provide some evidence of an emergent right for victims to receive compensation directly. The restitution of property is usually regarded as the default remedy that will normally be afforded priority.[23] It often entails the return of goods or property and is based on the civil law concept of *restitutio in integrum*, the idea of fully restoring an aggrieved party to their previous condition. It is defined in Article 35 of the ILC Articles as re-establishing 'the situation which existed before the wrongful act was committed' and may thus include other forms of reparation, considered below.

---

[20] S/Res/ 692.
[21] Bassiouni (2006) notes that at the end of its operational period the Commission had approved awards of approximately $52.5 billion (US) in respect of approximately 1.55 million claims.
[22] Malanczuk (1995).
[23] Shelton (1999), 94; (2002), 804; Leach (2005).

Article 31 reiterates the obligation in *Chorzów* to make full reparation to the injured state,[24] but beyond this, Article 33(1) provides that the State's obligations in any given case may extend beyond providing recompense to another state: secondary duties may be owed towards several states, or indeed the international community as a whole.[25] Article 33(2) then notes that the Articles are:

> without prejudice to any right, arising from the international responsibility of a State, which accrues directly to any person or entity other than a State

which, according to the Commentary, reflects the growing recognition that:

> individuals concerned should be regarded as the ultimate beneficiaries and in that sense as the holders of the relevant rights.[26]

It is thus envisaged that, in future, individual victims of violations of international law could use domestic courts or tribunals to obtain redress from violating states. It should be stressed, however, that the provision is still limited. In order for reparations to be made to a non-state entity, effective procedures would need to be in place at domestic level. This Article 'merely recognizes the possibility'.[27] These rights conferred by the ILC Articles remain state-centred and, while state responsibility can be invoked by states on behalf of the larger community, the Commentary is clear that the 'Articles do not deal with the possibility of the invocation of responsibility by persons or entities other than States'.[28] As such, the Articles in themselves will remain an ineffective tool for most victims of serious human rights abuses, but set in the context of an overall trend, they may well be said to constitute a positive step in the right direction.

Reparation in Human Rights Law

The post-war ascendancy of human rights law has partially overarched the significance of the development of the doctrine of state responsibility. Principles that once had their origin in the law of state responsibility have now been transplanted into human rights law. This means that if a state violates a human rights standard which it has ratified, it is under a duty to make reparation. As Saul has observed:

> [i]nternational human rights law has infused the inter-state paradigm of state responsibility . . . with a new concern and respect for the individual, irrespective of nationality.[29]

From the victim's perspective, one key difference between the two legal frameworks is nonetheless highly significant. Human rights law has incrementally

---

[24] An injury is defined as 'any damage, whether material or moral, caused by the internationally wrongful act'. The various forms of reparation, provided for by Art 34, include 'restitution, compensation and satisfaction, either singly or in combination'.

[25] ILC (2001), 233.

[26] *Ibid*, 234.

[27] *Ibid.*

[28] *Ibid.*

[29] Saul (2004), 534.

acknowledged the special status of individual victims as those who have primarily suffered the consequences of human rights violations. Its focus on rights as opposed to responsibilities means that individuals will usually be afforded a right to pursue redress directly from the offending state. In contrast to the provisions on state responsibility, individuals are accorded their own personality under human rights law; there is no a priori requirement that victims are represented or even supported by a state body. Human rights treaties have created directly accessible rights for individual victims. If a state breaches its obligations under the terms of the Treaty following the finding of a tribunal, the Treaty will usually require it to make reparations to the injured party.

The increasing emphasis placed on the value of providing reparation to victims reflects the gradual reconstruction of crime as less of a legalistic offence against the state and more of a social offence against individuals and communities. This position is reflected in a range of international instruments, foremost amongst them the 1985 Victims' Declaration. Principle 8 lays down the basic requirement that:

> offenders or third parties responsible for their behaviour should, where appropriate, make fair restitution to victims, their families or dependants.

In most jurisdictions, this will reflect the position taken in the domestic law of tort.[30] The Principle goes on to suggest that such restitution may include the return of property or payment for the harm or loss suffered; the reimbursement of any expenses incurred as a result of victimisation; the provision of services; and the 'restoration of rights'. Principle 9 stipulates that 'governments should review their practices, regulations and laws to consider restitution as an available sentencing option in criminal cases, in addition to other criminal sanctions'.

The Declaration recognises, however, that, in many cases, individual perpetrators will not be in a position to provide redress directly. In these circumstances, the State should assume the function of a safety net, providing compensation to victims and their families in those cases where there was a 'significant bodily injury or impairment of physical or mental health as a result of serious crimes'.[31] Thus, even where the State has no responsibility under international or national law to pay compensation, Principle 13 provides that '[t]he establishment, strengthening and expansion of national funds for compensation to victims should be encouraged'. Principle 14 provides that 'victims should receive the necessary material, medical, psychological and social assistance through governmental, voluntary, community-based and indigenous means'. It alludes to the idea that victims should be empowered to resume their lives to as full an extent as possible, and thus incorporates a range of measures that may be therapeutic or material. However, the Principles fail to elaborate on the detail concerning the precise scope of such assistance or support.

---

[30] Scott (ed) (2001), cited by Bassiouni (2006), 223 n 96.
[31] Art 12.

In 1989, work was undertaken to attempt to codify the nature of the right to reparation under international law. Theo Van Boven was commissioned as rapporteur to undertake a study on the 'right to restitution, compensation and rehabilitation for victims of human rights [abuses] and fundamental freedoms'. Following a series of meetings with bodies of experts, seminars and submissions from states and NGO's, Van Boven presented a set of Draft Principles to the Commission on Human Rights in 1994. The Commission then determined that more work should be undertaken, and appointed a new rapporteur, M Cherif Bassiouni, to revise Van Boven's work. The original set of Draft Principles was merged with the Joinet Principles of 1996 by Bassiouni, who presented his final report along with a fresh draft to the Commission in 2000.[32] After a brief period where momentum seemed to dwindle,[33] the process of final consultations began in 2002,[34] and the Basic Principles and Guidelines on the Right to a Remedy and Reparation for Victims of Violations of International Human Rights and Humanitarian Law were eventually adopted by the Commission on Human Rights in April 2005[35] and by the General Assembly in December 2005.[36]

The Basic Principles and Guidelines:

> intentionally adopted a victim-oriented perspective, organizing principles from all legal sources not according to instruments and sources, but according to the needs and rights of victims.[37]

They thus constitute a consolidation of existing international norms, rather than a new code designed to replace them. The Principles are limited to 'the identification of mechanisms, modalities, procedures and methods for the implementation of existing legal obligations under international human rights law and international humanitarian law'.[38] Underpinning the instrument is the idea that where an individual is a victim of a violation of an applicable international human rights or humanitarian law norm, then effective reparation must be made. Reparation must be prompt, adequate and effective and should be in proportion to the harm suffered, and should be available to victims 'without any discrimination of any kind or ground, without exception'.[39] Further evidence of the increasing emphasis on individual rights and the breakdown of the public / private divide is evident in the provisions which require that, where the State itself was not responsible for the violation, the party responsible should provide reparation to the victim.[40] If such a party is unidentifiable or is unable to provide redress, then the onus to compensate returns to the State.

---

[32] E/CN.4/2000/62.
[33] Bassiouni (2006) notes that the adoption of the draft text was delayed as a result of the Sep 2001 World Conference on Racism where the issue of victim compensation was contested by many States.
[34] E/CN.4/RES/2002/44.
[35] E/CN.4/2005/ L.10/Add.11.
[36] A/RES/60/147.
[37] E/CN.4/2003/63.
[38] A/RES/60/147.
[39] Principle 25.
[40] See further discussion in Ch 1, pp 27–8.

While the Basic Principles provide clarification on the nature of reparation and extent of the duty to make redress, like the 1985 Declaration beforehand, the Principles have no enforcement mechanism and their ultimate effectiveness is wholly dependent upon the action of individual states. Moreover, they have also been criticised on the grounds that they are vague, and fail to account for why victims of 'non-gross violations' should not be able to access reparation in the same way. Arguably this omission has led to something of a two-tier system, whereby international human rights law has deemed that some victims are more worthy than others.[41]

The Basic Principles deal with both human rights law and international humanitarian law, thereby recognising ongoing convergence between the two bodies of law.[42] However, from the perspective of crime victims, it is also regrettable that the Principles departed from the definitional approach of the 1985 Declaration, which recognised the commonality between victims of crime and victims of abuse of power.[43] Unlike the 1985 Victims Declaration, the 2005 Basic Principles apply primarily to victims of humanitarian and human rights abuses. In this sense, the instruments fail to encapsulate the principle of positive obligations which has played such a crucial role in both the European and Inter-American systems in enshrining in law those linkages between victims of state and non-state crime.[44]

The instrument, however, is not entirely irrelevant to the victim of non-state crime. Principle 17 reflects the general position that a non-state perpetrator should be the primary party responsible for providing redress to the victim or to the State if the latter has already provided reparation. The State exercises the same 'safety net' function under Principle 18 as it does under the 1985 Declaration; where the non-state party is unable or unwilling to provide reparation, the State should do so. Similar redress mechanisms are put in place for victims' families, which will normally be applicable to the dependants of victims who have died or become incapacitated as a result of the violation. Principle 19 obliges states to ensure that domestic judgments for reparations against individuals are enforced, and, likewise, foreign judgments against such non-state perpetrators should also be implemented. However, there is no suggestion that states should make reparation where they have failed to act against non-state violators or provide potential victims with adequate protection. While the instrument falls short of

---

[41] See eg, Roht-Arriaza (2004), who notes that 'reparations in cases of massive violence or repression have been paid only for a subset of the most egregious human rights violations' (at 163).

[42] See Bassiouni (2006), 253: 'The document does not address the substantive claims of human rights and international humanitarian law and it does not enumerate what falls under their respective ambits. It simply says that violations require remedies. However, it is clear from the comments and approaches of various Member States and the wording of the 2006 Basic Principles and Guidelines that there is significant resistance to conceptualising international human rights law and international humanitarian law as linked and unified'.

[43] See Ch 1, p 31.

[44] See Ch 4, pp 164–71.

what might have been expected in the context of expanding notions of human rights, it may be said that the instrument has nonetheless acted as a catalyst in expanding conceptions of 'reparation' and driving forward related policy initiatives.[45]

The forms of reparation referred to in the Basic Principles reflect the long-standing distinction made in international law between 'material' and 'symbolic' forms of redress. The former include proprietary and pecuniary measures, most notably restitution[46] and compensation.[47] The latter term is somewhat free-floating, but concepts such as 'rehabilitation',[48] 'satisfaction' and 'guarantees of non-repetition' are referred to in the instrument. These concepts are difficult to define, but may be said to encapsulate a wide range of measures, 'most having to do with a felt need for telling the story, for justice, and for measures to avoid repetition'.[49] Symbolic forms of reparation are particularly commonplace in cases in which the injury cannot be repaired, which may arise where the harm is 'moral' rather than 'material' in nature. A non-exhaustive list of the type of acts that may constitute 'satisfaction' is provided by Principle 22. They include the cessation of continuing violations; verification of the facts; full public disclosure of the truth; the search for the 'disappeared'; an official declaration or a judicial decision; restoring the dignity, reputation and legal and social rights of the victim and of persons closely connected with the victim; an apology, 'including public

---

[45] A right to reparation is also contained in the Updated Set of principles for the protection and promotion of human rights through action to combat impunity (E/CN.4/2005/102/Add.1). Principle 31 states: 'Any human rights violation gives rise to a right to reparation on the part of the victim or his or her beneficiaries, implying a duty on the part of the State to make reparation and the possibility for the victim to seek redress from the perpetrator'.

[46] Principle 19 refers to the restoration of the victim to his or her original state prior to the relevant violation. Restitution includes the 'restoration of liberty, enjoyment of human rights, identity, family life and citizenship, return to one's place of residence, restoration of employment and return of property'. The right has been applied in a number of post-conflict settings, including Chile, Argentina and the former Yugoslavia, as entailing a right to return to a home of origin, the return of property and restoration of legal rights. As such, it is often understood to refer to the restoration of rights, rather than financial compensation.

[47] Principle 20 of the UN Basic Principles provides that compensation should be provided for any economically assessable damage resulting from violations of international human rights and humanitarian law. This includes: (a) Physical or mental harm, including pain, suffering and emotional distress; (b) Lost opportunities, including education; (c) Material damages and loss of earnings, including loss of earning potential; (d) Harm to reputation or dignity; and (e) Costs required for legal or expert assistance, medicines and medical services, and psychological and social services. Typical examples would include the loss of wages, medical and hospital expenses, which may include counselling, and damaged or stolen property.

[48] Under Principle 21, rehabilitation refers to medical, psychological, legal and social services aimed at promoting the victim's healing. Cherif Bassiouni reiterated that rehabilitation should include medical and psychological care and other services as well as legal and social services, and it is acknowledged in the 1999 Basic Principles, which refer to 'the need of victims, many of whom come from the least-resourced sectors and groups of society, to be afforded medical, psychological, legal and social services'.

[49] Roht-Arriaza (2004), 159.

acknowledgement of the facts and acceptance of responsibility'; judicial and administrative sanctions against violators; and commemorations or tributes to victims.[50]

The way in which reparation is organised is often paramount to a victim's sense of justice,[51] and interestingly, research appears to suggest that victims place as high a priority on symbolic reparation as they do upon material recompense.[52] Such forms of reparation are particularly commonplace in post-conflict societies, where symbolic reparation may be offered as an alternative to formal prosecution, which is believed to have a beneficial role in helping victims move beyond anger and feelings of powerlessness by providing a sense of closure, as well as helping to reintegrate offenders back into society.[53] Such forms of reparation may also play a vital role in contributing to wider social reconstruction and inter-community reconciliation.[54]

While symbolic forms of reparation have featured prominently in both transitional justice and restorative justice literature, a risk nonetheless exists that justice may be seen as being belittled or degraded if not backed up by something more tangible, such as the restitution of property or financial compensation.[55] The best form of reparation is likely to constitute a mixture of symbolic and material awards, but what Zedner has labelled the 'elusive recipe for reparation' is often difficult to locate, let alone implement.[56] Thus while a right to reparation may well exist on a normative plain, it is unfortunately the case that mechanisms are rarely in place to allow victims to enforce reparations. As many international instruments rely on domestic mechanisms to be put in place so that victims are able to access a remedy, it is notoriously difficult for the efficacy of such institutions to be monitored at international level. If the State has been the perpetrator to begin with, then victims are reliant upon mechanisms of the same state that harmed them to award them restitution.

---

[50] Regarding the search for truth, see Ch 4, pp 180–203. In relation to 'guarantees of non-repetition', see Principle 23. Examples include: (a) Ensuring effective civilian control of military and security forces; (b) Ensuring that all civilian and military proceedings abide by international standards of due process, fairness and impartiality; (c) Strengthening the independence of the judiciary; (d) Protecting persons in the legal, medical and health-care professions, the media and other related professions, and human rights defenders; (e) Providing, on a priority and continued basis, human rights and international humanitarian law education to all sectors of society and training for law enforcement officials as well as military and security forces; (f) Promoting the observance of codes of conduct and ethical norms, in particular international standards, by public servants, including law enforcement, correctional, media, medical, psychological, social service and military personnel, as well as by economic enterprises; (g) Promoting mechanisms for preventing and monitoring social conflicts and their resolution; (h) Reviewing and reforming laws contributing to or allowing gross violations of international human rights law and serious violations of international humanitarian law.

[51] Wierda and de Grieff (2004).

[52] Retzinger and Scheff (1996); Shelton (1999); Braithwaite (2002).

[53] Minow (1998), 92.

[54] Roht-Arriaza (2004), 159.

[55] Shelton (1999); Roht-Arriaza (2004).

[56] Zedner (1994), 238.

Reparation in the European and Inter-American Human Rights Systems

Propelled by these international developments, the right to reparation is also emerging under regional human rights systems, most notably under the European and American Conventions. These systems are based on a direct relationship between the State and the individual, and in this way, the individual *per se* can hold the state responsible before the relevant court or tribunal. They are not, however, courts of first instance; in most cases, victims should have exhausted all domestic remedies.

Article 13 of the European Convention on Human Rights provides that:

> Everyone whose rights and freedoms as set forth in this Convention are violated shall have an effective remedy before a national authority notwithstanding that the violation has been committed by persons acting in an official capacity.

States have traditionally enjoyed a wide margin of appreciation on the applicability of Article 13, which has led to an inconsistent application of the concept of a remedy in the past 'aside from reiterating basic criteria of effectiveness, fairness and adequacy of redress'.[57]

The right to a remedy is enhanced by Article 41 which provides for 'just satisfaction' to the injured party, if domestic law allows for 'only partial reparation'.[58] It is usual that, where a breach of Article 13 is established, compensation will follow under Article 41. Traditionally, the Court has interpreted this provision so as to award pecuniary and non-pecuniary compensation, as well as costs and expenses.[59] The Court has refrained from ordering other forms of redress, such as quashing decisions of the domestic authorities or courts, rehabilitation, clearance of victims' names, striking down domestic legislation that is not Convention-compliant, or requiring a state to alter its legislation.[60] In this respect, the Convention jurisprudence is perhaps less developed than it ought to be; other international standards arguably offer a better guarantee of redress to victims of human rights violations. The Court has nonetheless acknowledged also that there are circumstances where compensation is inadequate or impossible, particularly in circumstances involving breaches of Articles 2 and 3 of the Convention.[61] As noted in the previous chapter, the development of the doctrine of positive obligations has led to the Court looking to remedies beyond compensation, devising a broad

---

[57] Bottigliero (2004), 148.

[58] Art 35. The question of what constitutes a local remedy remains somewhat unclear.

[59] Shelton (1999), 148–51.

[60] Leach (2005); Bottligiero (2004), 156.

[61] Leach (2005) points to cases such as *Akdivar v Turkey* (1997) 23 EHRR 143, *Orhan v Turkey* (App No 25656/94, 18 Jun 2002), where the applicants' houses were found to have been deliberately destroyed by the Turkish security forces. Leach notes that 'the Court has, in a rather formulaic way, rejected applicants' requests for restitution of their property, on the basis that restitution was 'in practice impossible' (at 154).

interpretation of the concept of a remedy.[62] In *Z v United Kingdom*,[63] the Court noted that the reparation requirements of Article 13 are distinct from any other investigatory or procedural requirements imposed upon the state, and compensation for the non-pecuniary damage flowing from the breach should in principle be part of the range of available remedies. It was further established in *Lyons v United Kingdom* that, as part of 'just satisfaction' there was an onus on the offending states to take legal measures upon the finding of a violation to ensure non-repetition.[64]

Like the European Convention, the American Convention also contains a general right to a remedy in Article 25.[65] This is enhanced by a far reaching provision in Article 63(1), which not only provides for the Court to order that compensation be paid, but also to order that the offending state takes appropriate remedial action.[66] This is a significant variation from the corresponding European provision, Article 41, under which the Court has no power to order states to take specific remedial action. It will be recalled that in the seminal case of *Velásquez Rodríguez*,[67] the Inter-American Court held that 'the duty to make adequate reparation' was a principle that followed automatically from a violation of an international obligation.[68] Such reparation might entail:

> the restoration of the prior situation, the reparation of the consequences of the violation, and the indemnification for patrimonial and non-patrimonial damages, including emotional harm.[69]

The duty to make reparation may thus encompass the identification of perpetrators, an effective criminal investigation and the imposition of punishment,[70] in addition to ensuring that victims received fair compensation.[71] However, in spite of the innovative range of remedies implied by the language used in its judgment,[72] the Court eventually only awarded monetary compensation in the *Velásquez Rodríguez* case.

---

[62] See generally Ch 4. In addition to the payment of compensation, Art 13 requires 'a thorough and effective investigation capable of leading to the identification and punishment of those responsible'— see *Kaya v Turkey* (1998) 28 EHRR 1, [107].

[63] (2002) 34 EHRR 3.

[64] App No 15227/03, 8 Jul 2003, [249–50]. See also *Aydin v Turkey*; *Askoy v Turkey* (1997) 23 EHRR 553.

[65] See discussion in Ch 4, pp 164–5.

[66] Art 63(1) states: 'If the Court finds that there has been a violation of a right or freedom protected by this Convention, the Court shall rule that the injured party be ensured the enjoyment of his right or freedom that was violated. It shall also rule, if appropriate, that the consequences of the measure or situation that constituted the breach of such right or freedom be remedied and that fair compensation be paid to the injured party'.

[67] (1989) 28 ILM 291.

[68] *Ibid*, at [25].

[69] *Ibid*, at [26].

[70] See Ch 4, pp 160–71.

[71] At *Velásquez Rodríguez*, [174].

[72] The Inter-American Commission, the families of the victims, and a number of international law experts acting as amici curiae had asked the court for much broader remedies, including an injunction requiring Honduras to criminally prosecute those responsible for disappearances, restructure the security apparatus, publicly condemn the practice of disappearances, and pay homage to the victims: Roht-Arriaza (1990), 474.

As with the European system, compensation will thus be the primary remedy where the right to life has been infringed and will include both pecuniary and non-pecuniary damages against those responsible. The question as to what might constitute 'fair compensation' is, of course, difficult to quantify—particularly in cases involving torture. It has been proposed by a number of commentators that victims of torture ought to receive a much higher compensation payment than they may nominally be entitled to under the civil law owing to the particularly harrowing and distressing nature of the violation.[73] It is further complicated by the fact that compensation for torture victims may be regarded as an attempt to 'buy justice', and may result in victims feeling insulted, particularly if the expectations of victims are not met. Periodically, however, the Inter-American Court has sought to put into effect the *Velasquez-Rodriguez* principles, in a variety of different contexts. Judgments of the Court have compelled offending states to amend domestic criminal codes, to locate the remains of disappeared persons, and to put in place rehabilitative measures for victims of state violence.[74] These are examples of what has been termed 'satisfaction' under the Basic Principles.

The progression towards a legally enforceable right of reparation for victims in both the American and European human rights systems is an important development for victims, given that international law has traditionally been slow to recognise their ability to seek compensation directly from perpetrators. While it is the norm for both the European and the Inter-American human rights courts to award compensation where there has been a finding of a violation, the courts have nonetheless recognised that there are cases where restitution may not be wholly adequate. Regional tribunals have largely followed the international trend in defining reparation in broad and generic terms, so that it encompasses a range of responses which may provide redress to the violation in question. It should be borne in mind, however, that access to regional courts for victims is relatively limited, insofar as these courts are not venues of first instance and domestic remedies must first be exhausted.

Lessons from International Criminal Law

Although the central aim of the International Criminal Court is the prosecution and trial of suspected human rights violators, the concept of reparation for victims is increasingly afforded a considerable degree of weight. The range of innovative mechanisms that allow for victim participation, documented in Chapter 3,[75] is complemented by an array of provisions that provide victims with means to access reparations.

[73] Sveaass and Lavik (2000).

[74] See discussion regarding the 'right to truth' in Ch 4, pp 180–203. See generally the *Trujillo Oroza* case (Series C, No 62, 2000). Also, in the *Barrios Altos* case (Series C, No 75, 2001), the Court approved the agreement signed by the State and the victims wherein the State recognised its obligation to provide diagnostic procedures, medicines, and specialised equipment.

[75] See Ch 3, pp 136–8.

Article 75(1) of the Rome Statute stipulates that the Court shall 'establish principles relating to reparations to, or in respect of, victims'. It may then 'determine the scope and extent of any damage, loss and injury to, or in respect of, victims' and, under paragraph (2)

> make an order directly against a convicted person specifying appropriate reparations to, or in respect of, victims, including restitution, compensation and rehabilitation.

This is evidently the most straightforward means of awarding reparations, although, as an alternative, the Court may order that reparations be made available through the Trust Fund established under Article 79.[76] Rule 85 stipulates that any 'natural persons who have suffered harm as a result of the commission of any crime within the jurisdiction of the Court' may receive compensation from the Trust Fund, which 'may include organizations or institutions that have sustained direct harm to any of their property'.[77] This not only applies to victims who file claims before the court, but also includes all victims of crimes within the jurisdiction of the Court, and their families.[78]

Rule 98 of the Rules on Evidence and Procedure provides guidance on how such reparations should be assessed. Awards may be made on either a collective or an individualised basis. In the case of individual awards, compensation will usually be awarded directly against the perpetrator.[79] Collective awards will usually be distributed from the Trust Fund:

> where the number of the victims and the scope, forms and modalities of reparations makes a collective award more appropriate.[80]

Whilst the decision to award reparations is entirely discretionary, the potential scope for reparation is broad and may encompass 'restitution, compensation, and rehabilitation', although it must be proportionate to the gravity of the violations and damage endured.

However, the extent to which the reparatory mechanisms of the ICC can be said to be fully 'restorative' is highly questionable.[81] While some reparation does

---

[76] Victims can access the Trust Fund even if they do not appear before the Court.

[77] Wierda and de Greiff (2004) note that R 85 may give rise to interpretation difficulties. They argue that, whereas narrow interpretation would only allow for the Fund to implement orders of the Court involving victims who have appeared before the Court in person, a broader interpretation would allow for a role for the Trust Fund to assist in defining who should benefit, including victims that have not participated in Court proceedings. International experience of recovering funds from perpetrators is deplorable.

[78] R 98. 5.

[79] R 98.1. Para (2) provides that the Court may order that awards for 'reparations against a convicted person be deposited with the Trust Fund where at the time of making the order it is impossible or impracticable to make individual awards directly to each victim'. See further Roht-Arriaza (2004), who notes that such mechanisms are likely to work best where only small numbers of victims access the court. It is true that only a minority of victims will have their cases dealt with by the International Criminal Court. As Roht-Arriaza observes, these tend to be the better educated and middle class, whereas many others never access the court or file claims. She also argues that 'individual reparations fail to capture the collective element of the harm in situations of mass conflict or repression'.

[80] Rule 98.3.

[81] Cf Popovski (2000); Findlay and Henham (2005).

feature in the Rome Statute, sanctions against perpetrators are generally retributive in character and do not aspire to promote victim / offender reconciliation. As previously noted, while the Court does give victims some opportunity to participate in proceedings, they are still largely adversarial in character and tend to be lawyer-dominated.[82] Nevertheless, the Statute itself provides further evidence of the increasing international consensus on the need to provide victims with comprehensive redress mechanisms.

In contrast to the potential for reparation that exists for the ICC, provision for reparation in other international criminal justice fora is not nearly as well developed. With regard to the ICTY, there is only a limited provision allowing for restitution for some victims. Under Article 24(3) of the Statute of the ICTY, the Trial chamber may order the 'return of any property or proceeds acquired by criminal conduct or duress to their rightful owners'. Rule 105 of the ICTY Rules of Procedure and Evidence provides that, upon a conviction and following a finding that property has been unlawfully taken, the Trial Chamber, at the request of the Prosecutor or ex officio, may hold a hearing on the specific question of restitution. The hearing will focus on the question of ownership: if the rightful owner of such property can be ascertained on the balance of probabilities, restitution may be ordered.

Rule 105 provides the only mechanism by which the ICTY can order any form of tangible reparation. In addition, however, Rule 106 stipulates that:

> pursuant to the relevant national legislation, a victim or persons claiming through the victim may bring an action in a national court or other competent body to obtain compensation.

This mechanism is unlikely to prove fruitful for many victims: not only is it extremely vague, but the Tribunal lacks any authority to order compensation payments. The burden is placed squarely upon victims to seek their own legal counsel and pursue the violator within domestic legal systems. Any decision to award compensation is left entirely to the discretion of national courts, with the only real assistance to victims in the proclamation being that ICTR and ICTY judgments 'shall be final and binding as to the criminal responsibility of the convicted person for such injury'. At the time of writing, there are no documented cases of the procedure having been utilised.[83] Furthermore, there is an a priori assumption that individual victims have access to national courts, which may well be ill-equipped to handle such cases.[84]

Redress mechanisms for victims under the ICTY leave a lot to be desired and fall a long way short of the much more developed provisions contained in the Rome

---

[82] See Ch 3, pp 137–8.

[83] R 106 was referred to briefly during the Case ICTR-96-7-T *Bagosora* (Decision on the Amicus Curiae) (1998), although no indication was given as to how precisely the rule might be applied in relation to the Belgian courts.

[84] Bassiouni (2006), 242–3.

Statute. This is perhaps attributable to the fact that the tribunal was established 'for the sole purpose of prosecuting persons responsible for serious violations of international law,[85] and was considerably more adversarial in character than the form of procedure envisaged by the International Criminal Court. As noted earlier, the role of victims before the Tribunal was much more akin to the purist common law conception of the victim as a witness to the prosecution, without any special standing.[86] Thus while efforts may be made in international tribunals to make reparation widely available for victims, ultimately only the small proportion of victims whose cases are heard directly by the court are likely to benefit.[87] For the rest, whose cases never make it to court, reparation may be extremely difficult to obtain.

Discussion

As regards victims of state violations, it is clear that most international fora now recognise the existence of a right to reparation, which is broadly defined to encompass both material and symbolic elements. While the forms and rationales for the provision of reparation are still subject to considerable debate, and practice remains inconsistent, the overall direction of current trends is encouraging. The recasting of the doctrine of state responsibility, the ratification in 2005 of the Basic Principles, and the development of the ICC's Trust Fund for Victims might together be said to constitute a new high water mark in terms of international standards. The concept of a right to reparation has moved from the periphery to become a focal point of debate in human rights and humanitarian law. However, it remains a concern that victims have only been able to access full reparation in a small minority of incidences, which is attributable to two main factors. First, there is the problem of resources. Many states, particularly those in the developing world are ill-placed to provide comprehensive financial packages to victims, meaning that many will have to go without a remedy.[88] Secondly, there is the problem of inadequate enforcement. Many of the instruments discussed in this section, including the Basic Principles, are only legally binding insofar as they reflect customary international law. As such, they only constitute a form of soft law, which carries little or no weight in domestic legal systems. Even in those cases where international treaties are binding (such as the regional human rights conventions and various UN conventions), the State must recognise the authority of international fora, or else be prepared to incorporate the relevant standards into national law and readily apply them through the domestic courts.

---

[85] UN Doc S/RES/827 1993).

[86] See Ch 3, pp 136–7.

[87] Wierda and de Greiff (2004).

[88] See further Lasco (2003), who notes regarding the Convention Against Torture, that the UN has established a Voluntary Fund for Victims of Torture which receives financial support from governments, organisations, and individuals.

Otherwise, there is relatively little international organisations are able to do to force compliance.

However, while a right to reparation for victims of abuse of power has at least been recognised on paper, the question as to whether victims of 'ordinary' crime have a similar right is much more difficult to answer. Whilst there are far fewer international standards against which domestic practices can be measured, both the Council of Europe and the European Union have been active in driving forward the concept in recent years. However, as a starting point, it can be noted that the European Convention itself fails to lay down any requirement for a signatory state to compensate a party for criminal injuries caused by another individual. As noted in the previous section, the right to a remedy under Article 13 will generally only come into play where a state actor has been at fault. Neither would victims of non-state crime be able to rely on Article 6 to obtain compensation, since the victim is not regarded as a party to the criminal trial.[89] One possible option might be for them to rely on Article 6(1) in their own right and claim they have been precluded from access to a court, although the fact that a civil remedy for damages would normally be available in domestic law, would mean that this too would be unlikely to constitute a valid avenue.[90]

The Council of Europe did, however, deal with the question of compensation for victims in a separate Treaty, the European Convention on the Compensation of Victims of Violent Crimes. As its title suggests, the Convention does not attempt to invoke any broader ideas about the various forms that reparation may take. Rather, it is limited to the payment of financial compensation. However, unlike the soft law apparatus of the UN Declarations, the Convention is legally binding upon signatory states, and requires them to ensure compensation for:

> those who have sustained serious bodily injury or impairment of health directly attributable to an intentional crime of violence . . . or the dependants of persons who have died as a result of such crime.[91]

Article 2 provides that, where compensation is not 'fully available' from other sources, the State shall contribute towards compensating those persons or their relatives 'who have sustained serious bodily injury or impairment of health directly attributable to an intentional crime of violence.[92] Payment should be made whether the offender has been prosecuted or not,[93] which reflects the international preference that the obligation to make reparation rests, in the first place, with the offender rather than the State.

---

[89] Art 6 contains the right to a fair trial. See Ch 2, pp 40–41.

[90] However, since Art 6 is not only restricted to criminal proceedings but, as Wadham and Arkinstall (2000) point out, this applies to all cases which involve the determination of 'civil rights and obligations', so where the member state has established a criminal injuries compensation scheme, it would seem that the usual fair trial guarantees would apply to these proceedings (at 1083). See also *Rolf Gustafson v Sweden* (Decision of the Court, 1 Jul 1997, App No 23196/94), at [37], where it was noted that a criminal injuries compensation scheme had created a 'civil right' for the purposes of Art 6.

[91] European Convention on the Compensation of Victims of Violent Crimes, *Preamble*.

[92] *Ibid*, Art 2(1).

[93] *Ibid*, Art 2(2).

Although the onus on the State to provide compensation under the Convention is relatively comprehensive, it only applies to those who are nationals or permanent residents of signatories to the Convention.[94] Article 8 also stipulates that a State may refuse compensation in those cases:

> (1) on account of the victims' conduct before, during or after the crime; (2) on account of the victims' involvement in organised crime; or (3) if a full award is contrary to a sense of justice or public policy.

Such caveats have been used by national governments to impose significant restrictions on providing access to state compensation schemes and that aspect has resulted in criticism from some commentators on the basis that such schemes often create a hierarchy of victims.[95] The Convention therefore only goes a very limited way towards creating a 'right to reparation'. Through the creation of policy-based exclusions and its failure to reflect the broader idea of 'reparation' which has been developed in human rights and international discourse, the degree of impact that the Convention has had in creating new legal rights for victims is highly questionable.

The Council of Europe has drafted two other relevant instruments that deal, inter alia, with the issue of victim compensation. Recommendation 85(11) imposes an obligation on public prosecutors to take the matter of compensation into account whenever they take a final decision on whether or not to prosecute.[96] In effect, this means that prosecuting authorities should consider the fact that a decision not to proceed with a prosecution might result in a victim not being afforded access to compensation, thus expanding the traditional notion of what constitutes the 'public interest' in prosecution decision-making.[97] In addition, it should be possible for a criminal court to order compensation by the offender to the victim,[98] which may take the form of either a penal sanction, or a substitute for a penal sanction.[99] Recommendation 87(21), which has recently been replaced and updated by Recommendation 06(8), stipulates that states should assist victims in obtaining compensation from the offender through both criminal and civil proceedings,[100] and should include equal access to private insurance schemes. In relation to state compensation, the Recommendation states that it is payable by the state to victims or their families in cases involving 'serious, intentional, violent crimes, including sexual violence'.[101] While these soft law measures are welcome in their own right, they largely reflect policies that are already in place in most Member States.

---

[94] European Convention on the Compensation of Victims of Violent Crimes, Art 3.
[95] Eg Miers (2000). See discussion below at pp 228–9.
[96] Recommendation 5.
[97] See Ch 2, pp 118–22.
[98] Rec 10.
[99] Rec 85(11), Guideline 11.
[100] *Ibid*, Guideline 7.
[101] *Ibid*, Guideline 8. In addition, there is an obligation under Rec 9 to evaluate the extent of insurance coverage available under public or private insurance schemes.

More significant from a legal perspective are the provisions of the EU Framework Decision, which is legally binding. Under Article 9, Member States are called to ensure that 'victims of criminal acts are entitled to obtain a decision within reasonable time limits on compensation by the offender' except where domestic law provides for an alternative means of payment. In addition, signatories are required to 'take appropriate measures to encourage the offender to provide adequate compensation to victims'.[102] The terms of the Framework Directive are broad and, as such, give Member States considerable scope for manoeuvre. It would be difficult to measure in any objective way, for example, what constitutes 'reasonable time limits' or 'appropriate measures'. Nonetheless, the initiative is nonetheless significant insofar as not only does it reflect the growing international consensus on the need for some form of reparation, but its provisions are also enforceable in domestic courts.

It will be apparent that the instruments that have been formulated by both the Council of Europe and the European Union do not adopt the vocabulary of 'reparation' at all. Furthermore, they place very little emphasis on the idea of other forms of non-pecuniary or non-proprietary forms of reparation. For example, the need for victim rehabilitation has been largely overlooked, as has the potential value of apologies, admissions of guilt, guarantees of non-repetition, or the restoration of rights, whether those rights relate to social status, employment, or the home or family life. In contrast to the relatively broad construction of 'reparation' in humanitarian and human rights law, it seems to be used in a narrow sense in many of the instruments that deal with victims of non-state crime. There is, nonetheless, a growing recognition among victims' groups and academic commentators that reparatory rights for crime victims should be viewed in a broader and more flexible light, and ought to encompass similar sorts of values as the standards which apply to victims of human rights abuses. Zedner provides some further indication as to what a broader concept of reparation might encompass for crime victims:

> Reparation is not synonymous with restitution, still less does it suggest a straightforward importation of civil into criminal law. Reparation should properly connote a wider set of aims. It involves more than 'making good' the damage done to property, body or psyche. It must entail recognition of the harm done to the social relationship between offender and victim, and the damage done to the victim's social rights in his or her property or person.[103]

Just as the cost of human rights atrocities and abuses cannot be quantified in solely economic terms, neither can the effects of 'ordinary' crime be measured in such a way. It is widely recognised that the effects of victimisation vary considerably. Some victims will be traumatised by what may appear to be a relatively trivial offence; others may be able to find closure and healing soon after falling

---

[102] EU Framework Decision, Art 9(2).
[103] Zedner (1994), 234.

victim to a serious offence.[104] Financial assistance may help some victims; for others it may be a low priority, and may even appear as an insulting attempt to buy them off. Whatever the consequences of an offence may be for an individual victim, it seems only logical that the type of reparation provided by the state or the offender corresponds to the needs and preferences of the individual concerned, and, as Zedner has indicated, it should take into account the social relationship which has been damaged by the act in question.

In recent years, there has been some evidence to suggest that this broader conception of reparation has begun to influence international standard-setting in relation to victims of non-state crime. A growing interest in the idea of reparation generally has gone hand-in-hand with the expansion of instruments that promote restorative justice, or mediation-based processes as alternatives to orthodox criminal procedure. In recent years, restorative justice has risen to a position of prominence on the international platform, and has driven forward the idea of reparation in many countries, particularly in the field of juvenile justice. While the concept is explored in greater detail in Chapter 6,[105] it is worth noting at this juncture that its exponential ascendancy constitutes a further reflection of the growing international consensus on the need to inject greater reparative elements into the penal system.

In summary then, the idea of a 'right to reparation' for victims of non-state crime may, as Bassiouni suggests, be best described as an emerging norm.[106] Although international benchmarks increasingly highlight the importance of reparation for victims, most are not justiciable in domestic courts, and are so broadly framed as to leave their future interpretation uncertain. Furthermore, they tend to cling to a rather narrow definition of 'reparation', placing considerable emphasis on the value of financial recompense whilst simultaneously sidelining other, more intangible, forms that have emerged under international human rights law. The cumulative effect of these developments, however, has been the exertion of downward pressure upon national governments to ensure that the idea of reparation and the core values that underpin it are incorporated within domestic criminal justice systems.

II. Realising Reparation in the Criminal Justice System

Even before many of the above-noted international norms had begun to emerge, the latter decades of the twentieth century witnessed a considerable expansion in the ability of crime victims within most western jurisdictions to utilise various

---

[104] Maguire (1980); Shapland et al (1985); Shapland and Hall (2007).
[105] See further Ch 6, pp 254–65.
[106] Bassiouni (2006), 223.

forms of redress mechanisms. For the most part, however, these mechanisms reflect the narrower view of 'reparation' as meaning some form of monetary compensation. Compensation, be it from the offender or the State, has a symbolic value; it affirms a public recognition of the victim's experience of being a victim of crime.[107] More recent times, however, have witnessed the ascendancy of broader reparative principles that are slowly beginning to permeate the penal system. This section traces the reparatory mechanisms that are available to victims in England and Wales, and asks what the future may hold as far as securing a much broader interpretation of 'reparation' within the domestic criminal justice system is concerned.

State Compensation

One major problem facing the majority of victims seeking compensation is that most offenders are not identified. Even where they are, as noted below, it is remarkably difficult for victims to obtain compensation directly from the perpetrator of the offence.[108] For this reason, many jurisdictions have established state compensation schemes to provide financial assistance to crime victims.[109] State compensation was first developed in the UK in 1964 to provide a method of compensation for 'innocent' victims of violence as an expression of societal sympathy towards them.[110] In spite of initial reluctance in policy circles,[111] the UK scheme was one of the first of its kind, and sought to provide financial redress to victims on a case-by-case basis through assessing individual harm suffered and expenses incurred, in rough approximation with damages that would be payable under the law of tort. The move largely put crime victims in the same position as those involved in industrial or motor accidents,[112] and was envisaged by victims' campaigner Margery Fry as an expansion of the welfare principle.[113] The applicant was required to give details of expenses, losses and sufferings, and each case was then adjudicated by the Criminal Injuries Compensation Board, before an award was determined on a discretionary ex gratia basis. Thus, any decision by the Board not to grant compensation could not be open to challenge in the courts; as such, it might be said to be a case of the State accepting responsibility rather than

---

[107] Shapland et al (1985).

[108] See below, pp 231–6.

[109] For an overview of European systems, see Greer (1996b); Brienen and Hoegen (2000). For a US perspective, see Saldana (1994); Underwood (2002).

[110] Goodey (2005),141) has located 4 primary rationales for the development of such schemes, these being: the legal duty of state to compensate victims for its failure to prevent crime; a moral duty to assist victims on humanitarian and welfare grounds; 'loss distribution' as a form of social insurance through the use of public funds; and as a benefit to the state as it afforded political credibility to those who introduce and administer compensation schemes.

[111] Rock (1990), 273.

[112] Williams (2005), 96.

[113] Fry (1951), 124.

liability.[114] As such, a victim's ability to obtain compensation through state funds may be regarded as an 'expectation' rather than a legally enforceable right.[115]

The Scheme was subject to major reform in the Criminal Injuries Compensation Act 1995. The Criminal Injuries Compensation Board was replaced by the Criminal Injuries Compensation Authority. Although similar in many respects, the new scheme is based on a system of tariffs.[116] The amount of compensation payable is tied to the level of the award. The scheme covers over 300 types of injury, which are classified into one of 25 bands. The bands nominally reflect the degree of pain and suffering incurred. The minimum threshold (at Level 1) is £1,000: so many minor injuries may not be covered. Level 25 represents the maximum amount payable for any single injury (£250,000). An overall cap of £500,000 means if a number of people applied following the death of a person, that figure would represent the maximum amount payable. There is no requirement that the offender be prosecuted, or even identified: an applicant merely has to show that he has received a personal injury that merits an award on a tariff scale in excess of £1000 (or that he or she is a dependant or relative of a victim of violence who has since died).[117] In this way, the Scheme has clear advantages over the offender-based programmes outlined below, which are evidently incapable of providing redress to victims where the offender cannot be identified. However, the nature of the new scheme remains controversial, given that injury is now assessed on an objective as opposed to a subjective basis, ignoring the fact that the impact can vary dramatically from one person to another. Its theoretical basis, which has been unclear from the start, has thus been thrown into further question by the use of the tariff scheme which is discernibly less victim-centred and much more ambiguous than its predecessor.[118]

A further inherent weakness in the scheme arises from the strict eligibility criteria that are imposed. Applicants must have been living in England, Scotland or Wales when the injury was sustained. Thus, if victims are injured abroad, they must claim within that particular jurisdiction. If injured in the UK, any such injury must be serious enough to qualify for at least the minimum award available under the scheme. The application of a minimum threshold may be viewed by some as necessary in the interests of public policy, but nonetheless serves to deny recompense to the great majority of victims who sustain minor injuries.

One of the criticisms that is most frequently levied at state compensation schemes is the fact that they appear to distinguish between 'deserving' and 'undeserving' victims. Most schemes, including that in the UK, only pay out in those cases where the victim is free from blame, thereby promoting the dangerously inaccurate concept of the 'ideal' victim and precluding 'deviant' victims from

---

[114] Williams (2005), 96. For an outline of the operation of the 'old' Scheme, see Miers (1997), 13–16.

[115] Goodey (2005), 142.

[116] Awards are also payable for loss of earnings and loss of earning capacity, but an overall cap of £500,000 is applied.

[117] Victims may appeal the award: first, to a higher level within CICA; then to the independent Criminal Injuries Compensation Appeals Panel.

[118] Dignan (2005); Goodey (2005); Freckleton (2004).

accessing any recompense.[119] Only those victims who strike a chord with society's view of the 'innocent' victim are deemed to deserve state support; those deemed to be undeserving are shunned. The 'ideal' victim will be happy to co-operate fully with the criminal justice system and the police. Failure to report an offence promptly, failure to make a statement, failure to participate in an identity parade, and failure to attend court, have all been cited as grounds for refusing compensation.[120]

The origins of this distinction between innocent and deviant victims can be traced to the original welfare philosophy underpinning the system: since ex gratia payments were conceived on the basis of societal sympathy for victims of violent crime, the character of the victim has always been at issue. The behaviour at the time of the incident in question may serve to reduce the amount of compensation paid. Such 'contributory misconduct' may arise, for example, where the victim of an offence was involved in a pub brawl.[121] A more controversial aspect of the scheme concerns the fact that victims will be denied compensation where they have criminal records, even though they have no connection with the injury-causing event.[122] Any convictions that are not spent under the Rehabilitation of Offenders Act 1974 will be taken into account on CICA's 'penalty points' system. Thus a victim of an assault who has previously been convicted of theft will not stand to benefit, and neither will the family members of a murder victim who had any unspent convictions.[123] Such a restrictive approach does not seem to be grounded in any solid rationale, other than to safeguard the State's own economic or political ends.[124]

Further criticisms have been levied at the scheme for its ambiguity on the question as to what constitutes a violent offence. The primary target of the scheme was always going to be victims of offences committed under sections 18, 20 or 47 of the Offences Against the Person Act, but beyond these 'core' assault offences, the ambit of the scheme is much more difficult to define. Victims injured as a result of arson are included, but victims of regulatory legislation, such as the Factories Act, are excluded.[125] Neither does the scheme cover victims who suffer psychiatric

---

[119] Miers (2000), 78–9.

[120] Spalek (2006), 100.

[121] See generally Miers (1997), 160. It is also the case that, under the 'old' scheme, victims of domestic violence were usually excluded until 1979.

[122] As Williams (2005), 96, points out, this reflected 'conventional wisdom' at the time the scheme came into operation, and has only been questioned in more recent years.

[123] Williams (2005), 95.

[124] See Miers (1990), 78: 'The problem firstly is that because delinquent victims resemble offenders too closely, and may have been formally so defined in the past, the possibility of their receiving compensation threatens the stereotype of the 'innocent' victim for whom such schemes are created. Secondly, this possibility subverts a prime objective of criminal injury schemes, which is to distinguish victims of crime from offenders where penal regimes are perceived to be too forgiving and too neglectful of the victim. The politicisation of the victim of crime requires that the taxpayer be asked to compensate only those victims who present 'deserving' characteristics, so it therefore becomes necessary to exclude the delinquent victim (however defined) from their beneficial provisions'.

[125] Dignan (2005), 44.

injury as the result of a burglary.[126] Victims who attempt to apprehend offenders are, however, included; yet victims of sexual offences which do not involve violence will be excluded. This particular debarment has been the source of considerable criticism; many such victims will have been groomed or even abused over a long period of time.[127] Victim Support has advocated that all victims of sexual offences should be entitled to compensation, regardless of whether violence was used.[128] Perhaps most concerning are the recent Home Office proposals to reform the scheme so that it is more focused on serious injuries.[129] While the document is somewhat vague, it is clear that there is an intention to cut back provision for minor injuries on the basis of the belief that such victims 'could be better served by radically improving practical and emotional support, rather than through relatively small payments from the Criminal Injuries Compensation Scheme, which arrive a long time after the incident'.[130]

Even though the scheme has been subject to criticism on a number of grounds, its very existence would seem to conform with the relatively unspecific international standards laid down concerning the responsibility of the state to provide compensation to crime victims in certain situations.[131] International standards, such as the European Convention on Compensation, neither preclude the application of upper or lower limits,[132] nor do they prohibit the reduction or refusal of compensation claims taking the applicants' circumstances into account.[133] State compensation schemes may serve to lessen the plight of some crime victims, and by in large fulfil the relatively undemanding obligations laid down in the international and European standards. However, they fall a long way short of providing a holistic form of reparation of the type that is now commonly envisaged as being desirable for victims of abuse of power. In some respects, the capacity of the State to offer these more flexible forms of reparation is limited. The lack of any direct input from the offender means that there are certain forms of reparation that will not automatically be available to the victim, such as a direct apology, a guarantee of non-repetition or even the intangible knowledge that 'something good' came out of the original offence. State compensation schemes tend to conceptualise monetary payments alone as being the appropriate means for putting right the harm that has been caused. Such a perspective falls short of emergent ideas about the flexible concept of reparation that is emerging in international humanitarian and human rights frameworks.

---

[126] Spalek (2006), 99.
[127] Williams (2005), 95.
[128] Victim Support (2003).
[129] Home Office (2004c).
[130] *Ibid*, 2.
[131] Eg 1985 UN Declaration, Principle 13; 2005 Declaration, Art 18; European Convention on Compensation, Art 1.
[132] Art 2.
[133] Art 8.

Reparation from the Offender

While most western countries now have some form of state compensation scheme in place for criminal injuries, many jurisdictions will seek to prioritise mechanisms that purport to achieve reparation directly from the offender.[134] Such mechanisms, however, are prone to two major shortcomings. First, as noted above, they can only be used where the offender is actually identified. Secondly, most offenders do not have the means to make substantial compensation payments to victims. In the UK, there are two main avenues for victims to achieve reparation directly from the offender: these are through a legal action in tort through the civil courts; or through a compensation order issued by a criminal court.

Civil Actions

The state-led nature of criminal justice means that criminal sanctions are primarily geared towards punishment of the offender in the name of the general public. Traditional common law doctrine deems that the relationship between the offender and victim is private in nature, and thereby falls within the remit of the civil, as opposed to the criminal law. The majority of crimes against the person or against property also constitute civil wrongs; therefore victims have always been able to pursue offenders for damages through the civil justice system. While international standards lay down a broad normative position that victims ought to be able to obtain compensation from offenders, they do not lay down a specific mode as to which avenues may be used to obtain such compensation. While the potential to make use of a civil avenue is acknowledged in some international instruments,[135] there appear to be no binding international standards that require crime victims to be able to pursue compensation through civil courts.

Civil actions by victims are extremely rare for a number of reasons. First, it imposes an unacceptable burden upon the victim. If a decision is taken not to prosecute the case, then the onus will fall on the victim to undertake investigations, collect the evidence and prove the case before the civil court. The prospect of a successful civil action will be increased if a criminal conviction has already occurred, but otherwise a civil action may prove a lengthy and time-consuming process. In those cases where a previous criminal hearing has taken place, it is fundamentally unfair to expect victims to commence an entirely new set of proceedings after the ordeal of the criminal trial. Requiring the victim to testify yet again to the court under stressful adversarial conditions concerning the nature and

---

[134] Goodey (2005), 144. While reparation directly from the offender may enable direct apologies and explanations as discussed above, there is a danger in under-valuing the role of the state compensation. Crawford (2000) remarks that: '[T]he public interest lies in public restoration to victims of crime through schemes of compensation . . . Under the benevolent veil of restorative justice, the state must not be allowed to abandon its responsibility' (at 303).

[135] See eg Rec 06(08), Principle 7.

extent of his or her injuries would leave many victims feeling deflated and disillusioned about the failure of the legal system to resolve the question of reparation in an efficient and satisfactory way.

Secondly, civil actions are rarely worthwhile financially. Such actions are expensive to commence and sustain, and full legal aid will rarely be available.[136] The exception may be in cases involving victims of corporate crime, whose perpetrators are likely to be in a much stronger position to provide recompense, and who may be backed by insurance. Most offenders, however, have very limited resources, and would simply not be able to afford to make large compensation payments.[137]

These hurdles for victims mean that recourse to civil action is rare; hence the clear preference in international standards for the victims to be able to access compensation directly through the criminal courts.[138] As Groenhuijsen suggests, recourse to the civil law is not a promising solution for crime victims, rather it is one of the historical roots of their problems since it tends to imply that the criminal justice system is not the appropriate forum to further their rights and interests.[139] The existence of a civil right of action is, in practical terms, irrelevant to the vast majority of victims.

Compensation Orders

Since 1973, courts in England and Wales have been empowered to order the offender to pay compensation as part of a sentence for 'any personal injury, loss or damage resulting from the offence'.[140] Originally introduced as an ancillary penalty, from 1982 courts were given the power to award compensation orders as penalties in their own right.[141] While it is still the norm for them to be awarded in conjunction with other penalties, the court may make a compensation order either instead of, or in addition to, any other penal sanction. The provisions concerning compensation orders are now contained in sections 130–4 of the Powers of Criminal Courts (Sentencing) Act 2000. Section 130(4) of the Act states that compensation:

> shall be of such amount as the court considers appropriate, having regard to any evidence and to any representations that are made by or on behalf of the accused or the prosecutor, the Court.

The legislation further provides that compensation should be afforded priority over fines. Thus where an offender has insufficient means to pay both, the Court

---

[136] Legal Aid for such cases is means-tested; meaning that most victims will be liable to make some contribution towards the costs of a civil action.

[137] Greer (1990).

[138] Victims' Declaration, Principle 9; Rec 85(11), Guideline 10.

[139] Groenhuijsen (2004), 75.

[140] Originally contained in the Criminal Justice Act 1972, the power is now contained in the Powers of Criminal Courts (Sentencing) Act 2000, s 130.

[141] Criminal Justice Act 1982, s 67.

should impose a compensation order rather than a fine.[142] Courts are under a duty to consider making orders in all cases and must now state reasons if not doing so.[143]

As with the state compensation scheme, the compensation order appears to reflect the relatively broad and unspecific international standards that govern compensation requirements for victims of non-state crime.[144] Once again, however, the effectiveness of any 'right' to compensation is open to question given the inherent limitations of the current scheme. Unlike civil damages, compensation orders must reflect the offender's ability to pay; an unrealistic burden on him or her may simply encourage them to resort to crime to obtain the necessary funds. As such, the maximum amount is capped at £5,000,[145] and the offender will usually be allowed to pay this over a period of time. The victim has no standing to influence this decision and must rely on the prosecutor to request that an order be made.[146] There is some evidence to suggest that the prosecution often fails to pass on adequate information required by the courts in order to facilitate the process,[147] which lends further weight to the argument advanced earlier that prosecutors are fundamentally unable to protect victims' interests.[148] Insufficient information is likely to mean that the court will give the benefit of the doubt to the offender where there is a question mark over his or her ability to pay. It would also appear to be the case that information is not readily made available to victims by any of the criminal justice agencies outside the courtroom. Maguire and Shapland, who surveyed the use of compensation orders in the late 1980s, found that the court often failed to inform victims about the terms the order or the reasons for non-payment.[149]

Compensation orders appear to be made on an inconsistent basis, and the amount awarded is usually small.[150] Unlike the state compensation arrangements, orders are not limited to offences involving violence,[151] nor are they limited to providing compensation for pecuniary loss. It was established in *Bond v Chief Constable of Kent*[152] that an order may be made solely on the basis of distress or anxiety experienced by the victim. Over the course of the past two decades, a trend is emerging that indicates that courts are prepared to make compensation orders with less frequency. Statistics indicate a significant drop in the number of orders

---

[142] Powers of Criminal Courts (Sentencing) Act 2000, s 130(12).

[143] Powers of Criminal Courts (Sentencing) Act 2000, s 130(3). This provision was originally contained in s104 Criminal Justice Act 1988. Cf the Sentencing Act 1997 (Tasmania), which made compensation orders compulsory for property damage or loss resulting from certain crimes.

[144] See 1985 UN Declaration, Principles 8–9; 2005 UN Basic Principles on Right to a Remedy, Principle 17; Council of Europe Rec 06(08), Principle 7; EU Framework Decision, Art 9.

[145] S 131(1).

[146] Neither does the victim have a right to appeal an order, or the lack thereof.

[147] Williams (2005),15.

[148] See Ch 4.

[149] Maguire and Shapland, (1990).

[150] Greer (1991), 168; Williams (2005), 99.

[151] An order may be made in case involving death, injury, loss or damage.

[152] (1982) 4 Cr App R (S) 314.

in both the magistrates' courts and the Crown Court between the late 1980s and the present.[153] Currently, just 14 per cent of those sentenced in the magistrates' courts and 7 per cent of those in the Crown Court are ordered to pay compensation.[154] Flood-Page and Mackie found that sentencers are not always following the law, in that compensation orders are not prioritised over fines and reasons are not given for failing to issue a compensation order.[155] Dignan suggests that a sharp increase in the proportionate use of custody cases was to blame,[156] and argues that sentencers are reluctant to realise their statutory responsibility to prioritise compensation orders, and are still imposing fines in contravention of their statutory duty.[157] To some extent, this may be attributed to a problem of perception, whereby compensation orders are perceived as being disproportionately severe by sentencers owing to the general lack of means of offenders to pay.[158] While recent statistics suggest this downward trend continues in the Crown Court, there was a steep rise of 56 per cent in the number of compensation orders made in magistrates' courts over the period 2000–2005.[159] This may reflect some success in the government's professed aim of radically increasing the amount of compensation recoverable in the criminal courts.[160]

The challenge of significantly raising the number of orders made at Crown Court level may prove arduous, since the negative attitude among the professional judiciary may be partially attributed to deeper structural factors. For many years, there has been a marked scepticism on the part of many judges and magistrates to mix aspects of civil and criminal law, which have traditionally been conceived in highly dichotomous terms in the common law system. Yet even within inquisitorial systems, judges and prosecutors have been found to be reluctant to mix compensation, which they perceive to be a civil matter, with the criminal law.[161] Reparation to victims is not regarded as a core objective of the criminal process, and it has been suggested that courts are unsure how they ought to factor restitution into the penal system.[162] It is, however, suggested below that this task need not be as complex as it may first appear.

Only rarely will victims receive compensation that is both full and immediate. It is much more likely that they will receive small, irregular amounts over a period of time, which only serves to prolong the effects of the offence on the victim. They will not, for example, be able to replace stolen or damaged property

---

[153] See further Ashworth (2005), 300–2.
[154] Home Office (2004c), 13.
[155] Flood-Page and Mackie (1998).
[156] Dignan (2005), 81.
[157] *Ibid.*
[158] Spalek (2006), 103.
[159] For an explanation of recent trends, see further Ashworth (2005), 299–301; Dignan (2005), 80–82.
[160] Home Office (2004c), 12–13.
[161] Brienen and Hoegen, 2000.
[162] See, eg, Wasik (1978); Shapland et al (1985), 134; Home Office (2004b).

immediately.[163] Moreover, even if the offender is able and willing to comply with a compensation order, a further weakness of the regime stems from the fact that it only serves to cover very specific material losses to victims who are deemed to be 'worthy'. As with any award obtained through the civil courts or the CICA, compensation will not be available to cover any psychological response. This requirement is certainly at odds with international standards,[164] and overlooks the fact that the emotional impact of victimisation may take many years to overcome.[165] For the offender, it is arguable that a compensation order does not amount to any genuine form of accountability. There is a real risk that they will be unable to distinguish between a compensation order and a fine:[166] both impose financial burdens, and thus few offenders are likely to consider the impact of their actions and are unlikely to feel personally accountable. From the point of view of both victim and offender, the compensation order does little to empower either party, since neither has any control over its allocation.

In spite of the above concerns, the opportunity to pursue compensation through the criminal courts enhances the victims' chances of obtaining some tangible or symbolic compensation, in contrast to the retributive model of criminal justice which offers none at all.[167] Brienen and Hoegen also contend that, from a European perspective, compensation orders are a relative success story and are better enforced and made more frequently than other mechanisms for recompensing victims in civil law jurisdictions.[168] However, the researchers noted that a fifth of all victims in England and Wales were led to believe that they were likely to receive compensation through the courts but did not receive any, and it is still not considered in all cases despite that being a legal requirement.[169]

There is, nonetheless, a strong moral case for awarding compensation in this way. As Groenhuijsen suggests, use of the criminal courts, prosecutors and judges, lend a form of 'constitutional authority' to such processes which may enhance overall satisfaction levels with the justice system.[170] As he asserts, 'compensation for victims is not only a private affair but is also to be regarded as serving demands

---

[163] Van Ness and Nolan (1998), 95–86, propose a means of sidestepping the problem of an offender's inability to pay. They argue that the systems of state compensation and offender compensation ought to be combined. Restitution should first be ordered, and should be based on a formula that takes into account the daily income of the offender. If the amount of harm to the victim is greater than the restitution ordered, the victim would then be able to apply for state compensation to 'top up' the amount they would receive. If the amount of harm to the victim were, however, to be less than the restitution ordered, the surplus would be placed into the state compensation fund.

[164] Principle 12(a) of the 1985 Victims' Declaration states compensation should be provided where victims have 'sustained significant bodily injury or impairment of physical or *mental health* as a result of serious crimes'. Similarly, Principle 8(6) of Recommendation 2006(08) states that compensation should cover treatment and rehabilitation for physical and psychological injuries.

[165] Shapland et al (1985); Classen et al (2005); Shapland and Hall (2007).

[166] Groenhuijsen (2004), 74.

[167] Zedner (1994), 247.

[168] Brienen and Hoegen (2000), 1099. See also below, Ch 6, pp 272–4 on the operation of the *partie civile* and the 'adhesion procedure'.

[169] Brienen and Hoegen (2000), 271–3.

[170] Groenhuijsen (2004), 72.

of public interest'.[171] Moreover, the fact that many offenders cannot afford to compensate victims in full may be a problem that has been over-emphasised, given the flexibility afforded to courts to vary the amount and terms of payment. Indeed, as noted above, it is clear from research that the actual amount of compensation seems to be a secondary concern of many victims, who are more concerned about whether the offender has made a personal contribution.[172] The compensation order model thus holds clear potential to deliver a mode of reparation that may be acceptable to many victims. However, much work clearly remains to be done in improving the way in which orders are enforced, and questions need to be asked concerning their apparent decline in recent years. Given that the attitudinal resistance on the part of the judiciary seems to be one explanation for this decline,[173] it is also clear that we need to unpack some of the deeper theoretical issues that have traditionally prevented reparatory measures gaining a foothold within the penal system.

III. Rethinking Reparation

The latter half of the twentieth century opened a range of new avenues through which victims were empowered, on paper at least, to pursue reparation from either the State or the offender. In the vast majority of cases, this will take the form of financial recompense, which fails to reflect the full meaning of the concept in international discourse. It should be borne in mind, however, that only in a minority of cases will reparation be available directly from the offender, and compensation orders tend to be viewed as an awkward adjunct to a penal system where punishment alone is viewed as the core objective of the official response to offending.

The prominence afforded to monetary compensation over broader forms of reparation or newly emergent forms of restorative justice is a reflection of the way in which crime is perceived as a public wrong and a matter for the state to address. There would appear to be an inherent assumption that victims' interests are somehow encapsulated within the public interest in denouncing and punishing unacceptable behaviour,[174] or that, in any case, infusing the victims' reparatory interests within the criminal justice system would create fresh tensions and ambi-

---

[171] Groenhuijsen (2004), 72.

[172] Greer (1996b), 693 at n 27 notes: 'Victims in Britain do not want "full" compensation in the civil sense—they tend to see compensation from the offender as a penal sanction to be tied in with penal objectives / sentencing aims. In general, they would prefer a smaller amount of compensation from the offender than a larger sum from the State'. Greer's view is confirmed by empirical research, which suggests that victims are often willing to accept partial compensation rather than insist on being compensated in full—see Shapland et al (1985); Kaiser and Kilchling (1996); Davis (1992).

[173] Flood-Page and Mackie (1998); Brienen and Hoegan (2000), Dignan (2005).

[174] Moore (1994).

guity concerning the function and organisation of both civil and criminal law.[175] While the public may well have a legitimate interest in the administration of criminal justice,[176] it is the victim who will have experienced the effects of the crime in a very real and tangible way. A purist conception of the criminal justice system as performing a purely public function not only denigrates victims,[177] but also serves to entrench the portrayal of offenders and victims in dichotomous terms with discrete and opposing interests.[178] This paradigm has served to alienate victims, and minimises their prospects of reparation, whether it be symbolic or material in form. What appears to be needed is a paradigm shift within domestic criminal justice that is reflective of the recent development of the right to reparation on the international platform.

It seems only logical that the structures and suppositional perceptions of crime and the criminal justice system ought to encapsulate the emerging consensus that crime impacts first and foremost upon its direct victims. This is not to deny the legitimate public interest in managing crime and reducing offending, but it is desirable that the structures of criminal justice, as well as its theoretical basis, should reflect the individual's right to reparation as well as the broader interests of the State.[179] The challenge that befalls domestic policymakers is to review existing criminal justice structures and procedures to ascertain whether these frameworks can be adjusted to facilitate a form of reparation that can satisfy both of these aspirations. Drawing on Epstein's theory of tort liability, Barnett proposes 'a single system of corrective justice that looks to the conduct, broadly defined, of the parties to the case with a view toward the protection of individual liberty and private property'.[180] In other words, he envisages some form of mechanism that integrates elements of the civil and criminal law into a unitary action.

Undoubtedly, such a radical move would be met with scepticism in some quarters and would be fraught with tensions, but many of these objections arise because of the incorrect perception of criminal and civil matters as being entirely divorced from one another. The private interests of the victim are regarded as falling within the remit of the civil, rather than the criminal courts. Yet it may be timely to pause for thought and re-examine whether it may be possible to conceptualise the 'private' interest as something that is quite distinct from the common law concept of civil damages. It is increasingly recognised that such a neat separation is difficult to justify in logical terms, as Walther explains:

---

[175] See Frehsee (1999), 246; Lombard (1996), 214.

[176] As explained by Duff (2003): 'They [crimes] infringe the values by which the political community defines itself as a law-governed polity: they are therefore wrongs for which the polity and its members are part-responsible in the sense that it is up to them, and not just up to the victim and offender as private individuals, to make provision for an appropriate response . . . [T]he political community is also owed something since it shares in the victim's wrong as a violation of its public values' (at 47–8).

[177] Duff (2003), 47.

[178] Dignan (2005), 179–86.

[179] See further Barnett (1977), 291, who argues that the right to reparation arises as 'the aggressive action of the criminal creates a debt to the victim'.

[180] Barnett (1977), 290, citing Epstein (1975), 441.

The variety of terms we encounter reflects the difficulty inherent in defining what 'making good' to the victim is actually about, and sheds light on the awkward, doctrinally unresolved standing of the victim's interests between the spheres of private and public law. This difficulty is easily obfuscated if we borrow a term from 'civil' or 'private' law and try to redefine it as an umbrella term for 'making amends' to a victim of crime. Both the terms 'restitution' and 'compensation' are too narrowly predefined by civil law to properly serve this purpose. Although the term 'reparation' also exists in civil law, it appears better suited for the umbrella function since, unlike 'restitution' and 'compensation', it does not per se predetermine the modalities of making good.[181]

This wider, more flexible concept of reparation would, on a theoretical level at least, be much better placed to realise the various non-pecuniary components of reparation that have developed for victims of abuse of power on the international platform. It could, for example, include apologies, explanation, guarantees of non-repetition, and access to truth.[182] In developing such a concept of reparation, the criminal justice system could distinguish itself from traditional doctrinal conceptions of compensation and restitution as developed by both the civil and the criminal justice systems. Reparation would address a much wider set of aims above and beyond either criminal injuries compensation or the law of tort. Instead, the resolution of the victim / offender conflict would be reconceptualised as part of the wider public interest, since the community is made up of 'victims, potential victims and the fellow citizens of victims'.[183]

It might be underlined, however, that a unitary form of reparation would nonetheless remain an essentially penal sanction, in order to reflect the idea that crime also harms society as a whole. If we regard punishment as 'anything that is unpleasant, a burden, or an imposition of some sort on an offender',[184] then it would seem that the criminal objective of punishing crime is capable of being met through reparation. While the payment of a financial penalty has very obvious onerous connotations, it can also be noted that much of the restorative justice literature has highlighted that symbolic gestures, and even restorative processes themselves, are often very difficult and highly emotive experiences for the offender.[185] As Randy Barnett has argued, the key difference in such a shift would be a change in the rationale for imposing punishment:

> The point is not that the offender deserves to suffer; it is rather that the offended party desires compensation . . . This represents the complete overthrow of the paradigm of punishment. No longer would the deterrence, reformation, disablement, or rehabilitation of the criminal be the guiding principle—of the judicial system. The attainment of these goals would be incidental to, and as a result of, reparations paid to the victim.[186]

---

[181] Walther (1996), 320.
[182] See Ch 6, p 290.
[183] Cavadino and Dignan (1996), 237.
[184] Daly, K (1999), 10.
[185] Braithwaite (1989); Duff (2003), 47; Strang (2002). See further Ch 6, p 263.
[186] Barnett (1977), 289.

A similar view is held by Anthony Duff, who has argued that restorative responses to crime and other forms of reparation ought to be viewed as penal measures since they involve the intentional infliction of a burden upon an offender for transgressing the criminal law.[187] Restoration, he argues, 'is not only compatible with retribution: it *requires* retribution'.[188] Thus, although according to common law theory, the criminal law may not specifically aim to resolve private conflicts, its objective in regulating offending behaviour may be furthered if reparative measures assist in terms of either reductivism, deterrence or any of the other well-rehearsed arguments concerning the objectives of the penal system.[189] As Groenhuijsen puts it, the distinction between punishment and reparation is 'a dogmatic aberration' which derives from a conceptual misunderstanding concerning crime and punishment:

> For the offender, there is no difference in the imposition of a fine on the one hand and an obligation to pay (the same amount of) restitution on the other. The proceeds of the crime have usually been spent a long time before, so the financial burden is equal in both situations. For the offender, the hardship—the pain—is neither affected by the recipient of the financial offer he has to make (the state or the victim) nor by its legal origin (tort / civil law v crime / punishment).[190]

Yet from the victim's perspective, the difference is immense. One will result in tangible compensation; the other will not. In contrasting the common law approach to the 'hybrid' form of action that is commonplace within many European jurisdictions,[191] Lerner observed a number of advantages of such a unitary criminal action:

> First, it is cheaper for the civil party (and more efficient for the justice system as a whole) to combine the civil and criminal proceedings rather than having two separate cases. The civil party can have a 'free ride' on the evidence at the criminal trial, and so be compensated at less expense. Secondly, the civil party serves to push the investigating judge . . . into vigorous investigation and presentation of the case . . . French legal writers often use the phrase 'conquering the inertia of the prosecutor' to describe the civil party's role.[192]

Victims would not be the only beneficiaries of such an approach. The injection of a civil interest into the somewhat elusive concept of the 'public interest' could lend additional legitimacy to the outcome of the case, thereby benefiting the criminal justice system as a whole. Weisstub also contends that the civil justice system could benefit from infusing itself with the symbolism of criminal sanctions, thereby showing itself to be 'consonant with public morality and conscience'.[193]

---

[187] Duff (2003).

[188] *Ibid*, 43.

[189] Eg, Goldstein (1982) notes that 'potential offenders are likely to be deterred from wrongdoing by the civil courts and punitive damages may be awarded there' (at 531).

[190] Groenhuijsen (2004), 74.

[191] See Ch 6, pp 272–4.

[192] Lerner (2001), 815.

[193] Weisstub (1986), 207.

There are also various economic arguments that could be used in support of this view: reparative sentences significantly lessen the financial burden on the taxpayer and a corresponding reduction in separate civil claims could reduce litigation in the courts.[194]

It may therefore be timely to stop perceiving the public interest of the State and the private interests of the victim in such strictly oppositional terms. Such a normative approach to defining reparation may well assist in helping domestic structures reflect international best practice, but the question as to how such a mechanism might work in practice is considerably more difficult to resolve. One option would be to attempt to remedy the situation within the current paradigm of criminal justice. Groenhuijsen argues that the existing paradigm is not so much inadequate as misunderstood. Arguably, the situation could thus be remedied through transplanting the *partie civile* mechanism to the English courts.[195] Civil jurisdictions have illustrated that victim claims can be accommodated within criminal actions. Although such schemes may be imperfect in practice,[196] on a theoretical level they reflect the individual harm experienced by the victim alongside the societal harm suffered by the public at large. Such a step would undoubtedly be met with strong opposition, and would be unlikely to work without a corresponding shift in attitude among practitioners.[197] Certainly, any move in this direction would also be met with ideological opposition in certain quarters. Challenges to our current ideological perceptions of the criminal and civil justice processes are not going to be readily accepted by everyone.

IV. Conclusions

The primary aim of this chapter was to demonstrate the growing importance attached to reparation in international and human rights discourse and assess the corresponding degree to which it is reflected in domestic criminal justice policy. In relation to the former, it is apparent that there is no one notion of 'reparation' from a victim perspective. However, a victim's right to reparation should be acknowledged in all cases where there is evidence that he or she has been a victim of an offence—be that offence a breach of human rights or humanitarian law or a breach of the domestic criminal law. Progress on the domestic scene has been intermittent, but with the recent proliferation of restorative justice initiatives, documented in the next chapter, and clear shifts in the normative alignment of criminal justice, significant advances are being made. On both the national and international platforms, it is easy to identify a growing trend not only acknowl-

---

[194] Zedner (1994), 233.
[195] However, legal transplants are not always as attractive as they may appear on paper. See Ch 6, p 289.
[196] See Ch 6, pp 272–4.
[197] See Ch 6, pp 285–90.

edging the harm suffered by victims, but also the various different ways in which such harm might be rectified. Although reparation is often viewed as being 'backward-looking on grounds of corrective justice',[198] if broadly construed to encompass ideas such as apologies, guarantees of non-repetition and other gestures of remorse, it may be conceived as being progressive and capable of re-equipping both the victim and offender to move forwards from the offence.

---

[198] Weiner (2005), 128.

6

A Place for Victims' Rights?

T HE DEVELOPMENTS CHARTED in this book illustrate how victims' rights have become firmly established as an integral component of human rights on the international platform. Although many of these advances have been primarily directed at victims of abuse of power, rather than at victims of non-state crime, both types of victims stand to benefit from the ongoing realignment of human rights and criminal justice parameters. On a domestic level, whilst the language of victims' rights is commonly used and abused to mask political enterprises and the 'war on crime',[1] there is also a genuine and deeply-rooted realisation that victims have a legitimate interest in the way that criminal justice is administrated, in terms of substance, processes and outcomes. Policymakers on both the domestic and international stages are beginning to acknowledge the fact that victims merit a more prominent role in criminal justice as opposed to their historically subservient status as informants and witnesses.

Whilst an array of different factors has contributed to this changing perception of the victim, foremost among them has been the process of globalisation, which has resulted in a huge proliferation of international norms and standards with regard to criminal justice and human rights generally. Consequently, there is a growing, albeit still imperfect, international consensus on the values and structures that ought to feature in any modern criminal justice system. From the perspective of victims, core values such as protection, participation, remedy, truth, reconciliation and reparation have come to be acknowledged as values which are mutually beneficial for both victims of non-state crime and victims of abuse of power. States are under a clear, positive duty to take legal and administrative steps to prevent violations occurring, and, where they do occur, states must investigate and prosecute them with a view to punishment. Importantly, it is recognised that this duty of protection extends to the courtroom itself, when victims are called on to testify as witnesses.

However, it is also apparent that not all of these values are subject to an equal degree of international consensus. There is, for example, considerable unity around goals such as protection and the right to a remedy. This is something that should be welcomed as a reflection of a concrete trend. The debate has, to a large extent, moved on, and now tends to focus on other values that are considerably more contentious. In particular, while participatory rights are certainly emerging, there is still some uncertainty as to the precise role victims ought to play in

---

[1] For a US perspective, see further Dubber (2002).

criminal proceedings. Commentators remain divided as to whether victims should be able to have an input into key decision-making processes concerning prosecution, plea bargaining, or sentencing. If it is accepted that victims ought to have some sort of role, then the nature of that role still needs to be delineated so as to avoid impacting upon the fair and objective administration of justice.

Nonetheless, in the longer term, there is no reason to believe that we cannot find answers to these challenges, as vexing as they might be. Certainly, from a global perspective, there is every prospect that we will see consensus continuing to grow where there has traditionally been division and dissent. Given the rapid progression of these norms and standards to date, it can be legitimately speculated that the detail will be fleshed out in forthcoming years. Rather than these developments marking the culmination of a process, it would seem that we are still very much in its early days. We can thus afford to be cautiously optimistic that current trends will continue for the foreseeable future, and will continue to provide a framework for the future direction of criminal justice reform.

It may be necessary, however, to sound a note of caution to avoid the risk of being swept along with the much-vaunted tide of globalisation. It should also be emphasised that normative trends will not always be reflected in practice. As such, it may be overly optimistic to assume that the proliferation of these norms will somehow revolutionise victim-related policymaking. For all the work that went into the UN Victims' Declaration of 1985 and the more recent Basic Principles on Reparation, these are ultimately soft law instruments. Putting these declaratory norms and principles into practice requires some form of legal mechanism in order to carry tangible benefits both for the benefit of victims of abuse of power in international law and for victims of non-state crime at a domestic level. From the point of view of victims of abuse of power, debates continue as to whose responsibility it ought to be to investigate grave human rights abuses, how the apprehension and prosecution of suspects should proceed, and who should pay compensation and provide services to victims.[2] However, from the perspective of the victim of non-state crime, perhaps we can afford to be a little more optimistic. While many of the international standards directly concerning them are also declaratory in nature, in the United Kingdom, at least, the Human Rights Act should ensure that the victim-related jurisprudence of the Strasbourg court is not ignored by the domestic courts and legislature.

I. Victims' Rights and Adversarial Justice

Even with widespread and comprehensive human rights standards in place, and even though some of these are binding in law, international trends are only ever

---

[2] See generally Mazzeschi (2003), Simonovic (2004), Bassiouni (2006), Simpson (2007), Pete and du Plessis (eds) (2007).

likely to have a limited impact upon the position of victims in the domestic criminal justice system as it currently stands. The reasons for this inherent limitation are primarily normative and structural in nature. Victims have no conceptual role within the adversarial system, and it is naturally conditioned to facilitate two parties, and only two parties. Thus the very *idea* that the victim is a legitimate stakeholder at all with rights in the adversarial system is still a source of considerable contention; there are many commentators and policymakers who remain sceptical about adopting terminology that refers to 'victims' rights'. Unfortunately, this perspective has hindered the development of victim-centred reforms in many common law jurisdictions. However, it is important that we ask why such scepticism continues to be so widespread given the direction of international trends and proliferation in standard-setting. Two major reasons are suggested. First, the concept of victims' rights is viewed as too vague and indeterminate to be a useful legal tool; and secondly, there is a fear that enshrining such rights in law will detract from due process. Each of these contentions is examined below.

The Nature of Victims' Rights

To a large extent, it is true that the precise nature and scope of victims' rights within contemporary criminal justice discourse remains uncertain. More needs to be done to clarify the nature and scope of emergent rights, but, as this book has sought to show, the parameters of such rights are gradually becoming more clearly defined. If a concept or idea is considered too vague to be given legal force, the answer is surely to find ways of making the concept less vague; not to conclude that it can never enter into law. Furthermore, it seems that to deny the place of victims' rights within criminal justice is to deny a *de facto* and *de jure* reality. Admittedly, there is no coherent statement of the *legal* rights victims are able to exercise within the English criminal justice system, but by virtue of the EU Framework Decision, Strasbourg jurisprudence and even our own domestic case law and legislation, victims have already acquired a number of rights within our legal order. This has been recognised by the Law Commission:

> [V]ictims of crimes have human rights as well, and if a country's rules of criminal law, procedure or evidence are ineffective to protect such victims, this deficiency sometimes enables them to complain that their rights under the Convention have been breached.[3]

As previous chapters have illustrated, victims have now well-established rights to protection in society generally, and whilst giving evidence at court. They can rely upon the procedural right to pursue private prosecutions, to have their views taken into account, and to have crimes against them investigated and appropriately punished. In addition, victims may seek judicial review of decisions of criminal justice agencies, sue offenders in the civil courts, and make a complaint where rights under the Code of Practice have been violated. Indeed, some of these

---

[3] Law Commission of England and Wales (1997), [5.22].

rights go beyond what is necessitated by minimum international standards. All of these rights have their foundations in law, and are thus fully justiciable.

Of course, official rhetoric and Government publications would tell us that victims have many more rights afforded to them by various soft law publications and the recently adopted Code of Practice. However, it may be argued that these 'rights' are not really 'rights' at all, since they are non-legal in nature and cannot be enforced in the courts. Victims may, for example, be entitled to compensation payable on an ex gratia basis or the court may make a compensation order in their favour if the offender is brought to justice. The Code of Practice grants them 'rights' to information, pre-trial contact with prosecutors, support at court, a reasonable level of facilities, an opportunity to provide a personal statement etc. Labels used in the past for these 'rights' have included 'expectations', 'entitlements' or 'service rights', but no matter which label is used and no matter how laudable these objectives may be, none of these standards constitute 'rights' in a legal sense since they cannot be enforced by the courts. Following the Domestic Violence, Crime and Victims Act, victims do have the legal right to utilise the complaints mechanisms contained therein. Yet, as Hall has observed, these procedures are external to the criminal justice system.[4] Without a form of justiciable redress, methods used to ensure that victims are able to rely on 'rights' created in Government publications are ultimately meaningless.

The adversarial system has then, to some extent, been reformed and refined in recent years to accommodate certain rights for victims. However, rights that exist on paper may not be reflected in practice. Many of them are severely limited. Successful private prosecutions, for instance, are exceedingly rare, and, following the decision in *Re McKerr*, victims are unable to pursue actions for Convention breaches that predate the Human Rights Act. Special measures, while undoubtedly improving the experience of vulnerable victims in court, do not change the fact that cross-examination is still a cornerstone of the adversarial system, and can be a harsh and degrading experience for many victims. Thus not all rights, even if firmly entrenched in law, will necessarily improve the plight of the victim in practice.[5]

A Zero-Sum Game?

A second objection to analysing victims' rights as a form of human rights stems from the perception that they risk interfering with the rights of the accused. In pitting victims' rights against those of offenders, it has been argued that the criminal process would be morally flawed since the defendant stands to lose out to the more morally acceptable victim.[6] The idea that the rights of victims and offenders are strictly oppositional is reflected by frequent resort to the metaphor of 'balance' in

---

[4] Hall (2007), 56.

[5] A further, and arguably more deep-seated obstacle, considered later in this Chapter, is that the adversarial system is fundamentally incapable of giving a firm platform to the sorts of rights and values that are becoming increasingly prominent on the international platform. See below, pp 249–54.

[6] See eg Spencer and Spencer (2001); Coen (2006).

political rhetoric and official publications.[7] Certainly some policy initiatives, launched in the name of 'victims', have done very little to assist them while actively encroaching upon the rights of the accused.[8] The potential for conflict has, however, been exaggerated, and it is wrong to state per se that the concept of victims' rights brings about a reduction in the rights of the accused. Fears of a trade-off of rights tend to stem from questionable assumptions, such as the idea that victims are inherently vengeful,[9] or that demeanour is a strong indicator of veracity.[10] Both these arguments have been used as a basis for minimising participation in sentencing or restricting the use of special measures for vulnerable witnesses, but neither is corroborated by empirical evidence.

Two further points are worth mentioning in relation to this 'zero sum game' argument. First, it does not necessarily follow that the interests of victims and offenders will always conflict. It is difficult to see how some rights, such as the provision of information, support at court, or the provision of good facilities, impact upon defendants at all. Indeed, the two groups share much in common, including similar socio-economic characteristics.[11] It is well established that there are a number of scenarios in which the victim and the defendant will share mutual concerns, such as the desire for a prompt and efficient trial process and to be provided with information about procedure.

Secondly, it is important to acknowledge that there are occasions when rights of victims and offenders will conflict, but this need not give rise to undue levels of concern. Convention case law abounds with incidences where two competing rights require the striking of an appropriate balance. For example, a victim may well object to a decision not to prosecute, to release a suspect on bail, to pursue a particular line of questioning in court, or to impose a community sentence. The fact that a clash of rights occurs does not mean that the rights of victims are somehow invalid, or that they should always be subservient to the rights of the accused. The fair trial standards laid down in the Convention are not absolute, and a fair trial does not mean a trial which is free from all possible detriment or disadvantage to the accused.[12] No one set of rights should prevail, and both sets of rights should be afforded equal respect. The Strasbourg Court has itself acknowledged that the victim / offender balancing act is not immune from this analysis:

> It is true that Article 6 does not explicitly require the interests of witnesses in general, and those of victims called upon to testify in particular, to be taken into consideration. However, their life, liberty or security of person may be at stake, as may interests coming generally within the ambit of Article 8 of the Convention . . . Contracting States should organise their criminal proceedings in such a way that those interests are not unjustifiably

---

[7] See further Sanders (2002); Jackson (1990), (2003); related discussion in Ch 1 at 9–25.

[8] Jackson (2003), 313. 2 examples cited are the erosion of the right to silence and the increased disclosure obligations on the defence.

[9] See Ch 3, pp 152–4.

[10] See Ch 2, pp 86–7.

[11] Dubber (2002), 155.

[12] Spencer (1994), 636.

imperilled. Against this background, principles of fair trial also require that in appropriate cases the interests of the defence are balanced against those of witnesses or victims called upon to testify.[13]

As Klug has argued, this is one of the key benefits in analysing victims' rights as human rights: the approach provides a framework whereby competing rights can be assessed.[14] There are relatively few attempts, however, to devise specific frameworks under which this can be carried out. Sanders and Young propose a quasi-utilitarian 'freedom model', which basically states that where competing sets of rights or values are in conflict, those that safeguard the freedom of others to the greatest extent should prevail.[15] This model is, however, somewhat limiting for victims, insofar as it would reject any direct input into decision-making processes as their contribution *may* (though not necessarily *will*) jeopardise the rights of the accused. Since this model falls short of maximising participation, it may not ultimately be capable of upholding the right to participation to the fullest extent, a trend which is rapidly emerging in international norms.[16]

The better solution, with the future potential to accommodate participatory rights, is to resolve conflicts of rights on a case-by-case basis using a principled rights-based framework that is constantly evolving to keep pace with international consensus. Admittedly, this could prove to be a vague and unpredictable exercise, but it seems to be the most satisfactory way of resolving conflicts. Trust should be placed in the courts and other criminal justice agencies to perform decision-making processes using a balancing exercise fairly, taking into account all relevant information, and acting within Convention standards and other international indicators of good practice. If necessary, the legislature could provide interpretative assistance.[17] The nature of the rights-balancing exercise may become easier over time, as the parameters of new rights become more sharply focused. This is nothing new, and the courts perform such an exercise all the time in relation to other rights both within and beyond the sphere of criminal justice.

Yet the functionality of such a balancing exercise is complicated further by the existence of the adversarial paradigm. As Goodey has observed, our trial system is a bad advert for the concept of a 'fair trial'.[18] It is certainly not the easiest backdrop against which to conduct a just and effective interest-balancing exercise. Indeed, it could be said to maximise the potential for conflict. Since oral cross-examination is regarded as the primary means of testing the testimony of a victim, curtailing it to any significant extent can be extremely difficult, as was highlighted in relation

---

[13] *Doorson v Netherlands* (1996) 22 EHRR 330, [70]. The wording of Article 6 itself states that it will only apply to an individual 'in the determination of a criminal charge against him', which means that victims will not be entitled to bring an action under the provision in their own right.

[14] Klug (2004).

[15] Sanders and Young (2007), 46–9.

[16] A further problem with the model is that it is not necessarily a straightforward task to determine the means of maximising the 'net' freedom: see Hall (2007), 61.

[17] As has been suggested by some Government ministers in the case of recent anti-terror legislation found to be incompatible with the Convention. See *The Observer*, 14 May 2006.

[18] Goodey (2005), 178.

to sexual history evidence in the case of *R v A*.[19] It is undeniable that the means of striking such balances are somewhat precarious, and yet effective and fair interest-balancing is what international best practice appears to demand. The adversarial system, however, is incapable of delivering a fair process of interest-balancing. The core structures and processes of the criminal trial place such a high value on confrontation and cross-examination that, if these practices were to be seen to be overly regulated, the accused's right to a fair trial in the adversarial system could well be seen to be jeopardised.

In *Van Mechelen v Netherlands*,[20] it will be recalled that any measures restricting the rights of the defence should be strictly necessary, and if a less restrictive measure can suffice, then it is that measure which should be applied.[21] There are many fundamental elements of the adversarial trial that are incapable of being effectively checked by specific measures introduced to protect the victim. Cross-examination is, for example, a process that will almost inevitably place complainants under considerable strain when testifying. Victims are therefore effectively denied reliance on their full Convention rights within an adversarial setting since cross-examination is typically one of the main tools used by the defence to challenge the prosecution evidence. Stringently curtailing the right of the defence to cross-examine a witness in an adversarial trial would, in most circumstances, contravene the Convention. However, as noted below, most inquisitorial systems do not have a conceptual equivalent of cross-examination and instead provide for other means of challenging the evidence of the prosecution.[22] Arguably, such systems are better placed to accommodate the emergent rights of victims in their capacities as witnesses to the same extent.

The Inherent Limits of Adversarial Justice

The core argument advanced in this book is that the adversarial system is inherently limited in the type of rights to which it is capable of giving effect. While attempts have been made in recent years to mitigate some of its astringencies, its long-term capability of safeguarding the types of rights that are emerging on the international stage such as protection, participation, justice, and reparation, is questionable.

Protection

Recently many crime prevention initiatives have been rolled out, and there have been increased efforts to protect witnesses in advance of trial. Furthermore, it has been acknowledged by the domestic courts that persons in vulnerable positions

---

[19] [2002] 1 AC 45. See Ch 2, pp 99–102.
[20] See Ch 2, p 94.
[21] *Van Mechelen v Netherlands* (1998) 25 EHRR 657, [59].
[22] See below, pp 278–81.

must be protected against the possibility of violence or abuse at the hands of both state and non-state actors, particularly relating to deaths in custody. These are all welcome developments, and there appear to be no *systemic* obstacles that prevent the realisation of the right to protection outside of the actual court process. However, the same cannot be said in relation to secondary victimisation that occurs within criminal trials. The nature of the gladiatorial combat that characterises the trial arena means that the vast majority of victims who come to court to give evidence are likely to experience some form of secondary victimisation owing to the structures of the adversarial system and the theoretical foundation upon which they are based.[23] Furthermore, in the case of those victims who are particularly vulnerable, such as child witnesses or complainants in rape cases, the adversarial system's attempts to accommodate them have been likened by Birch to an ultimately hapless effort to hammer a square peg into a round hole.[24]

The provisions of the Youth Justice and Criminal Evidence Act are forward-thinking and will undoubtedly be of considerable value to some victims who give evidence in court. Whilst empirical evidence suggests that the Act has been instrumental in providing a degree of relief from secondary victimisation, only a minority of victims will be eligible for some form of protection. Even those who are eligible for special measures will still have to be cross-examined. There are two particular sources of hardship for victims in their capacities as witnesses: adherence to the principle of orality and the value placed on cross-examination. Thus victims called to give evidence must testify live in the formal and daunting surroundings of a criminal courtroom, often in front of the alleged perpetrator of the offence. In many cases, they will then be cross-examined by counsel for the defence, who will use an array of techniques designed to make the witness stumble and fall when giving testimony. The Youth Justice and Criminal Evidence Act has done little to regulate these particular excesses of the adversarial model, and it is little wonder that research continues to report that victims feel that they are put on trial themselves. Toying with evidential rules, tightening trial procedures, or altering the rules contained in the professional Codes of Conduct are unlikely to change the way in which victims are treated in the criminal trial.

Participation

While the right to participation is still taking shape on the international stage, a consensus is clearly building that victims ought to have some role within the trial and other key decision-making processes. If, in time, international instruments should become more specific about the nature and form that participatory rights ought to take, adversarial systems may find it very difficult to conform to such standards. On a theoretical platform, the interests of the victim in common law systems are conceptualised as falling outside the criminal law, and should instead

---

[23] McBarnet (1981), Ellison (2001a), Sanders and Jones (2007).
[24] See also Birch (2000), 223.

be addressed in the civil courts using the law of tort. For this reason, victims remain conceptually isolated. In the adversarial trial, victims have no opportunity to put their own side of the story to the court in their own words, but must confine their explanation of events within the parameters of the questions posed by the advocates. They are not entitled to legal counsel to represent their interests, but are instead dependent upon the Crown prosecutor, who is obliged to combine his normative role as a minister of justice with new obligations to support victims and witnesses. However, the desire of victims to be heard and to be acknowledged is slowly being recognised, and has been the subject of considerable lip-service and policy initiatives in recent years. The Victims' Code of Practice outlines a right, for example, to make a Victim Personal Statement, and pilots are now underway to allow victims' relatives to make an oral statement at sentencing hearings in cases of murder or manslaughter. Although recent years have witnessed the forging of a much closer relationship between the CPS and victims, this does not change the fact that the interests of the victim continue to be conceptualised in a subservient position to the collective interests of society. This occurs throughout the criminal process: during the investigation and prosecution of offences, during the trial, and in the imposition of the penalty. While debates around the proper role of victims in decision-making are set to continue for some time to come, what is very clear is that our criminal justice system can *only* ever regard them, at best, as a useful tool for the State in relation to the investigation and prosecution of crime. A bipartisan system cannot become a tripartisan system without wholesale reform at a structural level, nor without a re-evaluation of the theoretical assumptions that underpin existing structures and institutions.

Justice

To some extent, the domestic courts have responded well to fresh requirements from the Strasbourg court concerning the rights of victims to an effective investigation. The full extent of the investigatory obligations under Articles 2 and 3 of the Convention is still to be ascertained. As things stand, these rights are still in their infancy and it remains to be seen how widely the courts will construe them in future years. Unlike the complex ideological debates raised by the idea of participatory rights, the potential to implement fully the various components of a right to a remedy seems less likely to be limited by the structural parameters of the criminal justice system, as they primarily concern the position of victims outside the courts.

There is, however, one particular aspect of the right to a remedy, which could be particularly difficult to realise in the adversarial system. The 'right to know' or the 'right to truth' has recently moved to a position of prominence in human rights discourse, particularly as regards victims of abuse of power. If standards for victims of state and non-state crime continue to cross-fertilise one another, we need to start thinking seriously about the place of truth-finding in the adversarial trial. It was noted in Chapter 4 that supporters of the adversarial model often claim, in its defence, that truth is best determined by the direct questioning of witnesses before the tribunal of fact.[25] As such, adversarial theory argues that demeanour and the ability of the witness to remain composed and relaxed during cross-examination are indicators of veracity. Such a perspective fails to take account of the psychological literature which indicates that giving evidence in an unfamiliar and stressful environment will almost certainly cause an adverse effect on the witness's ability to recall accurately past events. Research also indicates that aggressive questioning under cross-examination can arouse hostility in witnesses and thereby render their testimony in court less reliable. It is widely acknowledged that stress, much of which is attributable to the adversarial structures of the trial itself, impedes the ability of witnesses to give a true and accurate account of past events. The rationale for the existence of the cardinal principles and practices of the adversarial system must therefore be called into question. Too much faith has been placed upon the value of orality, demeanour, public hearings and cross-examination as beneficial fact-finding tools.

In addition to stress, the potential for truth-finding is also curtailed by the extent of party control of the evidence. Favourable evidence is promoted by the parties, whilst unfavourable evidence is underplayed.[26] There are few channels by which neutral evidence can be brought to the attention of the trier of fact. Witnesses do not have an opportunity to tell their story to the court. Instead, it is the advocates who tell the story, and who reconstruct the historical truth in the course of the trial. All witnesses are pawns in a much larger contest between the parties where the primary goal is to win. As Steffen neatly surmises:

> [t]ruth is but an incidental and dispensable element of the system. Attention shifts from the goal of truth-finding to the effectiveness of the game's players.[27]

Yet an effective and fair criminal justice system, which purports to weigh up evidence fairly and make a determination as to the guilt of the accused ought to place a paramount value upon truth-finding. Ultimately, those who rely on the system to arrive at the truth, namely victims and innocent defendants, will lose out. The 'truth' is constructed in advance of and in the process of the criminal trial. In the context of international criminal trials, Findlay and Henham argue that the trial ought to be re-envisaged as a search for truth rather than a process of penalty.[28] Trial decisions, they argue, should be:

> transformative and directed towards the restoration of the place of truth within justice as much as the restoration of the offender within the communities of justice and their victim communities.[29]

---

[25] See Ch 4, pp 186–8.
[26] Ellison (2001a), 159.
[27] Steffen (1988), 821.
[28] Findlay and Henham (2005), 348.
[29] *Ibid*, 313.

This too should be the case with our domestic trial. Adversarial justice is a poor mechanism for truth-finding, or for providing for reconciliation or restoration of both victim and offender. The prospects for realising a right to truth are largely non-existent while the adversarial system remains intact.

Reparation

The final 'right' that was analysed in this book was the right to reparation—to have harm made good. In spite of the fact that there seems to be widespread consensus that victims *ought* to be able to rely on such a right, not all agree that it should be delivered within the criminal justice system. Again, the single greatest obstacle to realising reparation within criminal justice stems from the purist conception of crime as a transgression by the individual against the state. Punishment, rather than reparation, is thus seen as the goal of criminal justice. While compensation may be ordered as part of the sentencing process, little thought has been given to ways of repairing harm other than through a monetary payment to the victim. This falls considerably short of the way in which reparation is conceptualised in international and human rights law; ideas such as 'satisfaction', 'truth' and 'guarantees of non-repetition' remain alien to the adversarial system. Yet it is fundamentally impossible to measure the effects of crime solely on a monetary basis, and it is argued that the time has now come to consider how we can rethink the concept of reparation, taking into account the needs and desires of individual victims. Research on that front clearly tells us that symbolic gestures, including apologies and community work, are often of greater value to most victims than being handed a specific amount of material compensation to reflect their losses. Reparation within our penal system should focus on rebuilding the social relationship that has been damaged by the victimisation; not simply trying to undo the effects of crime through monetary payments.

Unfortunately, it seems unlikely that there will be a policy overhaul, in the short term at least, that rethinks how punishment might be adapted to deliver a more holistic form of reparation to the victim and / or to the community. Our sentencing system remains fundamentally retributive in nature, and while popular punitivism continues to exert a major influence upon penal policy, this position is unlikely to change. As Barnett has noted, a system that revolves around retributivism offers no incentive for the victim to involve himself in the criminal justice process other than to satisfy his feelings of duty or revenge.[30] The time has now come to cease perceiving the public interest of the State and the private interests of the victims in such inimical terms and to search for a new way of sentencing offenders justly, whilst offering some measure of reparation to victims at the same time.

---

[30] Barnett (1977), 285.

Summary

Norms that are now emerging on the international platform have clearly had some impact upon the creation of new rights for victims within the English criminal justice system. However, the ability of the system to adapt and to conform fully to emerging standards of best practice is highly questionable. Courts can take steps to ensure victims are protected, have their cases properly investigated and have access to a remedy. Parliament has created mechanisms for providing some form of compensation to victims and, more recently, to give them a voice in the sentencing process. However, the elasticity of the adversarial paradigm is fast becoming over-stretched. As international trends continue to refine and develop the rights of victims, so pressure on the adversarial bubble increases. In the longer term, this is unsustainable and that bubble is likely to burst. To provide a full and comprehensive system for protecting the newly emerging rights of victims on the international platform, we need to give serious consideration to other ways of doing justice.

II. Alternative Approaches

There is a growing recognition that, in order to realise victims' rights effectively, we need a better model of criminal justice. While there is increasing acknowledgement of the systemic and value-laden problems that the adversarial paradigm produces, there remains considerable uncertainty and division as to what should be done to address the situation.[31] This section considers the feasibility of adopting two alternative methods for overhauling the adversarial nature of the criminal justice system. The first, radically increasing the use of restorative justice initiatives, could result in a more inclusionary means of sentencing in the vast majority of cases where the defendant pleads guilty. The second potential reform, the adoption of an inquisitorial method for the adjudication of guilt, could result in our trial process becoming better geared to accommodating the rights of victims in those cases where the accused contests the prosecution case.

Restorative Justice

Recently there has been a proliferation of initiatives based around mediation or restorative justice. The task of arriving at an agreed definition for the concept has been difficult, but Marshall's definition of restorative justice as:

---

[31] See further Pizzi (1999), ch 11.

> a process whereby parties with a stake in a specific offence collectively resolve how to deal with the aftermath of the offence and its implications for the future

seems to be broadly accepted.[32] It may thus be seen as something of an umbrella term, used to describe a diverse range of processes that are characterised by reparation, reintegration and participation of victims, offenders and communities and other stakeholders affected by the offence.[33] It is a victim-centred approach to criminal justice, which perceives crime in a very different manner from the way it is typically conceptualised in the adversarial system. As Howard Zehr has argued, crime is first and foremost 'a violation of people and relationships', and the restorative process aims to make amends for the harm that has been caused to victims, offenders and communities.[34] A wide variety of approaches have claims that they fall under the 'restorative' label, and there is no 'prototype' format for such a process. However, the most commonly adopted practices include direct mediation, indirect mediation, restorative cautioning, sentencing panels or circles, and conferencing.[35] Even within these broad categories, differences may be considerable in relation to the degree of formality, the stage of intervention, the facilitating body, extent of reconciliation, and the overall degree of 'restorativeness' they entail.[36] However, all might be said to fall under the umbrella of 'restorative justice' and are derived from the same normative framework that conceives victims, offenders and crime in a very different manner from the adversarial paradigm.

In placing an increased emphasis upon participation and reparation, international trends have certainly exerted a downward pressure upon national governments to develop policies based on restorative justice principles. The EU Framework Decision calls on Member States to promote mediation in criminal cases for offences which it considers appropriate for this sort of measure.[37] 'Mediation' is defined in Article 1(e) as:

> the search prior to or during criminal proceedings, for a negotiated solution between the victim and the author of the offence, mediated by a competent person.

As with the specific measures set out on compensation in Article 9,[38] the language of Article 10 is couched similarly in vague terms and confers a considerable degree of discretion upon Member States in terms of how specifically they choose to implement the provision.

---

[32] Marshall (1999), 5.

[33] Van Ness and Strong (2002).

[34] Zehr (2005), 181.

[35] See generally Dignan (2005), 107–26.

[36] See further Roche (2003), who argues that that it is of little use to simply assert whether or not a practice is restorative, but instead it is important to be able to determine how restorative it is by assessing both its process and values. See also McCold (2000).

[37] Art 10 states: '1. Each Member State shall seek to promote mediation in criminal cases for offences which it considers appropriate for this sort of measure. 2. Each Member State shall ensure that any agreement between the victim and the offender reached in the course of such mediation in criminal cases can be taken into account'.

[38] See Ch 5, p 225.

The Council of Europe issued a more elaborate set of principles in Recommendation (99)19, 'Concerning Mediation in Penal Matters'. It will be recalled, however, that this is a form of soft law that is non-binding. National governments are simply asked, in developing mediation schemes, to bear in mind the principles laid down in the Recommendation and to circulate the text as widely as possible. The Recommendation, which consists of 34 articles, recognises that there is a need for both victims and offenders to be actively involved in resolving cases themselves with the assistance of an impartial third party. The Articles generally reflect internationally recognised principles of best practice, including (inter alia), the importance of specific training, the principle of voluntariness, the need for judicial supervision, and the need to ensure that procedural human rights guarantees are safeguarded. In addition, Member States are called on to promote research and evaluation of mediation processes.

Inspired by the Council of Europe's Recommendation, the United Nations Vienna Declaration on Crime and Justice committed the Member States:[39]

> to introduce, where appropriate, national, regional and international action plans in support of victims of crime, such as mechanisms for mediation and restorative justice, and we establish 2002 as a target date for States to review their relevant practices, to develop further victim support services and awareness campaigns on the rights of victims and to consider the establishment of funds for victims, in addition to developing and implementing witness protection policies.[40]

Paragraph 28 of the Declaration further commits the Member States to the implementation of restorative justice policies that are 'respectful of the rights, needs and interests of victims, offenders, communities and all other parties'. At a subsequent meeting, the United Nations Congress on Crime Prevention examined restorative justice in its plenary sessions and formulated a draft proposal for Basic Principles on the Use of Restorative Justice Programmes in Criminal Matters. The instrument was adopted by the United Nations in August 2002.[41]

The Basic Principles stipulate that restorative justice programmes should be generally accessible at all stages of the penal procedure; that they should be used on a voluntarily basis; that participants should receive all relevant information and explanation; and that differences in aspects such as power imbalances, age, and mental capacity need to be taken into account in devising processes. Core due

---

[39] *Vienna Declaration on Crime and Justice: Meeting the Challenges of the 21st Century* (UN Doc A/CONF.187/4).

[40] *Ibid*, [27].

[41] ECOSOC Res. 2002/12. Note, however, that the value of mediation had already been recognised in a number of UN documents for some time. Principle 7 of the Declaration of Basic Principles of Justice for Victims of Crime and Abuse of Power calls for use of mediation, arbitration, customary justice, indigenous practices and other informal mechanisms where appropriate to facilitate conciliation and redress for victims; ECOSOC Resolution 1990/22 of 24 May 1990, *Victims of Crime and Abuse of Power*, requests the Secretary-General, together with all the entities of the United Nation's system and other appropriate organisations, to develop and institute means of conflict resolution and mediation; ECOSOC Resolution 1995/9 of 24 Jul 1995, *Guidelines for Cooperation and Technical Assistance in the Field of Urban Crime Prevention*, commits states to adopt mediation schemes as a device for reducing recidivism (see Guideline 3(d)(ii)).

process requirements should also be observed. Moreover, if restorative justice processes or outcomes are not possible or agreement cannot be reached, steps should be taken to support the offender to take responsibility for his actions to provide reparation to the victim and the community.

Domestic Practice

In spite of the ascendancy of restorative justice on the international platform, for the most part such mechanisms exist on an informal level within the UK. Martin Wright has astutely observed that 'laws on victim / offender mediation in Britain are like snakes in Ireland: they do not exist'.[42] However, there are a number of restorative schemes operating in the criminal justice system which offer victims some form of redress, although these tend to exist outside its formal parameters. Nonetheless, increasingly policymakers in the UK have sought to integrate aspects of restorative justice into the mainstream criminal justice system, with varying degrees of success. As has been the case in many jurisdictions, most of these restorative interventions have been targeted at young offenders, for whom many believe they work best in terms of diversion and reducing recidivism.[43]

Restorative principles were given a statutory footing in the Crime and Disorder Act 1998, which introduced a range of measures designed to tackle juvenile offending. Section 67 of the Act introduced 'reparation orders' as a low-level disposal for young offenders between the ages of 10 and 17.[44] These require young offenders to make specific reparation either to the individual victim or the community.[45] The restorative potential of reparation orders is clear, but, as Goodey suggests, while the language of restorative justice is heavily invoked by the legislation, its primary focus is the diversion of young offenders from crime, rather than making restoration to victims or the community.[46] The victim is given an opportunity to be consulted and involved at every stage. In line with orthodox restorative justice theory, the victim may be given an opportunity to have the harm put right; and the offender may be given an opportunity to make amends. However, research into the operation of reparation orders carried out by Dignan raises a number of significant concerns in relation to their operation. While the participation of victims was supposed to be voluntary, in some cases it was found that victims were not being consulted; and practice in four pilot areas was found

---

[42] Wright (1997).

[43] Johnstone (2002), 15.

[44] For more serious offenders, the legislation provides for an 'action plan order', which may combine forms of reparation with other (possibly punitive) elements aimed at designed to tackling the underlying causes of offending behaviour. Neither order can be made if the sentence is otherwise fixed by law.

[45] Such reparation should be proportionate to the seriousness of the offence, but should not exceed a total of 24 hours in aggregate. The Order may not be made to any person without their consent. In those cases where the victim of the offence does not wish to receive reparation directly, reparative measures may be undertaken which are likely to benefit the wider community.

[46] Goodey (2005), 204.

to be largely inconsistent.[47] To some extent, this was attributable to the fact that victims need to be identified, contacted and consulted, which requires courts to co-operate with the criminal justice agencies in granting adjournments, which they are often reluctant to do.[48] Dignan argues that, like the other measures contained in the 1998 Act, reparation orders cannot be regarded as 'truly restorative' since the sanction is coercively imposed by the court, rather than arrived at through some form of dialogue or consensus.[49] He observed that a substantial majority of reparation orders (80 per cent) had no impact on the direct victim, and almost two-thirds of orders (63 per cent) contained reparation directed at the community rather than the victims.[50] While community-based sanctions may well be capable of delivering a form of reintegration for the offender and a form of reparation to the broader community, the benefit that is conferred is intended to address a separate and more intangible injury than that suffered by the victim. The financial / proprietary loss experienced by the victim, alongside his or her emotional plight, is not directly addressed by community-based measures, which should thus be afforded less priority than those actions that provide reparations to direct victims.[51]

Under Part 1 of the Youth Justice and Criminal Evidence Act, referral orders became a mandatory court disposal for first time low-level juvenile offenders. Referral Orders will be given to most 10 to 17-year olds, providing they plead guilty and it is their first criminal conviction.[52] The scheme operates through diverting a young person away from court to a Youth Offender Panel. The Panel, which is intended to operate as a form of discussion forum, aims to offer the young person the opportunity to:

> make restoration to the victim, take responsibility for the consequences of their offending behaviour, and achieve reintegration into the law-abiding community.[53]

While similar mechanisms in other jurisdictions require that a young person must consent to taking part in such a programme, this is not the case with referral orders. Attendance is compulsory for both the young person and, if he / she is under the age of 16, a parent or other appropriate adult. A victim (or their representative), a supporter of the victim and anyone else 'capable of having a good influence on the offender' may also attend.[54] The panel meeting aims to conclude an agreement which will provide reparation to the victim or community and helps to address the young person's offending behaviour. Reparation may be achieved through a verbal or written apology, or even the repair of damaged property or monetary compensation. As regards the offender, specific interventions may

---

[47] Dignan (2002), 78.
[48] *Ibid*, 79.
[49] Dignan (2005), 111.
[50] Dignan (2002), 80.
[51] Van Ness and Nolan (1998), 88.
[52] Youth Justice and Criminal Evidence Act 1999, ss 1–2.
[53] Home Office (1999).
[54] Youth Justice and Criminal Evidence Act 1999, s 7(4)(b).

include family counselling, mentoring, victim awareness sessions and drugs or alcohol programmes.[55]

In their study of schemes piloted in 11 different areas, Newburn et al found that the restorative potential of the referral order was significantly hindered by the very low levels of victim participation: just 13 per cent had attended panel meetings. In practice, this meant that, as with reparation orders, it was much more common-place for reparation to be directed towards the somewhat elusive concept of 'the community', rather than to individual victims who had suffered direct harm. Whilst the research found that 82 per cent of contracts agreed at Youth Offender Panel meetings involved some form of reparation, this only took the form of direct reparation to victims in 7 per cent of all contracts. On a positive note, it is nonethe-less clear that the referral order scheme has integrated certain restorative prin-ciples into the youth justice system. The partial devolution of decision-making processes away from criminal justice professionals, and the statutory creation of a proper and meaningful opportunity for victims to be involved in such processes constitute a welcome shift away from the dichotomous, state-led conception of justice. Newburn et al's study concluded that panel sessions were 'constructive, deliberative and participatory forums'.[56] Nonetheless, it might be said that, given that they are only available for a range of relatively minor offences for a select range of offenders, and given that the principle of voluntariness has been compromised, the extent to which they encapsulate the core features of restorative justice remains questionable.

In contrast to England and Wales, Northern Ireland has opted to mainstream restorative justice in statute as the primary response to juvenile offending.[57] The Justice (Northern Ireland) Act 2002 provides that the vast majority of offences involving 10–17 year olds will be dealt with through one of two types of restora-tive youth conference: diversionary conferences and court-ordered conferences. Both types of conference take place with a view to a youth conference co-ordinator providing a recommendation to the prosecutor or court on how the young person should be dealt with for their offence.[58] A recent evaluation of the Northern Ireland scheme resulted in relatively positive findings as far as the provision of reparation was concerned.[59] In contrast to many other restorative initiatives, the level of victim participation was high: victims participated in over two-thirds

---

[55] Campbell et al (2006), 13. If there is no agreed outcome the Youth Offending Panel will report back to the court, who will then reconsider how the young person should be dealt with. A contract is enforceable and subject to monitoring and review by the Youth Offending Team. In the same way, if the young person fails to comply with the terms of the contract, the Youth Offending Team will refer the young person back to the court to consider re-sentencing.

[56] Newburn et al (2002), 62.

[57] The juvenile justice system was reformed in line with recommendations from the Criminal Justice Review, which was set up following the Belfast Agreement of 1998.

[58] Two preconditions must be in place for both types of conference. First, the young person must consent to the process and secondly they must admit that they have committed the offence. Where these conditions are not met the case will be referred to the Public Prosecution Service for a decision on whether to continue and, if so, the case will be dealt with through the ordinary court process.

[59] Campbell et al (2006).

(69 per cent) of the conferences, thus making reparation logistically more feasible.[60] Campbell et al found that, in 87 per cent of conferences, the young person apologised or agreed to apologise. Over three quarters of plans (76 per cent) also had elements to provide reparation, but mostly this reparation took the form of indirect reparation to the community or symbolic reparation to victims.[61]

Policymakers have been more reluctant to replicate such measures for adult offenders. Aside from compensation orders and the possibility of a civil action brought by the victim, there are few opportunities for adult offenders to make reparation. However, restorative cautioning is one model of restorative justice which has been growing in popularity in the UK. Increasingly common in Australia, New Zealand, and parts of the USA, police cautions are delivered using a restorative conference, either as an alternative to the orthodox caution or formal prosecution. Conferences are usually organised, managed and facilitated by the police to provide a forum for the police to bring together offenders and their victims, with their respective families and supporters. The model used in England and Wales was pioneered in Australia, and first used in the UK by Thames Valley police. As with many restorative schemes however, the chances of victims receiving reparation are considerably hindered by the fact that few victims choose to participate. An evaluation carried out by Hoyle et al in 2002 found that just 16 per cent of victims took part,[62] and very little direct, financial reparation was made to victims. An evaluation of a similar scheme in Northern Ireland which was limited to juvenile offenders found that while over 90 per cent of cases resulted in a written or verbal apology to the victim, few of the sessions resulted in any compensation or reparation.[63] In spite of these findings, the overall evaluations of both schemes were generally positive, and the Home Office has now encouraged all UK police forces to follow suit and establish similar practices.[64]

The use of restorative principles is also evident in a relatively new scheme of 'conditional cautions' for first-time or minor adult offenders. Introduced by the

---

[60] However, it is also important to underline that 60% of the victims who attended conferences were 'victim representatives' and 40% were actual victims themselves. Victim representatives, were usually individuals who were not directly affected by the specific offence, but instead gave the conference a general input of what it is like to be victimised. Victim representatives were often used in cases such as shoplifting or criminal damage to public property, or where there was some difficulty in getting a specific victim to attend the conference.

[61] Direct material reparation to victims was relatively rare. This can be explained in part by the very limited means of most young offenders, but it is also worth noting that the majority of victims (57%), did not request any form of material recompense. Moreover, in a number of cases reparation was not necessary as either no financial harm had been caused or the property had been recovered undamaged.

[62] Hill (2002) has suggested that while any sort of coercion to attend would obviously be undesirable, there was a risk in Thames Valley that the police had become so over-sensitised to the need not to apply pressure, that they did not take the opportunity to explain fully the potential benefits of the process to victims. Similarly, Hoyle (2002) noted that many of the Thames Valley facilitators gave victims a misleading idea of restorative justice: eg, in many cases victims were not told that they could bring along a supporter. As such, victims may have been inadvertently dissuaded from attending.

[63] O'Mahony and Doak (2004). However, the Northern Ireland scheme was introduced to cover juvenile offenders, and the vast majority of cases involved retail theft, where goods were normally recovered immediately.

[64] Dignan (2006), 272.

Criminal Justice Act 2003, conditional cautioning enables the CPS to issue a caution as an alternative to prosecution with a number of conditions attached. These conditions should be aimed at either rehabilitating the offender and / or ensuring that he or she makes reparation to the victim or the wider community,[65] and it is envisaged that restorative justice processes will form a part of, or will contribute towards these conditions. Participation in a scheme may form part of an offender's caution in and of itself, or the conditions themselves may represent the outcome of such a process.[66] Under section 23 of the 2003 Act, the CPS may only offer such a caution if the officer has evidence that the person has committed an offence; the relevant prosecutor decides that there is sufficient evidence to charge the person with the offence and grounds for giving a conditional caution; the offender admits the offence to the authorised person; an explanation of the effect of a caution and the warnings about the consequences of failure to observe the conditions has been given; and, finally, the offender signs a document that sets out details of the offence, an admission, consent to the caution and consent to the attached conditions.

The scheme pays only very limited lip-service to the idea of restorative justice for two main reasons. First, conditional cautions are not intended to replace traditional non-statutory police cautions, and are only used in a small minority of cases.[67] They were introduced as an alternative option where the imposition of conditions are seen as being a more effective way of addressing the offender's behaviour or making reparation to the victim or the community. Secondly, like many of the other measures listed above, it can be said to be only partly restorative, insofar as victims are not actively involved in the process[68] and, as Dignan observes, 'no attempt is made to "privilege" or "prioritise" restorative over rehabilitative interventions, even in cases involving direct victims'.[69]

In addition to the formal efforts on the periphery of the criminal justice system, there are a few informal schemes that attempt to use restorative principles through the use of conferencing or mediation. In 2001, the Government undertook to fund a number of these voluntary schemes and offered financial backing to their evaluation as part of its Crime Reduction Programme.[70] The schemes mostly concerned adult offenders, convicted of serious offences, including assaults, robberies, burglaries and grievous bodily harm. While evaluation is ongoing, preliminary reports suggest that

---

[65] Offenders who fail to comply with the conditions will usually be prosecuted for the original offence.

[66] Home Office (2004b).

[67] So-called 'simple' police cautions remain on a non-statutory footing and remain within the discretion of the police rather than the CPS.

[68] Under the Code of Practice, interviewers should, however, ascertain what the attitude of the victim would be to any offer of compensation. See Dignan (2005), 73.

[69] Dignan (2006), 273.

[70] The schemes, CONNECT, the Justice Research Consortium and REMEDI, are currently under evaluation by a team led by Professor Joanna Shapland at the University of Sheffield. The schemes were established primarily to concentrate on cases involving adult offenders at different stages of the criminal justice process, from pre-sentence through to release from prison. They are largely typical of those operating on a local level around the country.

reparation (either directly to victims or indirectly to communities) does not feature strongly.[71] As research documented in the previous chapter generally appears to confirm, most victims did not appear to want material reparation: more important for them was the idea of symbolic reparation, in the form of apologies and expressions of genuine remorse.[72]

Discussion

Recent years have seen a tentative, yet discernable, shift in government policy which places increasingly greater emphasis on reparation for crime victims. However, it should be apparent from the above discussion that not all measures that draw on restorative language or restorative-type themes can be regarded as 'restorative justice' in a pure sense. In the same way, just because a particular programme offers some form of reparation to the victim, this alone does not constitute a fully-fledged form of restorative justice. The extent to which a particular practice may be deemed to be restorative or not is difficult to measure, but as mentioned above, the question of restorativeness must be determined using a sliding scale which may measure a range of different variables.[73] Using these criteria, we can thus describe various schemes as either 'fully' or 'partially' restorative. While many of the programmes currently in place in the United Kingdom may be better described as 'partially' restorative, even where schemes are 'fully' restorative there is relatively little evidence available to suggest that restorative justice can fully and consistently restore victims in terms of the consequences of victimisation.[74] Like other forms of offender-based reparation, victims can only benefit in those cases where the offender is identified and admits the offence. Even then, the success of a restorative initiative will be ultimately dependent upon the degree to which both offender and victim desire to work within the restorative paradigm. The offender must be prepared to make amends voluntarily, and the victim must be prepared to accept. Otherwise, the use of the label 'restorative' will be largely inappropriate to describe either the process or its outcome.

If we recall some of the key themes and values that are reflected in international instruments, it is nonetheless clear that a paradigm built around restorative principles holds the potential to realise rights for victims, without compromising those of the offender. In contrast to the adversarial paradigm which inherently excludes victims by conceptualising crime as an offence against the State, restorative justice locates victims at the centre of its theoretical framework. In practice, this means that in 'fully' restorative systems, where offenders and victims are both identified and consent to the process, victims have an opportunity to give an account of past events in an informal and relaxed setting. They are free to comment on the facts,

---

[71] Shapland et al (2004); (2006).
[72] See Ch 5, pp 225, 238.
[73] Campbell et al (2006).
[74] Dignan (2005), 164.

how the offence affected them, and how they felt. They can use their own words and proceed at their own pace. They are not limited to answering questions carefully formulated by advocates designed to trip witnesses up or to minimise damage. Restorative justice provides a forum where victims can freely exercise the right to participation. Although some of the quasi-restorative schemes currently in place in the UK have suffered from low participation rates, this may be partly attributable to the way in which we as a society continue to perceive crime as an offence against the State, and where the working culture of the police, other criminal justice agencies and legal professionals see victims as outsiders to decision-making processes.

Furthermore, there is no reason why restorative processes should encroach upon the rights of the defence. No model currently adopted in the western world offers victims the final say as to how an offender should be dealt with. That power, quite rightly, should rest with a neutral arbiter, who is subject to legal control and oversight by the State. Instead, the victim is empowered to contribute to the decision-making process, without exercising a veto, and without jeopardising the rights of the offender. Research indicates that, from the offender's perspective, such input is often positive and is not generally motivated by feelings of anger or vindictiveness.[75]

Another key right that could be more easily effected through a restorative model than the conventional system is the right to reparation. While it may be more commonplace for reparation to be symbolic rather than material in nature, it is not always clear that victims actually *want* material reparation. There is evidence to suggest that victims who have gone through restorative processes are relatively content with purely symbolic outcomes.[76] Thus apologies, expressions of remorse, and forms of community work have become the most common types of reparation that tend to arise from restorative processes, and, in many cases, victims have indicated that they felt such gestures were sincere.[77] The inclusion of symbolic forms of reparations are welcome insofar as they reflect the wider meaning attributed to 'reparation' in humanitarian and human rights law, unlike compensation orders and state compensation schemes which tend to perceive reparation in purely material terms. There is, nonetheless, a risk that symbolic acts of reparation could become so commonplace that they become an expected norm and would thereby lose their restorative value. It was noted above that the total absence of tangible measures could result in injuries and harm being belittled or degraded;[78] Dignan argues that even written apologies can become 'routinised' and that this risk may be exacerbated where there exists an emphasis on community as opposed to direct victim involvement.[79]

[75] See Ch 3, above, pp 152–4.

[76] Marshall and Merry (1990); Umbreit et al (1994); Strang (2002); Campbell et al (2006).

[77] See Strang (2002), Campbell et al (2006). However, in relation to victims who received an apology in the Thames Valley restorative cautioning scheme, Hoyle et al (2002) report that only half felt the apology was probably or definitely genuine.

[78] See Ch 5, p 216.

[79] Dignan (2005), 153.

Restorative justice also offers victims the opportunity to pursue their right to truth. While still an emerging right on the international platform, it is gaining significant ground in human rights and transitional justice discourses and the idea of uncovering the facts and acknowledging harm is also beginning to infiltrate traditional understandings of criminal justice. It was argued in Chapter 4 that the truth was obscured through the processes of case construction and trial advocacy.[80] However, if more cases were diverted away from formal prosecution, this aspect of the process would be lost. In the absence of building a case to convince a jury, entering into plea negotiations, or preparing for sentencing hearings, the truth is much more likely to be preserved. Crucially however, unlike current practice relating to the acceptance of guilty pleas, the absence of a trial will not preclude victims from being able to tell their story.

In focusing on making amends for the harm caused by the offending behaviour, restorative models emphasise that healing conflicts cannot be effected through a financial settlement. Emotional harm is conceived as being of equal stature as material harm, and one means of amending the emotional aspect of the damage is through the cathartic effect of a truth process. Research reveals that victims are often relieved when they are able to 'put a face' to the offender, or if the reasons which led the offence to occur are explained to them.[81] Forgiveness and reconciliation may not always follow a restorative encounter, but without the truth being uncovered, neither of these goals can be effected. The restorative paradigm accepts that participation, truth-telling and reparation are all important, and, indeed, interlinked aspects of enabling victims and offenders to put a past incident behind them and move towards reconciliation and healing.[82]

There is a plethora of questions about the overall place of restorative justice within the wider criminal justice system, and fully-fledged restorative processes undoubtedly need a period of time to develop. The process of mainstreaming them onto a statutory platform is necessarily an incremental one. Questions remain as to whether the existing structures of the conventional paradigm can be enhanced to accommodate reparation in a meaningful way through harmonisation with restorative principles, or whether the conventional paradigm ought to be entirely usurped by a new restorative-based framework. A process of harmonisation of the two paradigms may take what is best from both and address the flaws in each system to create a strong, unitary model of criminal justice.[83] Other commentators, however, have argued that such an approach would mean that restorative perspectives and practices would be submerged by the predominance of existing formal structures;[84] or that the retributive paradigm is fundamentally incapable of accommodating restorative principles.[85] Here is not the place for

---

[80] See above Ch 4, pp 186–201.
[81] Umbreit and Roberts (1996); Strang (2002), 90; Hoyle et al (2002).
[82] Bazemore and Walgrave (1999), 4
[83] Dignan (2003); Van Ness (2003); Groenhuijsen (2004).
[84] Walgrave (2002).
[85] Zehr (2005); Braithwaite (2003).

detailed consideration of these issues, but if a restorative model is ever to replace the role of the conventional paradigm, the concept itself needs to be significantly developed and refined.[86]

The Inquisitorial Approach

While the restorative paradigm grants us some valuable insights into the ways in which the victim can participate in a meaningful way in decision-making processes, it cannot be adopted in those cases where the accused contests guilt. In these instances, it may be worth considering practice within the inquisitorial juris-dictions of continental Europe, where it is often contended that victims are treated more fairly.[87] The structures and values of the inquisitorial approach are very different from those of the adversarial model, and are grounded in a high degree of trust placed in the State. This can be contrasted with a basic underlying scepti-cism that seems to exist in adversarial jurisdictions about trusting the State to pro-duce the truth whilst simultaneously protecting the interests of the accused.[88] In the inquisitorial model, truth-finding is widely regarded as the overriding goal.[89] As such, it is sometimes said that the inquisitorial system emphasises the legiti-macy of trial outcomes, as opposed to the adversarial focus on the legitimacy of trial processes.[90]

The Structure of the Inquisitorial Process

While it is important not to generalise about the nature of inquisitorial proceed-ings,[91] Merryman has argued that criminal proceedings are usually divided into three distinct phases: the investigative phase, the examining phase, and the trial.[92] Each stage is formally documented, and is strictly governed by the principle of legality.[93] The investigative phase begins once a crime has been reported. It will be brought to the attention of the prosecutor, who will request a formal judicial investigation. In France, this request goes to a separate panel of three judges who are responsible for the charging process known as the *Chambre d'Instruction*. If the panel agrees that an investigation is warranted, it will appoint an examining magistrate (*juge d'instruction*), who will begin an investigation into all the

---

[86] Haines and O'Mahony (2006); Dignan (2005).

[87] Pizzi and Perron (1996); Bacik et al, (1998); Brienen and Hoegen, (2000); Ellison, (2001a).

[88] Jörg et al (1996), 45.

[89] See eg, Damaska (1973), 586.

[90] Law Reform Commission of Western Australia (1999), 79.

[91] These may vary considerably from country to country. See generally Van den Wyngaert (ed) (1993); Delmas-Marty and Spencer (eds) (2004).

[92] Merryman (1985), 129.

[93] This principle essentially states that where the prosecutor has sufficient grounds for suspecting that there has been a violation of pre-existing law, a charge must be brought against the suspect (Kühne (1993), 146).

circumstances surrounding the offence.[94] In other jurisdictions, including Germany and Austria, the prosecutor himself is viewed 'not as an adversary party of the defendant, but as a neutral representative of the State',[95] and controls the pre-trial investigation.

In addition to collecting information relating to the particular facts of the incident in question, the investigation also conducts an extensive inquiry into the suspect's *personnalité*, which includes the gathering of information on his upbringing, family life, education, job history, behaviour, financial situation and psychological make-up.[96] Once this evidence has been collected, the examining magistrate will begin the examination phase.[97] During this stage of the procedure, he or she will interview all pertinent witnesses, and interviews are usually recorded in a verbatim transcript.[98] Normally, the questioning of the lead suspect will form a central part of the examination phase. Although defendants cannot be compelled to answer questions, there is a strong expectation that they will do so and lawyers will normally instruct their clients to give truthful answers to all questions asked.[99] The examination phase can be lengthy: a wide range of witnesses are typically called, including the family, friends, co-workers and neighbours of the accused to gather a more rounded picture of the suspect's *personnalité*.[100]

The investigations and examinations conducted in the pre-trial phase will be recorded in the dossier, or case file. The dossier will usually consist of several hundred separate documents, including witness statements, expert reports and photographs.[101] The defence normally have an absolute right to inspect the full dossier prior to trial, and may make submissions to the investigating magistrate on any additional investigations or tests which ought to be instigated.[102] It is thereby vital that the dossier is both objective and complete. This is guaranteed, in theory at least, by the supervisory role exercised by the prosecutor over the police and also by the investigating magistrate, who has an overall duty to ensure that the investi-

---

[94] Lerner (2001), 797.

[95] Cho (2001), 3. However, Cho suggests that the degree of supervision in Germany is generally inadequate since, in practice, the police 'monopolise the requisite manpower, equipment, and experience, while the prosecutor lacks his own agents'.

[96] Lerner (2001), 824; Daly, M (1999), 67.

[97] In Germany and Italy, this office has been abolished and the prosecutor assumes full control over the criminal investigation: Van Kessel (1992), 411. Frase (1990) has argued that, in most French cases, the police tend to operate with 'minimal interference' from the judge (at 613).

[98] Lerner (2001), 797.

[99] *Ibid.*

[100] Daly, M (1999), 67–8. Daly notes that the investigation of *personnalité* is derived from the French legal maxim, *'On juge l'homme, pas les faits'* ('One judges the man, not the facts'). Both the prosecution and defence are prohibited from interviewing witnesses, although at this stage the defence will normally be able to exercise a right of allocution to protect his client's interests, calling certain matters to the attention of the court and advising the client on how he or she should respond to judicial questioning (Merryman (1985), 130). In contrast, the Spanish system permits a more adversarial style of argument before the examining magistrate, whereby the parties can request that he or she undertakes further investigations or the magistrate may dismiss the charges altogether (Thaman (1999), 239).

[101] McKillop (1997), 565–6.

[102] Frase (1990), 617.

gation is carried out fairly and impartially.[103] When the investigation has been completed, the examining magistrate will then determine whether there is reasonable cause for trial. In some jurisdictions, including France and Belgium, this decision is taken by an indicting chamber of three judges.[104] If it is decided that the case should proceed, the court then assumes control over the case, replacing the prosecutor and the investigating magistrate for the commencement of the trial proper.[105]

As a consequence of the way in which evidence is assembled in the pre-trial phase, the conduct of the trial bears little resemblance to its common law counterpart. Proceedings are structured in the form of an inquiry rather than a contest, which, depending on jurisdiction, will often be presided over by a single professional judge or a mixed panel comprising lay persons and other professional judges.[106] Daly has described the trial as 'anticlimactic', since the fact-finding has already been largely completed through the pre-trial investigation.[107] As such, proceedings are generally conducted with less formality than in adversarial jurisdictions.[108] The evidence has already been taken and the record made: the function of the trial is to present this evidence to the trier of fact and allow the prosecutor and defence to argue their respective cases on the basis of the evidence contained in the dossier.[109]

In most jurisdictions, the defendant is questioned before other witnesses, first by the presiding judge and then by the prosecutor and defence counsel. In some jurisdictions, questioning may be conducted indirectly through the trial judge. Other witnesses, including the *juge d'instruction*, are then usually questioned in a similar way, with most of their testimony being elicited through the relatively informal questioning of the presiding judge. Further evidence is presented in documentary form. After all the evidence has been received, parties will present their closing arguments before the trier of fact retires to consider the verdict.[110]

---

[103] *Ibid.*

[104] *Ibid*, 613.

[105] Van Kessel (1992), 413.

[106] Mixed panels are used in most inquisitorial jurisdictions. Eg, the French *Cour d'Assises* sits with a first instance jury comprising 9 lay jurors and 3 professional judges (including the presiding judge). A majority of 8 is needed to convict. The Court is only used to try serious crimes which carry a minimum sentence of 10 year's imprisonment: Lerner (2001), 796. Similarly, Spain and Russia both recently reformed their criminal justice systems and have reintroduced the use of lay jurors after they were abolished in the late nineteenth century. In Spain, the jury is composed of 9 jurors and 1 presiding judge, whereas Russia and Belgium both have common law-style juries comprising 12 laymen (Thaman (1999); Van Den Wyngaert (1993), 11). In contrast, Dutch courts are composed entirely of professional judges (Swart (1993), 280).

[107] Daly, M (1999), 66.

[108] Van Kessel (1992) noted that the presiding judge sits closer to the parties and to the public than in adversarial jurisdictions, and lawyers will generally address the judge with a greater degree of familiarity (at 413).

[109] Merryman (1985), 130.

[110] Van Kessel (1992), 413. Some jurisdictions, including Spain, allow all parties, including the victim, to make opening statements; a right that is not afforded to the parties in France or Russia (Thaman (1999), 245).

At a structural level, the inquisitorial process differs substantially from its adversarial counterpart, and these distinctions carry a number of advantages for victims. In contrast to the adversarial trial, where evidence is contemporaneously presented and tested by the parties, the examination of witnesses and the assessment of their credibility will have already been completed. The primary function of the inquisitorial trial is thus to assess the weight of individual pieces of evidence, which should mean that victims will not be extensively questioned about background information relating to their credibility. Any combat will have already taken place in the investigation and examination phases.[111] Although this may be a stressful or difficult experience for some victims, it does mean that they should not normally find their character under protracted attack if called to testify in the trial proper.

The second advantage for victims lies in the fact that proceedings are structured much less rigidly. Inquisitorial judges have a broad remit to lead and shape the trial as they see fit. Traditional features of the common law system, such as the right to cross-examination, the tightly regulated rules of evidence, and concepts such as abuse of process and burdens of proof do not feature strongly in inquisitorial models. From a victim's perspective, this should mean that he or she should be able to give testimony in a relatively free and unencumbered way, and that the judge should be able to exercise a broad range of discretionary powers to adapt proceedings so as to accommodate the special needs of vulnerable victims.

Thirdly, the lack of any clear-cut division between the 'prosecution case' and the 'defence case' means that witnesses are less likely to be regarded as the property of either party. Instead, they are viewed as witnesses of the court, and it would be unusual for them to be degraded through the type of point-scoring exercises that have been shown to be so problematic for them in the adversarial system. They are thereby not subjected to the same level of control. Instead, such witnesses will generally be able to give evidence adopting free narrative, answering only a few questions put to them by the judge or the parties. The tone and atmosphere of the inquisitorial trial is thus very different indeed from its adversarial counterpart.[112]

---

[111] Daly, M (1999), 66.

[112] As Lerner noted in his observation of the trial of Thierry Gaitaud at the French *Cour D'Assises* in 1999: 'Introduction of each witness was minimal ... [The judge] asked each witness "What do you have to tell us?" There was no direct or cross-examination as we know of it. The witness started off testifying in narrative form, usually for several minutes without interruption ... When the witness finished his or her story or the testimony got murky, Corneloup [the judge] began asking questions, directing the witness's attention to key points. He often read the former statements of a witness from the dossier in framing his questions. When he was done, he turned to the *assesseurs* and jurors to see if they had any questions, then to the prosecutor, then to defence counsel. Bilger [the prosecutor] and defence counsel usually asked between one and three questions each'. (at 804).

The Participation of Victims

Continental systems do not usually permit the victim to bring a private prosecution where the State declines to prosecute.[113] Instead, most jurisdictions permit the victim to request a review of the case through official channels, usually by a superior authority (eg Denmark, Luxembourg and Norway) or even by a court (eg Germany, Portugal and the Netherlands).[114] France, Spain and Belgium do not provide any opportunities to review a decision not to prosecute.[115] These countries do, however, permit the victim to set the prosecution process in motion where the *ministère publique* has declined to do so, through issuing a summons for the accused to appear in court (*citation directe*). Once this occurs, however, the public prosecutor must take over.[116]

In certain countries of the former Eastern block, the system of private prosecutions is fairly well established. Erez and Bienkowska's survey of victims in the Polish criminal justice system found that private prosecutions were effected in 22 per cent of the cases they analysed, and comprised 50 per cent of all the prosecutions for property-related offences, or where victims knew the offender personally.[117] Compared with those victims who did not prosecute privately, the authors noted a higher level of satisfaction in relation to the way in which victims perceived their treatment within the criminal justice system.[118]

However, in most inquisitorial systems where private prosecution is possible, it seems to be rarely used. In Germany, the *Privatkläger* procedure operates under certain limited circumstances set out in the Criminal Code.[119] It may be invoked if the prosecutor does not exercise his right to public prosecution or determines that there is insufficient evidence to proceed.[120] Nonetheless, the provision is virtually never used and is largely irrelevant since victims are unable to instruct the police to gather evidence.[121] Austria, Denmark, Norway and Switzerland also allow private prosecution in certain circumstances where the prosecutor has waived his right of prosecution, although here, too, the procedure is not widely

---

[113] However, in certain countries of the former Eastern block, the system of private prosecutions is fairly well established—see eg Erez and Bienkowska (1993).

[114] Brienen and Hoegen (2000), 1066–7.

[115] *Ibid*, 1066.

[116] Brienen and Hoegen (2000), 321; Vadillo (1993), 383.

[117] Erez and Bienkowska (1993). See esp pp 50–8: 'Victims in private prosecutions, more often than their counterparts in public ones, stated that they always received information about their rights . . . They also thought more frequently that the criminal justice system handled their victimization adequately . . . and they stated more often that they will co-operate with the criminal justice system in future victimization'.

[118] *Ibid*, 50.

[119] Brienen and Hoegen (2000) state that 'private prosecution is limited to trespassing, defamation, violation of confidentiality of mail, common assault, intimidation, vandalism, and comparable offences listed in s 374 StPO' (at 364). The authors proceed to note, however, that the victim must first 'constitute himself as a civil claimant before the examining magistrate' (*Ibid*, 1065).

[120] Art 374, StPO; Kühne (1993), 144.

[121] Kühne (1993), 144; Brienen and Hoegen (2000), 1065.

used.[122] As with its common law equivalent, the real value of private prosecution in the inquisitorial system would therefore appear to be purely symbolic.[123] One may therefore be tempted to conclude that, in fact, inquisitorial jurisdictions are no better structurally adapted to facilitate victims than adversarial ones. However, whereas in adversarial systems, victims are conceptually and structurally isolated, it appears that lack of use of the procedure on the continent may be attributable primarily to logistical and attitudinal reasons, rather than structural factors.

Given the fact that victims need to be highly motivated and well informed to pursue the case through the courts by themselves, it can be assumed that many find it easier to rely on the State to institute criminal proceedings. Although private prosecution is not widely practised in inquisitorial countries, other structures do exist that confer a proactive role upon the victim at the trial. This suggests that, in these jurisdictions, the criminal action and, in particular, the rationale underpinning its outcome, is conceived in a much broader and more inclusive way than the fairly stark public / private divide that has traditionally prevailed in the common law system of England.

As an alternative or in addition to private prosecution, some inquisitorial jurisdictions instead permit the victim to assist the prosecutor as a subsidiary counsel. The theoretical framework of this procedure recognises the special status of the complainant as the alleged victim of the criminal offence, whilst acknowledging at the same time the normative role of the State in prosecuting crime. Germany, Austria, Malta, Norway, Sweden and various eastern European countries operate some form of 'subsidiary prosecutor' schemes,[124] which allow victims an active role in both pre-trial decision-making and within trials themselves. The procedure will generally allow them to submit evidence, comment on representations made by the prosecution and defence, and express their opinions on key decisions taken.

In Germany, for example, victims of certain serious offences or the relatives of a murder victim may act as a subsidiary prosecutor (*Nebenkläger*).[125] A lawyer is often appointed for this purpose, although the cost will be borne by the complainant unless the accused is convicted.[126] By declaring his solidarity with the prosecution, the victim derives certain active participatory rights. These include a right to be present at all stages of the process; to put additional questions to witnesses; to provide additional evidence; and to make a statement or to present a claim for compensation. In this sense, the victim's lawyer can be an important ally

---

[122] Brienen and Hoegen (2000) cite an Austrian study by Krainz (1991), who found that just 3.5% of prosecutions were initiated privately (at 78). Regarding Norway, Denmark and Switzerland, the circumstances are also very clearly limited by law: see Brienen and Hoegen (2000), 218 (Denmark); 736 (Norway); 929 (Switzerland). See also Joutsen (1987b), 189.

[123] Brienen and Hoegen (2000), 1065.

[124] Joutsen (1987b), 191.

[125] Brienen and Hoegen (2000), 364; ss 395–402 StPO.

[126] Juy-Birmann (2002), 302.

to the public prosecutor, who nonetheless retains the burden of preparing and presenting the prosecution.[127]

Although some form of subsidiary prosecution has been an avenue open to victims in Germany since 1924,[128] it had fallen into virtual disuse until the rise of the victim on the policy agenda in the 1980s.[129] A survey by Kaiser conducted in 1989/90 found that subsidiary prosecutors participated in 14.3 per cent of cases,[130] and tended to play a predominantly passive role, intervening only occasionally to request that additional evidence be taken or to appeal against procedural decisions.[131] However, where victims did make use of the facility, most felt it had a positive effect upon their position within the system.[132] Erez and Bienkowska also evaluated the operation of the Polish subsidiary prosecution scheme. The researchers found that over a third of victims (36 per cent) whose cases went to trial acted as subsidiary prosecutors.[133] However, the survey also found that the main reason mentioned by victims for not exercising this privilege was that no one had informed them of this right (49 per cent).[134] As with those victims who had prosecuted offences privately, higher satisfaction rates were recorded for those victims who acted as subsidiary prosecutors than for those who did not.[135]

Although the procedure has the potential to help ease the plight of victims testifying in criminal proceedings, it is clearly underdeveloped in both Germany and Poland. Kury and Kaiser reported that 28.6 per cent of victims stated that they would have liked to have participated in the trial had they been made aware of their right to do so, and it would seem that, in general, victims in Germany are ill-informed of their rights to participate as a subsidiary prosecutor.[136] In one survey, a quarter of prosecutors stated that they never informed the victim of their rights, and only one in 10 stated that they always made such information available, as they are required to do under the law.[137] Most prosecutors stated that their duty to give such advice was 'quite simply forgotten' or that 'there was no suitable opportunity' to do so.[138]

A more optimistic picture of the subsidiary prosecution procedure in Germany is presented by Bacik et al. In these cases, where the complainant was a victim of

---

[127] *Ibid.* However, Bacik et al (1998) note that there is no official relationship between the public prosecutor and the subsidiary prosecutor: 'Although both wish to secure a conviction, the prosecutor also has a responsibility towards the defendant, and has a duty to seek out both the aggravating and mitigating factors' (at 68).

[128] Bacik et al (1998), 67.

[129] Sanders (1999), 12. The Victim Protection Act 1986 (*Opferschutzgesetz*) was particularly instrumental in creating new rights to participate actively in proceedings: Kaiser (1991), 548.

[130] Kaiser (1991), 604.

[131] *bid,* 605.

[132] *Ibid,* 602.

[133] Erez and Bienkowska (1993), 50. However, see Sanders (1999), who suggests that this figure is 'misleadingly high' since there was a relatively low response rate to the survey.

[134] Erez and Bienkowska (1993), 50.

[135] *Ibid,* 51.

[136] Kury and Kaiser (1991).

[137] Kury et al (1994), 75.

[138] *Ibid.*

rape or sexual assault, the authors found that the procedure was widely used, with up to 50 per cent of complainants relying upon it.[139] However, the researchers did express some uncertainty as to whether the procedure carried any real benefits for victims:

> There is some controversy over the effectiveness of the victim's lawyer. An opinion expressed by some state officials and prosecutors, was that the victim's lawyer serves no useful purpose, and simply duplicates the role of the prosecution. Thus, although all those interviewed agreed that it could be psychologically helpful for the victim to have her own lawyer present during the trial, this was not necessary either to ensure a conviction or to provide legal protection for the victim, since there is already a duty on both the prosecutor and the judge to protect her interests.[140]

Hence, while many victims would like to play such a role in the trial, they are regularly prevented from doing so by the reluctance of the legal profession to advise them of their rights and push forward their interests proactively. The main reason for this is that:

> [j]udges and prosecutors still regard the victim predominantly in his or her role as a witness, whereas the victim wants to be regarded as a party to the proceedings.[141]

Unlike the bipartisan nature of the adversarial trial, the structural framework of the inquisitorial system would facilitate a proactive role for the victim without much difficulty. The problem with the procedure is thus essentially an attitudinal one: victims are still perceived as outsiders to the criminal hearing. Bacik et al suggest that the victim is often conceived of as some sort of 'assistant' to the prosecutor, which could prove extremely problematic where the interests of the victim and the prosecution diverge.[142]

One possible way of sidestepping the particular difficulty highlighted by Bacik et al may be to accommodate the victim's counsel as an individual party to the proceedings, distinct from the prosecution, and capable of exercising a protective role within the trial whilst at the same time pursuing a reparative claim. An alternative model which allows for this is commonly referred to as the 'adhesion' or '*partie civile*' procedure. Participation of the victim as an independent civil party bears some similarity to the subsidiary prosecution model, although it has a distinct advantage in that it acknowledges the victim's status as a separate party to the trial. The procedure is widely utilised in France and Belgium, where the victim must formally demonstrate his or her intention of becoming a party to the proceedings by initiating an independent action before the *juge d'instruction* (*constitution de partie civile*) at any stage in the proceedings.[143] The procedure confers three important rights upon victims of crime. First, they can use the procedure to initi-

---

[139] Bacik et al (1998), 68.
[140] Bacik et al (1998), 67–8.
[141] Kury and Kaiser (1991), 5.
[142] Bacik et al (1998), 68.
[143] Or, as noted above, victims can initiate proceedings through issuing a summons to bring the accused directly before the trial court (*citation directe*—see Pradel (1993), 115).

ate a prosecution; secondly, they have the right to participate and be heard as a party in any prosecution; and thirdly, they have a right to pursue a claim for civil damages in the criminal action.[144]

However, while there is evidence to suggest that parties do exercise the right to be heard and to pursue civil claims, it appears that victim-initiated prosecutions in France are rarely instituted and depend heavily on the discretion of the examining magistrate.[145] Participation within the trial tends to be limited to the pursuit of the civil claim. The victim does not have a right to be involved directly in the public prosecution.[146] However, the *partie civile* (or their legal representative) will generally ask questions of witnesses (including the accused) after the assessors and jurors, but before the prosecutor. He or she also has a right to give a closing argument, although he or she is not permitted to object to questions put to the victim.[147] From the outset of proceedings, the victim can insist that the examining magistrate investigates and documents in the dossier any civil claim for damages. Similarly, the German 'adhesion' procedure, distinct from subsidiary prosecution described above, also makes it possible for civil damages to be claimed within the criminal action.[148] A civil claim may be made by notifying the clerk of the court: it is not necessary for victims to attend the trial or to be legally represented.[149] In contrast to subsidiary prosecution, Kaiser and Kilchling have reported that the adhesion procedure is 'very unusual', and suggest that while it is widely recognised, it attracts insufficient legal fees for attorneys, and a majority of jurists regarded it as an 'alien body' within criminal procedure.[150] Similarly, Frehsee noted that:

> [l]awyers who specialise in criminal law do not like to deal with civil law matters; they do not like to be misused as civil executory officers ... [T]he procedure is not routine; its management and control are rather awkward and ineffective.[151]

Kühne has noted that even where applications to utilise the procedure are made, judges often reject them.[152]

As with the above-noted reluctance to develop the subsidiary prosecution scheme, it is clear that these failings stem neither from the underlying structures of the inquisitorial system, nor from the unwillingness of victims to make use of available procedures,[153] but they are the result of ingrained perceptions of the civil claim as strongly subordinate to the main issue of the case, that being the criminal

---

[144] Frase (1990), 615.

[145] *Ibid.*

[146] Van Den Wyngaert (1996), 72.

[147] Bacik et al (1998), 59.

[148] Ss 403–6, StPO.

[149] Kaiser and Kilchling (1996), 265.

[150] *Ibid,* 561.

[151] Frehsee (1999), 242.

[152] Kühne (1993), 144.

[153] Kaiser and Kilchling (1996), 266. The authors also cite a study by Kilchling (1991) which showed that 90% of victims would have preferred to make use of such a procedure.

liability of the offender.[154] Practitioners in both common law and civil law jurisdictions both seem reluctant to grapple with the inevitable complexities that arise from a procedure that attempts to resolve both civil and criminal issues in a unitary action.

Protective Measures in the Criminal Trial

The importance attached to the pre-trial investigative phase means that oral evidence forms a relatively minor part of the trial proper. The decision will primarily be based upon the facts contained in the *dossier*. While most inquisitorial systems do subscribe to the principle of orality, this generally means that the judge should reach his or her decision on the basis of the evidence which has been directly laid before the court.[155] As this may include hearsay and other statements contained in the dossier, there is not always a need for victims to attend to give live evidence. Although the trial judge has the power to call witnesses, he or she may simply rely solely on the written statement of an absent witness that is read to the court through the *procès-verbal*,[156] providing he or she considers the evidence cogent enough to form the basis of *intime conviction*.[157]

This type of heavy reliance on the material contained in the dossier is commonplace in, inter alia, France, Belgium and in the Swiss canton of Zürich.[158] In these jurisdictions, it would appear that it is unusual for complainants to testify at the trial proper at all, particularly if they are seen as vulnerable. For example, Hamon notes that judges in France avoid ever making children attend the trial proper,[159] and Ellison has made similar observations in relation to rape complainants in the Netherlands.[160]

It is worth noting, however, that victims in these jurisdictions are not exempt from giving oral evidence altogether. Generally, they will still be expected to give oral evidence at the pre-trial hearing. However, as Ellison has observed, the setting of this hearing would seem to be much more relaxed and less trying for complainants than the prospect of giving evidence at the trial proper:

---

[154] Brienen and Hoegen (2000), 1069. Brienen and Hoegen made similar findings in relation to Austria, Turkey and Greece.

[155] Van Den Wyngaert (1993), 23; Kühne (1993), 148; Swart (1993), 297.

[156] Ie the part of the trial where oral evidence is received. See Chiaviaro, (2002); Pradel (1993), 119.

[157] Brienen and Hoegen (2000), 703.

[158] Van Den Wyngaert (1993), 23; Brienen and Hoegen (2000), 136 (Belgium); Kühne (1993), 148 (Germany); Swart (1993), 297; Ellison (2001a), 144 (Netherlands); Brienen and Hoegen (2000), 945–8 (Switzerland).

[159] Hamon (1989), 61.

[160] Ellison (2001a), 148. Rape complainants are only expected to appear before the trial proper in 'exceptional circumstances'. This will not, however, affect the right of the defence to present its arguments: Van Den Wyngaert (1993), 23. The author proceeds to note (in relation to the Belgian system), that while the 'philosophy of the Napoleonic Code' required all evidence gathered at the pre-trial stage to be reheard and subject to a 'public, contradictory debate' between the parties, in practice this no longer occurs in Belgium (at 34).

Such hearings take place in the relatively informal environment of the office of the examining magistrate and in private . . . The only persons present are the examining magistrate, the defence lawyer, and, at the examining magistrate's discretion, a support person . . . to lend the complainant 'moral support'. Complainants in the Netherlands are thus spared the acute embarrassment of giving evidence in public and the ordeal of facing the accused directly.[161]

Ellison proceeds to point out that while investigating magistrates in the Netherlands do have the discretion to arrange a face-to-face encounter between the accused and the accuser at the pre-trial stage, such confrontations appear to be rare in practice.[162]

In contrast, in other inquisitorial jurisdictions, including Germany, Austria and Spain, the courts are bound by the principle of immediacy, which requires all witnesses to be re-examined at the trial proper.[163] There are, however, exceptions to this rule that may apply where the witness is physically unable to give evidence,[164] or if the witness is a child.[165] In the Netherlands, Swart has contended that the principle has been 'almost entirely eroded by case law', which means that statements made by witnesses in the pre-trial stage are now increasingly admitted as valid testimony.[166]

Irrespective of whether or not individual jurisdictions require complainants to testify at the trial, attitudes in inquisitorial jurisdictions differ considerably from those held in adversarial systems about the alleged superiority of oral testimony. Even in those inquisitorial jurisdictions where complainants are expected to give oral testimony at the trial proper and to be questioned by the judge, the oral form is not regarded as intrinsically superior to any other form and, as such, much less emphasis is placed upon the demeanour of the witness as a means of gauging veracity.[167] Moreover, the fact that proceedings are judge-led as opposed to party-led will mean that advocates will not be able to exploit the principle of orality through the partisan manipulation of evidence that is so commonplace in adversarial jurisdictions.

By contrast, it has been noted that the principle of orality is exploited in the adversarial system through the advocates' curtailment of free narrative and the exertion of control over the responses of witnesses. This carries major ramifications for victims. Not only does it frequently result in secondary victimisation, but it also denies them any form of meaningful participation. Adversarial fact-finders hear a disjointed and prolonged account of events, subject to the rules of evidence and riddled by constant interruptions and suggestions from counsel. In the majority of inquisitorial jurisdictions, evidence is instead given in the form of a free narrative, and it is only at the end of this statement that a witness will be questioned about his or her evidence.[168]

---

[161] Ellison (2001a), 148.
[162] *Ibid.*
[163] Kühne (1993), 129; Vadillo (1993), 331.
[164] *Ibid.*
[165] Brienen and Hoegen (2000), 95.
[166] Swart (1993), 298.
[167] Lerner (2001), 801.
[168] Pizzi and Perron (1996), 42.

Witnesses can directly respond to the statements of other witnesses, and are also allowed to speak in natural voices in narrative form, unconstrained by cross-examination or evidentiary rules.[169] Pizzi and Perron have noted that it is not uncommon for victims of serious crimes, including rapes and serious assaults, to testify uninterrupted for 'thirty or forty minutes or longer'.[170]

The ability of complainants to tell their own story to the court using their own words helps to reduce secondary victimisation in a number of ways. First, it constitutes an important symbolic acknowledgement that the court is genuinely interested in the personal and individual nature of the victim's testimony. In turn, since witnesses are not identified with any one particular party, it might be surmised that complainants, and indeed all witnesses, may feel that their testimony is more personal and less contrived. The opportunity for free narrative and to give full, explanatory answers to questions is more likely to make victims feel that they have been listened to and less likely to make them feel sidelined or excluded.[171] Pizzi and Perron observed that witnesses 'seldom emerge from a trial feeling mishandled, as is so often the case in adversary procedure'.[172]

Secondly, Bacik et al found that the close control exerted by advocates over the testimony of rape complainants in Ireland rendered them much less articulate than the complainants they interviewed from inquisitorial jurisdictions.[173] Free narrative may thus alleviate the pressure on complainants who have often reported being made to feel as though they have to 'perform' at adversarial hearings,[174] and should also help to raise the confidence levels of complainants in advance of testifying, since they should be aware that their account of events will not be subjected to ongoing challenges and interruptions from the defence.

The lack of formal evidential rules means that there is relatively little statutory regulation on the use of protective measures in inquisitorial courtrooms. In general, the continental criminal codes contain very few provisions that are directly geared towards protecting victims or witnesses.[175] Instead, trial judges exercise a broad discretion as to what general steps might be taken to accommodate or protect them,[176] and the nature and extent of such measures vary considerably across jurisdictions. Generally, measures may include anonymity orders, holding some or all of the trial in camera, or restrictions on media reporting.[177] Some countries also make special provision for complainants to be questioned in the absence of the defendant. For example, Spanish law provides that the offender can be expelled from the court if he or she upsets the victim by behaving in an inappro-

---

[169] Pizzi and Perron (1996), 42.

[170] Joutsen (1987a), 42.

[171] The ability to relay free narrative to the court is increasingly recognised as carrying a therapeutic effect for the victim. See above, Ch 3, p 135.

[172] Pizzi and Perron (1996), 61.

[173] Bacik et al (1998), 29.

[174] Rock (1993), 56.

[175] Brienen and Hoegen (2000), 345.

[176] Hamon (1989), 58.

[177] See Bacik et al (1998), 42 (Belgium), 56 (France), 65 (Germany); Pradel (1993), 119 (France); Brienen and Hoegen (2000), 380 (Germany), 706 (Netherlands), 873 (Spain).

priate manner.[178] Under strict conditions, the Dutch courts may also allow a threatened witness to testify anonymously.[179] As noted previously, this practice has been accepted by the European Court of Human Rights, on condition that a conviction cannot be based 'solely or to a decisive extent' on anonymous testimony.[180]

As in adversarial trials, screens and video links are also used strategically to shield witnesses in inquisitorial countries. Bacik et al have indicated that they are used in France where the court considers that their use would enable the witness to give more effective evidence.[181] In many other jurisdictions, the use of such devices is expressly provided for in cases involving child witnesses.[182] For example, in Germany, the Witness Protection Act 1998 provides, inter alia, that the testimony of children under 16 can be pre-recorded, and that in certain circumstances the judge may question vulnerable and intimidated witnesses outside the court in a separate room (relayed to the main courtroom via a video link).[183] The judge will leave the court to question the child witness in a separate room, with the interview being relayed to the courtroom by video link.[184]

Brienen and Hoegen found that while the special needs of children during questioning are taken into consideration in 86 per cent of the twenty-two jurisdictions surveyed, the protections available to other victims were much more piecemeal.[185] Some jurisdictions certainly do have fairly comprehensive protections in place. Ellison notes that rape complainants will only usually testify in the Netherlands in exceptional circumstances; when this does occur, they will be able to make use of a televised link.[186] Similarly, Pizzi and Perron have outlined the special measures that a rape complainant can expect to have in place at a German trial:

> A rape victim at a German trial can seek to have the public removed from the courtroom when she is testifying, and this motion will be granted unless the judges determine that the public interest in hearing the victim's testimony outweighs the interests of the victim. Such motions are generally granted and thus provide some privacy for the victim by permitting her to testify with the public gallery cleared of spectators. The victim may also

---

[178] Brienen and Hoegen, (2000), 875.

[179] Ellison (2001a), 149.

[180] *Doorson*, above n 14, [76], see pp 247–8.

[181] Bacik et al (1998), 57.

[182] See Bacik et al (1998), 46, 60.

[183] Brienen and Hoegen (2000), 380. The authors note that the 'Mainz' model of interviewing witnesses outside the courtroom has been subject to heavy criticism, since the judge would not be able to see the occurrences and reactions to the testimony in the courtroom. Alternatively, the judge may order that the accused be excluded from the courtroom for the duration of the testimony 'if it is feared the witness will not speak the truth in his presence; if the witness is under 16 years of age and it is feared that questioning in the presence of the defendant may damage his well-being; or if the presence of the accused poses a serious threat to the health of any other witness (*ibid*, 381).

[184] Bacik et al (1998), 60.

[185] Brienen and Hoegen (2000), 1154. The authors note that under a third of jurisdictions (32%) provided for the questioning of the victim in the absence of the defendant and just 50% have enacted legislation to place limits on the type of questions that can be posed to vulnerable witnesses.

[186] See also Pizzi and Perron's account of protections available for rape complainants in German courts: (1996), 61.

move to have the defendant removed from the courtroom. Such a motion may be granted if the victim is under the age of sixteen, and the judges fear that she will suffer additional damage from having to testify in the presence of the accused.[187]

However, a more sceptical view of the protection of rape complainants in Germany is presented by Bacik et al, who note that the German provision is entirely dependent on the discretion of the judge.[188] They proceed to suggest that, in practice, the exclusion of the defendant from the courtroom does not happen very often, since it can be used as a ground for appeal.[189] The authors also note that of the five jurisdictions they surveyed in depth, only two of these (Denmark and Ireland) had any formal statutory means of protection that would *oblige* the court to make special provision for the testimony of adult rape complainants, whereas the measures were entirely discretionary in the other three jurisdictions.[190]

Given that inquisitorial systems seem to place relatively little importance on the need for an eye-to-eye confrontation between the accused and the accuser, it is surprising that, in contrast to the English adversarial system, a more developed system of protective measures is not in place in many inquisitorial jurisdictions. Pradel has suggested that the French courts, in particular, lag behind many other systems in their readiness to use innovative protective measures for vulnerable witnesses.[191] In general, measures themselves seem, if anything, less innovative than those available to complainants in adversarial trials under the Youth Justice and Criminal Evidence Act. This lower degree of protection could, however, be explained by the fact that complainants in inquisitorial systems are in less need of special procedural protection, since the process itself is less hostile and confrontational. The relatively business-like nature of the proceedings, and lack of bipartisan contest at their core, should mean that many victims in inquisitorial systems feel less tense and less apprehensive about the prospect of testifying than their counterparts in adversarial systems.

The Nature of Questioning

Zealous cross-examination in the adversarial system allows the accused to present a robust challenge to the case of the prosecution, which not only has a devastating effect on complainants, but also heightens the risk of obscuring the material truth.[192] In most inquisitorial systems, there is no conceptual equivalent of cross-examination, although the accused may rely on the principle of contradiction that effectively amounts to a right to challenge evidence adduced against him.[193]

---

[187] Pizzi and Perron (1996), 61.
[188] Bacik et al (1998), 64.
[189] *Ibid.* The relevant provision is s 247 of the StPO ('Removal of the Accused from the Courtroom').
[190] Bacik et al (1998).
[191] Pradel (1996), 160.
[192] Truth-finding in inquisitorial systems is discussed below at pp 281–3.
[193] Van Den Wyngaert (1993), 23.

Pradel notes that recent French case law has delineated two key aspects of the principle:

> First, it has been held that the principle of contradiction requires full disclosure to the person accused who must know the exact nature and cause of the allegations against him so that he is in a position to defend himself. Secondly, this principle allows the accused to benefit from the interrogation of the prosecution witnesses and to call his own witnesses.[194]

The manner in which the defence is able to exercise the principle of contradiction varies considerably between jurisdictions. Traditionally defence lawyers have had very limited opportunities to question the witness directly in France or Belgium;[195] although other jurisdictions, such as Spain and the Netherlands, permit the parties to play a subsidiary role in posing questions after the examining magistrate has conducted questioning.[196] Other civil law countries, including Italy and Denmark, even provide for a largely adversarial-style of cross-examination, although the judge retains very close control over the questions posed and generally ensures that witnesses are treated with respect.[197]

Inquisitorial systems are characterised by a lack of prescriptive rules as to the nature of questions that may be posed to witnesses.[198] However, where parties are afforded access to questioning witnesses directly, they will generally refrain from asking questions that are harmful or degrading to the witness.[199] Most commentators agree that questioning is much less aggressive in form, regardless of whether it is carried out by the parties or by the trial judge. Van Kessel, for example, notes that, by and large, questioning tends to be 'informal and more natural'[200] and Langbein has commented that the tone was 'crisp and business-like, but not hostile'.[201] Similarly, Damaska states:

> Anglo-American observers of the court scene are regularly struck by the rarity and the subdued nature of the challenges to the witnesses' credibility. If such a challenge occurs, it mainly focuses on the witness's reliability with respect to the facts to which he has been disposed and seldom escalates into a general attack on his character or reputation for untruthfulness.[202]

The apparently restrained tone of questioning carries obvious benefits for complainants.[203] As a result, Lerner observed that 'witnesses were relatively relaxed

---

[194] Pradel (1993), 120.

[195] Spencer (2002), 629. Spencer points out, however, that is very rare for the parties to make such a request.

[196] Ellison (2001a), 146 (Netherlands); Brienen and Hoegen (2000), 871 (Spain); Vadillo (1993), 396 (Spain).

[197] In relation to Italy, see Perrodet (2002), 381–2. Regarding Denmark, see Temkin (2002), 294. However, McEwan (1988) notes that in the Italian system, parties are not permitted to question children directly; this task is undertaken by the trial judge (at 821).

[198] Ellison (2001a), 152.

[199] *Ibid*, 149. Ellison states that such strategies are usually frowned upon by the courts.

[200] Van Kessel (1992), 464.

[201] Langbein (1977), 74.

[202] See also Damaska (1997a), 80.

[203] Van Kessel (1992) has also pointed out that the restrained nature of inquisitorial advocacy may also protect the accused against an aggressive, emotional prosecutor (at 443).

and often more forthcoming with information'.[204] Moreover, as Pizzi and Perron observed, the fact that the majority of the questions are posed by the judge can help to lessen the emotional impact of relaying detailed events about a distressing event, noting that:

> [i]t is often easier for victims to answer questions concerning painful, distasteful or embarrassing events when these questions come from professional judges who are expected to be both impartial and fair.[205]

Even where questions are put to the witnesses directly by the parties, both the less zealous tone and less intrusive content of these questions should render the experience of testifying in an inquisitorial courtroom a much less stressful ordeal than it would be in an adversarial arena. Pizzi and Perron have pointed out that since the inquisitorial fact-finder has plenty of information about the defendant's previous character and convictions, it would, in many cases, be a poor tactical move for the defence to overplay the significance of the victim's character record.[206]

There is, however, some doubt as to whether these apparent benefits are experienced by all witnesses. There is a significant body of evidence which suggests that, on occasions, testifying in inquisitorial jurisdictions can still be a trying experience for rape complainants. For example, Brienen and Hoegen point out that although the German Criminal Code provides that questions which possibly 'cast dishonour on a witness may only be posed if "unavoidable"',[207] the case law on this provision suggests that the credibility of witnesses is regularly challenged without defendants bearing any heavier consequences if their assertions are wrong.[208] Pizzi and Perron also note that 'acquaintance rape' cases are also problematic for complainants in Germany, since they are often characterised by a 'demanding and sustained questioning of the victim by the defence attorney'.[209] Ellison's research into the questioning of rape complainants in the Netherlands also suggests that rape victims there encounter similar problems,[210] as did the research carried out in the five different European jurisdictions surveyed by Bacik et al.[211]

Moreover, the absence of any formal evidentiary rules to regulate questioning in inquisitorial systems means that rape complainants do not have any formal degree

---

[204] Lerner (2001), 808.

[205] Pizzi and Perron (1996), 46.

[206] *Ibid*, 46–7.

[207] Brienen and Hoegen (2000), 381.

[208] *Ibid*. Similarly, the authors describe the questioning of rape complainants in the Spanish system as 'severe' (at 872).

[209] Pizzi and Perron (1996), 63.

[210] See Ellison (2001a), 151: 'The treatment of complainants . . . has been the subject of sustained criticism in the Netherlands. Defence lawyers stand specifically accused of engaging in improper questioning, and examining magistrates have been criticised for inadequate protection of complainants . . . In line with research findings in England and Wales and elsewhere, key common themes in defence questioning were identified. These included the complainant's clothing, evidence of physical resistance or absence thereof, delays in reporting, motivations for lying, and the consumption of drugs or alcohol prior to the rape'. However, she proceeds to suggest that while the use of sexual history evidence was once commonplace in the Netherlands, it has been used much less frequently in recent years.

[211] Bacik et al (1998), 34.

of protection against the use of sexual history evidence in most jurisdictions.[212] Bacik et al found that sexual history evidence was adduced in seven of the 20 cases they observed, and in four of these cases participants were asked about relationships with persons other than the accused. Most inquisitorial jurisdictions did not attempt to place any curbs on the use of sexual history evidence.[213] Nonetheless, the findings of Bacik et al seem to confirm that rape complainants in the adversarial system of Ireland found testifying more stressful than their counterparts in the inquisitorial systems. Complainants in Ireland were less confident, less articulate and experienced more stress than the victims interviewed in any other country.[214] The reason for this identified by the authors was 'the adversarial mode of trial, and in particular the style of cross-examination used in adversarial courts'.[215]

In sum, it appears to be the case that the nature of questions put to victims generally is much less confrontational and aggressive than in adversarial systems. However, it seems that rape complainants are not able to fully escape the derisory questioning relating to their personal lifestyles, dress sense, and previous sexual history. It could be argued therefore that while the theory, structures and processes underlying inquisitorial trials should ensure that secondary victimisation at court is minimised, there remain some attitudinal barriers within the legal profession that stifle the effects of these benefits for rape complainants. Nevertheless, it would still appear to be the case that, within most inquisitorial systems, victims in general are questioned in a more courteous and less intrusive manner.

The Place of Truth-finding

In contrast to the adversarial model of justice, truth-finding is often cited as the over-arching goal of the inquisitorial system.[216] The operation of an inquisitorial style corresponds with a widely held positive image of the State and a maximalist view of its functions.[217] A considerable degree of trust must be placed in the State and its agencies to investigate, prosecute and adjudicate objectively alleged criminal behaviour. This can be contrasted with a basic underlying scepticism that seems to exist in adversarial jurisdictions about trusting the State to produce the truth whilst simultaneously protecting the interests of the accused.[218] Whereas adversarial theory dictates that the truth is more likely to be elicited through a 'sharp clash of proofs',[219] the inquisitorial attitude dictates that the search for

---

[212] However, most jurisdictions do operate on some variation of the 'relevance' principle: '[T]he court decides whether questions about previous sexual history are relevant to establishing whether the defendant's belief in consent was justified'. (Brienan and Hoegen (2000), 381).

[213] One exception was, ironically, Denmark, which follows a quasi-adversarial mode of trial (Bacik et al, (1998), 47).

[214] *Ibid*, 7.

[215] *Ibid.*

[216] See eg, Damaska (1973), 586; Mack (1996), 68.

[217] Jörg (2003).

[218] Jörg et al (1996), 45.

[219] Landsman (1984), 2.

truth is best effected through what Damaska has termed a 'a self-propelled judicial inquiry . . . only slightly affected by party initiative'.[220]

The emphasis placed upon truth-finding is reflected in the general principles contained in the criminal codes of many inquisitorial jurisdictions. For example, the German Code of Criminal Procedure explicitly provides that the inherent objective of the German criminal justice system is to 'investigate thoroughly all the facts to arrive at the objective truth'.[221] Section 244(ii) of the Code also provides for the principle of material truth, which states that:

> in order to search out the truth, the court shall on its own motion extend the taking of evidence to all facts and means of proof that are important for the decision.[222]

The close judicial supervision of the preliminary fact-finding process means that the inquisitorial model arguably does a better job than its adversarial counterpart in ensuring that all relevant information is factored into key decision-making.

In contrast to the low priority placed on truth-finding by adversarial processes, many specific structures of the inquisitorial process are designed to maximise the potential for truth-finding. The model 'erects few evidentiary barriers that restrict the information the judge can consider in determining guilt'.[223] It is broadly accepted that a complex system of evidential rules is primarily needed in adversarial proceedings to safeguard the risk of lay persons attaching undue weight to potentially prejudicial evidence.[224] The lack of exclusionary rules in inquisitorial jurisdictions means that hearsay evidence and evidence of previous bad character are usually freely admitted.[225] The trier of fact is thereby entrusted with the ability to exercise due objective diligence when assessing the evidence, by attaching variable weight to different forms of evidence. For example, it might be assumed that whereas forensic DNA evidence placing the accused at the scene of the crime would be highly probative, hearsay evidence would attract comparatively little weight (although such evidence would not usually be excluded altogether). Instead, the court will usually take steps to test the reliability of second hand or third hand statements, by asking other witnesses and checking documents, and

---

[220] Damaska (1997a), 107.

[221] *Stafprozeordnung* [hereafter StPO], cited by Cho (2001), 2.

[222] *Ibid.*

[223] Pizzi and Marafiorti (1992), 7.

[224] Damaska (1997a), 26. See also Langbein (2003), 247–51.

[225] Although there is an absence of formal rules relating to the admissibility of evidence, two key principles are usually applied. First, the principle of free evaluation of evidence, enshrined in most of the criminal codes, means that the fact-finder should have access to all the relevant evidence before coming to a decision (see, eg s 261 StPO, as cited by Kühne (1993), 147). In many jurisdictions, this principle is considered alongside the principle of proportionality, which emphasises the need to balance the due process rights of individuals against the State's interest in fighting crime. However, the principle of proportionality is only likely to exclude evidence where it has been obtained illegally, and even then, it traditionally has only done so where the illegality has been the direct product of deliberate State action (Frase (1990), 567). However, recent years have seen an apparent trend towards wider exclusionary rules regulating illegally or improperly obtained evidence (see Thaman, (1999); Diehm (2001)). For a detailed assessment of exclusionary rules in France and Germany, see King (2002).

through considering the circumstances in which the original statements were made.[226] All evidence will therefore be weighed up, taking into account its differing weight and credibility.[227] Such evidence (particularly relating to the character of the defendant) is often seen as being crucial in enabling the trier of fact to form an *intime conviction* concerning the guilt or innocence of the accused, which reflects the standard of proof in criminal cases.[228]

It would therefore appear that most continental systems are less concerned with evidential problems than common law systems, and place a substantially higher degree of faith in the fact-finder to separate the more probative evidence from that which is overly prejudicial.[229] In contrast to the tightly regulated rules of evidence of the adversarial process, the continental rules of evidence allow for a wide array of information to be presented to the trier of fact. Since the collection of evidence is supervised by the investigating judge rather than the parties, this should avoid the selective filtering of information that occurs in the adversarial process. Relevant evidence is thereby much less likely to be excluded, and the lack of any evidential filtering of relevant information should mean that, in general, justice is more likely to be delivered to both victims and defendants.

Discussion

This section has identified a number of distinct advantages for victims who testify in inquisitorial proceedings. First, in certain jurisdictions, some victims will not have to give evidence at the trial proper at all. Secondly, where victims do give evidence, they can do so unimpeded and uninterrupted from the parties. Special measures are made available to child witnesses in many jurisdictions, and in some countries, other victims can make use of such measures too. However, it would seem that, on the whole, protective measures in inquisitorial countries are significantly less developed than in England and Wales. Thirdly, the nature and extent of the questioning will be very different. Questioning will be conducted mainly (and in some jurisdictions, exclusively) by the trial judge. Parties play a subsidiary role, with the judge maintaining tight control over the nature and extent of their

---

[226] Lerner (2001), 810.

[227] There is no solid reason for the belief that judges are better able to deal with prejudicial evidence than juries. Indeed, the recent decline of exclusionary rules in England and Wales would seem to suggest that such a paternalistic attitude towards juries is beginning to fade, and a high degree of trust is still placed in the jury to assess evidence fairly and attach different weight to different forms of evidence. Paternalism towards juries would seem to be a problem contrived exclusively by the common law. See eg Choo (1996) 33–7 (commenting on the ability of jurors to weigh up hearsay evidence).

[228] Frase (1990) has suggested that this encourages more defendants to testify, thus broadening the scope of the inquiry. Although the concept of *intime conviction* it has no direct English equivalent, Lerner (2001), 796, has suggested that it amounts to the fact-finder deciding whether he or she is 'deeply and thoroughly convinced'. The standard of proof thereby takes a very different form from the adversarial standard, which reflects the judge-led nature of proceedings.

[229] Pizzi and Perron (1996), 43.

questioning. Finally, inquisitorial models are much better equipped to offer victims, and indeed the fact-finder, a truthful account of past events.

In theory at least, complainants should be relieved of having to contend with the same degree of secondary victimisation which has traditionally plagued them in adversarial proceedings. The lack of a contest-based structure in inquisitorial trials should also mean that there should be few difficulties in accommodating direct input from victims in the trial as compared with the severe logistical and normative difficulties that would be encountered in attempting to integrate such a procedure in an adversarial framework. The fact that continental hearings are judge-led, as opposed to party-led, indicates that the participation of a third party would be much less problematic, and would be much less likely to be seen as a potential threat to the equality of arms.

Unfortunately, the theoretical potential of the inquisitorial system to accommodate the victim as a party to proceedings is partly impeded by the way in which systems of participation operate in practice. There is certainly some evidence to suggest that intrusive and aggressive questioning still occasionally occurs in rape cases, and victims are clearly not making use of the various mechanisms open to them that would allow them to participate in the trial. However, the reasons for these failings stem from attitudinal barriers from within the legal profession, rather than from the structures or underlying theory of the inquisitorial system. This view is confirmed by Brienen and Hoegen's finding that the negative attitude of legal professionals is primarily responsible for the poor implementation of victims' rights in continental Europe.[230] Unfortunately in both adversarial and inquisitorial systems, practitioners and policymakers appear reluctant to alter, develop or resource procedures that are capable of boosting the rights of the victim at trial, particularly in terms of granting them some form of participation.

The inquisitorial system, whilst imperfect in its current form, would nonetheless deliver a set of structures and normative values that are better placed to resolve rights-based conflicts between the rights of the accused and the rights of the victims. In most inquisitorial trials, the evidence of complainants can be properly tested without them having to experience the indignity of eyeball-to-eyeball confrontation and degrading cross-examination before an open court. Like the adversarial system, inquisitorial jurisdictions also place a strong emphasis on the need to uncover facts, but this task is generally effected through alternative methods. It is argued that these methods should be actively considered as alternatives to adversarial practices. Friedman, a staunch defender of the adversarial method, has conceded in respect of victims that '[g]ratuitous trauma should be prevented of course. But we cannot eliminate trauma from the process without gutting the system'.[231] This raises the question of whether the system should indeed be 'gutted', if an alternative system would be better equipped to administer justice just as effectively, whilst sparing victims the trauma of the adversarial contest.

---

[230] Brienen and Hoegen (2000), 1069–70, 1118.
[231] Friedman (1997), (1998), 709.

III. Looking to the Future

There is a curious irony which permeates adversarial and inquisitorial cultures in that both forms of jurisdiction display signs of dissatisfaction with their respective legal systems while looking to each other for potential solutions to common problems.[232] These include abstract concepts such as the need for enhanced transparency, accountability and legitimacy throughout the criminal process, as well as better ways of fact-finding and of providing specific protections for defendants and victims. As a bi-product of globalisation and enhanced communications, the possibilities for cross-fertilisation and harmonisation are widespread. Indeed, the impact of international harmonisation is already discernable in both adversarial and inquisitorial jurisdictions. In the latter, Van Kessel has identified a trend in continental jurisdictions, noting the development of the right to silence, the use of juries, exclusionary rules of evidence, and provisions to increase access to legal advice.[233] In 1988, Italy substituted its well established inquisitorial process in favour of an adversarial approach, only to abandon many of the reforms shortly afterwards on account of opposition from practitioners.[234] In the late 1990s, the French Parliament sent a team to England to evaluate the functioning of the adversarial procedure.[235] Jackson has also argued that the jurisprudence from Strasbourg has effected a shift in the way we tend to categorise systems according to the adversarial or inquisitorial spectrum, arguing instead that the Court has developed a new model of proof that is better characterised as 'participatory' as opposed to 'adversarial' or 'inquisitorial'. Certainly, we have every reason to be optimistic that the international consensus on such core values will transude into all criminal justice systems, and the need for reform of a more fundamental nature may well be acknowledged in time.

Reforming the Adversarial Paradigm

To some extent, these international shifts in attitude are reflected on a domestic level by a corresponding increase in dissatisfaction both among the general public and among academic commentators with the criminal justice system. These concerns have not only been raised as a result of growing despondency over the plight of victims, but can also be attributed to concerns stemming from recent highly publicised miscarriages of justice,[236] and to increasing demands for efficiency and

[232] Levels of public confidence in criminal justice seem uniformly low. See Page et al (2004); Hough and Roberts (2004).

[233] Van Kessel (1998), 806–11. See also Bradley (1993), 175.

[234] Law Reform Commission of Western Australia (1999), 90. The reason for Italy's initial adoption of adversarial features was 'an attempt to reduce the secretiveness and inefficiency that had permeated its criminal justice system' (Pizzi and Marafiorti (1992), 38).

[235] Law Reform Commission of Western Australia, (1999), 99 (n 4).

[236] Among those cases which received the most prominent media coverage were the Birmingham Six, Judith Ward, the Guildford Four, Derek Bentley, Sally Clark and Angela Cannings.

cost-effectiveness.[237] This has led to questioning of the value of the adversarial method; a trend that has been particularly apparent in the realm of civil justice for several years. The Woolf Report of 1996 contended that problems such as cost, delay and complexity derived to a large extent from the unrestrained adversarial culture of the system.[238] The Report proposed adopting certain inquisitorial-style features such as greater case management for judges, and a more co-operative pre-trial regime of discovery.[239] It was acknowledged by Lord Woolf that such a move would require a 'radical change of culture for all concerned'.[240] Glasser noted that the civil process was undergoing a 'slow erosion' of the basic practices of adversarial justice and of the orality principle in particular. This was occurring, he argued, in response to changing attitudes in modern litigation, because of increased pressure on public funds.[241] He concluded that:

> the classic model of the adversary system with its emphasis on the centrality of the oral process is bound to further lose its importance as court management of procedure increases.[242]

Outside the United Kingdom, other commentators and law reform bodies have arrived at similar conclusions. The Australian Law Reform Commission has similarly noted that many features of adversarialism lead to excessive costs, over-servicing, a lack of accountability and an unduly confrontational approach to dispute resolution.[243] In addition, recently developed Australian tribunals concerned with social security, immigration and human rights have been developed along inquisitorial as opposed to adversarial lines. It is widely accepted that they perform a more informal, accessible and cost effective job than their court-based counterparts.[244] As the South African Law Commission noted in 1989:

> [o]ne of the great and repeated complaints against the present system is directed against the adversary system and everything it implies.[245]

Reform to criminal justice now seems to be following the direction that civil justice reform has taken, with very specific components of the adversarial system coming under increased scrutiny.[246] The principle of orality and process of unfettered cross-examination have, in particular, been subject to considerable erosion. Aside from the range of special measures for victims and witnesses in court,

---

[237] Jackson (2002), 341.

[238] Woolf (1995), 26.

[239] Woolf (1996).

[240] Woolf, (1996), 7.

[241] Glasser (1993), 317.

[242] *Ibid.*

[243] Australian Law Reform Commission (1997), [1.8].

[244] Lavarach (1999), 19.

[245] South African Law Commission (1989), 11.

[246] Aside from new ideas about the treatment of victims and witnesses and the suitability of the adversarial paradigm for fact-finding, concerns have also been expressed about miscarriages of justice (Royal Commission on Criminal Justice (1993)); adjournments and delays (Audit Commission (2002)); the role of the Crown Prosecution Service (Glidewell (1998)); and the sentencing framework (Halliday (2001)).

Sir Robin Auld's *Review of the Criminal Courts in England and Wales*,[247] noted that many of the fundamental features of the adversarial trial causes distress and unfairness to witnesses,[248] acknowledging, in particular, the specific problems posed by cross-examination.[249] While judges were urged to become more pro-active in intervening in hostile cross-examinations, this is something which may be difficult to achieve while adversarial structures remain in place.[250] Some of the drawbacks of oral evidence were also noted, including the effects of stress and delay upon witnesses. Auld appears to have used these observations as a springboard for a number of his recommendations, which included the relaxation of the rules of admissibility on previous witness statements, the relaxation of the hearsay rule, and the extension of the use of televised evidence. Crucially, he seemed to accept that indirect testimony can, in certain circumstances, be as reliable and cogent as direct oral evidence. Ultimately, however, like the Philips Royal Commission of 1981[251] and the Runciman Royal Commission of 1993,[252] the Review was dismissive of the need for much more wholesale reform of the fundamental tenets of adversarial justice. The need for measures such as live television links and video-recordings to assist vulnerable witnesses has been broadly accepted, but English law reform bodies have never really questioned whether live cross-examination is the best method which can be used to test evidence, or whether any sort of *partie civile* approach could be injected into an adversarial trial process. Curiously, these ideas were not even considered in *Speaking Up for Justice*.

Other proposals contained in the Auld Review recommended the adoption of a number of inquisitorial-style features to the English system. These included the recommendation to codify the criminal law and law of evidence;[253] a greater managerial role for trial judges;[254] and further pre-trial co-operation between the parties.[255] In another apparent accession of an inquisitorial feature into the adversarial system, it was noted that the system should:

> move away from technical rules of inadmissibility to trusting judicial and lay fact finders to give relevant evidence the weight it deserves.[256]

As such, judges would play a much more pro-active role in the trial, and have a much broader discretion in relation to the admissibility of evidence.[257]

---

[247] Auld (2002).

[248] Auld (2002), [11.30].

[249] *Ibid.*

[250] *Ibid.*, at ch 7. See discussion in Ch 2, above, pp 94–7.

[251] Royal Commission on Criminal Procedure (1981), [1.8].

[252] Royal Commission on Criminal Justice (1993), 4.

[253] Auld (2002), ch 1.

[254] Similar proposals were made in respect of the civil justice system by Lord Woolf some years earlier in respect of the civil justice system. See Woolf (1996), [3].

[255] Auld (2002), [2.13].

[256] Auld (2002), [2.17].

[257] As Auld himself acknowledged: '[T]he boundaries between the adversarial and inquisitorial systems of trial are blurring; our judges and magistrates are already assuming an increasingly active role in the preparation of cases for trial and becoming more interventionist in the course of it than has been traditional'. *Ibid*, [11.104].

Justice Act 2003 and the Criminal Procedure Rules 2005 gave leg-
nost of these reforms, signifying a shift away from a rigid regime
vidential rules towards a broader freedom of proof. The hearsay
ne substantial erosion,[258] as has the principle of orality.[259] The
ure Rules 2005 begin by laying down a new 'overriding objective',
that courts and everyone involved in a criminal case must pursue: to deal with the
case justly.[260] While this task will involve taking into account the 'interests of witnesses, victims and jurors', it is regrettable that the use of rights-based language
that is so commonplace in Government white papers and non-binding protocols
was not reflected in the drafting of the legislation. Still, in looking at the nature of
the legislation as a whole, it is welcome evidence that law reform in criminal justice is increasingly revolving around internationally accepted values, and that victims are no longer relegated to the sidelines. Moreover, one can detect a further
shift away from traditional adversarial practice, with a new range of powers being
conferred on judges to actively manage the preparation of cases waiting to be
heard.[261]

Following these two pieces of legislation, concern has been expressed not so
much about the extent to which they make inroads into the adversarial tradition,
but rather the fact that reform seemed to be proceeding on an ad hoc basis, without any clear sense of direction. The Law Society, in its response to *Justice for All*,
expressed concern over:

> the increasing trend to graft inquisitorial elements onto our existing adversarial system
> without the essential safeguards required in an inquisitorial system such as judicial over-
> sight of police investigations.[262]

It further noted that an 'uncomfortable hybrid' seemed to be emerging, without
any proper process of debate and discussion of reasons for selecting which procedures to adopt and which to disregard.[263] The fact that policymakers and law
reform bodies appear increasingly willing to draw from other national and international models of procedure is to be welcomed, but without coherent long-term
direction the continuing drip effect of international harmonisation risks diffusing:

> the worst tendencies of combativeness in the Anglo-American system, while retaining
> some of the salutary features of the continental inquisitorial system.[264]

Perhaps quite unintentionally, the Auld Review and the subsequent Criminal
Justice Act have triggered a broader debate about the suitability of the adversarial

---

[258] See s 114 and Ch 2, pp 84–5.

[259] Pt 8 of the Act 2003 extends the use of live links in criminal proceedings enabling witnesses other
than vulnerable witnesses who are in the United Kingdom but unable to come to court to give evidence
via a live link without appearing in court. See also the Crime (International Co-operation) Act 2000,
which allows evidence requested by foreign countries to be taken by telephone.

[260] Criminal Procedure Rules 2005, r 1.1.

[261] Criminal Procedure Rules 2005, r 3.

[262] Law Society (2002).

[263] See also Corker (2002); Fitzpatrick (2002).

[264] Edwards (1997), 855.

structures to deliver justice for both victims and offenders. As evidential rules, criminal justice structures and procedures have undergone radical change, so too the principles which have traditionally underpinned them have declined. Orality, cross-examination and third party exclusion are core attributes of the adversarial paradigm which are inherently incapable of delivering effective protection to the newly emergent rights of victims, and it is quite possible that we are entering an era of transition towards a model that is more aptly structured to deliver and protect the rights of both victims and offenders, as well as a more accurate means of fact-finding.

A wholesale shift to an inquisitorial model is unlikely to happen in the short term. The adversarial system appears to be entrenched in England, and indeed in the rest of the United Kingdom. The prospect of uprooting longstanding criminal justice structures has few proponents within the legal profession, criminal justice agencies, or even government as a whole. There seems to be an innate sense of superiority in many quarters about the advantages of the adversarial system; with corresponding scepticism about the inquisitorial procedures. Questions have been raised, for example, as to the extent to which inquisitorial processes are placed to protect the due process rights of the accused,[265] or whether, in any case, the financial and logistical costs of a transition would really be worthwhile.[266] Furthermore, some legal sociologists and comparative scholars have questioned whether it is at all possible to transplant criminal justice systems into different cultural settings.[267] Any attempt to undertake such radical reform is likely to be extremely costly and contentious, and, as such, would carry major political risks. The enormity of this task means that any government will be extremely sceptical about embarking on such a course of reform.

The decline of the sanctity of adversarial justice reflects an undercurrent of dissatisfaction with the traditional common law approach to defining criminal offending as a crime against the State. This has also led to a questioning of the legitimacy of the retributivist paradigm that characterises the sentencing process. Like the trial process, sentencing is state-led and excludes the victim. Offenders are punished on the basis that they have breached society's rules, and it is therefore this 'public interest' that has acted to ensure that sentencing frameworks are maintained within a retributive mode. Our conception of crime as an offence solely affecting public interest has meant that sentencing processes continue to be formal, lawyer-dominated and minimise the prospect of participation for both victims and offenders. As Van Ness and Nolan have argued, there is a

---

[265] See especially Landsman (1984), 48–51. See also Friedman (1997), Amodio and Selvaggi (1999). Such reservations are not restricted to academic commentators: see comments of Simon LJ in *D v National Society for the Prevention of Cruelty to Children* [1978] AC 171, 231.

[266] See eg Luban (1988): '[T]he adversary system, despite its imperfections, irrationalities, loopholes and perversities, seems to do as good a job as any at finding truth and protecting legal rights ... Second, some adjudicatory system is necessary. Third, it's the way we have always done things. These things constitute a pragmatic argument: if a social institution does a reasonable enough job of its sort that the costs of replacing it outweigh the benefits, and if we need that sort of job done, we should stay with what we have' (at 82).

[267] See eg Damaska (1997b).

fundamental 'clash of values' between the orthodox criminal paradigm and the restorative paradigm.[268] However, just as any attempt to reform sentencing processes could assist reparation and participation to some degree, the extent to which orthodox procedures can accommodate such values is necessarily limited.[269]

In terms of future directions, recent trends in the growth of restorative justice and the growing appreciation of the value of reparation indicate we are rethinking the rationale and processes underlying the sentencing system and the role of victims within it. Measures that provide reparation for victims are still thin on the ground and remain on the fringes of the criminal justice system, yet they nonetheless continue to make creeping inroads. Since the development of criminal injuries compensation in the 1960s, the range of mechanisms that are capable of providing some form of reparation to victims has grown substantially, and includes compensation orders, reparation orders, referral orders and a new stream of voluntary restorative schemes operating outside the formal parameters of the criminal justice system. Indeed, Northern Ireland and New Zealand have both sought to mainstream restorative justice within their formal juvenile justice systems, and victims in these jurisdictions are now given genuine opportunities to participate in criminal justice processes and contribute to case disposals.[270] Further, the advent of the Victim Personal Statement scheme and the piloting of victim's advocates suggest the way in which policymakers and the courts understand the contemporary role of victims is changing; no longer is the victim perceived as an outsider to the central action. Instead, it is widely acknowledged that processes and outcomes that fail to accord with a victim's sense of justice are likely to make them feel resentful and destroy their faith in social institutions.[271]

What we are therefore seeing in relation to victims' rights is a clear trend towards their realisation. Just as international and human rights standards have acted to elevate the position of the victim, so too, our domestic system seems to be responding—albeit slowly. However, even on the domestic platform, there has been a growing recognition that the paradigmatic exclusion of victims is unlikely to be sustainable in the longer term. It is also being increasingly questioned as to whether solutions to this structural alienation can be found within the confines of the adversarial process. Much can be learnt from the practices of inquisitorial jurisdictions and newly developed international criminal tribunals. Indeed, there already are signs, following the reforms of the Auld Report and the Criminal Justice Act 2003, that the adversarial system is being eroded on a number of fronts. From the victim's perspective, there is reason to be optimistic that far-reaching reform of the adversarial model may be forthcoming in the not too distant future.

To date, however, the approach of the Government and the courts has been to try to protect the interests of victims within the confines of longstanding and

---

[268] Van Ness and Nolan (1998), 81.
[269] *Ibid.*
[270] See Doak and O'Mahony (2006) and Morris et al (1993) respectively.
[271] Wemmers (1996).

outdated conceptions about the normative function of the criminal trial, the best ways to ascertain facts, the best ways to punish offenders, and the best ways of delivering justice to victims. While there have been various attempts to curtail the excesses of the adversarial trial and the difficulties of victims in accessing reparation, it is a matter of some regret that recent changes in law and policy have not been of a more fundamental nature. Yet, even if the reforms do carry limited potential in easing the plight of the victim at court, their significance should not be underestimated. Legislative developments and trends can develop a momentum of their own if propelled by wider political and international developments. In an era of rapid harmonisation of rights, rules and procedures, the climate is ripe for reform. The call in this book is for policymakers and academics to engage much more readily and more seriously with the idea of 'best practice' which emanates from international harmonisation. We need to look beyond the confines of our own legal system and our own cultural perceptions of the trial and criminal justice and take on board lessons from elsewhere. The inquisitorial method is imperfect; and the restorative justice paradigm is underdeveloped; but perhaps these systems provide a better structural and normative framework in which the core rights discussed in this book can be realised.

Charting a course for such far-reaching reform is also replete with risks. Victim-orientated reforms that are ill-conceived may only serve to muddy the waters and create fresh problems for other players. Without a strategic framework for reform, a messy and unworkable hybrid system might result, which may do a worse job in delivering justice than anything that has gone before. Within discrete criminal justice systems, each element hangs on another, and any transplantation would therefore have to involve a simultaneous reorientation of the values, goals and broader criminal justice structures of the adversarial system. It may thus be timely to take a step backwards and reconsider the key aims and values that our criminal justice system seeks to promote, before undertaking a more radical overhaul of structures and processes around which these values revolve. On the international platform, a consensus of values has been instrumental in creating new rights for victims in both human rights discourse and international criminal justice discourse. Thus, on a domestic level, this search for new values should be the starting point for a more fundamental search for better structures. In formulating these new values, it is essential that any contemporary, liberal model of justice takes on board the nature and direction of the international trends, but we also need to rethink the purpose of the criminal justice system.

When thinking specifically of how we can build the rights of the victim into our new conceptions of values and criminal justice, we must bear in mind that 'rights' must be enforceable through formal legal mechanisms, and not remain a mere aspiration through the publication of protocols, guidelines, charters and the signing up to various non-binding standards. Furthermore, care must be taken not only to be responsive to those rights which have some teeth within the legal order—such as the Strasbourg case law or the EU Framework Directive. Policymaking for the longer term should aim to go beyond this and draw from emerging norms too; including those that have not quite yet secured a firm foothold or consensus. Among these emerging rights, a right to participate is fast being recognised. So too is a right to truth, as is the need to reconceptualise the idea of 'reparation' in such a way so that it does not equate to monetary compensation. While the adversarial paradigm may be able to adapt itself to realise some of these rights, it cannot do so for all of them. Fundamentally, at the core, is still the conception that crime constitutes an offence against the State and, as such, that victims have no precise interest in either the process or the outcome. While the various elements of the adversarial system can be reformed, tightened and loosened, the underlying structures and dichotomous ethos of the system remain in place. It remains, at a structural and ideological level, a bipartisan contest between the State and the accused.

In his 1987 survey of victims' rights in Europe,[272] Joutsen correctly predicted that victim-orientated reforms would be forthcoming, but were unlikely to occur in the wholesale manner that would turn the adversarial system on its head. He speculated that victims' rights would develop according to certain specific offences, such as rape, or in relation to specific individual rights, such as to present a victim impact statement at the sentencing stage of the process.[273] These have indeed been the type of reforms which have been instigated in most jurisdictions. The modes of trial, sentencing and the functional parameters of the criminal justice system generally, have all remained largely unchanged. In the years to come however, both the concept and content of victims' rights are likely to be subjected to considerable development and refinement, both on the national and international stage. The time for fragmentary tinkering with the parameters of the adversarial system may be drawing to a close. A future Review of the Criminal Courts or a future Royal Commission may herald the advent of a new and more holistic integration of victims' rights within the criminal justice system.

[272] Joutsen (1987b).
[273] Joutsen (1987a), 122–3.

BIBLIOGRAPHY

Abrahms, D, Viky, G, Masser, B, and Gerd, B (2003) 'Perceptions of stranger and acquaintance rape: The role of benevolent and hostile sexism in victim blame and rape proclivity' 84 *Journal of Personality and Social Psychology* 111.

Abramovsky, A (1992) 'Victim Impact Statements: Adversely Impacting upon Judicial Fairness' 8 *St John's Journal of Legal Commentary* at 21.

Adler, Z (1987) *Rape on Trial* (London, Kegan Paul).

Aldana-Pindell, R (2002) 'In Vindication of Justifiable Victims' Rights to Truth and Justice for State Sponsored Crimes' 35 *Vanderbilt Journal of Transnational Law* 1399.

—— (2004) 'An Emerging Universality of Justiciable Victims' Rights in the Criminal Process to Curtail Impunity for State—Sponsored Crimes' 26 *Human Rights Quarterly* 605.

Alvarez, JE (1999) 'Crimes of State / Crimes of Hate: Lessons from Rwanda' 24 *Yale Journal of International Law* 365.

Amann, D (2000) 'Harmonic Convergence? Constitutional Criminal Procedure in an International Context' 75 *Indiana Law Journal* 809.

Ambos, K (2003) 'International Criminal Procedure: 'Adversarial', 'Inquisitorial' or Mixed?' 3 *International Criminal Law Review* 1.

Amnesty International (1996) 'Fairness to Defendants at the International Criminal Court: Proposals to Strengthen the Draft Statute and its Protection of Defendants' Rights' 1 *International Criminal Court Briefing Series.*

Amodio, E, and Selvaggi, E (1999) 'An Accusatorial System in a Civil Law Country: The 1988 Italian Code of Criminal Procedure' 62 *Templeton Law Review* 1213.

Anderson, T, Schum, D, Twining, W (2006) *Analysis of Evidence* (Cambridge, Cambridge University Press).

Angle, H, Malam, S, and Carey, C (2003) *Witness Satisfaction: Findings from the Witness Satisfaction Survey 2002* (London, Home Office).

Antkowiak, T (2002) 'Truth as Right and Remedy in International Human Rights Experience' 23 *Michigan Journal of International Law* 977.

Ashworth, A (1986) 'Punishment and Compensation: Victims, Offenders and the State' 6 *Oxford Journal of Legal Studies* 86.

—— (1987) 'The "Public Interest" Element in Prosecutions' *Criminal Law Review* 595.

—— (1992) 'What Victims of Crime Deserve' paper presented to the Fulbright Commission on Penal Theory and Penal Practice, University of Stirling, September 1992.

—— (1993a) 'Some Doubts About Restorative Justice' 4 *Criminal Law Forum* 277.

—— (1993b) 'Victim Impact Statements and Sentencing' *Criminal Law Review* 498.

—— (1998) *The Criminal Process: An Evaluative Study*, 2nd edn (Oxford, Oxford University Press).

—— (2000) 'Victims' Rights, Defendants' Rights and Criminal Procedure' in A Crawford and J Goodey (eds), *Integrating a Victim Perspective Within Criminal Justice* (Aldershot, Ashgate).

Ashworth, A (2002) 'Responsibilities, Rights and Restorative Justice' 42 *British Journal of Criminology* 578.

—— (2004) 'Criminal Justice Reform: Principles, Human Rights and Public Protection' *Criminal Law Review* 516.

—— (2005) *Sentencing and Criminal Justice* (Cambridge, Cambridge University Press).

Ashworth, A, and Redmayne, M (2005) *The Criminal Process*, 3rd edn (Oxford, Oxford University Press).

Attorney General (2005) *Guidelines on the Acceptance of Pleas and the Prosecutor's Role in the Sentencing Exercise* (London, Department of Constitutional Affairs).

Audit Commission (2002) *The Route to Justice: Improving the Pathway of Offenders Through the Criminal Justice System* (London, Audit Commission).

Auld, Sir R (2002) *Review of the Criminal Courts of England and Wales* (Cmnd 9376) (London, HMSO).

Australian Law Reform Commission (1992) *Children's Evidence: Closed Circuit Television*, Report 63 (Canberra, Australian Law Reform Commission).

—— (1997) *Review of the Adversarial System of Litigation: Rethinking the Federal Civil Litigation System*, Issues Paper 20 (Canberra, Australian Government Publishing Service).

Bacik, I, Maunsell, C, and Grogan, S (1998) *The Legal Process and Victims of Rape* (Dublin, Irish Rape Crisis Centre).

Baker, JH (2002) *An Introduction to English Legal History*, 4th edn (London, Butterworths).

Baker, AW, and Duncan, SP (1984) 'Child sexual abuse: A study of prevalence in Great Britain' 9 *Child Abuse and Neglect* 457.

Bankowski, Z (1981) 'The Value of Truth: Fact Scepticism Revisited' (1981) 3 *Legal Studies* 257.

Barnett, RE (1977) 'Restitution: A New Paradigm of Criminal Justice' 87 *Ethics* 279.

Bassiouni, MC (2000) 'The Right to Restitution, Compensation and Rehabilitation for Victims of Gross Violations of Human Rights and Fundamental Freedoms', UN Doc E/CN.4/2000/62, 18 January 2000.

—— (2006) 'International Recognition of Victims' Rights' 6 *Human Rights Law Review* 203.

Bauman, Z (2006) *Liquid Fear* (Cambridge, Polity Press).

Bayley, J (1991) 'The Concept of Victimhood' in D Sank and D Caplan (eds) *To Be a Victim: Encounters with Crime and Injustice* (New York, Pelum Press).

Bazemore, G (1996) 'Three Paradigms For Juvenile Justice' in B Galaway and J Hudson (eds), *Restorative Justice: International Perspectives* (New York, Criminal Justice Press) Monsey.

Bazemore, G, and Walgrave, L (1999) 'Restorative Juvenile Justice: In Search of Fundamentals and an Outline for Systemic Reform' in G Bazemore and L Walgrave (eds), *Restorative Juvenile Justice: Repairing The Harm Of Youth Crime* (New York, Willow Tree Press).

Beck, U (1992) *Risk Society: Towards a New Modernity* (London, Sage).

Bennet, WL, and Feldman, M (1981) *Reconstructing Reality in the Courtroom* (Brunswick, Rutgers University Press).

Bentham, J (1827) *Rationale of Judicial Evidence* Vol 1 (London, Hunt and Clarke) (New York, Garland 1978).

Bentley, D (1998) *English Criminal Justice in the Nineteenth Century* (London, Hambleton).

Bernstein, P (1998) *Against the Gods: The Remarkable Story of Risk* (New York, John Wiley & Sons).

Bingham, T (2006) 'Assessing contentious eyewitness evidence: A judicial review' in A Heaton-Armstrong, E Shepherd, G Gudjonsson, and D Wolchover (eds) *Witness Testimony Psychological, Investigative and Evidential Perspectives* (Oxford, Oxford University Press).

Birch, D (2000) 'A Better Deal for Vulnerable Witnesses?' *Criminal Law Review* 223.

Birch, D, and Powell, R (2004) *Meeting the challenges of Pigot: Pre-trial cross-examination under s.28 of the Youth Justice and Criminal Evidence Act 1999* (unpublished).

Blake, M, and Ashworth, A (1998) 'Some Ethical Issues in Prosecuting and Defending Criminal Cases' *Criminal Law Review* 16.

Bohn, DK and Holz, KA (1996) 'Sequelae of abuse: Health effects of childhood sexual abuse, domestic battering, and rape' 41 *Journal of Nurse-Midwifery* 442.

Borooah, VK, and Carcach, C (1997) 'Crime and fear—evidence from Australia' 37 *British Journal of Criminology* 635.

Bottigliero, I (2004) *Redress for Victims of Crimes Under International Law* (Leiden, Martinus Nijhoff Publishers).

Bottoms, A (1995) 'The philosophy and politics of punishment and sentencing' in C Clarkson & R Morgan (eds) *The Politics of Sentencing Reform* (Oxford, Clarendon Press).

Boyd, A (1984) *The Informers: A Chilling Account of Supergrasses in Northern Ireland* (Galway, Mercier Press).

Bradley, C (1993) 'The Emerging International Consensus as to Criminal Procedure Rules' 14 *Michigan Journal of International Law* 171.

Braithwaite, J (1989) *Crime, Shame and Reintegration* (Cambridge, Cambridge University Press).

—— (2002) *Restorative Justice and Responsive Regulation* (Oxford, Oxford University Press).

—— (2003) 'Principles of Restorative Justice' in A Von Hirsch, J Roberts, AE Bottoms, K Roach, K, and M Schiff (eds), *Restorative Justice and Criminal Justice: Competing or Reconcilable Paradigms?* (Oxford, Hart Publishing).

Braithwaite, J, and Daly, K (1998) 'Masculinities, violence, and communitarian control' in SL Miller (ed), *Crime Control and Women: Feminist Implications of Criminal Justice Policy* (Newbury Park, CA, Sage).

Brennan, C (2001) 'The Victim Personal Statement: Who is the Victim?' 4 *Web Journal of Current Legal Issues*.

Brennan, M, and Brennan, R (1988) *Strange Language: Child Victims under Cross-Examination* (Wagga Wagga, Riverina Murray Institute of Higher Education).

Brereton, D (1997) 'How different are Rape Trials? A Comparison of the Cross-Examination of Complainants in Rape and Assault Trials' 37 *British Journal of Criminology* 242.

Brienen, M, and Hoegen, H (2000) *Victims of Crime in 22 European Criminal Justice Systems: The Implementation of Recommendation (85) 11 of the Council of Europe on the Position of the Victim in the Framework of Criminal Law and Procedure* (Niemegen, Wolf Legal Productions).

Brown, B, Burman, M, and Jamieson, L (1992) *Sexual History and Sexual Character Evidence in Scottish Sexual Offence Trials* (Edinburgh, Scottish Office Central Research Unit Papers).

Brown, SE (1984) 'Police responses to wife beating: neglect of a crime of violence' 12 *Journal of Criminal Justice* 277.

Brownlee, ID, Mulcahy, PA and Walker, CP (1994) 'Pre-Trial Reviews, Court Efficiency and Justice: a Study in Leeds and Bradford Magistrates' Courts' 33 *Howard Journal of Criminal Justice* 109.

Bryett, K, and Osborne, P (2000) *Criminal Prosecution Procedure and Practice: International Perspectives*, Report 16, Review of the Criminal Justice System in Northern Ireland (HMSO, London).

Burton, M (2000) 'Prosecution decisions in cases of domestic violence involving children' 22 *Journal of Social Welfare and Family Law* 175.

Burton, M, Evans, R and Sanders, A (2006) *Are Special Measures for Vulnerable and Intimidated Witnesses Working? Evidence from the criminal justice agencies*, Home Office Online Report 01/06 (London, Home Office).

Buruma, Y (2004) 'Doubts on the Upsurge of the Victim's Role in Criminal Law' in H Kaptein and M Malsch (eds), *Crime, Victims, and Justice, Essays on Principles and Practice* (Aldershot, Ashgate).

Butler, Judge Gerald (1999) *Inquiry into Crown Prosecution Service Decision-Making in Relation to Deaths in Custody and Related Matters* (London, HMSO).

Buzawa, ES and Buzawa, CG (1990), *Domestic Violence: The Criminal Justice Response* (Newbury Park, CA, Sage).

Cairns, D (1998) *Advocacy and the Making of the Adversarial Trial 1800–1865* (Oxford, Clarendon Press).

Calvert-Smith, Sir D (2002) *Summary of Findings of the Review on the Crown Prosecution Service's Handling of the Damilola Taylor Case* (London, CPS).

Cammiss, S (2006)' The management of domestic violence cases in the mode of trial hearing: prosecutorial control and marginalizing victims' 46 *British Journal of Criminology* 704.

Campbell, C, Devlin, R, O'Mahony, D, Doak, J, Jackson, J, Corrigan, T, and McEvoy, K (2006) *Evaluation of the Northern Ireland Youth Conference Service NIO Research and Statistics Series: Report No 12* (Northern Ireland Office, Belfast).

Cardenas, J (1986) 'The Crime Victim in the Prosecutorial Process' 9 *Harvard Journal of Law and Public Policy* 357.

Carson, D (2003) 'Therapeutic Jurisprudence and Adversarial Justice: Questioning Limits' 4 *Western Criminology Review* 124.

Cascardi, M and O'Leary, KD (1992) 'Depressive symptomatology, self-esteem, and self blame in battered women' 7 *Journal of Family Violence* 249.

Cavadino, M, and Dignan, J (1996) 'Towards a Framework for Conceptualising and Evaluating Models of Criminal Justice from a Victim's Perspective' 4 *International Review of Victimology* 153.

—— (1997) 'Reparation, Retribution and Rights' 4 *International Review of Victimology* 233.

Ceci, SJ, Powell, MB and Principe, GF (2002) 'The scientific status of children's memory and testimony' in DL Faigman, DH Kaye, MJ Saks & J Sanders (eds), M*odern Scientific Evidence: The Law and Science of Expert Testimony*, Vol 2 (St Paul, MN, West Pub Co).

Chalmers, J, Duff P, and Leverick F (2007) 'Victim impact statements: can work, do work (for those who bother to make them)' *Criminal Law Review* 360.

Chambers, G, and Millar, A (1986) *Prosecuting Sexual Assault* (Edinburgh, HMSO).

Chiaviaro, M (2002) 'Private Parties: the rights of the defendant and the victim' in M Delmas-Marty, and JR Spencer (eds), *European Criminal Procedures* (Cambridge, Cambridge University Press).

Cho, K (2001) 'Procedural Weakness of German Justice and its Unique Exclusionary Rules Based on the Right of Personality' 15 *Temple International and Comparative Law Journal* 1.

Choo, A (1996) *Hearsay and Confrontation* (Oxford, Oxford University Press).

Choo, A and Nash, S (2003) 'Evidence Law in England and Wales: The Impact of the Human Rights Act 1998' 7 *International Journal of Evidence and Proof* 31.

Choudry, S and Herring, J (2006) 'Righting Domestic Violence' 20 *International Journal of Law and the Family* 95.

Christie, N (1977) 'Conflicts as Property' 17 *British Journal of Criminology* 1.

—— (1986) 'The Ideal Victim' in E Fattah (ed), *From Crime Policy to Victim Policy* (Basingstoke, Macmillan).

Clare, I, and Gudjonson, G, (1993) 'Interrogative suggestibility, confabulation, and acquiescence in people with mild learning disabilities: Implications for reliability during police interrogations' 32 *British Journal of Clinical Psychology* 295.

Clarke, J, Gewirtz, S and McLaughlin, E (2000) *New Managerialism, New Welfare?* (London, Sage).

Clarke, J, Newman, J, Smith, N, Vidler, E, and Westmarland, L (2007) *Creating Citizen-Consumers* (London, Sage).

Classen, CC, Palesh, OG and Aggarwal, R (2005) 'Sexual Revictimization: A Review of the Empirical Literature' 6 *Trauma, Violence and Abuse* 103.

Coen, R (2006) 'The Rise of the Victim—A Path to Punitiveness?' 16 *Irish Criminal Law Journal* 10.

Cohen, S (1972) *Folk Devils and Moral Panics* (London, MacGibbon and Kee).

—— (1995) 'State Crimes of Previous Regimes: Knowledge, Accountability, And The Policing Of The Past' 20 *Law and Social Inquiry* 7.

Cole, D (2001) 'Psychodrama and the Training of Trial Lawyers: Finding the Story' 21 *North Illinois University Law Review* 1.

Cooper, D (2005) 'Pigot Unfulfilled: Video-recorded Cross-Examination under Section 28 of the Youth Justice and Criminal Evidence Act 1999' *Criminal Law Review* 456.

Cordon, I, Goodman, G, and Anderson, S (2003) 'Children in Court' in PJ Van Koppen and SD Penrod (ed), *Adversarial versus Inquisitorial Justice* (New York, Kluwer).

Corker, D (2002) 'The Worst of Both Worlds' 152 *New Law Journal* 1741.

Corriero, M (2002) 'The Involvement and Protection of Children in Truth and Justice-Seeking Processes: the Special Court for Sierra Leone' 18 *New York Law School Journal of Human Rights* 337.

Costigan, G (1931) 'The Full Remarks on Advocacy of Lord Brougham and Lord Chief Justice Cockburn at the Dinner to M Berryer on November 8, 1864' 19 *California Law Review* 521.

Costigan, R, and Thomas, P (2000) 'Anonymous Witnesses' 51 *Northern Ireland Legal Quarterly* 326.

Crawford, A (2000) 'Salient Themes Towards a Victim Perspective and the Limitations of Restorative Justice: Some Concluding Comments' in A Crawford and J Goodey (eds), *Integrating a Victim Perspective Within Criminal Justice* (Aldershot, Ashgate).

Cretney, A, and Davis, G (1996) *Punishing Violence* (London, Routledge).

—— (1997) 'Prosecuting Domestic Assault: Victims Failing Courts or Courts Failing Victims?' 36 *Howard Journal of Criminal Justice* 146.

Criminal Bar Association (2003) *Response to 'Pre-Trial Witness Interviews by Prosecutors, A Consultation Paper'* (London, Criminal Bar Association).

Criminal Law Revision Committee (1984) *Sexual Offences* (Cmnd 9213) (London, HMSO).

Crown Prosecution Service (1993) *Statement on the Treatment of Victims and Witnesses* (London, CPS).

—— (2002a) *Farquharson Guidelines on The Role of and Responsibilities of the Prosecution Advocate,* 2nd edn (London, CPS).

—— (2002b) *DPP Issues Findings in Damilola Taylor Case* (Press Release), 19 December (London, CPS).

—— (2003a) *Pre-trial Witness Interviews by Prosecutors: A Consultation Paper* (London, CPS).

—— (2003b) *Legal Guidance* (London, CPS).

—— (2004) *Code for Crown Prosecutors* (London, CPS).

—— (2005a) *The Prosecutors Pledge* (London, CPS).

—— (2005b) *Pre-trial witness interviews: Code of Practice* (London, CPS).

—— (2006) *A Standard for Communication between Victims, Witnesses and the Prosecuting Advocate* (London, CPS).

Daly, K (1999) 'Revisiting the Relationship between Retributive and Restorative Justice' in H Strang and J Braithewaite (eds), *Restorative Justice from Philosophy to Practice* (Dartmouth, Aldershot).

Daly, M (1999) 'Legal Ethics: Some Thoughts on the Differences in Criminal Trials in Civil and Common Law Legal Systems' 2 *Journal of the Institute for the Study of Legal Ethics* 65.

Damaska, M (1973) 'Evidentiary Barriers to Conviction and Two Models of Criminal Procedure' 121 *University of Pennsylvania Law Review* 506.

—— (1975) 'Structures of authority and comparative criminal procedure' 84 *Yale Law Journal* 480.

—— (1997a) *Evidence Law Adrift* (New Haven, Yale University Press).

—— (1997b) 'The Uncertain Fate of Evidentiary Transplants: Anglo-American and Continental Experiments' 45 *American Journal of Comparative Law* 839.

—— (2004) 'Negotiated Justice in International Criminal Courts' 2 *Journal of International Criminal Justice* 1018.

Danet, B, and Bogoch, B (1980) 'Fixed Fight or Free for All? An Empirical Study of Combativeness in the Adversary System of Justice' *British Journal of Law & Society* 36.

Darbyshire, P, Maughan, A and Stewart, A (2002) 'What Can the English Legal System Learn from Jury Research Published up to 2001?' Supplementary Paper to the Auld Review, available online at http://www.kingston.ac.uk/~ku00596/elsres01.pdf [accessed 26 July 2007].

Davis, G (1992) *Making Amends: Mediation and Reparation in Criminal Justice* (London, Routledge).

Davies, G, Hoyano, L, Keenan, C, Maitland, L, and Morgan, R (1999) *An Assessment of the Admissibility and Sufficiency of Evidence in Child Abuse Prosecutions* (London, HMSO).

Davies, G, and Noon, E (1991) *An Evaluation of the Live Link for Child Witnesses* (London, Home Office).

Davies, G, and Westcott, H (1999) *Interviewing Children Under the Memorandum of Good Practice: A Research Review* (London, Home Office).

—— (2006) 'Investigative Interviewing with Children: Progress and Pitfalls' in A Heaton-Armstrong, E Shepherd, G Gudjonsson, and D Wolchover (eds) *Witness Testimony Psychological, Investigative and Evidential Perspectives* (Oxford, Oxford University Press).

Davies, G, Wilson, C, Mitchell, R, and Milsom, J (1995) *Videotaping Children's Evidence: An Evaluation* (London, Home Office).

De Than, C (2003) 'Positive Obligations under the European Convention on Human Rights: Towards the Human Rights of Victims and Vulnerable Witnesses' 67 *Journal of Criminal Law* 165.

Delmas-Marty, M and Spencer, JR (eds) (2004) *European Criminal Procedures* (Cambridge, Cambridge University Press).

Dennis, IH (2007) *The Law of Evidence*, 3rd edn (London, Sweet & Maxwell).

Dent, H (1986) 'An experimental study of the effectiveness of different techniques of questioning mentally handicapped witnesses' *British Journal of Clinical Psychology* 13.

Department of Constitutional Affairs (2005) *Hearing The Relatives Of Murder And Manslaughter Victims* (London, DCA).

—— (2006) *Hearing the Relatives of Murder and Manslaughter Victims: The Government's plans to give the bereaved relatives of murder and manslaughter victims a say in criminal proceedings* (London, DCA).

Department of Health (2000), *Protecting Children, Supporting Parents : A Consultation Document on the Physical Punishment of Children* (London, Department of Health).

Department of Justice, Equality and Law Reform (Ireland) (1998) *Discussion Paper on the Law of Sexual Offences* (Dublin, Dept of Justice, Equality and Law Reform).

Diehm, J (2001) 'The Introduction of Jury Trials and Other Adversarial Elements into the Former Soviet Union and Other Inquisitorial Countries' 11 *Journal of Transnational Law and Policy* 1.

Dignan, J (1992) 'Repairing the damage: can reparation be made to work in the service of diversion?' 32 *British Journal of Criminology* 453.

—— (2002) 'Reparation Orders' in B Williams (ed), *Reparation And Victim—Focused Social Work* (London, Jessica Kingsley).

—— (2003) 'Towards a Systematic Model of Restorative Justice' in A Von Hirsch, J Roberts, AE Bottoms, K Roach, K, and M Schiff (eds), *Restorative Justice and Criminal Justice: Competing or Reconcilable Paradigms?* (Oxford, Hart Publishing).

—— (2005) *Understanding Victims and Restorative Justice* (Maidenhead, Open University Press).

—— (2006) 'Restorative Justice in Criminal Justice and Criminal Court Settings' in G Johnstone and D van Ness (eds) *Handbook of Restorative Justice* (Cullompton, Willan Publishing).

Director of Public Prosecutions for Northern Ireland (2003) *Victims, Witnesses and the Prosecution* (Belfast, DPP for NI).

Doak, J (2005) 'Victims' Rights in Criminal Trials: Prospects for Participation' 32 *Journal of Law and Society* 294.

Doak, J, and O'Mahony, D (2006) 'The vengeful victim? Assessing the attitudes of victims participating in restorative youth conferencing' 13 *International Review of Victimology* 157.

Du Cann, R (1993) *The Art of the Advocate* (London, Penguin).

Du Plessis, M, and Pete, S (eds) (2007) *Repairing The Past? : International Perspectives on Reparations for Gross Human Rights Abuses* (Antwerp, Intersentia Press).

Dubber, MD (2002) *Victims in the War on Crime* (New York, New York University Press).

Duff, A (2003) 'Restoration and Retribution' in A Von Hirsch, J Roberts, AE Bottoms, K Roach, K, and M Schiff (eds), *Restorative Justice and Criminal Justice: Competing or Reconcilable Paradigms?* (Oxford, Hart Publishing).

Duff, A, Farmer, L, Marshall, S, and Tadros, V (eds) (2004), *The Trial on Trial*, Vol 1 (Oxford, Hart Publishing).

Dugger, A (1996) 'Victim Impact Evidence in Capital Sentencing: A History of Incompatibility' 23 *American Journal of Criminal Law* 375.

Dworkin, R (1978) *Taking Rights Seriously* (Cambridge MA, Harvard).

Eades, D (1995) *Language in Evidence* (Sydney, UNSW Press).

Easton, S (2000) 'The Use of Sexual History Evidence in Rape Trials' in M Childs and L Ellison (eds), *Feminist Perspectives on Evidence* (London, Cavendish).

Edwards, H (1997) 'Comments on Mirjan Damaska's "Of Evidentiary Transplants"' 45 *American Journal of Comparative Law* 853.

Edwards, I (2004) 'An ambiguous participant: The Crime Victim and Criminal Justice Decision-Making' 44 *British Journal of Criminology* 967.

Edwards, MG (1999) *Adversarial Trial Structure and Truth Finding in Criminal Cases* (University of Wales, Aberystwyth, Unpublished MPhil Thesis).

Eggleston, R (1975) 'What is wrong with the adversary system?' *Australian Law Journal* 428.

Ekman, P (2001) *Telling Lies* (New York, Norton).

Elias, G (1986a) 'Community Control, Criminal Justice and Victim Services' in E Fattah (ed) *From Crime Policy to Victim Policy* (London, Macmillan).

—— (1986b) *The Politics of Victimization* (New York, Oxford University Press).

—— (1990) *Victims Still: The Political Manipulation of Crime Victims* (London, Sage).

Elliott, R (1998) *Vulnerable and Intimidated Witnesses: A Review of the Literature* (London, Home Office).

Ellison, L (1998) 'Cross-examination of Rape Complainants' *Criminal Law Review* 606.

—— (2001a) *The Adversarial Process and the Vulnerable Witness* (Oxford, Oxford University Press).

—— (2001b) 'The Mosaic Art: Cross-examination and the Vulnerable Witness' 21 *Legal Studies* 353.

—— (2003) 'Responding to victim withdrawal in domestic violence prosecutions' *Criminal Law Review* 760.

—— (2007) 'Witness preparation and the prosecution of rape' 27 *Legal Studies* 171.

Emmerson, B, and Ashworth, A (2001) *Human Rights and Criminal Justice* (London, Sweet & Maxwell).

Epstein, R (1975) 'Intentional Harms' 3 *Journal of Legal Studies* 402.

Erez, E (2000) 'Integrating A Victim Perspective In Criminal Justice Through Victim Impact Statements' in A Crawford and J Goodey (eds), *Integrating a Victim Perspective Within Criminal Justice* (Aldershot, Ashgate).

Erez, E, and Bienkowska, E (1993) 'Victim Participation in Proceedings and Satisfaction with Justice in the Continental Systems: The Case of Poland' 21 *Journal of Criminal Justice* 47.

Erez, E, Roeger, L, and Morgan, F (1997) 'Victim Harm, Impact Statements and Victim Satisfaction with Justice: An Australian Experience' 5 *International Review of Victimology* 37.

Erez, E, and Rogers, L (1999) 'Victim Impact Statements and Sentencing Outcomes and Processes: The Perspective of Legal Professions' 39 *British Journal of Criminology* 216.

Erez, E, and Tontodonato, P (1990) 'The Effect of Victim Participation in Sentencing on Sentence Outcome' 28 *Criminology* 451.

—— (1992) 'Victim participation in sentencing and satisfaction with justice' 9 *Justice Quarterly* 393.

Ericson, K, Perlman, N and Isaacs, B (1994) 'Witness competency, communication issues and people with developmental disabilities' 22 *Developmental Disabilities Bulletin* 101.

Ericson, R (1981) *Making Crime: A Study of Detective Work* (Toronto, Butterworths).

European Commission (1999) *Crime Victims in the European Union: Reflections on Standards and Action* (COM/ 1999/359) (Brussels, European Commission).

Farrall, S, and Gadd, D (2004) 'The Frequency of the Fear of Crime' 44 *British Journal of Criminology* 127.

Faulkner, D (2001) *Crime, State and Citizen* (Winchester, Waterside Press).

Fenwick, HM (1995) 'Rights of Victims in the Criminal Justice System: Rhetoric or Reality?' *Criminal Law Review* 843.

—— (1997) 'Procedural Rights of Victims of Crime: Public or Private Ordering of the Criminal Justice Process?' 60 *Modern Law Review* 317.

Ferraro, KF (1995) *Fear of Crime: Interpreting Victimization Risk* (New York, SUNY Press).

Field, S and Roberts, P (2002) 'Racism and Police Investigations: Individual Redress, Public Interests and Collective Change after the Race Relations (Amendment) Act 2000' 22 *Legal Studies* 493.

Fielding, N (2006) *Courting Violence* (Oxford, Oxford University Press).

Findlay, M (2002) 'Internationalised Criminal Trial and Access to Justice' 2 *International Criminal Law Review* 237.

Findlay, M, and Henham, R (2005) *Transforming International Criminal Justice: Retributive and Restorative Justice in the Trial Process* (Cullompton, Willan).

Fitzpatrick, B (2002) 'Tinkering or transformation? Proposals and Principles in the White Paper, "Justice for All"' 5 *Web Journal of Current Legal Issues.*

Flin, R, Stevenson, Y, and Davies, G (1989) 'Children's Knowledge of Court Proceedings' 80 *British Journal of Psychology* 285.

Flood-Page, C, and Mackie, A (1998) *Sentencing Practice: An Examination Of Decisions In The Magistrates' Courts And The Crown Court In The Mid-1990s*, Research Study 180 (London, Home Office).

Frank, J (1949) *Courts on Trial: Myth and Reality in American Justice* (Princeton, Princeton University Press).

Frankel, ME (1975) 'The Search for Truth: An Umpireal View' 123 *University of Pennsylvania Law Review* 1031.

Frase, RS (1990) 'Comparative criminal justice as a guide to American law reform: how do the French do it, how can we find out and why should we care?' 78 *California Law Review* 538.

Freckleton, I (2004) 'Compensation For Crime Victims' in H Kaptein and M Malsch (eds), *Crime, Victims And Justice: Essays on Principles and Practice* (Aldershot, Ashgate).

Freedman, M (1975) 'Judge Frankel's Search for Truth' 123 *University of Pennsylvania Law Review* 1060.

Frehsee, D (1999) 'Restitution and the Offender-Victim Arrangement in German Criminal Law: Development and Theoretical Implications' 2 *Buffalo Criminal Law Review* 235.

Friedman, R (1997) 'Confrontation Rights of Criminal Defendants' in JF Nijboer and JM Reijntjes (eds), *Proceedings of the First World Conference on New Trends in Criminal Investigation and Evidence* (The Hague, Open University of the Netherlands).

—— (1998) 'Hearsay and Confrontation: Thoughts from Across the Water' *Criminal Law Review* 697.

Fry, M (1951) *Arms Of The Law* (London, Gollancz).

Fyfe, NR, and McKay, H (2000) 'Desperately Seeking Safety' 40 *British Journal of Criminology* 675.

Garland, D (1990) *Punishment and Modern Society* (Chicago, University of Chicago Press).

Garland, D (2001) *The Culture of Control: Crime and Social Order in Contemporary Society* (Oxford, Oxford University Press).

Gearty, C (2002) 'Osman Unravels' (2002) 65 *Modern Law Review* 87.

Geis, G (1990) 'Crime victims—practices and prospects' in A Lurigio, WG Skogan and RC Davis (eds), *Victims of Crime: Problems, Policies, Programs* (Newbury Park, CA, Sage).

General Council of the Bar (2004a) *Code of Conduct for Barristers in England and Wales*, 8th edn (London, General Council of the Bar).

—— (2004b) *Written Standards for the Conduct of Professional Work* (London, General Council of the Bar).

—— (2005) *Guidance on Witness Preparation* (London, General Council of the Bar).

Gillespie, A, and Bettinson, V (2007) 'Preventing Secondary Victimisation Through Anonymity' 70 *Modern Law Review* 114.

Glaser, D and Frosh, S, (1988) *Child Sexual Abuse* (London, Macmillan).

Glasser, C (1993) 'Civil Procedures and the Lawyers—The Adversary System and the Decline of the Orality Principle' 56 *Modern Law Review* 307.

Glidewell, I (1998) *Review of The Crown Prosecution Service* (Cmnd 3960) (London, Home Office).

Glissan, J, and Tilmouth, S (1998) *Advocacy in Practice: Being the Third Edition of Cross Examination: Practice and Procedure* (Melbourne, Butterworths).

Goldstein, A (1982) 'Defining The Role Of The Victim In Criminal Prosecution' 52 *Mississippi Law Journal* 515.

Goodey, J (2005) *Victims and Victimology: Research, Policy and Practice* (Harlow, Pearson Longman).

Goodman, G, Taub, EP, Jones, D, England, P, Port, L, Rudy, L, and Rado, L (1992) *Testifying in Criminal Court: Emotional Effects on Child Sexual Assault Victims* (Chicago, University of Chicago Press).

Goodpaster, G (1987) 'On the theory of the American Adversary Criminal Trial' 78 *Journal of Criminal Law and Criminology* 118.

Graham, J, Woodfield, K, Tibble, M, and Kitchen, S (2004) *Testaments of Harm: A Qualitative Evaluation of the Victim Personal Statements Scheme* (London, National Centre for Social Research (Great Britain)).

Greer, C (1995) *Supergrasses: A Study in Anti-Terrorist Law Enforcement in Northern Ireland* (Oxford, Clarendon Press).

Greer, DS (1971) 'Anything But The Truth? The Reliability of Testimony in Criminal Trials' 11 *British Journal of Criminology* 147.

—— (1990) *Compensation for Criminal Injury* (Belfast, SLS).

—— (1991) *Criminal Injuries Compensation* (London, Sweet & Maxwell).

—— (1994) 'A Transatlantic Perspective on the Compensation of Crime Victims in the United States' 85 *Journal of Criminal Law & Criminology* 333.

—— (1996a) 'Ireland' in D Greer (ed), *Compensating Crime Victims* (Freiburg, Max Planck Institute).

—— (1996b) 'Concluding Observations: The European Convention and State Compensation of Crime Victims in Principle and Practice' in D Greer (ed), *Compensating Crime Victims* (Freiburg, Max Planck Institute).

Groenhuijsen, M (2004) 'Victims' Rights and Restorative Justice: Piecemeal Reform of the Criminal Justice System or a Change of Paradigm?' in H Kaptein and M Malsch (eds), *Crime, Victims, and Justice: Essays on Principles and Practice* (Ashgate, Aldershot).

Grohovsky, J (2000) 'Giving Voice to Victims: Why the Criminal Justice System in England and Wales Should Allow Victims to Speak Up for Themselves' 64 *Journal of Criminal Law* 416.

Guastello, C (2005) 'Victim Impact Statements: Institutionalised Revenge' 37 *Arizona State Law Journal* 1321.

Gudjonsson, G (1992) *The Psychology of Interrogations, Confessions and Testimony* (Chichester, John Wiley & Sons).

—— (2006) 'The Psychological Vulnerabilies of Witnesses and the Risk of False Assusations and False Confessions' in A Heaton-Armstrong, E Shepherd, G Gudjonsson, and D Wolchover (eds) *Witness Testimony Psychological, Investigative and Evidential Perspectives* (Oxford, Oxford University Press).

Haines, K, and O'Mahony, D (2006) 'Restorative Approaches, Young People and Youth Justice' in B Goldson and J Muncie (eds), *Youth Crime and Justice* (London, Sage Publications).

Hale, C (1996) 'Fear of crime: A review of the literature' 4 *International Review of Victimology* 79.

Hale, Sir M (1736) *The History of the Pleas of the Crown* (Reprint, 1972) (London, Professional Books).

Hall, DJ (1991) 'Victims' Voices in Criminal Court: The Need for Restraint' 28 *American Criminal Law Review* 233.

Hall, M (2007) *Putting Victims of Crime at the Heart of Criminal Justice: Practice, Politics and Philosophy* (University of Sheffield, Unpublished PhD Thesis).

Halliday, Sir J (2001) *Making Punishments Work—Report of a Review of the Sentencing Framework for England and Wales* (London, Home Office).

Hamlyn, B, Phelps, A, Turtle, J, and Sattar, G (2004) *Are Special Measures Working? Evidence from Surveys of Vulnerable and Intimidated Witnesses*, Home Office Research Study 283 (Home Office, London).

Hamon, H (1989) 'The Testimony of the Child Victim in Intra-Familial Sexual Abuse' in J Spencer, G Nicholson, R Flin, and R Bull (eds), *Children's Evidence in Legal Proceedings* (Cambridge, Faculty of Law).

Harber, K and Pennebaker, J (1992), 'Overcoming Traumatic Memories' in S Christianson (ed) *The Handbook of Emotion and Memory: Research and Theory* (London: Lawrence Erlbaum Associates).

Harber, K and Wenberg, C (2005) Emotional Disclosure and Closeness Toward Offenders 31 Personality and Social Psychology Bulletin 734.

Harris, R (1892) *Hints on Advocacy* (Boston, MA, Little Brown).

Hayner, PB (1994) 'Fifteen Truth Commissions—1974 To 1994: A Comparative Study' 16 *Human Rights Quarterly* 597.

Hedderman, C (1987) *Children's Evidence: the Need for Corroboration*, Research and Planning Unit Paper 41 (Home Office, London).

Henderson, E (2001) *Cross-Examination: A Critical Examination* (University of Cambridge, Unpublished PhD Thesis).

Henham, R (2004) 'Some reflections on the role of the victims in the International Criminal Trial Process' 11 *International Review of Victimology* 201.

Henham, R and Drumbl, M (2005) 'Plea Bargaining at the International Criminal Tribunal for the Former Yugoslavia' 16 *Criminal Law Forum* 49.

Hester, M (2006) 'Making it through the Criminal Justice System: Attrition and Domestic Violence' 5 *Social Policy and Society* 71.

Hill, R (2002) 'Restorative Justice and the Absent Victim: New Data from the Thames Valley' 9 *International Review of Victimology* 273.

Hillenbrand, S (1989) 'Legal Aid to Crime Victims" in E Fattah (ed) *The Plight of Crime Victims in Modern Society* (Basingstoke, Macmillan).

Hillenbrand S, and Smith BE (1989), *Victim Rights Legislation: An Assessment of its Impact on Criminal Justice Practitioners and Victims* (Chicago, American Bar Association).

HMCPSI (2002) A *Report on the Joint Inspection into the Investigation and Prosecution of Cases Involving Allegations of Rape* (London, Home Office).

HMCPSI / HMIC (2007) *Without Consent: A Report on the Joint Review of the Investigation and Prosecution of Rape Offences* (London, Home Office).

Hohfeld, W (1919) *Fundamental Legal Conceptions as Applied in Judicial Reasoning* (New Haven, Yale University Press).

Holstrom, L, and Burgess, AW (1974) 'Rape Trauma Syndrome' 131 *American Journal of Psychiatry* 981.

Home Office (1990) *Victim's Charter* (London, Home Office).

—— (1996) *Victim's Charter*, 2nd edn (London, Home Office).

—— (1998) *Speaking Up for Justice, Report of the Interdepartmental Working Group on the Treatment of Vulnerable or Intimidated Witnesses in the Criminal Justice System* (London, Home Office).

—— (1999) *The Referral Order: Draft Circular Version 3* (London, HMSO).

—— (2002a) *Justice for All* (Cmnd 5563) (London, HMSO).

—— (2002b) *Early Special Measures Meetings between Crown Prosecutors and Vulnerable or Intimidated Witnesses* (London, HMSO).

—— (2004a) *No Witness, No Justice: The National Victim and Witness Care Programme* (London, Home Office).

—— (2004b) *Conditional Cautioning: Code of Practice* (London, Home Office).

—— (2004c) *Compensation and Support for Victims of Crime: A Consultation Paper on Proposals to Amend the Criminal Injuries Compensation Scheme and Provide a Wide Range of Support for Victims* (London, Home Office).

—— (2005a) *The Witness Charter: New standards of care for witnesses in the criminal justice system: Consultation* (London, Home Office).

—— (2005b) *Rebuilding Lives: Supporting Victims of Crime* (London, The Stationery Office).

—— (2006a) *Rebalancing the Criminal Justice System in Favour of the Law-abiding Majority* (London, Home Office).

—— (2006b) *Working With Intimidated Witnesses: A Manual For Police And Practitioners Responsible For Identifying And Supporting Intimidated Witnesses* (London, Home Office).

—— (2006c) *Convicting Rapists and Protecting Victims* (London, Home Office).

—— (2007) *Child Sex Offender Review* (London, Home Office).

Hope, T, and Sparks, R (2000) 'Introduction: Risk, Insecurity and the Politics of Law and Order' in T Hope and R Sparks (eds), *Crime, Risk And Insecurity* (London, Routledge).

Horne, L, Glasgow, D, Cox, A, and Calam, R (1991) 'Sexual abuse of children by children' 3 *Journal of Child Law* 147.

Hough, M, and Park, A (2002) 'How malleable are attitudes to crime and punishment?' Findings from a British deliberative poll in J Roberts and M Hough (eds), *Changing Attitudes to Punishment* (Cullompton, Willan Publishing).

Hough, M, and Roberts, J (2004) *Confidence in justice: an international review*, Home Office Findings No 243 (London, Home Office).

Hoyano, L (2000) 'Variations on a theme by Pigot: special measures directions for child witnesses' *Criminal Law Review* 250.

—— (2007) 'The Child Witness Review: Much Ado about too Little' *Criminal Law Review* 849.

Hoyle, C (1998) *Negotiating Domestic Violence* (Oxford, Oxford University Press).

—— (2002) 'Securing Restorative Justice for the Non-Participating Victim' in C Hoyle and R Young (ed) *New Visions of Crime Victims* (Oxford, Hart Publishing).

Hoyle, C, Cape, E, Morgan, R and Sanders, A (1998) *Evaluation of the One Stop Shop and Victim Pilot Statement Projects* (London, Home Office).

Hoyle, C, Young, R, and Hill, R (2002) *Proceed with Caution: An Evaluation of the Thamas Valley Police Initiative in Restorative Cautioning* (York, Rowntree).

Hudson, B (1998) 'Restorative Justice: The challenge of sexual and racial violence' 25 *Journal of Law and Society* 237.

International Committee of the Red Cross (2005) *Customary International Humanitarian Law: Volume I, Rules* (Cambridge, Cambridge Press University).

International Criminal Court (2005) *Code of Judicial Ethics, ICC-BD/02-01-05* (ICC, The Hague).

International Law Commission (2001) *Report: Fifty-Third Session* (New York, United Nations).

Irish Law Reform Commission (1988) *Rape and Allied Offences* (Dublin, Irish Law Reform Commission).

—— (1997) *Rape: A Consultation Paper* (Dublin, Irish Law Reform Commission).

Ironside, P (2002) 'Rwandan Gacaca: Seeking Alternative Means To Justice, Peace, And Reconciliation' 15 *New York International Law Review* 31.

Jackson, JD (1990) 'Getting Criminal Justice Out Of Balance' in S Livingstone and J Morison (eds), *Law, Society and Change* (Aldershot, Ashgate).

—— (2002) 'The Adversary Trial and Trial by Judge Alone' in M McConville and G Wilson (eds), *The Oxford Handbook of the Criminal Justice Process* (Oxford, Oxford University Press).

—— (2003) 'Justice for All: Putting Victims at the Heart of Criminal Justice?' 30 *Journal of Law and Society* 309.

—— (2004) 'Putting Victims at the Heart of Criminal Justice? The Gap Between Rhetoric and Reality' in E Cape (ed), *Reconcilable Rights? Analysing the Tension between Victims and Defendants* (London, Legal Action Group).

—— (2005) 'The Effect of Human Rights on Criminal Evidentiary Processes: Towards Convergence, Divergence or Realignment?' 68 *Modern Law Review* 737.

Jackson, JD, and Doran, S (1995) *Judge Without Jury: Diplock Trials and the Adversary System* (Oxford, Clarendon Press).

Jarvis Thompson, J (1992) *The Realm of Rights* (Cambridge MA, Harvard).

Jeans, JW (1975) *Trial Advocacy* (St Paul, West Publishing Co).

Johnstone, G (2002) *Restorative Justice: Ideas, Values, Debates* (Cullompton, Willan Publishing).

Jorda, C, and de Hemptinne, J (2002) 'The Status and the Role of the Victim' in A Cassese, P Gaeta and J Jones (eds), *The Rome Statue of the International Criminal Court: A Commentary* (Oxford, Oxford University Press).

Jordan, J (2001), 'Worlds apart? Women, rape and the police reporting process' 41 *British Journal of Criminology* 679.

Jörg, N, (2003) 'Convergences of Criminal Justice Systems: Building Bridges – Building the Gaps: Defence and Defences', paper presented at the 17th International Conference of the *International Society for the Reform of Criminal Law* (The Hague, 24–28 August 2003).

Jörg, N, Field, S, and Brants, C (1996) 'Are Inquisitorial and Adversarial Systems Converging?' in C Harding, P Fennell, N Jörg, and B Swart (eds), *Criminal Justice in Europe* (Oxford, Oxford University Press).

Joutsen, M (1987a) 'Listening to the Victim: The Victim's Role in European Criminal Justice Systems' 34 *Wayne Law Review* 95.

—— (1987b) *The Role of the Victim of Crime in European Criminal Justice Systems: A Cross-National Study of the Role of the Victim* (Helsinki, HEUNI).

Jung, H (2004) 'Nothing But the Truth? Some Facts, Impressions and Confessions about Truth in Criminal Procedure' in A Duff, L Farmer, S Marshall and V Tadros (eds), *The Trial on Trial*, Vol 1 (Oxford, Hart Publishing).

JUSTICE (1998) *Victims in Criminal Justice, Report of the JUSTICE Committee on the Role of Victims in Criminal Justice* (London, JUSTICE).

Juy-Birmann, R (2002) 'The German System' in M Delmas-Marty and J Spencer (eds), *European Criminal Procedures* (Cambridge, Cambridge University Press).

Kaiser, M (1991) 'The Status of the Victim in the Criminal Justice System According to the Victim Protection Act' in G Kaiser, H Kury, and HJ Albrecht (eds), *Victims and Criminal Justice: Legal Protection, Restitution and Support* (Freiburg, Max Planck Institute).

Kaiser, M, and Kilchling, M (1996) 'Germany' in D Greer (ed), *Compensating Crime Victims* (Freiburg, Max Planck Institute).

Karmen, A (1992) 'Who's Against Victims' Rights?' 8 *St John's Journal of Legal Commentary* 157.

Keating, H (2006) 'Protecting or punishing children: physical punishment, human rights and English law reform' 26 *Legal Studies* 394.

Kebbell, MR, Hatton, C, and Johnson, SD (2004) 'Witnesses with intellectual disabilities in court: What questions are asked and what influence do they have?' 9 *Legal and Criminological Psychology* 23.

Kebbell, MR and Johnson, D (2000) 'Lawyers' Questioning: The Effects of Confusing Questions on Witness Confidence and Accuracy' (2000) 24 *Law & Human Behaviour* 629–641.

Kelly, L, Lovett, J and Regan, L (2005) A Gap or Chasm? Attrition in Reported Rape Cases, Home Office Research Study No 293 (London, Home Office).

Kelly, L, Temkin, J, Griffiths, S (2006) *Section 41: An Evaluation of New Legislation Limiting Sexual History in Rape Trials*, Home Office Online Report 20/06 (London, Home Office).

Kibble, N (2004) *Judicial Perspectives on Section 41 of the Youth Justice and Criminal Evidence Act 1999* (London, Criminal Bar Association).

Kilchling, M (1991) 'Interests of the Victim and the Public Prosecution—First Results of a National Survey' in G Kaiser, H Kury, and HJ Albrecht (eds), *Victims and Criminal Justice: Legal Protection, Restitution and Support* (Freiburg, Max Planck Institute).

Kilpatrick, DG, Beatty, D, and Smith Howley, S (1998) *The Rights of Crime Victims—Does Legal Protection Make A Difference?* (Washington DC, US Dept of Justice).

King, M (2002) 'Security, Scale, Form, and Function: The Search for truth and the Exclusion of Evidence in Adversarial and Inquisitorial Justice Systems' 12 *International Legal Perspectives* 185.

King, P (2000) *Crime, Justice and Discretion in England 1740–1820* (Oxford, Oxford University Press).

Kirchengast, T (2006) *The Victim in Criminal Law and Justice* (Basingstoke, Palgrave Macmillan).

Klerman, D (2000) *Settlement and Decline of Private Prosecution in Thirteenth Century England* (Oakland, Independent Institute).

Klug, F (2004) 'Human Rights and Victims' in E Cape (ed), *Reconcilable Rights? Analysing the Tension between Victims and Defendants* (London, Legal Action Group).

Koenig Kellas, J and Trees, A (2006) 'Finding Meaning in Difficult Family Experiences: Sense-Making and Interaction Processes During Joint Family Storytelling' 6(1) *Journal of Family Communication* 49.

Koffman, L (1996) *Crime Surveys and Victims of Crime* (Cardiff, University of Wales Press).

Konradi, A (1997) 'Too little, too late: prosecutors' pre-court preparation of rape survivors' 22 *Law and Social Inquiry* 1.

Krainz, K (1991) 'The Position of Injured Parties in the Austrian Criminal Procedure' in G Kaiser, H Kury, and HJ Albrecht (eds), *Victims and Criminal Justice: Legal Protection, Restitution and Support* (Freiburg, Max Planck Institute).

Kramer, M (ed) (2001) *Rights, Wrongs and Responsibilities* (Basingstoke, Palgrave Macmillan).

Kühne, HH (1993) 'Germany' in C Van Den Wyngaert (ed), *Criminal Procedure Systems in the European Community* (London, Butterworths).

Kury, H, and Kaiser, M (1991) 'The Victim's Position within the Criminal Proceedings—An Empirical Study' in G Kaiser, H Kury, and HJ Albrecht (eds), *Victims and Criminal Justice: Legal Protection, Restitution and Support* (Freiburg, Max Planck Institute).

Kury, H, Kaiser, M, and Teske, JR (1994) 'The Position of the Victim in Criminal Procedure—Results of a German Study,' 3 *International Review of Victimology* 69.

Landsman, S (1984) *The Adversary System, a Description and Defence* (Washington, The American Enterprise Institute).

Langbein, JH (1977) *Comparative Criminal Procedure: Germany* (St Paul, West Publishing).

—— (2003) *The Origins of the Adversary Criminal Trial* (Oxford, Oxford University Press).

Lasco, C (2003) 'Repairing the irreparable: current and future approaches to reparations' 10 *Human Rights Brief* 18.

Laudan, L (2006) *Truth, Error, and Criminal Law: An Essay in Legal Epistemology* (Cambridge, Cambridge University Press).

Lavarach, M (1999) 'Fighting the Fiends from Finance' in H Stacy and M Lavarch (eds), *Beyond the Adversarial System* (Sydney, Federation Press).

Law Commission of England and Wales (1997) *Evidence in Criminal Proceedings: Hearsay and Related Topics* (Paper No 245) (London, Law Commission).

—— (2001) *Evidence Of Bad Character In Criminal Proceedings* (Paper No 273) (London, Law Commission).

Law Reform Commission of Western Australia (1999) *Review of the Criminal and Civil Justice System in Western Australia: Final Report* (Project 92) (Perth, Law Reform Commission of Western Australia).

Law Society (2002) *Response to the Criminal Justice White Paper 'Justice for All'* (London, Law Society).

—— (2003a) *Guide to the Professional Conduct of Solicitors*, 8th edn (London, Law Society).

—— (2003b) *Response to the CPS Consultation Paper on Pre-Trial Interviews by Prosecutors* (London, Law Society).

Leach, P (2005) 'Beyond The Bug River—A New Dawn for Redress before the European Court of Human Rights?' 2 *European Human Rights Law Review* 148.

Lees, S (1996) *Carnal Knowledge: Rape on Trial* (London, Hamish Hamilton).

Lees, S, and Gregory, J (1993) *Rape and Sexual Assault: a Study of Attrition* (London, Islington Borough Council).

Lerner, R (2001) 'The Intersection of Two Systems: An American on Trial for an American Murder in the French *Cour d'Assises*' 3 *University of Illinois Law Review* 791.

Leverick, F, (2004) 'What has the ECHR done for victims?' 11 *International Review of Victimology* 177.

Liberty (2003a) *Liberty's Response to the CPS Consultation on Pre-Trial Interviews* (London, Liberty).

—— (2003b) *Briefing on the Criminal Justice Bill for the House of Lords* (London, Liberty).

—— (2005) *Summary of the Prevention of Terrorism Act 2005* (London, Liberty).

Livingstone, SW, and Doak, J (2000) 'Human Rights and Criminal Justice' Report 14, *Review of the Criminal Justice System in Northern Ireland* (London, HMSO).

Loftus, E, Wolchover, D, and Page, D (2006) 'General Review of the Psychology of Witness Testimony' in A Heaton-Armstrong, E Shepherd, G Gudjonsson, and D Wolchover (eds) *Witness Testimony Psychological, Investigative and Evidential Perspectives* (Oxford, Oxford University Press).

Lombard, F (1996) 'France' in D Greer (ed), *Compensating Crime Victims* (Freiburg, Max Planck Institute).

Luban, D (1988) *Lawyers and Justice: An Ethical Study* (Princeton, Princeton University Press).

Lubet, S (2001) *Nothing But the Truth* (New York, New York University Press).

Luhmann, N (1989) 'Law as a Social System' 83 *Northwestern University Law Review* 136.

MacCormick, N, and Garland, D (1998) 'Sovereign States and Vengeful Victims: The Problem of the Right to Punish' in A Ashworth and M Wasik (eds), *Fundamentals of Sentencing Theory* (Oxford, Clarendon Press).

Mack, R (1996) 'It's Broke so Let's Fix It: Using a Quasi-Inquisitorial Approach to Limit the Impact of Bias in the American Criminal Justice System' 7 *Indiana International and Comparative Law Review* 63.

MacPherson, Sir W (1999) *The Stephen Lawrence Inquiry: Report of an Inquiry by Sir William MacPherson of Cluny* (Cmnd 4262) (London, HMSO).

Maguire, M (1980) 'The Impact of Burglary on Victims' 20 *British Journal of Criminology* 261.

—— (1985) 'Victims' Needs and Victim Services: Indications from Research' 10 *Victimology* 539.

Maguire, M, and Shapland, J (1990) 'The "Victims Movement" In Europe' in AJ Lurigio, WG Skogan, and RC Davies (eds), *Victims Of Crime: Problems, Policies and Programs* (London, Sage).

Malanczuk, P (1995) 'International Business and New Rules Of State Responsibility?—The Law Applied by the United Nations (Security Council) Compensation Commission for Claims Against Iraq' in KH Böckstiegel (ed), *Perspectives of Air Law, Space Law and International Business Law for the Next Century* (Cologne, Carl Heymanns).

Markesinis, BS (ed) (1994) *The Gradual Convergence: Foreign Ideas, Foreign Influences, and English Law on the Eve of the 21st Century* (Oxford, Clarendon Press).

Marshall, TF (1999) *Restorative Justice: An Overview* (London, HMSO).

Marshall, TF, and Merry, S (1990) *Crime and Accountability: Victim / Offender Mediation in Practice* (London, HMSO).

Massaro, T (1988) 'The Dignity Value of Face-to-Face Confrontations' 40 *Florida Law Review* 863.

Matravers, M (2004) ' "More Than Just Illogical": Truth and Jury Nullification' in A Duff, L Farmer, S Marshall and V Tadros (eds), *The Trial on Trial*, Vol 1 (Oxford, Hart Publishing).

Mattinson, J, and Mirrlees-Black, C (2000), *Attitudes to Crime and Criminal Justice: Findings from the 1998 British Crime Survey*, Home Office Research Study 200 (London, Home Office).

Mawby, R, and Gill, ML (1987) *Crime Victims : Needs, Services, and the Voluntary Sector* (New York, Tavistock).

Mawby, R, and Walklate, S (1994) *Critical Victimology: International Perspectives* (Thousand Oaks, Sage Publications).

Maxwell, G, and Morris, A (1993) *Family, Victims and Culture: Youth Justice in New Zealand* (Wellington, Social Policy Agency and Institute of Criminology, Victoria University of Wellington).

May, A (2003) *The Bar and the Old Bailey 1750–1850* (Chapel Hill, University of North Carolina Press).

May R, and Wierda, M (2002) *International Criminal Evidence* (New York, Transnational Publishers).

Mayhew, P, and Van Kesteren, J (2002) 'Cross-national attitudes to punishment' in JV Roberts and M Hough (eds), *Changing Attitudes to Punishment, Public opinion, Crime and Justice* (Devon, Willan Publishing).

Maynard, W (1994), *Witness Intimidation Strategies for Prevention*, Police Research Group Crime Detection and Prevention Series Paper No 55 (London, HMSO).

Mazzeschi, R (2003) 'Reparation claims by individuals for state breaches of humanitarian law and human rights: an overview' (2003) 1 *Journal of International Criminal Justice* 339.

McBarnet, D (1981) *Conviction, the State and the Construction of Justice* (London, Macmillan).

—— (1983) 'Victim in the Witness Box—Confronting Victimology's Stereotype' 7 *Contemporary Crises* 293.

McCold, P (2000) 'Towards a Holistic Vision of Restorative Juvenile Justice: A Reply to the Maximalist Model' 3 *Contemporary Justice Review* 357.

McColgan, A (1996) 'Common Law and the Relevance of Sexual History Evidence' *Oxford Journal of Legal Studies* 275.

McConville, M (2002) 'Plea Bargaining' in M McConville and G Wilson (eds), *The Oxford Handbook of the Criminal Justice Process* (Oxford, Oxford University Press).

McConville, M, Hodgson, J, Bridges, L, and Pavlovic, A (1994) *Standing Accused: The Organisation and Practice of Criminal Defence Lawyers in Britain* (Oxford, Clarendon Press).

McConville, M, Sanders, A, and Leng, R (1991) *The Case for the Prosecution* (London, Routledge).

McDonald, W (1976) 'Towards a Bicentennial Revolution in Criminal Justice: The Return of the Victim' 13 *American Criminal Law Review* 649.

McEwan, J (1988) 'Child Evidence: More Proposals for Reform' *Criminal Law Review* 813.

—— (1998) *Evidence and the Adversarial Process*, 2nd edn (Oxford, Hart Publishing).

—— (2000) 'In Defence of Vulnerable Witnesses: The Youth Justice and Criminal Evidence Act 1999' 4 *International Journal of Evidence and Proof* 29.

McKee, L (2005) *Families, Violence and Social Change* (Maidenhead, Open University Press).

McKillop, B (1997) 'Anatomy of a French Murder Case' 45 *American Journal of Comparative Law* 527.

Mekjian, G, and Varughese, M (2005) 'Hearing the victim's voice: analysis of victims' advocate participation in the trial proceeding of the International Criminal Court' 17 *Pace International Law Review* 1.

MENCAP (1997) *Barriers to Justice* (London, MENCAP).

Merryman, JH (1985) *The Civil Law Tradition* (Stanford, Stanford University Press).

Miers, D (1990) *Compensation for Criminal Injuries* (London, Butterworths).

—— (1997) *State Compensation for Criminal Injuries* (London, Blackstone).

—— (2000) 'Taking the Law into Their Own Hands: Victims as Offenders' in A Crawford and J Goodey (eds), *Integrating A Victim Perspective Within Criminal Justice* (Aldershot, Ashgate).

Miles, J (1995) 'The Role of the Victim in the Criminal Process: Fairness to the Victim and Fairness to the Accused' 19 *Criminal Law Journal* 193.

Milne, R, and Bull, R (1999) *Investigating Interviewing: Psychology and Practice* (Chichester, Wiley).

Minow, M (1998) *Between Vengeance and Forgiveness: Facing History After Genocide and Mass Violence* (New York, Houghton Mifflin).

Moore, DB (1994) *A New Approach to Juvenile Justice: An Evaluation of Family Conferencing in Wagga Wagga*. Report to the Australian Criminology Research Council Centre for Rural Social Research (Wagga Wagga, Charles Sturt University-Riverina,).

Morgan, J, Winkel, FW, and Williams, K (1996) 'Protection of and Compensation for Vicims of Crime' in C Harding, P Fennell, N Jörg, and B Swart (eds), *Criminal Justice in Europe* (Oxford, Oxford University Press).

Morgan, R, and Sanders, A (1999) *The Use of Victim Statements* (London, Home Office).

Morris, A, Maxwell, G, and Robertson, J (1993) 'Giving Victims A Voice: A New Zealand Experiment' 32 *Howard Journal Of Criminal Justice* 304.

Mortimer, A, and Shepherd, E (1999) 'The Frailty of Children's Testimony' in A Heaton-Armstrong, E Shepherd, G Gudjonsson, and D Wolchover (eds) *Witness Testimony Psychological, Investigative and Evidential Perspectives* (Oxford, Oxford University Press).

Mowbray, A (2004) *The Development of Positive Obligations under the European Convention on Human Rights by the European Court of Human Rights* (Oxford, Hart Publishing).

Muller, K (2001) 'An Inquisitorial Approach to the Evidence of Children' 4 *Crime Research in South Africa.*

Munday, R (1993) 'Comparative Law and English Law's Character Evidence Rules' 13 *Oxford Journal of Legal Studies* 589.

Murch, M, Borkowski, M, and Myers, J (1996) 'A Decade of International Reform to Accommodate Child Witnesses' in B Bottoms and G Goodman (eds) *International Perspective on Child Abuse and Children's Testimony: Psychological Research and the Law* (Thousand Oaks, CA, Sage).

Murphy, G, and Clare, I (2006) 'The Effect of Learning Disabilities on Witness Testimony' in A Heaton-Armstrong, E Shepherd, G Gudjonsson, and D Wolchover (eds) *Witness Testimony Psychological, Investigative and Evidential Perspectives* (Oxford, Oxford University Press).

Murphy, WJ (2001) 'The Victim Advocacy and Research Group: Serving a Growing Need to Provide Rape Victims with Personal Legal Representation to Protect Privacy Rights and to Fight Gender Bias in the Criminal Justice System' 11 *Journal of Social Distress and the Homeless* 123.

Mythen, G, and Walklate, S (eds) (2006) *Beyond the Risk Society: Critical Reflections on Risk and Human Security* (Milton Keynes, McGraw Hill / Open University Press).

Nash, CL, and West, DJ (1985) 'Sexual Molestation of Young Girls' in DJ West (ed) *Sexual Victimization* (Aldershot, Gower).

Nash, M (2006) *Public Protection and the Criminal Justice Process* (Oxford, Oxford University Press).

New Zealand Law Commission (1999) *Evidence*, Report 55(1) (Wellington, New Zealand Law Commission).

Newburn, T, Crawford, A, Earle, R, Goldie, S, Hale, C, Masters, G, Netten, A, Saunders, R, Sharpe, K, and Uglow, S (2002) *The Introduction of Referral Orders into the Youth Justice System, Home Office Research Study 242* (London, Home Office).

Ni Aolain, F (2002) *The Politics of Force* (Belfast, Blackstaff).

Niarchos, CN (1995) 'Women, War, and Rape: Challenges Facing the International Tribunal for the Former Yugoslavia' 17 *Human Rights Quarterly* 649.

Nobles, R, and Schiff, D (2000) *Understanding Miscarriages of Justice* (Oxford, Oxford University Press).

O'Kelly, CME, Kebbell, MR, Hatton, C, and Johnson, SD (2003) 'Judicial intervention in court cases involving witnesses with and without learning disabilities' 8 *Legal and Criminological Psychology* 229.

O'Mahony, D, and Doak, J (2004) 'Restorative Justice: Is More Better?' 43 *Howard Journal* 484.

O'Malley, P (2004) *Risk, Uncertainty and Government* (London, Glasshouse Press).

Office for Criminal Justice Reform (2005) *Code of Practice for Victims of Crime* (London, HMSO).

—— (2007), *Improving the Criminal Trial Process for Young Witnesses: A Consultation Paper* (London, Ministry of Justice).

Orbuch, T, Harvey, J, Davis, S and Merbach, N (1994), 'Account-Making and Confiding as Acts of Meaning in Response to Sexual Assault' 9 *Journal of Family Violence* 249.

Page, B, Wake, R, and Ames, A (2004) *Public confidence in the criminal justice system, Home Office Findings No 221* (London, Home Office).

Pannick, D (1992) *Advocates* (Oxford, Oxford University Press).

Pennington, N, and Hastie, R (1993) 'The Story Model for Juror Decision Making' in R Hastie, *Inside the Juror: The Psychology of Juror Decision Making* (Cambridge, Cambridge University Press).

Perrodet, A (2002) 'The Italian System' in M Delmas-Marty and J Spencer (eds) *European Criminal Procedures* (Cambridge, Cambridge University Press).

Pigot, Judge T (1989) *Report of the Advisory Group on Video Evidence* (London, HMSO).

Pizzi, W (1999) *Trials Without Truth* (New York, New York University Press).

Pizzi, W, and Marafiorti, L (1992) 'The New Italian Code of Criminal Procedure: The Difficulties of Building an Adversarial Trial System on a Civil Law Foundation' 17 *Yale Journal of International Law* 1.

Pizzi, W, and Perron, W (1996) 'Crime victims in German Courtrooms: a Comparative Perspective on American Problems' 32 *Stanford Journal of International Law* 37.

Plotnikoff, J, and Woolfson, R (1998) *Witness Care in Magistrates' Courts and the Youth Court*, Home Office Research Findings No 68 (London, Home Office).

—— (2004) *In their own words: the experiences of 50 young witnesses in criminal proceedings* (London, NSPCC).

—— (2007) *The 'Go-Between': evaluation of intermediary pathfinder projects* (London, Ministry of Justice).

Pollock, F, and Maitland, F (1898) *The History of English Law, Vol 2*, 2nd edn (Cambridge, Cambridge University Press).

Popovski, V (2000) 'The International Criminal Court: A Synthesis of Retributive and Restorative Justice' 15 *International Relations* 3.

Powell, RL (2006) 'Security and the Right to Security in European Court of Human Rights Jurisprudence', Working paper available at SSRN: http://ssrn.com/abstract=959257 [accessed 24 July 2007].

Pradel, J (1993) 'France' in C Van Den Wyngaert (ed) *Criminal Procedure Systems in the European Community* (London, Butterworths).

—— (1996) 'La Protection du témoin contre les pressions' *Revue Internationale de Criminologie et de Police Technique* 160.

Redmayne, M (2003) 'Myths, relationships and coincidences: the new problems of sexual history' 7 *International Journal of Evidence and Proof* 75.

Reeves, H (1985) 'Victim Support Services: The UK Model' 10 *Victimology* 679.

—— (1997) *The Treatment of Rape and Child victims as Witnesses of Crime* (University of Leeds, Anne Spencer Memorial Lecture).

Reeves, H, and Mulley, J (2000) 'The New Status of Victims in the UK: Opportunities and Threat' in A Crawford and J Goodey (eds) *Integrating a Victim Perspective Within Criminal Justice* (Aldershot, Ashgate).

Rehman, J (2002) 'The Influence of International Human Rights Law Upon Criminal Justice Systems' 66 *Journal of Criminal Law* 510.

Reiner, R (2000) 'Crime Control in Britain' 34 *British Journal of Criminology* 71.

Renaud, G (2001) 'Credibility And Demeanour: An Examination Based on the World of Literature' on-line article at http://www.trussel.com/maig/credibil.htm [accessed 24 July 2007].

Retzinger, S, and Scheff, T (1996) 'Strategy for community conferences: Emotions and social bonds' in B Galway and J Hudson (eds) *Restorative Justice* (New York, Criminal Justice Press).

Riding, A (1999) 'The Crown Court Witness Service: Little Help in the Witness Box' 38 *Howard Journal* 411.

Rieke, RD, and Stutman, R (1994) *Communication in Legal Advocacy* (Columbia, University of South Carolina Press).

Riley, P (1982) *Will and Political Legitimacy: A Critical Exposition of Social Contract Theory in Hobbes, Locke, Rousseau, Kant, and Hegel* (Cambridge, MA, Harvard University Press).

Risinger, DM (2004) 'Unsafe Verdicts: The Need for Reformed Standards for the Trial and Review of Factual Innocence Claims' 41 *Houston Law Review* 1281.

Roberts, J, and Erez, E (2004) 'Communication in Sentencing: Exploring the Expressive Function of Victim Impact Statements' 10 *International Review of Victimology* 223.

Roberts, P (2002) 'On Method: The Ascent of Comparative Criminal Justice' 22 *Oxford Journal of Legal Studies* 539.

Roche, D (2003) *Accountability in Restorative Justice* (Oxford, Oxford University Press).

Rock, P (1990) *Helping Victims of Crime: The Home Office and the Rise of Victim Support in England and Wales* (Oxford, Clarendon Press).

—— (1991) 'The Victim in Court Project at the Crown Court at Wood Green' 30 *Howard Journal of Criminal Justice* 301.

—— (1993) *The Social World of an English Crown Court: witnesses and professionals in the Crown Court Centre at Wood Green* (Oxford, Clarendon Press).

—— (1998) *After Homicide* (Oxford, Clarendon Press).

—— (2004) *Constructing Victims' Rights: The Home Office, New Labour and Victims* (Oxford, Clarendon Press).

Rogers, J (2003) 'Applying the Doctrine of Positive Obligations in the European Convention on Human Rights to Domestic Substantive Criminal Law in Domestic Proceedings' *Criminal Law Review* 690.

Roht-Arriaza, N (1990) 'State Responsibility to Investigate and Prosecute Grave Human Rights Violations in International Law' 78 *California Law Review* 451.

—— (1995) 'Punishment, Redress, and Pardon: Theoretical and Psychological Approaches' in N Roht-Arriaza (ed) *Impunity And Human Rights In International Law And Practice* (USA, Oxford University Press) 13.

—— (2004) 'Reparations Decisions and Dilemmas' 27 *Hastings International and Comparative Law Review* 157.

Roht-Arriaza, N, and Mariezcurrena, J (2006) *Transnational Justice in the Twenty-First Century: Beyond Truth Versus Justice* (Cambridge, Cambridge University Press).

Royal Commission on Criminal Justice (1993) *Report* (Cmnd 2263) (London: HMSO).

Royal Commission on Criminal Procedure (1981) *Report* (Cmnd 8092) (London: HMSO).

Saldana, RH (1994) *Crime Victim Compensation Programs: A Reference Guide to the Programs in the U.S* (Mount Vernon, WA: Quartzite Books).

Sanders, A (1999) *Taking Account of Victims in the Criminal Justice System: A Review of the Literature* (Edinburgh, Scottish Office Central Research Unit).

—— (2002) 'Victim Participation in an Exclusionary Criminal Justice System' in C Hoyle and R Young (eds) *New Visions of Crime Victims* (Oxford, Hart Publishing).

—— (2004) 'Involving Victims in Sentencing: a conflict with defendants' rights?' in E Cape (ed) *Reconcilable Rights? Analysing the Tension between Victims and Defendants* (London, Legal Action Group).

Sanders, A, Creation, J, Bird, S, and Weber, L (1996) *Victims with Learning Disabilities: Negotiating the Criminal Justice System*, Home Office Research Findings No 44 (London, Home Office).

Sanders, A, Hoyle, C, Morgan, R, and Cape, E (2001) 'Victim Impact Statements: Don't work, Can't work' *Criminal Law Review* 437.

Sanders, A, and Jones, I (2007) 'The Victim in Court' in S Walklate (ed) *Handbook of Victims and Victimology* (Cullompton, Willan).

Sanders, A, and Young, R (2007) *Criminal Justice*, 3rd edn (Oxford, Oxford University Press).

Santiago, JM, McCall-Perez, F, Gorcey, M, and Beigel, A, 'Long-term psychological effects of rape in 35 rape victims' (1985) 142 *American Journal of Psychiatry* 1338.

Saul, B (2004) 'Compensation for Unlawful Death in International Law: A Focus on the Inter-American Court of Human Rights' 19 *American University International Law Review* 523.

Schafer, S (1968) *The Victim and His Criminal* (New York, Random House).

Scott, C (ed) (2001) *Torture as Tort: Comparative Perspectives on The Development of Transnational Human Rights Litigation* (Oxford, Hart Publishing).

Scottish Law Commission (1990) *The Evidence of Children and Other Potentially Vulnerable Witnesses* (Edinburgh, HMSO).

Sebba, L (1996) *Third Parties* (Columbus, Ohio State University Press).

—— (1997) 'Will the "Victim Revolution" Trigger a Reorientation of the Criminal Justice System?' 1 *Israel Law Review* 379.

Seipp, DJ (1996) 'The Distinction between Crime and Tort in Early Common Law' 76 *Boston University Law Review* 59.

Shapland, J (1988) 'Fiefs and Peasants: Accomplishing Change for Victims in the Criminal Justice System' in M Maguire and J Poiting (eds) *Victims of Crime: A New Deal?* (Milton Keynes, Open University Press).

—— (2000) 'Victims and the Criminal Process: A Public Service Ethos for Criminal Justice' in S Doran and J Jackson (eds) *The Judicial Role in Criminal Proceedings* (Oxford, Hart Publishing).

Shapland, J, Atkinson, A, Atkinson, H, Chapman, B, Colledge, E, Dignan, J, Howes, M, Johnstone, J, Robinson, G, and Sorsby, A (2006) *Restorative Justice in Practice—findings from the second phase of the evaluation of three schemes*, Home Office Research Findings 274 (London, Home Office).

Shapland, J, Atkinson, A, Colledge, E, Dignan, J, Howes, M, Johnstone, J, Pennant, R, Robinson, G, and Sorsby, A (2004) *Implementing Restorative Justice Schemes—A Report on the First Year*. Home Office Online Report 32/04 (London, Home Office).

Shapland, J, and Bell, E (1998) 'Victims in the Magistrates' Courts and Crown Court' *Criminal Law Review* 537.

Shapland, J, and Cohen, D (1987) 'Facilities for Victims: the Role of the Police and the Courts' *Criminal Law Review* 28.

Shapland, J and Hall, M (2007) 'What do we know about the effect of crime on victims?' 14(2) *International Review of Victimology* 175.

—— (2008) 'Courts and Victims: The Trial Process, Reparation and Sentencing' in A Bottoms (ed) *Victims In The Criminal Justice System: A Need For 'Rebalancing'?* (Cullompton, Willan Publishing) [forthcoming].

Shapland, J, Willmore, J, and Duff, P (1985) *Victims and the Criminal Justice System* (Aldershot, Gower).

Shaw, M (1998) 'The International Criminal Court—Some Procedural and Evidential Issues' 3 *Journal of Armed Conflict Law* 65.

Shelton, D (1999) *Remedies in International Human Rights Law*, 2nd edn (Oxford, Oxford University Press).

—— (2002) 'Righting Wrongs: Reparations in the Articles on State Responsibility' 96 *American Journal of International Law* 833.

Short, J, Williams, E and Christie, B (1976) *The Social Psychology of Telecommunications* (New York, Wiley).

Simester, A, and Sullivan, GR (2003) *Criminal Law: Theory and Doctrine* (Oxford, Hart Publishing).

Simonovic, I (2004) 'Dealing with the legacy of past war crimes and human rights abuses: experiences and trends' 2 *Journal of International Criminal Justice* 701.

Simpson, G (2007) *Law, War and Crime: War Crimes Trials and the Reinvention of International Law* (London, Polity Press).

Skolnick, JH (1966) *Justice Without Trial: Law Enforcement in Democratic Society* (New York, Wiley).

Skryms, B (1996) *The Evolution of the Social Contract* (Cambridge, Cambridge University Press).

Smith, D (1997) 'Case Construction and the Goals of Criminal Process' 37 *British Journal of Criminology* 319.

Smith, JC, and Hogan, B (2005) *Criminal Law*, 11th edn (Oxford, Oxford University Press).

Smyth, JM, & Pennebaker, JW (1999) 'Sharing One's Story: Translating Emotional Experiences into Words as a Coping Tool' in CR Snyder (ed) *Coping: The Psychology of What Works* (New York and Oxford, Oxford University Press).

South African law Commission (1989) *Protection of the Child Witness*, Working Paper 28, Project 71 (Pretoria, South African Law Commission).

Spalek, B (2006) *Crime Victims: Theory, Policy And Practice* (Basingstoke, Palgrave Macmillan).

Spencer, JR (1994) 'Orality and the Evidence of Absent Witnesses' *Criminal Law Review* 628.

—— (2000) 'The Youth Justice and Criminal Evidence Act 1999: the Evidence Provisions' *Archbold News*, 28 January 2000.

—— (2002) 'Evidence' in M Delmas-Marty and J Spencer (eds) *European Criminal Procedures* (Cambridge, Cambridge University Press).

—— (2004) 'Criminal Procedure: The Rights of the Victim versus the Rights of the Defendant' in E Cape (ed) *Reconcilable Rights? Analysing the Tension between Victims and Defendants* (London, Legal Action Group).

—— (2006) *Evidence of Bad Character* (Oxford, Hart Publishing).

Spencer JR, and Flin, R (1993) *The Evidence of Children*, 2nd edn (London, Blackstone).

Spencer, J, and Spencer, M (2001) *Witness Protection and the Integrity of the Criminal Trial*, paper presented at the Second World Conference on the Investigation of Crime (Durban, Institute of Human Rights and Criminal Justice Studies).

Stahn, C, Olásolo, H, and Gibson, K (2006) 'Participation of Victims in Pre-Trial Proceedings of the ICC' 4 *Journal of International Criminal Justice* 219.

Steffen, S (1988) 'Truth as Second Fiddle: Re-Evaluating the Place of Truth in the Adversarial Ensemble' 4 *Utah Law Review* 799.

Stern, K, and Chahal, S (2006) 'Articles 2 and 3 of the European Convention on Human Rights: the investigative obligation: Part 2' July, *Legal Action*, 23.

Stone, M (1995) *Cross-Examination in Criminal Trials* 2nd edn (London, Butterworths).

Strang, H (2002) *Repair Or Revenge: Victims And Restorative Justice, Clarendon Studies In Criminology* (Oxford, Oxford University Press).

Swart, A (1993) 'The Netherlands' in C Van Den Wyngaert (ed) *Criminal Procedure Systems in the European Community* (London, Butterworths).

Sveaass, N, and Lavik, NJ (2000) 'Psychological Aspects of Human Rights Violations: the Importance of Justice and Reconciliation' 69 *Nordic Journal Of International Law* 35.

Tarling, R, Dowds, L, and Budd, T (2000) *Victim and witness intimidation: findings from the British Crime Survey* (London, Home Office).

Taslitz, A (1999) *Rape and the Culture of the Courtroom* (New York, New York University Press).

Temkin, J (2000) 'Prosecuting and Defending Rape: Perspectives from the Bar' 27 *Journal of Law and Society* 219.

—— (2002) *Rape and the Legal Process*, 2nd edn (Oxford, Oxford University Press).

Thaman, S (1999) 'Europe's New Jury Systems: The Cases of Spain and Russia' 62 *Law and Contemporary Problems* 233.

Thibaut, J, and Walker, L (1978) 'A Theory of Procedure' 66 *California Law Review* 541.

Thomas, T (2004) 'When Public Protection Becomes Punishment? The UK Use of Civil Measures to Contain the Sex Offender' 10 *European Journal On Criminal Policy And Research* 337.

Tonry, MH (2004) *Punishment and Politics : evidence and emulation in the making of English crime control policy* (Cullompton, Willan Publishing).

Twining, W (1994) *Rethinking Evidence: Exploratory Essays* (Chicago, Northwestern University Press).

Umbreit, M, Coates, R, and Kalanj, B (1994) *Victim Meets Offender: The Impact of Restorative Justice and Mediation* (Monsey, Criminal Justice Press).

Umbreit, M, and Roberts, A (1996) *Mediation of Criminal Conflict in England: An Assessment of Services in Coventry and Leeds* (St Paul, MN, Centre for Restorative Justice and Mediation, University of Minnesota).

Underwood, TL (2002) 'Concepts of Victim Assistance' in TL Underwood and C Edmunds (eds) *Victim Assistance: Exploring Individual Practice, Organizational Policy, and Societal Responses* (New York, Springer).

United Nations (1955) *Annotations On The Text Of The Draft International Covenants On Human Rights* (UN Doc A/2929) (Geneva, United Nations).

—— (1999) *Offenders and Victims: Accountability and Fairness in the Criminal Justice Process* (UN Doc A/ CONF.187/8) (Vienna, United Nations).

United Nations Human Rights Committee (1992) *General Comment 6, Article 6, Compilation of General Comments and General Recommendations Adopted by Human Rights Treaty Bodies,* UN Doc HRI\GEN\1\Rev.1 At 6 (1994) (Geneva, Office Of High Commissioner For Human Rights).

Vadillo, R (1993) 'Spain' in C Van Den Wyngaert (ed) *Criminal Procedure Systems in the European Community* (London, Butterworths).

Van Boven, T (1993) *The Right to Restitution, Compensation and Rehabilitation for Victims of Gross Violations of Human Rights and Fundamental Freedoms* (UN Doc E/CN.4/SUB.2/1993/8) (Geneva, United Nations).

Van den Wyngaert, C (ed) (1993) *Criminal Procedure Systems in the European Community* (London, Butterworths).

—— 'Belgium' in C Van Den Wyngaert (ed) *Criminal Procedure Systems in the European Community* (London, Butterworths).

—— (1996) 'Belgium' in D Greer (ed) *Compensating Crime Victims* (Freiburg, Max Planck Institute).

Van Kessel, G (1992) 'Adversary Excesses in the American Criminal Trial' 67 *Notre Dame Law Review* 403.

—— (1998) 'European Perspectives on the Accused as a Source of Testimonial Evidence' 100 *West Virginia Law Review* 799.

Van Ness, D (1996) 'Restorative Justice and International Human Rights' in B Galaway and J Hudson (eds) *Restorative Justice: International Perspectives* (Monsey, NY, Criminal Justice Press).

—— (2003) 'Proposed basic principles on the use of restorative justice: Recognizing the aims and limits of restorative justice' in A Von Hirsch, J Roberts, AE Bottoms, K Roach, K, and M Schiff (eds) *Restorative Justice and Criminal Justice: Competing or Reconcilable Paradigms?* (Oxford, Hart Publishing).

Van Ness, DW, and Nolan, P (1998) 'Legislating for Restorative Justice' 10 *Regent University Law Review* 53.

Van Ness, DW, and Strong, K (2002) *Restoring Justice,* 2nd edn (Cincinnati, OH, Anderson Publishing Co).

Victim Support (1988) *The Victim in Court: Report of a Working Party Chaired by Lady Ralphs* (London, Victim Support).

—— (1995) *The Rights of Victims of Crime: A Policy Paper* (London, Victim Support).

—— (1996a) *Women, Rape and the Criminal Justice System* (London, Victim Support).

—— (1996b) *Victims, Witnesses and the Criminal Trial* (London, Victim Support).

—— (2003) *Insult To Injury: How the Criminal Injuries Compensation System is Failing Victims of Crime* (London, Victim Support).

Von Hirsh, A (1993) *Censure and Sanctions* (Oxford, Clarendon Press).

Wadham J, and Arkinstall, J (2000) 'The Human Rights Act and The Rights of Victims of Crime' 150 *New Law Journal* 1023.

Walgrave, L (2002) 'Restorative Justice and the Law: Socio-Ethical and Juridical Foundations for a Systemic Approach' in L Walgrave (ed) *Restorative Justice and the Law* (Cullompton, Willan Publishing).

Walker, N, and Telford, M (2000) *Designing Criminal Justice: The System in Comparative Perspective, Report 14, Review of the Criminal Justice System in Northern Ireland* (London, HMSO).

Walklate, S (2001) 'The Victims' Lobby' in M Ryan, S Savage and D Wall (eds) *Policy Networks in Criminal Justice* (London, Palgrave Macmillan).

Walsh, D (2000) *Bloody Sunday and the Rule of Law in Northern Ireland* (London, Palgrave Macmillan).

Walther, S (1996) 'Reparation and Criminal Justice: Can they be integrated?' 30 *Israel Law Review* 316.

Wasik, M (1978) 'The Place of Compensation in the Penal System' *Criminal Law Review* 599.

Waterman, AH, Blades, M, and Spencer, C (2000) 'Do Children Try to Answer Nonsensical Questions?' 18 *British Journal of Developmental Psychology* 211.

Weigend, T (2003) 'Truth, the Jury and the Adversarial System: Is the Criminal Process about Truth?' 26 *Harvard Journal of Law and Public Policy* 157.

Weiner, MA (2005) 'Defeating Hatred With Truth: An Argument in Support of a Truth Commission as part of the Solution to the Israeli-Palestinian Conflict' *38 Connecticut Law Review* 123.

Weisstub, D (1986) 'Victims of Crime in the Criminal Justice System' in E Fattah (ed) *From Crime Policy to Victim Policy* (London, Macmillan).

Wellborn, OG (1991) 'Demeanour' *76 Cornell Law Review* 1075.

Wemmers, J (1995) 'Victims in the Dutch Criminal Justice System' 3 *International Review of Victimology* 323.

—— (1996) *Victims in the Criminal Justice System* (Amsterdam, Kugler).

Wemmers, J, and Cyr, K (2004) 'Victims' Perspectives on Restorative Justice: How Much Involvement Are Victims Looking For?' 11 *International Review of Victimology* 259.

Whitehead, E (2001) *Witness Satisfaction: findings from the Witness Satisfaction Survey 2000*, Home Office Research Study 230 (London, Home Office).

Wierda, M, and De Greiff, P (2004) *Reparations and the International Criminal Court: a Prospective Role for the Trust Fund for Victims* (New York, International Centre for Transitional Justice).

Wigmore, JH (1937) *The Science of Judicial Proof as Given by Logic, Psychology, and General Experience and Illustrated in Judicial Trials*, 3rd edn (Boston, Little Brown).

—— (1940) *A Treatise on the Anglo-American System of Evidence in Trials at Common Law*, 3rd edn (Boston, Brown & Co).

Wilcox, A, Young, R, and Hoyle, C (2004) *Two-year Resanctioning Study: A Comparison of Restorative and Traditional Cautions*, Home Office Report 57/04 (London, Home Office).

Williams, B (1999) 'The Victim's Charter: Citizens as Consumers of Criminal Justice Services' 38 *Howard Journal of Criminal Justice* 384.

—— (2005) *Victims of Crime and Community Justice* (London, Jessica Kingsley).

Woolf, H (1995) *Access to Justice: Interim Report to the Lord Chancellor on the Civil Justice System in England and Wales* (London, Lord Chancellor's Department).

—— (1996) *Access to Justice: Final Report* (London, HMSO).

Wright, M (1997) 'Victim/Offender Mediation in the United Kingdom: Legal Background and Practice,' paper presented at *Seminar on Mediation Between Juvenile Offenders and their Victims* (Popowo, Poland, 22–24 October).

Yaroshefsky, E (1989) 'Balancing Victims' Rights and Vigorous Advocacy for the Defendant' *Annual Survey of American Law* 135.

Young, A (2001) *The Role of the Victim in the Criminal Process* (Ottawa, Department of Justice).

Zauberman, R (2000) 'Victims as Consumers of the Criminal Justice System' in A Crawford and J Goodey (eds), *Integrating a Victim Perspective within Criminal Justice* (Aldershot, Ashgate).

Zedner, L (1994) 'Reparation and Retribution: Are they Reconcilable?' 57 *Modern Law Review* 228.

Zehr, H (2005) *Changing Lenses: A New Focus for Crime and Justice*. 3rd edn (Waterloo, ON, Herald Press).

Zuckerman, A (1992) 'Miscarriage of Justice—a Root Treatment' *Criminal Law Review* 323.

INDEX